2001 SUPPLEMENT

THE LAW OF DEMOCRACY

LEGAL STRUCTURE OF THE POLITICAL PROCESS

by

SAMUEL ISSACHAROFF
Professor of Law, Columbia Law School

PAMELA S. KARLAN
Kenneth and Harle Montgomery Professor of Public Interest Law, Stanford Law School

RICHARD H. PILDES
Professor of Law, New York University School of Law

NEW YORK, NEW YORK

FOUNDATION PRESS

2001

SUMMARY OF CONTENTS

*

TABLE OF CONTENTS

*

CHAPTER TWO

Page 22, before *Minor v. Happersett*:

Although it is commonly thought that the franchise, once extended, is rarely retracted, particularly in a democratic culture such as that of the United States, that has not always been so. The case of women and the vote provides one contrary example. When New Jersey adopted its post-American Revolution state constitution in 1776, and when it passed its election laws in 1890, those laws granted the vote to "all inhabitants" otherwise qualified; the breadth of this grant was intentional and it was understood to include property-holding women and black residents. New Jersey was the only state to enfranchise women for all elections (some select women could vote in specific local elections, such as in Kentucky in 1838, which then permitted propertied widows and unmarried women to vote in school elections). But even in New Jersey, purportedly in response to women voting together and affecting election outcomes, LINDA KERBER, NO CONSTITUTIONAL RIGHT TO BE LADIES 94 (1998), by 1807 the New Jersey legislature withdrew the broad franchise and legislated that "no person shall vote in any state or county election for officers in the government of the United States or of this state, unless such person be a free, white male citizen." ALEXANDER KEYSSAR, THE RIGHT TO VOTE: THE CONTESTED HISTORY OF DEMOCRACY IN THE UNITED STATES 54, 175 (2000).

Page 28, after note 3:

Some suffrage advocates argued, with some irony no doubt, that at least widows should get to vote because the Fifteenth Amendment prohibited discrimination on the basis of "previous condition of servitude." Kerber, at 102.

Page 29, after note 4:

Note that Susan B. Anthony's strategy, which led fifty other women to register in Rochester with her, was to seek prosecution so that she could get her arguments before a jury (Anthony promised to indemnify the election inspectors should they be prosecuted for permitting her to vote). For weeks, Anthony and Matilda Gage went on speaking tours throughout the counties in which Anthony was to be tried (the federal prosecutors succeeded in having the trial moved once). Reportedly, several of the jurors had been prepared to acquit, had the judge not directed a verdict of guilty. Adam Winkler, *A Revolution Too Soon: Woman Suffragists and the "Living Constitution," 1869-1875*, ____ (forthcoming 2001). Anthony announced she would never pay the fine assigned, and the judge declined to jail her for fear of turning her into a martyr. The suffragists arguments were often grounded in the writings of traditional liberal political theorists; in particular, Anthony at the end of her life wrote in her copy of JOHN STUART MILL'S THE SUBJECTION OF WOMEN, "This book has been the law for me since 1869." Kerber, at 99.

Page 33, after note 9:

Although *Adkins* was the only contemporary Supreme Court case to suggest a transformative possibility for the Nineteenth Amendment, as opposed to what became the dominant mode of construing the Amendment, which is as a narrow, rule-like provision that affects only the specific right to vote, there were other institutions in the era who did construe the Amendment as having gravitational pull on issues of women's equality more generally. Thus, Congress passed the Cable Act in 1922 which permitted women who married certain foreign nationals to retain their American citizenship -- thus restricting traditional rules of coverture concerning domicile (in which a wife's domicile followed her husband's). The statute was expressly justified as warranted by the Nineteenth Amendment. Relying on the Amendment, one federal district judge refused to apply the common-law doctrine that absolved a wife of responsibility for crimes jointly committed with her husband. Another judge in a tax case concluded that the Amendment enabled a woman to choose her own domicile; the court thus rejected the government's claim that common-law coverture principles made the wife's domicile her husband's. Some state courts gave narrower constructions to provisions denying women the right to contract, explicitly invoking the Amendment.

The one area where state courts were most willing to extend the Amendment beyond the right to vote was to the category of "political rights" more generally. Thus, the Maine Supreme Court held that the Amendment pre-empted state constitutional provisions that had barred women from holding public office. And in the jury cases, discussed in the casebook at p.33, while split, often found women now eligible. But these appear to be all the examples of the momentary gravitational pull the Nineteenth Amendment had beyond the right to vote itself. These examples are drawn from Reva B. Siegel, *Collective Memory and the Nineteenth Amendment: Reasoning about "the Woman Question" in the Discourse of Sex Discrimination*, in HISTORY, MEMORY, AND THE LAW 131 (A. SARAT and T. KEARNS eds. 1999). In contrast to judicial interpretation of the Fourteenth Amendment, Siegel concludes: "Courts have adopted a rule-based construction of the [Nineteenth] amendment that reads its language acontextually – without reference to the sociopolitical commitments of those who opposed and advocated reform of the Constitution. Consequently, as currently interpreted, the Nineteenth Amendment bars sex-based restrictions on voting -- no more." *Id.*, at 143.

NOTE ON THE WOMAN'S SUFFRAGE MOVEMENT

Page 33, after note 9:

Recent years have seen an outpouring of legal and historical scholarship on the women's suffrage movement.

1. For a fine, concise recent history, see ALEXANDER KEYSSAR, THE RIGHT TO VOTE: THE CONTESTED HISTORY OF DEMOCRACY IN THE UNITED STATES 172-223 (2000). Keyssar describes women's suffrage as the largest mass movement for the expansion of the franchise in American history. Advocates pursued a national strategy of formal constitutional amendment and legislation, and when that failed, they turned to state-by-state efforts, given that control over the franchise remained at the state level. Some victories ensued, mostly in Western states which were trying to attract settlers. Wyoming was the first to enfranchise women, as a territory in 1869 and with statehood in 1889. Utah, Idaho, and Colorado had by the mid-1890s done likewise. But popular referenda failed elsewhere. Given the byzantine federal structure of voting rights, partial enfranchisement did occur many places. The most common involved schools; in response to suffragist pressure, by 1890 twenty states permitted women to vote on matters affecting schooling. Women were also permitted in many places to vote on liquor licensing, and sometimes in municipal elections. *Id.*, at 186-87.

The arguments in favor of women's suffrage varied and shifted over time, in part reflecting deep divisions within the movement, in part reflecting changes in the larger political culture. So too with the arguments against the vote. In the immediate aftermath of the Civil War, advocates embraced a broad republican justification, with a more universal and egalitarian conception of citizenship and the vote. But while blacks eventually succeeded with the Fifteenth Amendment, women failed. One reason was that the party of civil rights, the Republican Party, feared that endorsing women's rights would jeopardize the difficult effort to establish the right to vote for blacks. Another reason was that there was no discernable partisan advantage to enfranchising women, unlike blacks, who would obviously vote overwhelmingly Republican. Nor did the Republican Party perceive women to need the vote for self-protection in the way Southern blacks did. *Id.*, at 180.

But there was also a racist component to the argument for women's suffrage, which became more prevalent in the 1870s and 1880s, as well as strong elitist and class-based arguments that became even more pronounced later. As blacks became enfranchised and more immigrants arrived, women's suffrage was justified on the ground that white native-born women would ensure the political dominance of "Americans" against the potential power of blacks, Chinese, aliens, and transients. *Id.*, at 191. In the 1890s, there was a broad middle- and upper-class disenchantment with democracy and the emergence of various new restrictions on the franchise, such as literacy tests. Some suffragists, having moved away from the broad republican justification of the vote, endorsed this retrenchment and sought to fit women's suffrage within it. Thus, Stanton in an 1895 article entitled "Educated Suffrage" proposed doing away with the "ignorant foreign vote" by instituting tests for "intelligent reading and writing." *Id.*, at 199. Carrie Catt, head of the National Women's Suffrage Association, reflected the views of the Progressive Era when she similarly argued in the wake of the 1890 Census: "Today, there has arisen in America a class of men not intelligent, not patriotic, not moral, nor yet not pedigreed. In caucuses and conventions, it is they who nominate officials, at the polls through corrupt means, it is they who elect them and by bribery, it is they who secure passage of many a legislative measure." *Id.*, at 198.

As Keyssar puts it, the women's suffrage movement was unusual also in that it faced a strong countermovement of citizens opposed to their own enfranchisement. Women along with men argued that suffrage and political participation by women would deform natural gender roles and destroy family life. The demand for suffrage came centrally from middle-class women, women from families engaged in the professions, trade, commerce, and educated women. But many upper-class women became leaders of antisuffrage organizations and campaigns; rural women were also less responsive and difficult to organize; and urban working-class women did not embrace a movement that did not seem receptive to the foreign born and did not directly address economic issues. *Id.*, at 193. By the mid-1900s, suffragists concluded that they had to move back toward a more inclusive vision of the franchise, and the turning point in the suffrage movement came around 1910 when working-class interest, expressed through organizations like the AFL, joined forces with the suffragist movement. The role of women in World War I gave a further legitimating push to the movement, and in 1918, Congress approved the Nineteenth Amendment and sent it for ratification to the states. Rejected through most of the South, the amendment was approved in the West, Northeast, Midwest (including Oklahoma), and Kentucky, Arkansas, Texas, and, by a margin of one vote, in Tennessee, which made Tennessee the thirty-sixth state necessary and made the Amendment law on August 18, 1920.

Ironically, though the electorate nearly doubled in size between 1910 and 1920 as a result, voting patterns and partisan alignments appear to have been not affected significantly. *Id.*, at 218.

2. In *A Revolution Too Soon: Woman Suffragists and the "Living Constitution," 1869-1875,* (forthcoming 2001), Adam Winkler documents the constitutional arguments and political motivations behind the *Minor* litigation. Suffragists had first hoped that the franchise would come at the same time with the enfranchisement of black citizens in the Fifteenth Amendment, and when that failed, they pursued congressional endorsement of a Sixteenth Amendment to guarantee female suffrage. But in the opening address of the Woman Suffrage Convention in St. Louis, Missouri in late 1869, Virgina Minor had boldly claimed that the Fourteenth Amendment already secured women's right to vote. When legislative efforts failed, even though the Grant Administration and Republican Party was seemingly sympathetic, suffragists picked up Minor's strategy and pursued it in several forms, including the efforts of Minor and Susan B. Anthony to actually register and vote, followed by litigation when their right to do was denied.

Winkler argues that the theory of constitutional interpretation deployed in these litigations was the first major example of an "evolving jurisprudence" mode of argument. Throughout the 19th century, constitutional theory and practice emphasized originalist modes of interpretation. Because the original intent of the Fourteenth and Fifteenth Amendments, still so recent in time, were widely recognized not to support women's suffrage, Minor, Stanton, and others argued that the status of women had been evolving in law and that these changes should be read into the Fourteenth Amendment to make voting a right of citizenship that women too now possessed. As evidence of these legal changes, suffragists pointed out that women in some states could sue and be sued; make contracts in their own name even though married; could do business in their own names; obtain passports; had the right to inherit property in their own name though married; and similar developments. They also attacked the premises of originalist jurisprudence. *Minor* rejected these efforts to assert a more evolutive approach to constitutional interpretation and re-asserted the conventional originalist methodology. Thus, this first effort to "evolutive interpretation" failed, in part because it was too close in time to the originalist history it sought to reject, and also in part, Winkler suggests, because suffragists sought to use the method to achieve a dramatic transformation for which no constitutional groundwork had been laid. Winkler argues that later uses of this method, as in the civil rights and "right to privacy" arenas, worked in part because they operated in more piecemeal fashion and built up step-by-step small victories as a foundation to larger assaults on originalism. On the general problem of how aggressively reformers should pursue legal change in the face of various constraints, see the interesting analysis in Dan Kahan, *Gentle Nudges v. Hard Shoves: Solving the Sticky Norms Problem*, 67 U. CHI. L. REV. 607 (2000).

3. In NO CONSTITUTIONAL RIGHT TO BE LADIES 81-124 (1998), historian Linda Kerber recovers the history of one of the central modes through which suffragists struggled for the right to vote. They articulated a conception of citizenship and the relationship between its burdens and rights that hearkened back to the "no taxation without representation" principles of the American Revolution. In the post-Civil War era, many women owned property, and activists began to refuse to pay taxes as long as they were not permitted to vote. One contemporaneous study concluded that women paid one-eleventh of all taxes collected in Massachusetts (or one-twelfth, if poll taxes were included, which women could not pay). A particularly vivid way the unfair burden argument was illustrated noted that in Newton, Massachusetts, one woman paid as much tax to the state as 1,424 male voters. Similarly, the women in the state overall were calculated to have paid six times the amount of tax as the bottom 80% of men who voted in statewide elections (and who paid only poll taxes, since they had no taxable property).

One of the most noticed tax revolt episodes involved two wealthy sisters in their seventies and eighties who refused to pay what were the highest property taxes in their Vermont town, as long as they could not vote. For seven years, the Smith sisters publicly fought the town, in print and public contests, and their cows and land were seized for non-payment of taxes. The Smith sisters attacked the legitimating concept of virtual representation, by which husbands were thought to represent the interests of wives, by asserting that women and men had distinct interests. They also made claims based in part on appeals to women's "special virtues:" they argued that women were more honest, better citizens, more moral than men, and that women "are never seen round the grogshops." They also argued that local governments dealt with issues of "civic housekeeping," such as the cleanliness of water supplies and sewers, or the safety of roads, on which women's domestic expertise would be an advantage. Not only were women denied the right to vote on these issues, they could not talk in town meetings addressing them. After more than a decade of litigation, the Smiths finally were relieved of their tax default status, but on technical grounds not reaching the question of principle their protest meant to raise. The notoriety of their tax protest, however, fueled similar tax protests elsewhere.

4. In *Collective Memory and the Nineteenth Amendment: Reasoning about "the Woman Question" in the Discourse of Sex Discrimination*, in HISTORY, MEMORY, AND THE LAW 131 (A. SARAT and T. KEARNS eds. 1999), Reva B. Siegel explores the differences in the way the law treats race versus sex discrimination. This difference is reflected in provocatively diverse methods of interpretation of the Fourteenth versus the Nineteenth Amendment. Siegel argues that claims of racial discrimination are typically rooted in narrative accounts that focus on the role of formal legal racism and, concomitantly, understand the Fourteenth Amendment as a constitutional commitment to transcend this history. In contrast, legal claims today about sex equality lack a similar historical structure. "Where claims of race discrimination invoke a lengthy national history of state-sanctioned coercion, claims about sex discrimination often refer to a history of social attitudes that are the product of custom and consensus." *Id.*, at 132. Moreover, Siegel argues:

> The prevailing understanding of the Nineteenth and Fourteenth Amendments thus illustrates how the social memory of gender relations shapes and is shaped by acts of constitutional interpretation. In the quest for the vote, generations of American women resisted their pervasive legal disempowerment and raised core concerns about the organizing principles and institutions of American life. Their struggle provoked wide-ranging debate that explored the relations of the sexes, both in the family and in the state. This national, multigenerational debate about the norms that should structure public and private life ultimately produced a constitutional commitment to revise foundational structures of the Republic. During the 1920s, at least some courts responded to the ratification of the Nineteenth Amendment in ways that reflected the social meaning and institutional preoccupations of the women suffrage campaign. But this response was both hesitant and fleeting, and the meaning of the suffrage struggle soon faded from popular and legal consciousness. When, decades later, the Court finally began to develop a body of constitutional doctrine protecting women's rights under the Fourteenth Amendment, it did not build upon the memory of the woman suffrage campaign, but instead proceeded to elaborate a body of sex discrimination doctrine that is fundamentally indifferent to the history of women's struggles in the American legal system. Thus, the very body of law that currently protects women's rights is elaborated in terms that (1) efface the history of women's resistance to legal imposition and (2) obscure the specific institutional sites of that struggle.

Id., at 141. For an earlier version of this view, see also W. William Hodes, *Women and the Constitution: Some Legal History and a New Approach to the Nineteenth Amendment*, 25 RUTGERS L. REV. 26, 50 (1970) (arguing that "the 19th amendment really had very little to do with the vote, but instead established the total equality of women with men. Under such an interpretation, there is a national right in all women to suffer no discrimination of any kind *because of their sex.*").

5. With respect to methods of constitutional interpretation, recall that the Fifteenth, Nineteenth, and Twentysixth Amendments are drafted in virtually

identical language. They prohibit denial or abridgement of the right to vote on grounds of race, gender, and age over 18 years. If Professor Siegel's arguments are correct about the transformative reading of the Nineteenth Amendment, should that mean that the Fifteenth and Twentysixth Amendments should – or indeed, must – be interpreted in similarly transformative ways? Or if there is some difference in how these Amendments should be interpreted, must that difference be found in something outside their written texts, which speak in nearly identical language? The Supreme Court, as you know from Chapter 2, has never given the Fifteenth Amendment an expansive or transformative reading, nor has the Twentysixth Amendment been the font of significant constitutional development. Should we read these Amendments "intratextually," so that the words "the right to vote," "denied," and "abridged" are given the same meaning across the Amendments? For an argument in favor of such a method of interpretation, see Akhil R. Amar, *Intratextualism*, 112 HARV. L. REV. 747, 748 (1999) ("In deploying this technique, the interpreter tries to read a contested word or phrase that appears in the Constitution in light of another passage in the Constitution featuring the same (or a very similar) word or phrase."). But in light of the Court's readings of the Fifteenth and Twentysixth Amendments, would intratextualism then not require rejection of Siegel's interpretive approach to the Nineteenth Amendment?

6. For a well-regarded three-hour documentary on the history of the woman's suffrage movement by noted director Ken Burns, go to http://www/pbs.org/stantonanthony/.

FURTHER NOTES ON FELON DISFRANCHISEMENT

Page 40, after note 4:

5.   Currently, three states -- Maine, Vermont, and Massachusetts -- extend the franchise to all offenders (Massachusetts has a measure on the ballot for Nov., 2000 that would ban inmates from voting). Twenty-one states permit ex-offenders to vote but disenfranchise incarcerated and unincarcerated offenders; fourteen other states disenfranchise for life all offenders who have not been pardoned.   Andrew Shapiro, Note, *Challenging Criminal Disenfranchisement Under the Voting Rights Act: A New Strategy*, 103 YALE L.J. 537, 556 (1993).

6. Given dramatic increases in incarceration rates in recent years, and the disproportionate incarceration rates of black men in particular, the aggregate racial impact of felon disfranchisement laws is becoming an increasing focus of public debate and litigation. Nationally, 13 percent of black men cannot vote because of criminal records; in Alabama and Florida, nearly one in three black men are permanently disfranchised. No other democracy appears to disfranchise as many people due to criminal records. Tamar Lewin, *Crime Costs Many Black Men the Vote, Study Says*, N.Y. Times, Oct. 23, 1998, at A-14. A class-action suit has been filed recently in the federal district court for the Southern District of Florida challenging the Florida disfranchisement provision on the ground that it rests on racially discriminatory purposes in violation of the Fourteenth Amendment and the Voting Rights Act.

7.   In light of increased focus on issues of race and felony disfranchisement, we provide more information here on the important litigation in *Baker v. Pataki*, 85 F.3d 919 (2d Cir. 1996) (en banc), noted in the casebook at p.39. *Baker* challenged New York laws that denied the vote to incarcerated and paroled felons (but not to felons serving suspended sentences or sentences of probation). Plaintiffs argued that these felon-disfranchisement provisions violated section 2 of the Voting Rights Act, as amended in 1982. Amended section 2 prohibits the use of any "voting qualification" that "results" in a denial or abridgement of the vote on account of race or color. (Section 2 is treated in depth in the casebook in Chapter 7. See particularly the casebook's discussion of *Ortiz v. City of Philadelphia*, at pages 543-45.)

Plaintiffs argued that there were race-based disparities in New York's conviction rate and sentencing practices, and that in combination with these disparities, New York's felon-disfranchisement law violated the VRA's "results" test. The District Court dismissed the complaint for failure to state a claim. After a panel of the Second Circuit reversed that decision, the Second Circuit voted to hear the case *en banc*. The Second Circuit then split 5-5, the result being that the District Court's dismissal decision was affirmed. Several judges, however, wrote opinions explaining their views on an issue that will surely return to the courts soon. These opinions exemplify the complex interplay between the constitutional power of Congress to regulate voting, the Voting Rights Act, and state-election laws.

Judges Mahoney, Miner, Walker, McLaughlin, and Jacobs concluded that section 2 does not reach felon-disfranchisement laws, for if the Voting Rights Act did so, Congress would have exceeded its enforcement powers. On this view, the mere fact that felon-disfranchisement laws might have the effect of disproportionately denying the vote to blacks and Hispanics would not be sufficient to justify a congressional ban on those laws. Congress' powers to enforce the Fourteenth and Fifteenth Amendments though appropriate legislation extends, in this view, only to laws that perpetuate the effects of past (or present) *purposeful* discrimination. These judges went on to argue that the widespread historical practice of felon disfranchisement, combined with the textual recognition of this practice in the Fourteenth Amendment, precluded such laws from being characterized as perpetuating the effects of past discrimination.

Judges Feinberg, Newman, Meskill, Kearse, and Parker disagreed. They concluded that, as a matter of statutory interpretation, section 2 of the Voting Rights Act should be construed to apply to felon-disfranchisement laws. Moreover, these judges also concluded that Congress had the constitutional power to enact a provision with this scope. They argued that, while the Fourteenth Amendment's text does make clear that states have the power to deny the vote to felons, the states do not have the power to do so "on the basis of race." They rejected the view that Congress only had the power to ban voting practices only if the ban addressed "historical discrimination of an unconstitutional kind." Even if this were the constitutional standard, however, these judges argued that there was sufficient evidence that state felon-disfranchisement laws had often been used to deny the vote because of race. These judges would therefore have remanded the case for trial on whether New York's law in fact violated section 2. Plaintiffs had also argued that New York's law itself directly violated the Constitution, under both the Fourteenth and Fifteenth Amendments. The *en banc* court did not address the constitutional claims. The constitutional claims thus survived the 5-5 affirmance of the district court's dismissal of the VRA claims but apparently the plaintiffs abandoned their attempt to prove purposeful discrimination.

Does Congress have the power to ban state felon-disfranchisement laws? What findings would Congress have to make to justify such a ban? Does the view of Judge Mahoney and his colleagues lead to the conclusion that section 2 of the Voting Rights Act, as amended in 1982, is unconstitutional? Or only unconstitutional as applied to felon-disfranchisement laws? These are extremely complex and important questions; they go to the heart of the relationship between national and state power under the Constitution with respect to voting. They cannot be fully explored until you have studied Chapters 5, 6, and 7 of the casebook and its supplemental materials on the *City of Boerne* case and its doctrinal aftermath. You should consider these questions now and revisit them later in the course.

8. One recent study suggests that felon disfranchisement is not just a matter of the rights of disfranchised voters, but might also have significant, national electoral and policy consequences. *See* Christopher Uggen and Jeff Manza, *The Political Consequences of Felon Disfranchisement Laws in the United States* (Draft, Aug. 11, 2000) (presented to the American Sociological Association). Given the dramatic rise in incarceration rates in the last decade, the authors estimate that in 1998 over 4.7 million United States citizens – a noteworthy 2.36 percent of the voting age population – were disenfranchised due to felony convictions. In individual states, the figures are even more striking; in Florida, for example, a remarkable 8.55 percent of the voting-age population was disfranchised in the 1998 election (Florida is one of the states that permanently deny convicted felons the right to vote, unless re-instated by

pardon).

To determine what the voter turnout and preference of disenfranchised felons would have been in past elections, the authors "matched" regional felon populations to non-felon populations in terms of socio-demographic attributes generally considered to contribute to voter turnout and preferences. The attributes used were gender, race, age, income, labor force status, marital status and education. The results of this matching indicate that, on average since 1972, thirty-two percent of disfranchised voters would have voted in presidential elections, twenty-nine percent in senatorial elections held in presidential election years, and seventeen percent in senatorial elections held in non-presidential election years. With few exceptions, these hypothetical voters would have strongly preferred Democratic to Republican candidates, based on the socio-demographic characteristics of the disfranchised. The study assumes that the experience of criminal conviction itself does not affect electoral behavior.

What does this mean in terms of actual election results for either Senators or Presidents? The authors speculate that if disfranchised felons had been allowed to vote in senatorial elections since 1972, they may have erased the Republican margin of victory in at least seven contests. In other words, seven Democratic Senators since 1972 would have been elected rather than their Republican counterparts -- include such important Republicans as Sen. Mitch McConnell (Ky.), Sen. Connie Mack (Fla.), and Sen. John Warner (Va.). Assuming that the Democrats elected in the absence of disfranchisement would have held their seats as long as the Republicans who defeated them, the Democrats might well have held majority control of the Senate from 1986 to 2000. If this result holds up statistically, it offers a dramatic picture of the political consequences of laws that ban felons and ex-felons from voting.

The level of incarceration in the United States has increased dramatically in the last forty years. Turning to close Presidential elections, the authors speculate, based on their empirical analysis, that had the current level of incarceration existed at the time of the 1960 Presidential election, it is very likely that Richard Nixon would have defeated John Kennedy in the popular vote and possible that Nixon would have won the electoral college vote as well.

Page 53, after note 2:

Note that the case *Harper* overruled, *Breedlove v. Suttles*, 302 U.S. 277 (1937), in which the Court had upheld poll taxes, contained a gender dimension not discussed in *Harper*. The $1 Georgia poll tax in *Breedlove* exempted women who did not register to vote as well as the blind. As part of the constitutional challenge to the poll tax, the ACLU challenged this gender-based exemption on behalf of a male plaintiff (Norman Breedlove, who cumulatively owed $13.50 in poll taxes) as both a violation of the Fourteenth and the Nineteenth Amendments. To the former, the Court responded that "discrimination in favor of all women being permissible," the selective exemption for a subset of women was constitutional. Women could "be exempted on the basis of special considerations to which they are naturally entitled. In view of burdens necessarily borne by them for the preservation of the race, the State reasonably may exempt them from poll taxes." *Id.*, at 282 (citing, inter alia, *Muller v. Oregon*, 208 U.S. 412 (1908)). To the Nineteenth Amendment argument, the Court replied "[i]t is fanciful to suggest that the Georgia law is a mere disguise

under which to deny or abridge the right of men to vote on account of their sex."
Id., at 284. Poll taxes, of course, weighed more heavily on women than men, given that women's median income was substantially below that of men (unless the male paid the tax of, for example, his wife), and the "special treatment" provision of Georgia law might be thought to have encouraged women and men to think of a woman going to the polls as an expensive luxury.

Page 68, add the following new section before Chapter 2 C:

B.

2. TERRITORIAL DISENFRANCHISEMENT

In addition to section 2 of the Fourteenth Amendment (treated in *Richardson v. Ramirez*, in the casebook at pp. 33-40), several provisions of Articles I and II of the Constitution might have special resonance for challenges to certain forms of disenfranchisement. Two current examples concern the voting rights of U.S. citizens who live in Puerto Rico or in the District of Columbia.

The following two principal cases raise interesting issues in their own right. They also pose important questions about the relationship between the electoral provisions of the original Constitution and the Fourteenth Amendment, as well as about dynamic versus originalist methods of constitutional interpretation.

Igartua De La Rosa v. United States
___ F.3d ___ (1st Cir. 2000) (per curiam)

Before Torruella, Chief Judge, Lynch and Lipez, Circuit Judges

.... [Eleven] citizens of the United States residing in Puerto Rico [allege] they are being deprived of the right to vote for the candidates to the offices of President and Vice-President of the United States, a condition which they view to be a "violation of their constitutional rights to the same privileges and immunities, treaty rights, due process and equal protection of the laws" enjoyed by United States citizens residing in the States....

After several intervening procedural events, on August 29, 2000 the district court entered a ... Final Judgment:

(1) Declaring "that the United States Citizens residing in Puerto Rico have the right to vote in Presidential elections and that its electoral votes must be counted in Congress"; [and]

(2) Concluding "that the Government of Puerto Rico has the obligation to organize the means by which the United States citizens residing in Puerto Rico will vote in the upcoming and subsequent Presidential elections and to provide for the appointment of Presidential electors," and ordering "the Government of Puerto Rico to act with all possible

expediency to create such mechanism"; ....

On September 10, 2000 the Legislature of Puerto Rico enacted Law No. 403 for the purpose of allowing the citizens of the United States of America domiciled in Puerto Rico to vote in the election for the offices of President and Vice-President of the United States, and to establish the procedures and mechanisms to effectuate said vote. This bill was signed into law on September 10, 2000 and became effective immediately....

For the reasons stated herein, we reverse and vacate the Final Judgment and Final Opinion and Order and remand with instructions to dismiss the action....

I

In [*Igartua De La Rosa v. United States*, 842 F. Supp. 607 (D.P.R. 1994), *aff'd*, 32 F.3d 8 (1st Cir. 1994), cert. denied, 514 U.S. 1049 (1995) (*Igartua I*)], a case brought by the same lead plaintiff and lawyer who appears currently before us, this court held with undeniable clarity that the Constitution of the United States does not confer upon United States citizens residing in Puerto Rico a right to participate in the national election for President and Vice-President. Addressing precisely the argument presented to the district court in this case, this court recognized that Article II of the Constitution explicitly provides that the President of the United States shall be elected by electors who are chosen by the States, in such manner as each state's legislature may direct. We concluded that Puerto Rico, which is not a State, may not designate electors to the electoral college, and therefore that the residents of Puerto Rico have no constitutional right to participate in the national election of the President and Vice-President.

Since our decision in *Igartua I* in 1994, Puerto Rico has not become a State, nor has the United States amended the Constitution to allow United States citizens residing in Puerto Rico to vote for President, as it did for United States citizens residing in the District of Columbia with the Twenty-Third Amendment to the Constitution. Absent such a change in the status of Puerto Rico or an amendment to the Constitution of the United States, our decision in *Igartua I* controls this case, unless there has been intervening controlling or compelling authority....

There are two exceptions to the rule that earlier decisions are binding. First, an earlier panel decision "may be undermined by controlling authority, subsequently announced, such as an opinion of the Supreme Court." The second exception is for "those relatively rare instances in which authority that postdates the original decision, although not directly controlling, nevertheless offers a sound reason for believing that the former panel, in light of fresh development, would change its collective mind." The Commonwealth [of Puerto Rico, which has intervened in this lawsuit to support the plaintiffs,] argues that those exceptions are met here in light of two Supreme Court decisions: *Rice v. Cayetano*, 528 U.S. 495 (2000), and *U.S. Term Limits v. Thornton*, 514 U.S. 779 (1995). Neither case support the Commonwealth's argument.

The Court in *Rice* struck down a Hawaii statute that imposed race-based voting qualifications based on the Fifteenth Amendment's mandate that neither the National Government nor the states may deny or abridge the right to vote on account of race. This Fifteenth Amendment ruling on racial voting classifications does not impact the reasoning in *Igartua I* that Article II governs the right to vote in presidential elections. The reliance on the Court's holding in *U.S. Term Limits* similarly is inapt. The Court ruled that States lack the power to impose qualifications for offices of the United States Congress in addition to those set forth in the Constitution. The Court's language describing the "fundamental principle of our representative democracy" ... serves to amplify the Court's holding that the states cannot impose restrictions on federal elections, but also does not alter the Article II analysis in *Igartua I*. Thus, neither case stands for the proposition that the right to vote in the presidential election is derived from any source other than Article II of the Constitution....

TORRUELLA, Circuit Judge (concurring).

As I did in *Igartua I*, I join the Court's opinion in this appeal because I believe it to be technically and, as the law now stands, legally correct in its conclusion that the Constitution does not guarantee United States citizens residing in Puerto Rico the right to vote in the national Presidential election.... I am, however, compelled to write separately because I can no longer remain silent to the subjacent question, because from my perspective, there are larger issues at stake.

I.

More than 100 years ago, at the conclusion of the Spanish-American War of 1898, Puerto Rico was ceded to the United States by Spain. Despite lofty rhetoric at the time extolling the virtues of American democracy, the United States has since exercised almost unfettered power over Puerto Rico and the nearly 4,000,000 United States citizens who currently reside there [This is a larger population than 26 States]. Although persons born in Puerto Rico are citizens of the United States at birth, and thereby "owe[] allegiance to the United States," while residing in Puerto Rico they enjoy fewer rights than citizens of the United States that reside in the fifty States, or even in foreign countries. Undoubtedly the most glaring evidence of this egregious disparity is the fact that they do not elect a single voting representative to a federal government that exercises almost absolute power over them.

This anomalous situation arises primarily as a result of the decisions of the Supreme Court in the *Insular Cases,* which established as early as 1901 the plenary power of Congress over Puerto Rico under the so-called "territorial" clause of the Constitution [U.S. Constn., Art. IV, Sec. 3, cl.2]. In a series of narrowly divided decisions, the Court held that Puerto Rico was an "unincorporated territory," and as a result part of the United States for some purposes and not for others. As such, Congress was held to have plenary power over the internal and external affairs of the Island, subject not even to the Bill of Rights except insofar as those guarantees might be explicitly extended to the Island by Congress....

[T]he Supreme Court in 1922 in *Balzac v. Porto Rico*, 258 U.S. 298 (1922), established the inferior nature of the United States citizenship held by residents of Puerto Rico by concluding that the Constitution's protection of these new citizens was limited to those rights deemed by the Court to be "fundamental." *Cf. Yick Wo v. Hopkins*, 118 U.S. 356 (1886) (voting is "a fundamental political right, because [it is] preservative of all rights").

II.

Since Balzac the civil rights of United States citizens residing in Puerto Rico, particularly their national political rights, have remained dormant at best, subject to the vagaries of Congress, and the conspicuous inattention of the judiciary. The granting of so-called "Commonwealth" status in 1952, itself an enigmatic condition which merely allowed the residents of Puerto Rico limited self-government, did nothing to correct Puerto Rico's fundamental condition of national unempowerment, embodied most notably in the lack of voting representation in the Congress and the ineligibility to vote for President and Vice-President. The United States citizens residing in Puerto Rico to this day continue to have no real say in the choice of those who, from afar, really govern them, nor as to the enactment, application, and administration of the myriad of federal laws and regulations that control almost every aspect of their daily affairs....

The present conundrum cannot be justified or perpetuated further under the subterfuge of labeling it a "political question." Undoubtedly, this situation is "political" in the sense that it involves the political rights of a substantial number of United States citizens. It is also "political" because it is one that should, in the normal course of things, be resolved by the political process and the political branches of government. But in the final analysis, this problem is no more "political" than that presented to and resolved by the Supreme Court in *Brown v. Board of Education*, 347 U.S. 483 (1954) . . .

The United States citizens residing in Puerto Rico are caught in an untenable Catch-22. The national disenfranchisement of these citizens ensures that they will never be able, through the political processes, to rectify the denial of their civil rights in those very political processes. This uninterrupted condition clearly provides solid basis for judicial intervention at some point, one for which there is resounding precedent.

III

In this 211th year of the United States Constitution, and 102nd year of United States presence in Puerto Rico, United States citizenship must mean more than merely the freedom to travel to and from the United States. This citizenship should not, cannot, be devalued to such a low scale.

After more than a century of United States possession of Puerto Rico, there continues to be tremendous debate over the status of the Island and the nature of its relationship with the United States. Certainly the citizens of Puerto Rico are divided on the issue, a condition which has permitted the federal government to externalize this question. What is established, for the time being at least, is that the federal courts continue to recognize the almost absolute power of Congress to unilaterally dictate the affairs of Puerto Rico and her people. So long as that is the case, the practicality of the matter is that Puerto Rico remains a colony with little prospect of exerting effective political pressure on the elected branches of government to take corrective action.

The contemporary society of United States citizens residing in Puerto Rico hardly deserves colonial treatment by the United States, assuming that such treatment is ever justified....

The perpetuation of this colonial condition runs against the very principles upon which this Nation was founded. Indefinite colonial rule by the United States is not something that was contemplated by the Founding Fathers nor authorized per secula seculorum by the Constitution. And far from being a matter of local concern to the United States citizens in Puerto Rico only, the inequality to which these citizens are subjected is an injury to every American, because as surely as the current situation causes irreparable harm to United States citizens residing in Puerto Rico, it just as powerfully denigrates the entire Nation and the Constitution.

Although this is not the case, nor perhaps the time, for a federal court to take remedial action to correct what is a patently intolerable situation, it is time to serve notice upon the political branches of government that it is incumbent upon them, in the first instance, to take appropriate steps to correct what amounts to an outrageous disregard for the rights of a substantial segment of its citizenry. A failure to do so countenances corrective judicial action....

Adams v. Clinton
90 F. Supp. 2d 35 (D.D.C. 2000) (three-judge court) (per curiam), aff'd
___ U.S. ___ (2000)

Before Garland, Circuit Judge, and Oberdorfer and Kollar-Kotelly, District Judges

In these consolidated lawsuits, seventy-five residents of the District of Columbia, along with the District of Columbia itself, challenge as unconstitutional the denial of their right to elect representatives to the Congress of the United States. Plaintiffs argue that their exclusion from representation is unjust. They note that the citizens of the District pay federal taxes and defend the United States in times of war, yet are denied any vote in the Congress that levies those taxes and declares those wars. This, they continue, contravenes a central tenet of our nation's ideals: that governments "derive their just powers from the consent of the governed." The Declaration of Independence, ¶ 2.

None of the parties contests the justice of plaintiffs' cause. President Clinton and the other defendants, however, maintain that the dictates of the Constitution and the decisions of the Supreme Court bar us from providing the relief plaintiffs seek. Any such relief, they say, must come through the political process.

Plaintiffs' grievances are serious, and we have given them the most serious consideration. In the end, however, we are constrained to agree with defendants that the remedies plaintiffs request are beyond this court's authority to grant....

IV

....Article I, section 2, clause 1 of the Constitution provides:

> The House of Representatives shall be composed of Members chosen every second Year by the People of the several States, and the Electors in each State shall have the Qualifications requisite for Electors of the most numerous Branch of the State Legislature.

U.S. Const. art. I, § 2, cl. 1. Although standing alone the phrase "people of the several States" could be read as meaning all the people of the "United States" and not simply those who are citizens of individual states, the Article's subsequent and repeated references to "state[s]" -- beginning with the balance of the same clause quoted above -- make clear that the former was not intended. *See, e.g., id.* (electors "in each State" shall have qualifications of electors of most numerous branch "of the State Legislature"); *id.* art. I, § 2, cl. 2 (each representative shall "be an Inhabitant of that State" in which he or she is chosen); *id.* art. I, § 2, cl. 3 (representatives shall be "apportioned among the several States which may be included within this Union"); *id.* ("each State shall have at Least one Representative"); *id.* art. I, § 2, cl. 4 (the Executive Authority of the "State" shall fill vacancies); *id.* art. I, § 4, cl. 1 (the legislature of "each State" shall prescribe times, places, and manner of holding elections for representatives). Indeed, for this reason ... residents of United States territories are not entitled to vote in federal elections, notwithstanding that they are United States citizens.

.... [Plaintiffs] contend that District residents can fairly be characterized as citizens of a "state," as the term was intended in Article I, under either of two theories. First, they argue that the District of Columbia itself may be treated as a state through which its citizens may vote.   Second, they contend that District citizens may vote in congressional elections through the State of Maryland, based on their "residual" citizenship in that state -- the state from whose territory the current District was originally carved. In the following sections we consider the validity of each theory.

A

As plaintiffs correctly note, the Supreme Court has on occasion interpreted the constitutional term "state" to include the District. ... . As they concede, however, the Court also has interpreted the term "state" to exclude the District. ...

The measure of "whether the District of Columbia constitutes a 'State or Territory' within the meaning of any particular . . . constitutional provision depends upon the character and aim of the specific provision involved." *District of Columbia v. Carter*, 409 U.S. 418 (1973)....

1. We begin with the language of Article I, which makes clear just how deeply Congressional representation is tied to the structure of statehood....

Including the District within the definition of "state" is ... inconsistent with the provisions of clause 3 of Article I, section 2, the clause that directly addresses the issue of congressional apportionment. That clause provides that "Representatives . . . shall be apportioned among the several States which may be included within this Union, according to their respective numbers." U.S. Const. art. I, § 2, cl. 3.

That provision plainly contemplates true states and not the District, which neither was one of the original states nor has been "admitted by the Congress into this Union." *Id.* art. IV, § 3, cl. 1. Indeed, the "Seat of Government" contemplated by the Constitution is subsequently described in Article I as a "District," in contrast to the "particular States" whose cessions of territory were expected to create it. And, as if to remove any doubt, clause 3 goes on to identify specifically those thirteen entities it regards as the immediate post-ratification states, and to assign each an initial apportionment of representatives until an "actual Enumeration" of "each State's" "respective Numbers" can be accomplished. *Id.* art. I, § 2, cl. 3. The District is not included within that initial apportionment....

2. We conclude from our analysis of the text that the Constitution does not contemplate that the District may serve as a state for purposes of the apportionment of congressional representatives. That textual evidence is supported by historical evidence concerning the general understanding at the time of the District's creation.

It is true, as plaintiffs note, that the voting rights of District residents received little express attention at the time of the Constitution's drafting. *See generally* Peter Raven-Hansen, *Congressional Representation for the District of Columbia: A Constitutional Analysis*, 12 HARV. J. LEGIS. 167, 172 (1975). As plaintiffs suggest, this lack of attention may have been due to the fact that the District's geographic location had not yet been determined, and that even once selected, the territory had relatively few residents. It is also true, as our dissenting colleague argues, that the historical rationale for the District Clause -- ensuring that Congress would not have to depend upon another sovereign for its protection -- would not by itself require the exclusion of District residents from the congressional franchise....

Such evidence as does exist, however, indicates a contemporary understanding that residents of the District would not have a vote in the national Congress. At the New York ratifying convention, for example, Thomas Tredwell argued that "the plan of the federal city, sir, departs from every principle of freedom . . . subjecting the inhabitants of that district to the exclusive legislation of Congress, in whose appointment they have no share or vote." On the same day at that convention, Alexander Hamilton proposed that the Constitution be amended to provide: "When the Number of Persons in the District or Territory to be laid out for the Seat of the Government of the United States . . . amount to [an unspecified number] . . . Provision shall be made by Congress for having a District representation in that Body." The proposed amendment failed.

Considerably more evidence of the contemporary understanding emerges from examination of the period immediately surrounding Congress' assumption of exclusive jurisdiction over the land ceded for the District by Maryland and Virginia. During that period, some residents of the District sought to dissuade Congress from passing the

Organic Act of 1801, through which jurisdiction was to be assumed. They believed that, under the Constitution, once Congress assumed jurisdiction they would necessarily lose their vote and be "reduced to the mortifying situation, of being subject to laws made, or to be made, by we know not whom; by agents, not of our choice, in no degree responsible to us." Members of Congress opposed to the Organic Act made the same argument. Even those who supported the Act appeared to agree that, under the Constitution, once Congress assumed jurisdiction the residents would automatically lose their right to vote....

Within a few years of the assumption of congressional jurisdiction, still others saw retrocession of the District to Maryland and Virginia as the only remedy for the "political slavery" of nonrepresentation. In 1803, a bill calling for retrocession was introduced in Congress. Although the bill was defeated, the residents of the former Virginia territory eventually succeeded in obtaining retrocession in 1846.

Although the foregoing represents positive evidence of a contemporary understanding that District residents would not (and did not) have the right to vote in Congress, perhaps more important is the absence of evidence to the contrary....

3. Finally, we note that every other court to have considered the question -- whether in dictum or in holding -- has concluded that residents of the District do not have the right to vote for members of Congress....

B

As an alternative to the argument that the District may be considered a state under Article I, [some of the] plaintiffs contend that residents of the District should be permitted to vote in congressional elections through Maryland, based on a theory of "residual" citizenship in that state. This theory depends heavily on the fact that residents of the land ceded by Maryland apparently continued to vote in Maryland elections during the period between the Act of 1790, by which Congress accepted the cession, and the Organic Act of 1801, by which Congress assumed jurisdiction and provided for the government of the District....

[T]his theory ... has already been rejected in a decision binding upon this court. In *Albaugh v. Tawes*, a three-judge district court considered a suit seeking a declaratory judgment "that the District of Columbia is a part of the State of Maryland for purposes of United States Senator elections." 233 F. Supp. 576 (D. Md. 1964).... The court rejected plaintiffs' claims, noting the Supreme Court's decision in *Reily v. Lamar* [6 U.S. (2 Cranch) 344 (1805)] that former residents of Maryland lost their state citizenship upon "the separation of the District of Columbia from the State of Maryland."...

The Supreme Court affirmed the decision of the three-judge court [in a summary affirmance opinion].

3.   [Among plaintiffs' arguments is the contention that the creation of the District could not constitutionally have withdrawn the right to vote in Maryland].... The original residents of the District were among the people of the states by virtue of their citizenship in Maryland, plaintiffs argue, and they therefore had an inalienable right to vote that could not be withdrawn. Moreover, plaintiffs contend that right continues to inhere in those who currently are residents of the District....

We cannot accept the argument that current residents of the District retain residual rights because other people, living 200 years earlier in the same place, had such rights. In the United States, personal rights generally do not "run with the land." Even if it could be argued that the right to vote was a privilege that irrevocably vested from 'the moment the United States Constitution was ratified" in "every citizen living in what were then the thirteen states of the union," including the portions of Maryland and Virginia that would later become the District, the argument would not extend to the present plaintiffs. By virtue of the passage of 200 years, all of the plaintiffs -- whether by birth or a combination of birth and their ancestors' migration -- arrived on the scene after the land already had become a district whose residents, by constitutional contemplation, lacked a vote in the national Congress. Whatever rights the original residents of the area may have had, none of them are alive to press them before this court....

4. We next consider an additional argument advanced in support of a right to vote in Maryland elections, this one based not only on the historical relationship between the District and Maryland, but also on the Supreme Court's ruling that residents of a federal enclave must be permitted to vote in the state from which the enclave was created. In *Evans v. Cornman*, the Supreme Court struck down under the Fourteenth Amendment's Equal Protection Clause a Maryland residency requirement that prevented persons living on the grounds of the National Institute of Health (NIH) from voting in state and federal elections. 398 U.S. 419 (1970). NIH had become a federal reservation in 1953, when Maryland ceded jurisdiction over the property to the United States. Fifteen years later, the state denied NIH residents the right to vote.

The Court began its analysis by noting that:

Appellees clearly live within the geographical boundaries of the State of Maryland, and they are treated as state residents in the census and in determining congressional apportionment. They are not residents of Maryland only if the NIH ceased to be a part of Maryland when the enclave was created. However, that "fiction of a state within a state" was specifically rejected by this Court ... and it cannot be resurrected here to deny appellees the right to vote.

It then proceeded to consider whether the state could deny plaintiffs the vote on the ground that they were neither substantially interested in nor affected by state electoral decisions. Maryland alleged that the plaintiffs were substantially less interested in state affairs than other Maryland residents because, under the Enclaves Clause, U.S. CONST. art. I, § 8, cl. 17, Congress had the power to exercise exclusive jurisdiction over the NIH.

The Supreme Court rejected the state's argument, noting that "the relationship between federal enclaves and the States in which they are located" had "changed considerably" over the years. In particular, it noted that Congress had passed a series of statutes expressly permitting states to extend many of their laws to cover enclave residents, including their criminal, tax, unemployment, and workers' compensation laws. Moreover, it noted that plaintiffs were "required to register their automobiles in Maryland and obtain drivers' permits and license plates from the State; they are subject to the process and jurisdiction of State courts; they themselves can resort to those courts in divorce and child adoption proceedings; and they send their children to Maryland public schools." All of this led the Court to conclude that

> In their day-to-day affairs, residents of the NIH grounds are just as interested in and connected with electoral decisions as they were prior to 1953 when the area came under federal jurisdiction and as are their neighbors who live off the enclave. In nearly every election, federal, state, and local, for offices from the Presidency to the school board, and on the entire variety of other ballot propositions, appellees have a stake equal to that of other Maryland residents.

Accordingly, Evans held that NIH residents were "entitled under the Fourteenth Amendment to protect that stake by exercising the equal right to vote."

Plaintiffs here argue that since the residents of federal enclaves are entitled to vote under Evans, the residents of the District should be so entitled as well. There is some appeal to that argument, as Congress's authority to govern enclaves is identical to its authority over the District, and is conferred by the same clause of the Constitution. *See* U.S. Const. art. I, § 8 ("The Congress shall have Power . . . . to exercise exclusive Legislation in all Cases whatsoever, over such District . . . as may, by Cession of particular States . . . become the Seat of the Government . . ., and to exercise like Authority over all Places purchased by the Consent of the Legislature of the State in which the Same shall be, for the Erection of Forts, Magazines, Arsenals, dock-Yards, and other needful Buildings . . . .") [The Court notes that the Constitution indicates that the District is created by "Cession" of particular States, while enclaves are purchsed with State consent "in which the Same [enclave' shall be," but concludes that whatever the possible significance of this difference, it has no bearing on this case].

But the fact that Congress may have identical authority over both the District and the enclaves is not dispositive, because the ultimate result in Evans rested on the fact that Congress had not exercised that authority over NIH. As noted above, Congress had passed statutes permitting Maryland to exercise its own authority in the enclave, and Maryland had done so extensively. It was Maryland's exercise of authority over the plaintiffs in that case -- in areas as disparate as motor vehicle regulation, state court jurisdiction, and public education -- that gave them "a stake equal to that of other Maryland residents." The case before us is plainly not analogous in this respect. Congress has ceded none of its authority over the District back to Maryland, and Maryland has not purported to exercise any of its authority in the District.

Plaintiffs do not dispute this distinction, and as a consequence do not contend that they have a right to vote in elections for the Maryland state legislature. Instead, they argue that while the absence of the exercise of Maryland authority over District residents might mean they have an insufficient interest in elections to Maryland's own legislature, "District citizens have an equally vital stake in elections to Congress" as other Maryland residents. Finding District residents qualified to vote for Congress but not for the Maryland legislature, however, would turn Article I on its head. As we have noted, Article I, section 2 states that "the [congressional] Electors in each State shall have the Qualifications requisite for Electors of the most numerous Branch of the State Legislature." U.S. Const. art. I, § 2, cl. 1. Plaintiffs' enclave theory, by contrast, would permit residents of the District to vote in Maryland's congressional elections notwithstanding that they lack -- even under an Evans theory -- precisely those qualifications....

V

In this Part, we consider plaintiffs' arguments based on provisions of the Constitution other than Article I. These include the Equal Protection, Privileges or Immunities, Due Process, and Republican Guarantee Clauses.

A

We first address the contention of the plaintiffs (and of out dissenting colleague) that the District's lack of representation in the

House deprives its residents of the equal protection of the laws. . . .The plaintiffs allege that the lack of representation renders them unequal to the residents of the fifty states and of the federal enclaves. And they further contend that because the right to vote is fundamental, such unequal treatment cannot be upheld unless it satisfies strict scrutiny -- that is, unless it is "narrowly tailored to serve a compelling" government interest....

We do not disagree that defendants have failed to offer a compelling justification for denying District residents the right to vote in Congress. As the dissent argues, denial of the franchise is not necessary for the effective functioning of the seat of government. The problem, however, is that strict scrutiny does not apply in this case. Although equal protection analysis scrutinizes the validity of classifications drawn by executive and legislative authorities, the classification complained of here is not the product of presidential, congressional, or state action. Instead, as we have just concluded, the voting qualification of which plaintiffs complain is one drawn by the Constitution itself. The Equal Protection Clause does not protect the right of all citizens to vote, but rather the right "of all *qualified* citizens to vote." *Reynolds v. Sims*, 377 U.S. 533 (1964) (emphasis added). "The right to vote in federal elections is conferred by Art. I, § 2, of the Constitution," *Harper v. Virginia Bd. of Elections*, 383 U.S. 663 (1966), and the right to equal protection cannot overcome the line explicitly drawn by that Article. . . .

.... Plaintiffs assert that, even if Article I were intended to deprive District residents of congressional representation ... that deprivation cannot continue in light of the expansive application of the principle [of one person, one vote] in modern equal protection analysis.

But the one person, one vote cases themselves make clear that the structural provisions of the Constitution necessarily limit the principle's application in federal elections. In *Reynolds v. Sims*, for example, the Court recognized that the allocation "to each of the 50 States, regardless of population" of two senators and at least one representative was inconsistent with one person, one vote. Nonetheless, the Court said, "The system of representation in the two Houses of the Federal Congress is one ingrained in our Constitution, as part of the law of the land." Moreover, and particularly relevant here, the Court declared that "the developing history and growth of our republic cannot cloud the fact that, at the time of the inception of the system of representation in the Federal Congress, a compromise between the larger and smaller states on this matter averted a deadlock in the Constitutional Convention which had threatened to abort the birth of our Nation." This, the Court said, rendered the composition of the House and Senate constitutionally compelled, and thus "inapposite and irrelevant to state legislative districting schemes."

In Gray v. Sanders, the Court had previously reached the same conclusion regarding the electoral college system used in presidential elections, which does not allocate voting strength in strict proportion to population, but which is nonetheless mandated by Article II, section 1 and the Twelfth Amendment. And subsequently, in *Department of Commerce v. Montana*, 503 U.S. 442 (1992), the Court noted two additional (and one of the same) limitations upon the one person, one vote principle. That "general admonition," the Court said, "is constrained by three requirements. The number of Representatives shall not exceed one for every 30,000 persons; each State shall have at least one Representative; and the district boundaries may not cross state lines."

In sum, notwithstanding the force of the one person, one vote principle in our constitutional jurisprudence, that doctrine cannot serve as a vehicle for challenging the structure the Constitution itself imposes upon the Congress.... [T]he differing treatment is the consequence not of legislative determinations but of constitutional distinctions. This court is without authority to scrutinize those distinctions to determine whether they are irrational, compelling, or anything in between.

B

Plaintiff also contend that the right to vote for members of Congress is a privilege of national citizenship....

We do not disagree that the "right to vote for national officers" is a "right[] and privilege[] of national citizenship." *Twining v. New Jersey*, 211 U.S. 78 (1908). Nor do we dispute Justice Kennedy's statements, in a concurrence repeatedly cited by plaintiffs, that this right arises out of the "relationship between the people of the Nation and their National Government, with which the States may not interfere." *U.S. Term Limits, Inc. v. Thornton*, 514 U.S. 779 (1995) (Kennedy, J., concurring). Indeed, as we noted above, it is Article I, section 2 that confers "the right to vote in federal elections." That, however, can hardly be the end of the inquiry, as even plaintiffs concede that residents of the territories do not have the right to vote in congressional elections, notwithstanding that they, too, are national (American) citizens.

Rather, it is precisely because it is Article I that confers the federal right to vote that we must look to that Article to provide its content and define its boundaries. Article I grants that right only to those who "have the Qualifications requisite for Electors of the most numerous Branch of the State Legislature." U.S. Const. art. I, § 2, cl. 1. Furthermore, it apportions representatives only "among the several States which may be included within this Union." *Id.* art. I, § 2, cl. 3. Thus, in Justice Kennedy's own words, the "Constitution uses state boundaries to fix the size of congressional delegations." Because we have previously concluded that the District cannot be characterized as a state for these purposes, and because therefore the constitutional provision that creates the federal right to vote does not include District residents within its terms, denial of the vote to those residents does not abridge their national privileges or immunities....

VI

As we have noted, many courts have found a contradiction between the democratic ideals upon which this country was founded and the exclusion of District residents from congressional representation. All, however, have concluded that it is the Constitution and judicial precedent that create the contradiction....

Like our predecessors, we are not blind to the inequity of the situation plaintiffs seek to change. But longstanding judicial precedent, as well as the Constitution's text and history, persuade us that this court lacks authority to grant plaintiffs the relief they seek. If they are to obtain it, they must plead their cause in other venues. Accordingly, plaintiffs' motions for summary judgment are denied, and defendants' motions to dismiss are granted with respect to those claims that challenge the constitutionality of the apportionment of the House of Representatives....

OBERDORFER, J, dissenting in part ....

.... I would hold that both Article I and principles of equal protection require this Court to declare that qualified residents of the District have a constitutional right to vote for voting representation in the House of Representatives....

.... Voting nationally has evolved from 18th century suffrage limited to white, property-owning, tax-paying males, over the age of 21, to the virtual universal suffrage today enjoyed by all but minors, felons, and the people of the District of Columbia....

In *Wesberry [v. Sanders* (1964)], the Supreme Court . . . . concluded that the Constitution requires that districts be apportioned so as to satisfy as nearly as possible the maxim "one person, one vote." The plain statement in Wesberry bears repeating:

> No right is more precious in a free country than that of having a voice in the election of those who make the laws under which, as good citizens, we must live. Other rights, even the most basic, are illusory if the right to vote is undermined. Our Constitution leaves no room for classification of people in a way that unnecessarily abridges that right.

For people in the District of Columbia, Congress is the ultimate "exclusive" legislature. The Secretary's continued failure to include the people of the District of Columbia in apportionment contributes to their heretofore permanent disenfranchisement in their ultimate legislature -- Congress -- because the place where they live, once part of the State of Maryland, is not now literally a State. Those who would interfere with the exercise of the "precious" right to vote have a heavy burden of persuasion and proof that their interference is "necessary." To put it simply, the defendants have failed to persuade me that it is necessary for the Secretary to exclude the people of the District from apportionment and thus interfere with their voting for a Member of the House of Representatives....

Given that the people living in the District from 1790-1800 had and exercised a constitutionally-protected right to vote for Congressional representation, and that that right was not, and could not have been, lost or waived in 1801 when the federal government assumed exclusive jurisdiction over the District, the question remains whether, under *Wesberry*, anything else necessitates defendants' continuing to deny or interfere with the right of their political posterity to vote for voting representation in the House of Representatives. Looking at the literal text of Article I and any necessary inferences therefrom, the 23rd amendment, nonvoting by citizens in the territories, and the lapse of time since the inhabitants of the District last voted in 1800, my answer is "nothing else."

1. Plain Language

The plain language of the Constitution does not necessitate denying the people of the District the right to voting representation in Congress. Neither the Seat of Government clause nor any other provision of Article I addresses, much less directly precludes, congressional representation for the people of the District. If the Framers intended to deny voting representation in Congress to the inhabitants of the Seat of Government, the Seat of Government clause was an appropriate place to say so. It does not....

2. Inferences from the use of the word "State"

The use of the word "State" in the various provisions of Article I concerning the election of members of the House of Representatives does not necessitate denying the people of the District the right to voting representation in Congress. The defendants maintain, in effect, that the use of the word "State" in these provisions creates a necessary inference that people not in a "State," therefore, people in the District of Columbia, cannot choose or be a Representative....

a. Structure and Purpose of Article I

There is nothing in the use of the word "States" in the provisions of Article I pertaining to the election of members of the House of Representatives that expressly precludes recognition of a right for the inhabitants of the District to vote for voting representation in Congress. More importantly, no policy purpose would be served by adopting such an interpretation. The primary purpose of the references to "States" in Article I is apparent when one considers that it was a priority of the Framers to set up a mechanism to create a national form of representative government.... In 1787, the 13 original States were the obvious and, actually, only political subdivisions capable together of conducting national elections....

[T]he majority of the references to "States" in Article I can best be understood as specifying and using the most practical mechanisms available in the 18th century by which the people scattered among the several States could select their national representatives. So understood, their employment in the circumstances that obtained in the late 18th century should not preclude employment by the people of the District of the election apparatus only available to them since the 1960's through which to regain representation in the House of Representatives enjoyed by their political forebears until 1801.

The requirement that a Representative be an inhabitant of the State which he or she represents, *see* U.S. Const. art. I, § 2, is the only reference to States in the context of choosing Representatives that is not related to using the States as a mechanism for selecting Representatives. It seems obvious, however, that the primary, if not sole, purpose of that requirement was to see to it that each Representative live among the people represented. It should be obvious that this requirement was not aimed at denying the right of the people of the District to vote for voting representation in the House of Representatives. At most, it means that if the inhabitants of the District enjoyed representation by a member from the District, their Representative should reside there....

b. Historical Materials

The relevant historical materials do not necessitate a conclusion that the Framers intended to deny to the inhabitants of the yet-to-be-selected Seat of Government the right to vote for voting representation in Congress through the use of the term "States" in Article I....

(v) Organic Act

There were statements made at the time of the enactment of the Organic Act in 1801 which assume that its enactment would have the effect of terminating the right of inhabitants of the District to vote for voting representation in the House of Representatives. I do not consider those statements to be persuasive evidence that the Framers' of the Constitution intended such a outcome to result from their use of the term "States" or from the language of any other provision in the Constitution. The Organic Act debates occurred over fourteen years after the Constitutional Convention and over ten years after the First Congress selected the location of the Seat of Government. The views of individual participants in those debates, even if they could be attributed to the Sixth Congress as a whole, would be an unreliable indication of the understanding of the Founders during the time before the location of the Seat of Government had been determined. Defendants do not suggest that those who made the statements participated in the Convention or were "au courant" in 1787. Moreover, given the modest size of the District's population in 1801, the drafters of the Organic Act might well have assumed, without knowing, that the Framers had simply not considered providing affirmatively, yet not affirmatively precluding, for the District's relatively few inhabitants. A member of Congress and two Senators representing 8,000 souls could have very awkward and disruptive of the power balance. Had populous New York or Philadelphia been chosen as the permanent Seat of Government, however--certainly a possibility in 1787 -- it seems unlikely that 1801 Congressmen would have seen the denial of voting representation for the District's population as the Framers' manifest design. These facts make it, in my view, unreasonable to assume that the views expressed at the time of the adoption of the Organic Act reliably reflect any decision by the Framers, which were have necessarily been formed without knowing whether the site of the Seat of Government would be New York, Philadelphia, or some other place, urban or rural....

d. Democratic principles

As reiterated by the Supreme Court in *Term Limits* and *Powell*, interpretation of the Constitution, particularly Article I, should be guided by the fundamental democratic principles upon which this nation was founded. Absent any persuasive evidence that the Framers' intent in using the term "State" was to deny the inhabitants of the District the right to vote for voting representation in the House of Representatives, a consideration of fundamental democratic principles further supports the conclusion that the use of that term does not necessitate that result.

A republican, that is representative, form of government, is a keystone in the Constitution's structure, a keystone hewn directly from the Declaration of Independence; the denial of representation was one of the provocations that generated the Declaration and the War that implemented it....

The importance of voting by the people in a representative democracy, such as the Constitution established, is so obvious that it is difficult to articulate its provenance. Yet, there is no dispute that voting by the people and the existence of a representative democracy are inextricably linked. One simply cannot exist without the other....

Thus, the very structure of the national government, subjected by the Constitution to the ultimate sovereignty of the people, strongly negates the argument that either the Article I references to "States," or the absence of any mention of voting for the people of the District in the District Clause, necessarily precludes voting by and representation of the people of the District. Accordingly, the democratic principles reflected in the structure of the government created pursuant to the Constitution weigh decisively against the negative inference proposed by the defendants -- an inference that would result in the denial of the right to vote for voting representation in the legislature with exclusive authority over the District....

5. Lapse of Time

The mere fact that nonvoting by the people of the District has been a continuous and unbroken practice since 1801 does not necessitate denying the people of the District today the right to vote for voting representation in the House of Representatives. The Supreme Court has never hesitated to recognize constitutional rights, no matter when recognition is sought and no matter how long practices to the contrary have continued....[citing *Brown v. Board of Education, Reynolds v. Sims, and Roe v. Wade, Harper v. Virginia Board of Elections*, and other cases].

For years, many voter apportionment issues never reached the courts because it was accepted doctrine that the apportionment of legislative districts involved a political question beyond the reach of the judiciary. It was not until the Court's 1962 decision in Baker ... that the courts began to address many long-suffered voting rights deprivations. Thus, as a practical matter, until *Baker v. Carr*, a suit like the plaintiffs would have been an exercise in futility.

III

EQUAL PROTECTION

Basic equal protection principles require government, state and national, to treat similarly situated persons equally, particularly with respect to constitutionally-based rights and privileges. The equal protection clause embodies a three-tiered system of review. . . . .

With respect to voting, the Supreme Court has held that the right to cast votes of equal weight in the selection of representatives to a legislature is a fundamental right whose denial must be subject to the strictest scrutiny....

[T]he federal government treats the people of the District of Columbia differently from people residing in States, who are apportioned seats in the House of Representatives. In addition, the people of the District are treated differently from people residing in federal enclaves, over which Congress holds the same constitutional power of "exclusive legislation" that it holds over the people of the District. U.S. Const. art. I, § 8. Yet, the inhabitants of enclaves are included in apportionment and vote in Congressional elections in the state within which the federal enclave exists.... Finally, the people of the District are treated differently from United States citizens who reside overseas, who, by virtue of the Uniformed and Overseas Citizens Absentee Voting Act (Overseas Voting Act), vote in Congressional elections in the state where they most recently lived....

NOTES AND QUESTIONS

1. One of the most neglected topics in American constitutionalism involves the constitutional issues surrounding the era of United States' "imperialism," the era in the late 19th and early 20th centuries in which the United States sought to influence, acquire, or govern territories previously under the control of earlier "empires," such as Spain -- including Puerto Rico, the Phillipines, Guam, and to some extent Cuba. From the perspective of democratic principles and constitutional law, the potential acquisition or governance of these territories raised novel questions: could the United States hold territories in which the residents were denied the privileges of United States citizenship, particularly the right to vote? If it were permissible to do for a short period of time, could the United States do so indefinitely, as a matter of constitutional law as well as political morality. As *De La Rosa* illustrates, many of these questions obviously still remain. For an introduction to these issues and their history, see Sanford Levinson, *Why the Canon Should Be Expanded to Include* The Insular Cases *and the Saga of American Expansionism*, 17 CON. COMM. 239 (2000). There is also a direct link between these issues and the disenfranchisement of black voters in the American South in the same period, discussed in the casebook at pages 68-107. A principal reason the federal government acquiesced so readily in the massive disfranchisement of black voters in the South was that the government (the Republican Party, then in control) as well as much northern opinion believed in restricting suffrage in these newly acquired territories -- and justified that belief with arguments that strongly resembled those deployed by Southern defenders of black disfranchisement. *See* Richard H. Pildes, *Democracy, Anti-Democracy, and the Canon*, 17 CONST. COMM. 293, 305 (2000).

2. For further discussion of Puerto Rican suffrage, see Amber L. Cottle, Comment, *Silent Citizens: United States Territorial Residents and the Right to Vote in Presidential Elections*, 1995 U. CHI. LEGAL F. 315.

3. In *De La Rosa*, consider Judge Toruella's *Carolene Products* argument. Note that one of the rationales for heightened scrutiny for discrimination against aliens is their political powerlessness. Is there a parallel between his analysis and the issue raised in *Colegrove v. Green* (discussed in the casebook at 117-22), about the efficacy of political solutions to problems of disenfranchisement?

4. Judge Toruella's position depends in part on the fact that the Constitution provides for the selection of the President and Vice-President by the states (through the Electoral College) rather than by popular election. Would he have taken a different position had Igartua challenged the failure to provide Puerto Rico with voting representation in Congress? But now consider the issues in *Adams v. Clinton*, in which the claim was for congressional representation. Should the textual argument for congressional representation be considered stronger, weaker, or the same as the argument for voting in presidential elections?

5. In addition to whether American citizens who live in Puerto Rico should be entitled to vote in presidential (or congressional) elections, there is a more complicated constitutional and statutory question raised by the frequent movement of American citizens from Puerto Rico to the mainland and back again. These issues were addressed most recently in *Romeu v. Cohen*, ___ F. Supp. 2d ___ (S.D.N.Y. 2000).

The plaintiff was a U.S. citizen who had lived (and voted in) New York from 1994 through 1999. In 1999, he moved to Puerto Rico and registered to vote there. Nevertheless, he wanted to vote in the 2000 presidential election.

The Uniformed and Overseas Citizens Absentee Voting Act (UOCAVA), 42 U.S.C. §§ 1973ff to 1973ff-6, and New York Election Law § 11-200(1) (NYEL) allow "overseas" voters to continue voting in their previous domicile. But there is an arguable gap in coverage, as we shall see.

UOCAVA contains two important definitional provisions. First, it defines "overseas voter" as:

> (B) a person who resides outside the United States and is qualified to vote in the last place in which the person was domiciled before leaving the United States; or

> (C) a person who resides outside the United States and (but for such residence) would be qualified to vote in the last place in which the person was domiciled before leaving the United States.

42 U.S.C. § 1973ff-6(5). Second, it defines "United States," when that term is "used in the territorial sense" as "the several States, the District of Columbia, the Commonwealth of Puerto Rico, Guam, the Virgin Islands, and American Samoa." 42 U.S.C. § 1973ff-6(8). Under the plain language of the UOCAVA, an American citizen who lives in Puerto Rico does not "resid[e] outside the United States." Romeu was therefore not a protected "overseas voter." At the same time, NYEL does permit continued voting by out-of-staters in a special class NYEL defines as a "special federal voter." But because Romeu voted in another United States jurisdiction, albeit a territory or possession, he was not eligible under NYEL for "special federal voter" status.

Romeu claimed that American citizens now living in Puerto Rico who previously lived and voted in one of the fifty states should retain that fundamental right to vote when they moved to Puerto Rico. He argued that UOCAVA and NYEL unconstitutionally deprived him of such a right.

Judge Scheindlin rejected that argument:

The problem for Romeu is that, while he might have a fundamental right to vote in Presidential elections as a resident of Puerto Rico, he does not have a fundamental right to demand an absentee ballot from New York State. The Supreme Court has held that states can impose reasonable residency requirements on the ballot....

As a resident of and registered voter in Puerto Rico, Romeu is no longer qualified to vote in New York State.... From New York's perspective, it does not matter whether Romeu moved to Puerto Rico or to New Jersey. He no longer lives in New York and is no longer qualified to vote there. The UOCAVA and NYEL respect this principle by not providing absentee ballots to people who move to another state or one of the territories. Romeu's inability to vote in Presidential elections stems from his status as a current resident of a territory, not a former resident of New York State....

Given *Igartua I*, denying Romeu the right to vote in presidential elections because of his current status as a resident of Puerto Rico, the statutes therefore violated no constitutional provision.

Romeu also argued that UOCAVA and NYEL violated his right to travel by forcing him to choose between retaining his right to vote in Presidential elections and moving to Puerto Rico. In *Saenz v. Roe*, 526 U.S. 489 (1999), the Supreme Court had explained that the constitutionally protected right to travel included, inter alia, "the right of a citizen of one State to enter and to leave another State," and that laws that burden the right to travel are subject to strict scrutiny.

The district court rejected this claim as well:

First, neither the UOCAVA nor NYEL deprive [Romeu] of his right to vote in Presidential elections generally. As explained above, Romeu's status as a resident of Puerto Rico causes that deprivation.... Second, New York residents who merely travel to Puerto Rico are not deprived of the right to vote in Presidential elections in New York. In fact, the [Voting Rights Act] specifically provided that each state had to allow all duly qualified residents of that state who were absent from that state on the date of the Presidential election to vote by absentee ballot, so long as the resident applied for an absentee ballot at least seven days prior to the Presidential election....

Properly understood, Romeu's argument is that the UOCAVA and NYEL penalize his right to move to Puerto Rico by depriving him of his right to vote in Presidential elections in New York State. In support of his argument, Romeu relies heavily on Dunn [v. Blumstein], in which the Supreme Court held that durational residency requirements for voting unconstitutionally burdened the right to vote and the right to travel. [But] Dunn explicitly "emphasized . . . the difference between bona fide residence requirements and durational residence requirements." Far from holding that a bona fide residency requirement constituted an impermissible burden on the right to travel, the Supreme Court stated:

> An appropriately defined and uniformly applied requirement of bona fide residence may be necessary to preserve the basic conception of a political community, and therefore could withstand close constitutional scrutiny.

Having moved to Puerto Rico in May 1999, Romeu does not have a right to receive an absentee ballot from any state, including New York. See Saenz (explaining that "for those travelers who elect to become permanent residents," the right to travel protects "the right to be treated like other citizens of that state").

Finally, Romeu claimed that UOCAVA and NYEL violated the Equal Protection Clause by allowing American citizens living outside the United States to vote while failing to confer that same status on American citizens living in Puerto Rico. Because the statute was facially neutral, the District Court declined to apply strict scrutiny. Although discrimination against Puerto Ricans might constitute racial discrimination -- thereby triggering strict scrutiny -- the district court held that the plaintiff had failed to prove that the facially neutral statute was in fact intended to single out Puerto Ricans for disparate treatment: "[B]oth the UOCAVA and NYEL allow United States citizens of Hispanic, African-American or Indian descent residing in any of the fifty states to receive an absentee ballot when they move outside the United States. Conversely, all United States citizens, including Anglo-American citizens, are unable to receive an absentee ballot under the UOCAVA and NYEL once they have moved to Puerto Rico."

Note that in deciding to apply rationality review, the district court relied heavily on *Katzenbach v. Morgan*, 384 U.S. 641 (1966), presented in the casebook at p. 277-280. As a reminder, in that case the Supreme Court had *upheld* Congress' decision in the Voting Rights Act to *extend* the franchise to a certain class of Puerto Rico educated voters who had later become residents of a State, such as New York. In *Morgan*, however, the Court applied rational-basis review to judge a legislative decision of Congress to extend the franchise. In part, Congress had relied on findings regarding electoral discrimination in New York against this class of Puerto Rico educated voters. Should *Morgan* provide authority for applying only rational basis review, when the claim is that electoral laws *deny* the franchise to a class of Puerto Rico "associated" voters in the context Romeu was raising? The district court went on to find that the rational-basis standard was met because of the constitutional limitations permitting only "State" voters to vote.

6. For discussions of D.C. enfranchisement, see Jamin B. Raskin, *Is This America? The District of Columbia and the Right to Vote*, 34 HARV. C.R.-C.L. L. REV. 39 (1999); Peter Raven-Hansen, *Congressional Representation for the District of Columbia: A Constitutional Analysis*, 12 HARV. J. LEGIS. 167 (1975).

7. The plaintiffs in *Adams* also challenged the District's lack of representation in the Senate. That claim is currently pending before a single-

judge district court. (The three-judge held, as a statutory matter, that that claim was not properly before it.) Given that the District has fewer people than all but two or three states, would providing it with two Senators unfairly *over*represent its population? Note as a constitutional matter that representation in the Senate and the House seem to be linked. Does this argue as a practical matter for a solution in which District voters vote within a pre-existing state, like Maryland, where their numbers would be roughly the size of a single congressional district?

8. Note that the District of Columbia, like Puerto Rico, is a majority-minority jurisdiction. According to the 1990 Census, the District population was 65.8% African American, 27.4% white, and 2.2% Hispanic. Note also that, since the ratification of the Twenty-Third Amendment in 1961, which gave D.C. residents the ability to vote in the presidential election, by assigning three electoral college votes to the District, the District has always cast its electoral votes for a Democrat. Do these demographic factors suggest anything about the likelihood of D.C.'s residents acquiring congressional representation through the political process? Do they also suggest, in light of the analysis in *Dunn v. Blumstein* and *Carrington v. Rash* possible constitutional problems with "fencing out" District voters?

9. What are the implications of the Twenty-Third Amendment? Most courts and commentators suggest that its affirmative conferral of an ability to vote in presidential elections carries a negative inference: by failing to mention congressional elections for District residents, or the right to vote in presidential elections for territorial residents, it implicitly condones the continuation of those exclusions. In this light, consider Professor Raskin's suggestion:

> Reading the Twenty-third Amendment to preclude a constitutional claim for voting representation in Congress offends the dynamic of democratic enlargement that defines the Constitution. Consider for example the Twenty-fourth Amendment, added to the Constitution in 1964 to ban all poll taxes in federal elections. During the enactment and ratification debates, there was much discussion about whether the Amendment should extend to poll taxes in state elections as well, and a deliberate decision was made to limit the Amendment's scope. Just two years later, in *Harper v. Virginia Board of Elections*, the Supreme Court found that Virginia's state election poll tax violated the Equal Protection Clause, although such a claim had been regarded as ridiculous by those who understood the Twenty-fourth Amendment's silence on the subject to imply that state poll taxes remained valid. This holding prompted angry dissenting opinions from Justices Black and Harlan, who argued that the Court was betraying "the original meaning of the Constitution," and ignoring the fact that poll taxes "have been a traditional part of our political structure." The majority determined, however, that "notions of what constitutes equal treatment for the purposes of the Equal Protection Clause do change." These words seem custom-made for the situation of the District of Columbia.

Raskin, *supra*, at 85.

10. Does Congress have the power to provide representation to District voters without a constitutional amendment? Note that in other electoral contexts, Congress has used its powers under the Fourteenth Amendment and the Seat of Government Clause to treat the District as though it were a state for both statutory and constitutional purposes. *See, e.g.,* 2 U.S.C. § 431 (1994) (Federal Election Campaign Act); 42 U.S.C. § 1973ee-6(5) (1994) (voting accessibility for the elderly and handicapped); 42 U.S.C. § 1973ff-6(6) (1994) (Uniformed and Overseas Citizens Absentee Voting Act of 1986); 42 U.S.C. § 1973gg-1(4) (1994) (National Voter Registration Act of 1993). Could Congress simply provide that for purposes of the various provisions in 2 U.S.C. that deal with the apportionment of representatives among the states, the District is a state?

Page 75, after note 6:

1. A recent article by one of this casebook's authors notes that the *Giles* case is completely absent from modern sources that define "the canon" of American constitutional law: *Giles* is not even mentioned in the leading Constitutional Law casebooks, nor does it appear in Professor Tribe's important treatise, AMERICAN CONSTITUTIONAL LAW (3d.ed. 2000). What do you think accounts for this startling absence of a case dealing with such central issues of democratic citizenship and American constitutional law? Why should *Plessy v. Ferguson*, 163 U.S. 537 (1896), permitting segregated public facilities, be so well-known, yet *Giles v. Harris,* permitting the removal of black citizens from democracy, be so obscure? *See generally* Richard H. Pildes, *Democracy, Anti-Democracy, and the Canon*, 17 CONST. COMM. 293 (2000).

2. What is the relationship between Congressional power to control the shape of American democracy and the Supreme Court's power through constitutional decisionmaking? Given the Court's insistence that Congress decide the constitutionality and legitimacy of disfranchisment, what tools did Congress have available to it? One possibility is Section 2 of the Fourteenth Amendment, which was one of the most contested features at the time of the Amendment's adoption, but which turned out to be little used. Congress could have sought to reduce the representation of Southern states in the United States House of Representatives, in proportion to the extent of disfranchisement.

3. *Giles* raises enduring and fundamental questions about the power of courts to resist political repression or bring about effective change. Was Justice Holmes correct in his view that any Supreme Court decision holding unconstitutional Alabama's blatant circumvention of the Fifteenth Amendment would have been "an empty form" and that in the South of the late 19th and early 20th centuries, "if the conspiracy [to disfranchise black voters] and the intent exist, a name on a piece of paper [that is, a court order] will not defeat them"? It is important not to romanticize the power of courts, or at the least, not to be anachronistic about how effective Supreme Court decisions in 1903 might have been, given the increasing legitimacy of the Supreme Court in the century since. *Giles* forces attention to the question of precisely where the power of courts in any political system, including that of the United States Supreme Court, comes from.

But just as judicial romanticism has its dangers, "realism" also can become a complacent and all-too-easy stance. Was Holmes appropriately "realistic" about his blatant political assessment of the likely effects of judicial intervention -- or using "realism" as a way to excuse the Court's cowardice, or perhaps even to excuse his own personal agreement with black disfranchisement? By the time of *Giles*, many beacons of "enlightened" New England opinion had become disenchanted with the Fifteenth Amendment's implementation. In 1901, *The Atlantic Monthly*, for example, pronounced itself supportive in principle of political equality between races, but also proclaimed that black enfranchisement had been a "grave error" and a wrong-headed "short cut to equality" that had bestowed "the sudden gift of the ballot to men wholly unprepared to use it wisely." As a result, the Fifteenth Amendment had "proved disastrous." LXXXVIII, *The Atlantic Monthly* 433, 434, 436 (Oct. 1901). Given this position even from entities such as *The Atlantic Monthly*, perhaps Holmes' own views were similar.

From the perspective of the present, "realism" about the past also raises the danger of a false sense of historical necessity and determinism. There is surely a tendency to see what happened in the past as inevitable; the fact that black voters were disfranchised from *Giles* until the 1965 Voting Rights Act, can make it seem that black disenfranchisement was inevitable, no matter what Holmes and the Court did. Yet close attention to the social, legal, and political history of issues involving race can suggest much more contingency in the way the treatment of race developed in American law – and hence suggest that certain actions, at certain times, could indeed have influenced the subsequent path of race relations. Many in the present would no doubt be surprised to learn, for example, that on the very eve of disfranchisment in North Carolina, there were still substantial, interracial political coalitions that allowed a fusion of political parties, with black and white support, to control the North Carolina legislature as late as 1894-1898. Yet in 1900, that State's disenfranchising Constitution was passed. *Giles* was only three years later.

Pildes, *supra*, argues that the political context of disenfranchisement was more unpredictable, more fluid and up for grabs in many places, than would be suggested by the "realism" of Holmes' view that black disenfranchisement was inevitable and unstoppable. As evidence, Pildes notes that the disfranchising Constitutions were often passed with slim majorities, even though black voters were almost totally excluded from the vote. Thus, the 1900 North Carolina Constitution passed with 58.6% of the vote; in Alabama, only 57% of white voters supported the 1901 Constitution -- and even that margin of victory almost certainly required overwhelming fraud in vote counting. Permanent disfranchisement through constitutional means was resisted because it would disenfranchise many uneducated and poor whites, as well as blacks. Given the precariousness with which white supremacists managed to enshrine their position into state constitutions, is it actually "realistic" to think that a contrary Supreme Court decision in *Giles* would not have slowed the process of disfranchisement down enough, at least in certain places, such as North Carolina, so as to have avoided permanent, Constitutional, destruction of the suffrage for much of the 20th century? For a contrary view, taking the position that a decision for Giles would have made no difference to the 20th century development of black political participation see Michael J. Klarman, *The Plessy Era*, 1998 S. Ct. Rev. 303.

Page 115, after note 3:

4. *Mail-in Voting.* Would voter participation – and more informed voting – be enhanced by doing away with voting at public polls on a single day

and switching to a vote-by-mail system? For the first time in history, this system was used in the 2000 Presidential elections in one state. By statewide initiative, Oregon in 1998 enacted a statewide vote-by-mail system, after having used the system for several years in some local and special elections. In May 2000, Oregon became the first state to use an all-mail ballot for primary elections. For the presidential elections, ballots were mailed starting October 20, 2000 -- nearly three weeks before the rest of the country went to the polls on November 7th. Voters could vote anytime during that period; the ballot also included 26 initiatives and numerous candidate races in addition to the Presidency. There are no more polling places in Oregon. Voters filled in ballots at home and mailed them in or took them to drop boxes.

Proponents predict the system to increase turnout by at least 10 percent. The state also stands to save $3 million on election costs. Opponents argue that the system will be an invitation to fraud and that it will allow political consultants and interest groups to monitor the voting patterns and manipulate them more easily. In 1998, a Virginia-based watchdog group, the Voting Integrity Project, filed a suit arguing that the system violated federal law requirements that congressional and presidential elections take place on the same day in November. The federal district court dismissed the case; it is now on appeal to the Ninth Circuit Court of Appeals. In light of how close the 2000 Presidential election was, including in Oregon in particular, should voters be permitted to cast ballots up to three weeks in advance of the election? Should the courts find this new practice consistent with the "single-election day" requirement of federal law, discussed in the next paragraph?

Are the states prohibited by federal law from experimenting with voting in this way? The Supreme Court has indeed held that certain forms of early congressional elections do conflict with the relevant federal statutes and hence are pre-empted. 2 U.S.C. Sec. 7 provides that the "Tuesday next after the 1st Monday in November, in every even numbered, year, is established as the day for the election, in each of the States . . . of the United States, of Representatives and Delegates to the Congress . . ." The same statutory rules apply to electing Senators and Presidential electors. In *Foster v. Love*, 522 U.S. 67 (1997), the Court held that Louisiana's non-partisan primary structure (which the Court endorsed in other respects in *California Democratic Party v. Jones*, 120 S.Ct. 2402 (2000)), violated these laws. Under Louisiana law, all candidates appeared on the same primary ballot, regardless of party; if any candidate received a majority of votes in the primary, he or she was elected without any further action on federal election day. Because the "final selection" of candidates could conclude (and 80 percent of the time, did) before federal election day, the system violated federal election law.

Texas recently established an early voting system that permits voting to begin seventeen days before federal election day. The Fifth Circuit upheld that system and distinguished *Foster* in *Voting Integrity Project v. Bomer*, 199 F.3d 773 (5th Cir. 2000). The court noted that absentee voting, which occurs in every state, would otherwise violate the "federal election day" law. For general discussion, see Edward B. Moreton, Jr., *Voting by Mail*, 58 S. CAL. L. REV. 1261 (1985). Even if a candidate is not finally chosen until election day, as with the Oregon system, does the fact that Oregon's system permits voting for national elections to extend as far in advance of national election day as three weeks put the Oregon law in tension with the purposes of the federal "single-election day" statute?

5. *Who Doesn't Vote?* Conventional wisdom holds that, because the poor, the less-educated, and minorities are over-represented among non-voters, any increase in voter turnout, including that prompted by a compulsory voting system, would benefit progressive causes and Democratic candidates. A recent empirical study, however, downplays the potential partisan consequences of increased voter turnout, concluding that non-voters have sufficiently similar preferences to those who vote that increased voting would not affect election results. *See* Benjamin Highton and Raymond E. Wolfinger, *The Political Implications of Higher Turnout* (Dec. 1999) (draft of paper to be published in the British Journal of Political Science, on file with editors). Based on the stated preferences of voters and non-voters, the authors first provide an estimate as to what aggregate voter preferences would have been in 1992 and 1996 had all eligible citizens participated in the elections. In 1992, Bill Clinton's margin of victory would have increased by only 1.3 points. On the other hand, these same estimating techniques conclude that in 1996, Clinton's margin of victory would have increased by almost 18 points. This would seem a dramatic indication that non-voters could indeed matter, but the authors dismiss this result as a historical anomaly when viewed in light of similar analyses of previous elections. For evidence of non-voter preferences converging with those of voters, in elections from 1960-1988, the authors cite RUY TEIXEIRA, THE DISAPPEARING AMERICAN VOTER (1992). While the 1996 "electorate" (including non-voters) would have been moderately more liberal on economic issues than that of the actual electorate, this "electorate's" position (including non-voters) on abortion, gays in the military, and school prayer would have been slightly more conservative.

Second, to test the hypothesis that the actual preferences of unengaged and unmobilized non-voters would be transformed were they actually to vote -- and in particular, that political participation itself would make these non-voters more liberal -- the authors next disregard the stated preferences of non-voters and ascribe to them the preferences of economically cognate voters who did actually vote. The assumption here is that these actual voters reflect the preferences that the non-voters of similar economic status would have were they to vote. Assuming universal turnout by this combined electorate of actual voters and non-voters in 1992 and 1996, the authors conclude that there is even less empirical reason to accept the conventional wisdom that higher turnout would be a boon for the left.

Finally, the authors argue that the reason why nonvoters do not show a greater inclination towards liberal positions is that they are not mostly poor, less educated and minority, but only disproportionately so. Nonvoters are even more disproportionately young and transient. Thus, "the notion that nonvoting is concentrated among a single group or a set of related groups is incorrect." *Id.*, at 18.

CHAPTER THREE

Page 155, after note 2:

2a. In January 1999, the Supreme Court decided the issue of statistical sampling for the 2000 Census in *Department of Commerce v. United States House of Representatives*, 525 U.S. 316 (1999). In an effort to address the growing problem of undercounting, the Census Bureau announced a plan to use statistical sampling for the purpose of apportioning Congressional seats to the States as part of the 2000 Census. However, the United States House of Representatives sought an injunction against the challenged sampling procedure. The case posed a significant constitutional question: whether the Census Clause prohibited the Census Bureau's use of statistical sampling methods by the Census Bureau. But the Court decided the case on statutory grounds, holding that the particular sampling method involved violated the Census Act, 13 U.S.C. § 195. The Court declined to hear the constitutional question presented. The Court interpreted the Act to allow for the use of sampling in gathering demographic data but read the statute to prohibit statistical sampling for the purpose of apportioning Congressional seats. Thus, whether or not this use of statistical sampling would violate the Census Clause of the Constitution should a future amendment to the Census Act eliminate the statutory bar is still unclear.

The result in the Census Case is that sampling is not permitted for apportioning seats among the states for representation in the House of Representatives. But the Court also indicated that the Census Act permits -- and might perhaps require -- that sampling be used to compile the demographic data for the myriad other purposes for which the Census is used. This includes the state redistricting process, which is based on the Census data. Thus, the Secretary of Commerce currently plans to release the Census data in two forms: the first, without sampling, for apportionment of the House; the second, with sampling, for several other potential purposes.

It is a virtual certainty that this will result in intense political struggles and litigation during the upcoming redistricting process. There will be contests over whether states are required or merely permitted to use the adjusted Census figures, which will be based on sampling techniques. If states are merely permitted, but not required, to use the adjusted figures, there will be vigorous struggles over whether to do so in fact. For a good, accessible summary of these and other legal issues involving the 2000 Census, see NATHANIEL PERSILY, 2000 CENSUS DATA: NEW FORMAT AND NEW CHALLENGES, IN THE REAL Y2K PROBLEM: CENSUS 2000 DATA AND REDISTRICTING TECHNOLOGY 1-27 (N. Persily, ed., 2000).

Several states have already passed laws requiring the use of unadjusted data for redistricting. Many of these states are subject to the special "preclearance" provision of section 5 of the Voting Rights Act of 1965 (discussed at length in Chapter 5 of the casebook). This provision requires states with a history of depressed political participation and restrictive voting practices to get federal approval prior to making any changes in laws involving voting and elections, including redistricting measures. In order to get such approval, the state must show that the new law has neither a discriminatory purpose nor a discriminatory effect. Virginia passed a statute requiring the use of unadjusted data, see Va. Code Ann. §§ 24.2-301.1 and -304.1 and then sought preclearance in a declaratory judgment action before the United States District Court for the District of Columbia. In *Virginia v. Reno*, ___ F. Supp. 2d ___ (D.D.C. 2000) (three-judge court), the court dismissed the state's claims as not yet ripe for review, since the Census Bureau has not yet definitively decided whether to provide adjusted data in time for redistricting.

Persily also notes a potentially major problem that the intersection of *Shaw v. Reno,* 509 U.S. 630 (1993), and the Census data will pose for the first time in the 2001 redistricting process. As of now, the only form in which Census data will be released to the states in time for their redistricting will include only the following information: (1) aggregate and voting-age population figures; (2) figures on each racial group and those of Hispanic origin. Not until 2002-03 will the rest of the information from the Census, including the detailed socio-economic data from the long Census forms, be available. Shaw and its progeny -- which are treated in depth in Chapter 8 -- require that race not be "the predominant factor" in drawing election districts. Yet the Census data that will be available will make race the only tabulated factor in addition to raw population numbers. What does this mean for how states will comply with the Voting Rights Act, or otherwise seek to take race into account, in the upcoming redistrictings?

Page 173, before note 5:

5b. One of the most important recent tests at the local-government level of the "one person, one vote" principle involves Business Improvement Districts ("BIDs"). BIDs are state- or locally-authorized entities established to promote business activity within a specific geographic sub-area of a city. A major example is New York City's Grand Central Business Improvement District (GCBID), established through state law in 1988, which includes 337 properties, including Grand Central Station, spread over 75 blocks in midtown Manhattan including Grand Central Station -- an area approximately the size of downtown Los Angeles. GCBID is responsible for capital improvements and services, such as security, sanitation, social services for the homeless, maintenance, tourist information, and retail improvements. The city levies and collects an additional assessment from property owners within the district, in addition to ordinary municipal taxes. These funds are GCBID's primary source of revenue. The state-law established governing structure of BIDs deviate from the one person, one vote rule. Property owners and tenants within the district vote, but the authorizing statute requires that a majority of GCBID's members represent property owners. Property owners thus may vote for 31 board members, commercial tenants may elect 16 board members, and residential tenants may elect one board member.

Tenants of a cooperative apartment building in the district challenged the voting privilege property owners had over residents. The Second Circuit, in a two-to-one vote, rejected this challenge. *See Kessler v. Grand Central District Management Association, Inc.*, 158 F.3d 92 (2d Cir. 1998). The court concluded that GCBID was "a district that exists for a special, limited purpose, that [the governing board]'s activities have a disproportionate effect on property owners, and that [the governing board] has no primary responsibilities or general powers typical of a governmental agency." *Id.* at 108. In the court's view, the BID's purpose was to promote business in the district; this was a limited purpose that did not supplant the City's primary responsibility for providing traditional governmental services in the district. GCBID also lacked the traditional governmental power to impose taxes or enforce laws, and the City retained control over the BID's budget and scope of activities. Moreover, the burden of the special assessment fell disproportionately on property owners, for they were exclusively responsible for paying the assessment. The Second Circuit therefore applied the *Salyer-Ball* doctrine and required that the voting rules bear only "a reasonable relationship to the purposes of the GCBID." *Id.* at 108. That the district needed collective action of property owners to pursue the improvement projects, and that property owners might not agree to the additional assessment on their property absent principal control over how the money would be spent, was sufficient to meet this "reasonableness" standard.

The dissent found BIDs more analogous to the governmental units at issue in *Avery* and *Hadley*: "It is the importance of the government functions, and their applicability to a broad range of citizens, which makes the one person, one vote constitutional requirement applicable. Local government may not, by carving up its civic services and functions into a multitude of 'specializations,' each one subject to privatization, immunize the municipality from the strictures of one person, one vote." *Id.* at 126. GCBID provided an array of traditional governmental functions, its activities affected all those who lived and worked within its jurisdiction, and it enjoyed broad discretion over its activities. Hence, the dissent would have required one person, one vote.

Should BIDs be seen as essentially public entities, to which one person, one vote should apply? Or are they like the water districts in *Salyer* and *Ball*, which the Court characterized as "essentially business enterprises" and only of public character in a "nominal" sense? Are these the right terms in which the one vote, one person issue should be framed? Do these "innovative" structures of local government allow for the smuggling back in of property-based views of citizenship? In Richard Briffault, *A Government for Our Time? Business Improvement Districts and Urban Governance*, 99 COLUM. L. REV. 365, 373 (1999), Professor Briffault argues that BIDs reflect the uncertain state of contemporary ideas of governance:

> The conflict over BIDs mirrors the contemporary debate over the roles of the public and private sectors in American society. Yet, in its assumption of a sharp public-private divide, the argument about BIDs unintentionally reflects the limitations of that debate. Like many other aspects of governance in late-twentieth-century America, BIDs are neither wholly public nor fully private, but, rather, combine attributes of both public and private. BIDs are publicly created, they wield public powers, they provide public services, and they are subject to public control. Their empowerment of business and landowner interests and their provision of extra services to business districts based on special assessments paid within those

districts, however, are distinctly "private" elements at odds with some of the basic features of public governance. Indeed, it is precisely because they are part of the public sector that the organization and financing of, and the enhanced services provided by, BIDs may seem so troubling. BIDs constitute a distinct challenge to the democratic accountability of public institutions and the equal treatment normally required in the provision of public services.

Yet Briffault concludes that the property-voter preference ought to be constitutional:

> Although the property owners paying BID assessments may be able to diffuse those costs throughout the district, the assessment payers do bear the costs of the BID in the first instance. Their support is typically critical for the establishment of the BID and for its continuation. A state could reasonably conclude that BIDs are a useful means of providing urban services and that property owner voting control would facilitate creation of the BID. As long as a BID's regulatory and fiscal powers are limited, and the city government has the capacity to oversee and control BID operations, property owner voting may be a constitutionally permissible component of local government innovation. Id., at 444-45.

Even if constitutional, does this privatization of local government services undermine democratic values? For worries along those lines from the same author, see Richard Briffault, *The Rise of Sublocal Structures in Urban Governance,* 82 MINN. L. REV.. 503, 509 (1997) ("these structures may be able to improve the efficiency of local operations, but they are unlikely to improve the prospects for political participation by ordinary citizens in big-city governance.").

Page 173, replace note 5 with the following:

Even if some elections are exempted from the requirements of one-person, one-vote, this does not necessarily exempt them from other constitutional and statutory commands. For example, judicial elections are not covered by one-person, one-vote, see supra note 1, yet they are covered by provisions of the Voting Rights Act of 1965 that forbid racial discrimination in voting, see *Chisom v. Roemer,* 501 U.S. 380 (1991). See also, Glenn P. Smith, Note, *Interest Exceptions to One-Resident, One-Vote: Better Results from the Voting Rights Act,* 74 TEX. L. REV. 1153 (1996).

In *Rice v. Cayetano,* 528 U.S. 495 (2000), the Supreme Court confronted the question whether Hawaii could restrict the franchise for elections to choose the trustees of the Office of Hawaiian Affairs to persons who were descendants of people inhabiting the Hawaiian Islands in 1778. (The Office administered programs designed for the benefit of such individuals.) Hawaii argued that this limitation on the franchise was sustainable under the reasoning of *Salyer* and *Ball.* The Supreme Court rejected that analysis:

We would not find those cases dispositive.... The question before us is not the one-person, one-vote requirement of the Fourteenth Amendment, but the race neutrality command of the Fifteenth Amendment. Our special purpose district cases have not suggested that compliance with the one-person, one-vote rule of the Fourteenth Amendment somehow excuses compliance with the Fifteenth Amendment. We reject that argument here.... The Fifteenth Amendment has independent meaning and force. A State may not deny or abridge the right to vote on account of race, and this law does so.

Rice appears as a principal case in the Supplement to Chapter 8.

CHAPTER FOUR

Page 201, after note 2:

2a. Note that the Court evaluates the burden of the write-in ban in isolation from other elements of the Hawaiian electoral structure as a whole. For a critique that argues ballot regulations should be assessed not in isolation from each other, but in terms of their cumulative effects on the right to meaningful participation, Samuel Issacharoff and Richard H. Pildes, *Politics as Markets: Partisan Lockups of the Democratic Process*, 50 STAN. L. REV. 643, 671 (1998):

> Moreover, this ban on write-in voting did not operate in isolation, nor are the stakes trivial. In addition to shutting down the write-in option, state laws make it exceptionally difficult for new parties and independent candidates to get on the ballot. For a candidate who wants to run as an independent, the difficulty does not lie in getting a place on the ballot, for only a handful of signatures are required. Rather, the independent's real difficulty lies in the fact that voters who wish to vote for an independent must pay an enormous price. Hawaii law, in effect, requires primary voters to choose only a single ballot for all offices. In order to vote for an independent candidate for one office, for example, the voter loses the ability to vote in any other race.   The same monopoly-enhancing restriction applies to voters who want to vote for a third-party candidate. These restrictions have even more bite in a one-party State in which the winner of the primary election, if a Democrat, is almost certainly going to win the general election. Consequently,   the cumulative structure of Hawaii's laws eviscerates any nascent resistance to the Democratic monopoly.

Should courts take these cumulative effects into account in determining whether electoral burdens are undue? Recall the ways the cumulative effects of the poll tax, described in note 1 of *Harper v. Virginia Board of Elections*, casebook p.42, worked to make the system more obstructive than the mere tax itself in isolation.

Page 212, after note 3:

6. What should be the standard of review for ballot access challenges? Even after the decision in *Rockefeller v. Powers*, discussed at p.211 of the casebook, Senator John McCain was not going to be able to get on the Republican Party primary ballot for the 2000 elections. He therefore challenged the post-1996 ballot access rules, and in *Molinari v. Powers*, 82 F. Supp. 2d 57 (EDNY, 2000), the same district judge that had invalidated the ballot access rules for the 1996 Presidential primary elections again invalidated the more recent rules. The "reformed" rules had required that primary candidates had to collect 5,000 signatures statewide and imposed a geographic distributional requirement that candidates also had to collect (under highly regulated circumstances) the signatures of at least 0.5% of the registered Republicans in each congressional district. The court found those regulations to be irrational and an undue burden on First Amendment rights:

> [T]he New York ballot access scheme as applied to the Primary poses an undue burden in its totality on the right to vote under the First Amendment . . . Specifically, I am referring to the related requirements . . . that (i) each witness to a designating petition must either be a registered Republican voter residing in the congressional district of the delegate candidate for whom he or she is witnessing signatures, or, in the alternative, must be a notary public or commissioner of deeds . . and (ii) the town/city "trap" . . .

> [T]o invalidate a petition [because of a failure to satisfy the second requirement] deprives the voter who signed the petition of the right to participate in the primary process by placing on the ballot candidates whom he or she supports. It also deprives the delegate candidates of a place on the ballot . . . Moreover, it does this for no rational, much less compelling, reason . . .

> The proffered reasons for the residence requirement simply cannot justify the burden the residence requirement places on the petition gathering process. In essence, the residence requirement reduces by approximately 2.9 to 3 million voters the pool of Republicans available to volunteer to petition for signatures in any particular district . . . While the effect of the residence requirement on a presidential candidate like Mr. Forbes or Senator McCain is significant . . . the requirement poses no burden for the candidate supported by the Republican Party or the Republican State Committee . . . Indeed, it is this fact that provides the only comprehensible reason for the residence requirement . . .

> The requirement in New York that witnesses reside in the same congressional district as the delegate candidates for whom they are circulating petitions is even more burdensome to core political speech than the one at issue in [Buckley v. Valeo] . . . My judgment is that the requirements that a witness reside in the congressional district in which he or she is witnessing a signature and that a witness or signer separately list the town or city in which he or she resides in addition to his or her residence address fail under any test.

Should courts sustain any rationally-based ballot qualification? Should the intent to restrict access be separately considered? How different is it from prior cases that the District Court evaluated "the scheme" in "its totality" – as opposed to assessing any one provision in isolation – in order to conclude that the scheme itself posed an undue burden? Compare this with the approach of the Supreme Court in *Burdick v. Takushi*, casebook at 193, and the critique of that decision above in note 2a.

7. Before the *McCain* litigation, the Republican Party presidential primary rules had been stunningly effective in keeping insurgent Republicans off the primary ballot. Never before had a candidate who was not the choice of the state party's leaders (such as Bush in 2000 or Dole in 1996) and who relied on federal matching funds (unlike Forbes, in 1996, who was self-financed) been able to surmount the ballot-access hurdles and create a competitive Republican primary. For a comprehensive study of the ballot-access struggles in New York, including a detailed history of the *McCain* litigation by one of the lawyers who represented McCain, see Nathaniel Persily, *The Regulation of Party Nomination Methods: California Democratic Party v. Jones, John McCain, and Beyond*, 17 N.Y.U. L. Rev. ___ (forthcoming 2001). In the wake of *McCain*, Republican party-leaders have proposed legislation that would enable a presidential primary candidate to appear on the state primary ballot if that candidate (1) was certified to receive federal matching funds or that he/she had met the federal matching fund requirements (at least $5,000 from each state); (2) was certified by the State Board of Elections as being nationally known and recognized candidate whose candidacy is "generally and seriously advocated or recognized" by the national or State news media; (3) had collected 5,000 signatures statewide. Notice that these new ballot-access rules, for presidential primaries, would shift the focus to the national status of the candidate, as opposed to his or her ability to gather signatures district-by-district in New York.

8. A survey of recent ballot access cases shows that the trend in the lower federal courts is to uphold most state ballot access restrictions. *See, e.g., Wood v. Meadows*, 207 F.3d 708 (4th Cir. 2000) (holding that under a rational basis level of scrutiny, state interests in administrative convenience, limiting the number of candidates on general election ballot, requiring candidates to show a modicum of support, and designating the primary date as one where the full field of valid candidates is identified outweighed the burden imposed on independent candidates by law requiring them to file statements of candidacy signed by one-half of one percent of all registered Virginia voters with at least 200 signatures from each congressional district five months prior to general elections); *The Council of Alternative Political Parties v. Hooks*, 179 F.3d 64 (3d Cir. 1999) (upholding New Jersey election law denying independent and "alternative political party" gubernatorial candidates seeking general ballot access through primary nominations and requiring them to file nominating petitions with 800 signatures by the major parties' primary date); *Schulz v. Williams*, 44 F.3d 48 (2d Cir. 1994) (holding New York election law requiring independents wishing to nominate candidate for statewide office to gather the signatures of 15,000 registered voters, indicating their election district, assembly district and ward within a 42-day period from July 12 to August 23 to be constitutional under a rational basis level of scrutiny); *Socialist Workers Party v. Hechler*, 890 F.2d 1303 (4th Cir. 1989) (upholding West Virginia election law that barred voters signing nominating petition for minor party candidate from also participating in major party primary and requiring minor party candidate to file certificate of candidacy one month prior to major party

primaries); *Libertarian Party of Virginia v. Davis,* 766 F.2d 865 (4th Cir. 1985) (upholding Virginia election law requiring minor party seeking general ballot access to submit petition signed by one-half of 1% of all registered voters, including at least 200 voters from each congressional district because justified by state interest in securing candidates with a modicum of numerical and geographic support); *Taman v. Illinois Board of Elections,* 2000 U.S. Dist. LEXIS 5962 (N.D. Ill.) (holding that a petition requirement of 2131 signatures for judicial candidates cannot be considered an undue burden for a candidate seeking county-wide office in a county of over five million population); *Wood v. Quinn,* 2000 U.S. Dist. LEXIS 10233 (E.D. Va.) (holding that law requiring independent senatorial candidates submit petitions containing 10,000 signatures from each of 400 congressional districts witnessed by petitioner from same congressional district is constitutional); *The Patriot Party of Pennsylvania v. Mitchell,* 826 F. Supp. 926 (E.D. Pa. 1993) (finding constitutional an Illinois law requiring political party to obtain 15% of the registered vote in order to be deemed a "major political party" and that those who do not achieve such a threshold must repeatedly demonstrate voter support through nominating petitions or election support because the law serves to further the state's compelling interest in screening out frivolous candidates); *but see, Tobin for Governor v. The Illinois State Board of Elections,* 2000 U.S. Dist. LEXIS 10983 (N.D. Ill.) (election law that requires that candidate nomination petition be signed by a registered voters is unconstitutional under *Buckley v. ACLF*); *Molinari v. Powers,* 82 F.Supp. 2d 57 (E.D.N.Y. 2000) (finding two aspects of Republican nominating requirements, e.g.,: (1) witness to petition must be registered Republican residing in congressional district of delegate candidate for whom he is witnessing signatures, and (2) petition signer must list larger town/city unit within which their village of residence is located; to be unconstitutional burdens on rights of candidates).

Page 224, after note 5:

6. For a sophisticated treatment of the complex interplay between *The White Primary Cases,* the Voting Rights Act, and the constitutional associational rights of political parties, see *LaRouche, Jr. v. Fowler,* 152 F. 3d 974 (D.C. Cir. 1998) (per Garland, J.). LaRouche sought the Democratic Party's nomination for President in 1996 and had allegedly won two delegates to the party's national convention through votes he had received in primary elections in two states. But applying an internal Democratic Party rule, the Chairman of the Party ruled that LaRouche was not a bona fide Democrat, was not to be treated as a qualified candidate, and that state parties should disregard any votes cast for him. This ruling was based on LaRouche's political beliefs, which the DNC Chairman characterized as "explicitly racist and anti-Semitic, and otherwise utterly contrary to the fundamental beliefs . . . of the Democratic Party." Concluding that viewpoint discrimination is "the *sine qua non* of a political party," the Court held that even if political parties were treated as state actors, they need only show that an internal party rule "rationally advance some legitimate interest of the party" to withstand constitutional scrutiny. The Court therefore rejected LaRouche's First Amendment challenge to the party's exclusion of his candidacy.

Page 244, Before the beginning of Section D.

CALIFORNIA DEMOCRATIC PARTY, ET AL. v. BILL JONES, SECRETARY OF STATE OF CALIFORNIA, ET AL.
120 S. Ct. 2402 (2000)

JUSTICE SCALIA delivered the opinion of the Court.

This case presents the question whether the State of California may, consistent with the First Amendment to the United States Constitution, use a so-called "blanket" primary to determine a political party's nominee for the general election.

* * *

. . . In 1996 the citizens of California adopted by initiative Proposition 198. Promoted largely as a measure that would "weaken" party "hard-liners" and ease the way for "moderate problem-solvers," Proposition 198 changed California's partisan primary from a closed primary to a blanket primary. Under the new system, "all persons entitled to vote, including those not affiliated with any political party, shall have the right to vote . . . for any candidate regardless of the candidate's political affiliation." Cal. Elec. Code Ann. § 2001 (West Supp. 2000); see also § 2151. Whereas under the closed primary each voter received a ballot limited to candidates of his own party, as a result of Proposition 198 each voter's primary ballot now lists every candidate regardless of party affiliation and allows the voter to choose freely among them. It remains the case, however, that the candidate of each party who wins the greatest number of votes "is the nominee of that party at the ensuing general election." Cal. Elec. Code Ann. § 15451 (West 1996).

* * *

I

Respondents rest their defense of the blanket primary upon the proposition that primaries play an integral role in citizens' selection of public officials. As a consequence, they contend, primaries are public rather than private proceedings, and the States may and must play a role in ensuring that they serve the public interest. Proposition 198, respondents conclude, is simply a rather pedestrian example of a State's regulating its system of elections.

We have recognized, of course, that States have a major role to play in structuring and monitoring the election process, including primaries. . . What we have not held, however, is that the processes by which political parties select their nominees are, as respondents would have it, wholly public affairs that States may regulate freely. To the contrary, we have continually stressed that when States regulate parties' internal processes they must act within limits imposed by the Constitution.

* * *

Representative democracy in any populous unit of governance is unimaginable without the ability of citizens to band together in promoting among the electorate candidates who espouse their political views. The formation of national political parties was almost concurrent with the formation of the Republic itself. Consistent with this tradition, the Court has recognized that the First Amendment protects "the freedom to join together in furtherance of common political beliefs," which "necessarily presupposes the freedom to identify the people who constitute the association, and to limit the association to those people only." That is to say, a corollary of the right to associate is the right not to associate. . .

In no area is the political association's right to exclude more important than in the process of selecting its nominee. That process often determines the party's positions on the most significant public policy issues of the day, and even when those positions are predetermined it is the nominee who becomes the party's ambassador to the general electorate in winning it over to the party's views. . .

Unsurprisingly, our cases vigorously affirm the special place the First Amendment reserves for, and the special protection it accords, the process by which a political party "selects a standard bearer who best represents the party's ideologies and preferences." The moment of choosing the party's nominee, we have said, is "the crucial juncture at which the appeal to common principles may be translated into concerted action, and hence to political power in the community."

      * * *

California's blanket primary violates [these] principles. Proposition 198 forces political parties to associate with -- to have their nominees, and hence their positions, determined by -- those who, at best, have refused to affiliate with the party, and, at worst, have expressly affiliated with a rival. In this respect, it is qualitatively different from a closed primary. Under that system, even when it is made quite easy for a voter to change his party affiliation the day of the primary, and thus, in some sense, to "cross over," at least he must formally *become a member of the party;* and once he does so, he is limited to voting for candidates of that party.

The evidence in this case demonstrates that under California's blanket primary system, the prospect of having a party's nominee determined by adherents of an opposing party is far from remote -- indeed, it is a clear and present danger. For example, in one 1997 survey of California voters 37 percent of Republicans said that they planned to vote in the 1998 Democratic gubernatorial primary, and 20 percent of Democrats said they planned to vote in the 1998 Republican United States Senate primary. . .

The record also supports the obvious proposition that these substantial numbers of voters who help select the nominees of parties they have chosen not to join often have policy views that diverge from those of the party faithful. The 1997 survey of California voters revealed significantly different policy preferences between party members and primary voters who "crossed over" from another party. One expert went so far as to describe it as "inevitable [under Proposition 198] that parties will be forced in some circumstances to give their official designation to a candidate who's not preferred by a majority or even plurality of party members."

* * *

In any event, the deleterious effects of Proposition 198 are not limited to altering the identity of the nominee. Even when the person favored by a majority of the party members prevails, he will have prevailed by taking somewhat different positions -- and, should he be elected, will continue to take somewhat different positions in order to be *renominated*. . . It is unnecessary to cumulate evidence of this phenomenon, since, after all, the whole *purpose* of Proposition 198 was to favor nominees with "moderate" positions. It encourages candidates -- and officeholders who hope to be renominated -- to curry favor with persons whose views are more "centrist" than those of the party base. In effect, Proposition 198 has simply moved the general election one step earlier in the process, at the expense of the parties' ability to perform the "basic function" of choosing their own leaders.

* * *

In sum, Proposition 198 forces petitioners to adulterate their candidate-selection process -- the "basic function of a political party," -- by opening it up to persons wholly unaffiliated with the party. Such forced association has the likely outcome -- indeed, in this case the *intended* outcome -- of changing the parties' message. We can think of no heavier burden on a political party's associational freedom. Proposition 198 is therefore unconstitutional unless it is narrowly tailored to serve a compelling state interest. It is to that question which we now turn.

III

Respondents proffer seven state interests they claim are compelling. Two of them -- producing elected officials who better represent the electorate and expanding candidate debate beyond the scope of partisan concerns -- are simply circumlocution for producing nominees and nominee positions other than those the parties would choose if left to their own devices. . . Both of these supposed interests, therefore, reduce to nothing more than a stark repudiation of freedom of political association: Parties should not be free to select their own nominees because those nominees, and the positions taken by those nominees, will not be congenial to the majority.

* * *

Respondents' third asserted compelling interest is that the blanket primary is the only way to ensure that disenfranchised persons enjoy the right to an effective vote. By "disenfranchised," respondents do not mean those who cannot vote; they mean simply independents and members of the minority party in "safe" districts. These persons are disenfranchised, according to respondents, because under a closed primary they are unable to participate in what amounts to the determinative election -- the majority party's primary; the only way to ensure they have an "effective" vote is to force the party to open its primary to them. This also appears to be nothing more than reformulation of an asserted state interest we have already rejected -- recharacterizing nonparty members' keen desire to participate in selection of the party's nominee as "disenfranchisement" if that desire is not fulfilled. We have said, however, that a "nonmember's desire to participate in the party's affairs is overborne by the countervailing and legitimate right of the party to determine its own membership qualifications."

    * * *

Respondents' remaining four asserted state interests -- promoting fairness, affording voters greater choice, increasing voter participation, and protecting privacy -- are not, like the others, automatically out of the running; but neither are they, *in the circumstances of this case*, compelling. That determination is not to be made in the abstract, by asking whether fairness, privacy, etc., are highly significant values; but rather by asking whether the *aspect* of fairness, privacy, etc., addressed by the law at issue is highly significant. And for all four of these asserted interests, we find it not to be.

    * * *

Finally, we may observe that even if all these state interests were compelling ones, Proposition 198 is not a narrowly tailored means of furthering them. Respondents could protect them all by resorting to a *nonpartisan* blanket primary. Generally speaking, under such a system, the State determines what qualifications it requires for a candidate to have a place on the primary ballot -- which may include nomination by established parties and voter-petition requirements for independent candidates. Each voter, regardless of party affiliation, may then vote for any candidate, and the top two vote getters (or however many the State prescribes) then move on to the general election. This system has all the characteristics of the partisan blanket primary, save the constitutionally crucial one: Primary voters are not choosing a party's nominee. Under a nonpartisan blanket primary, a State may ensure more choice, greater participation, increased "privacy," and a sense of "fairness" -- all without severely burdening a political party's First Amendment right of association.

    * * *

Respondents' legitimate state interests and petitioners' First Amendment rights are not inherently incompatible. To the extent they are in this case, the State of California has made them so by forcing political parties to associate with those who do not share their beliefs. And it has done this at the "crucial juncture" at which party members traditionally find their collective voice and select their spokesman. The burden Proposition 198 places on petitioners' rights of political association is both severe and unnecessary. The judgment for the Court of Appeals for the Ninth Circuit is reversed.

    It is so ordered.

JUSTICE STEVENS, with whom JUSTICE GINSBURG joins as to Part I, dissenting.

* * *

A State's power to determine how its officials are to be elected is a quintessential attribute of sovereignty. This case is about the State of California's power to decide who may vote in an election conducted, and paid for, by the State. The United States Constitution imposes constraints on the States' power to limit access to the polls, but we have never before held or suggested that it imposes any constraints on States' power to authorize additional citizens to participate in any state election for a state office. In my view, principles of federalism require us to respect the policy choice made by the State's voters in approving Proposition 198.

The blanket primary system instituted by Proposition 198 does not abridge "the ability of citizens to band together in promoting among the electorate candidates who espouse their political views." *Ante,* at 6. The Court's contrary conclusion rests on the premise that a political party's freedom of expressive association includes a "right not to associate," which in turn includes a right to exclude voters unaffiliated with the party from participating in the selection of that party's nominee in a primary election. *Ante,* at 6-7. In drawing this conclusion, however, the Court blurs two distinctions that are critical: (1) the distinction between a private organization's right to define itself and its messages, on the one hand, and the State's right to define the obligations of citizens and organizations performing public functions, on the other; and (2) the distinction between laws that abridge participation in the political process and those that encourage such participation.

* * *

. . . The reason a State may impose. . .significant restriction[s] on a party's associational freedoms is that both the general election and the primary are quintessential forms of state action. It is because the primary is state action that an organization -- whether it calls itself a political party or just a "Jaybird" association -- may not deny non-Caucasians the right to participate in the selection of its nominees. The Court is quite right in stating that those cases "do not stand for the proposition that party affairs are [*wholly*] public affairs, free of First Amendment protections." *Ante,* at 6. They do, however, stand for the proposition that primary elections, unlike most "party affairs," are state action. The protections that the First Amendment affords to the "internal processes" of a political party, *ibid.*, do not encompass a right to exclude nonmembers from voting in a state-required, state-financed primary election.

The so-called "right not to associate" that the Court relies upon, then, is simply inapplicable to participation in a state election. A political party, like any other association, may refuse to allow non-members to participate in the party's decisions when it is conducting its own affairs; n6 California's blanket primary system does not infringe this principle. *Ante,* at 2-3, n. 2. But an election, unlike a convention or caucus, is a public affair. Although it is true that we have extended First Amendment protection to a party's right to invite independents to participate in its primaries. . . [we have never] held or suggested that the "right not to associate" imposes a limit on the State's power to open up its primary elections to all voters eligible to vote in a general election. In my view, while state rules abridging participation in its elections should be closely scrutinized, the First Amendment does not inhibit the State from acting to broaden voter access to state-run, state-financed elections. When a State acts not to limit democratic participation but to expand the ability of individuals to participate in the democratic process, it is acting not as a foe of the First Amendment but as a friend and ally.

* * *

In my view, the First Amendment does not mandate that a putatively private association be granted the power to dictate the organizational structure of state-run, state-financed primary elections. It is not this Court's constitutional function to choose between the competing visions of what makes democracy work -- party autonomy and discipline versus progressive inclusion of the entire electorate in the process of selecting their public officials -- that are held by the litigants in this case. . . That choice belongs to the people.

Even if the "right not to associate" did authorize the Court to review the State's policy choice, its evaluation of the competing interests at stake is seriously flawed. For example, the Court's conclusion that a blanket primary severely burdens the parties' associational interests in selecting their standard bearers does not appear to be borne out by experience with blanket primaries. . . Following a bench trial and the receipt of expert witness reports, the District Court found that "there is little evidence that raiding [by members of an opposing party] will be a factor under the blanket primary. On this point there is almost unanimity among the political scientists who were called as experts by the plaintiffs and defendants." While the Court is entitled to test this finding by making an independent examination of the record, the evidence it cites -- including the results of the June 1998 primaries, *ante*, at 10-11, which should not be considered because they are not in the record -- does not come close to demonstrating that the District Court's factual finding is clearly erroneous.

As to the Court's concern that benevolent crossover voting impinges on party associational interests, *ante*, at 11, the District Court found that experience with a blanket primary in Washington and other evidence "suggested that there will be particular elections in which there will be a substantial amount of cross-over voting . . . although the cross-over vote will rarely change the outcome of any election and in the typical contest will not be at significantly higher levels than in open primary states." In my view, an empirically debatable assumption about the relative number and effect of likely crossover voters in a blanket primary, as opposed to an open primary or a nominally closed primary with only a brief pre-registration requirement, is too thin a reed to support a credible First Amendment distinction. . .

On the other side of the balance, I would rank as "substantial, indeed compelling," just as the District Court did, California's interest in fostering democratic government by "increasing the representativeness of elected officials, giving voters greater choice, and increasing voter turnout and participation in [electoral processes]." The Court's glib rejection of the State's interest in increasing voter participation, *ante*, at 17, is particularly regrettable. In an era of dramatically declining voter participation, States should be free to experiment with reforms designed to make the democratic process more robust by involving the entire electorate in the process of selecting those who will serve as government officials. Opening the nominating process to all and encouraging voters to participate in any election that draws their interest is one obvious means of achieving this goal. I would also give some weight to the First Amendment associational interests of nonmembers of a party seeking to participate in the primary process, to the fundamental right of such nonmembers to cast a meaningful vote for the candidate of their choice . . . and to the preference of almost 60% of California voters -- including a majority of registered Democrats and Republicans -- for a blanket primary. . . In my view, a State is unquestionably entitled to rely on this combination of interests in deciding who may vote in a primary election conducted by the State. It is indeed strange to find that the First Amendment forecloses this decision.

[Part II of the opinion is omitted]

NOTES AND QUESTIONS

1. To what extent can the Court's sweeping First Amendment "right not to associate" be confined to the specific form of a blanket primary? Doesn't any state regulation of how candidates are nominated threaten to infringe the right to be free of unwanted associations? Ironically, this is the exact argument that was raised (unsuccessfully) by political parties to the initial imposition of primary nomination processes at the turn of the last century. *See generally* Adam Winkler, *Voters' Rights And Parties' Wrongs: Early Political Party Regulation in the State Courts, 1886-1915,* 100 COLUM. L. REV. 873 (2000). Don't all primary processes dilute the ability of the parties to define out those who are not deemed true partisans of the party's views?

2. Indeed, American political parties are distinct from political parties in other Western democracies precisely because, since the turn of the century with the rise of the mandatory primary elections, the law has regulated American parties, including their candidate selection processes, in a vastly more substantial and intrusive way than in European systems. British law banned party labels on parliamentary ballots before 1970, and since then, these labels are added when desired by individual candidates. Australia puts no party labels on ballots and simply treats parties as other private associations, subject to general laws rather than party-specific regulations. How much of the distinct American regulation of party nomination processes can or should be justified by American electoral rules, which provide the major parties special access to the ballot and permit the use of party labels on the ballot? Yet even those systems that provide for official ballot recognition of party labels do not have the regulation of party nominations that has long been characteristic of American politics. Only Germany, Turkey, and

Norway regulate party candidate selection at all; yet even these regulations merely stipulate that dues-paying party members must be entitled to participate in what is essentially a selection process run by the parties themselves without regulation (these comparisons are as of 1986). This has led one of the leading studies of American political parties to pose the central question as being: "Why has the United States alone among democratic nations subjected *parties* to so much legal regulation and control?" LEON EPSTEIN, POLITICAL PARTIES IN THE AMERICAN MOLD 158 (1986). Epstein goes on to show, in a fascinating historical study, what processes and arguments have led to the traditionally more extensive regulation of parties and candidate selection in the United States than elsewhere. Part of his answer is that Americans have long been more prone to view (and experience?) political parties as corrupt: "Nowhere else in the western democratic world did parties look so evil, at least to middle-class citizens, as they did in the United States." *Id.*, at 159.

In light of both the longstanding legal tradition of party regulation in the United States, and the purportedly distinctive American concern for the venality of parties and their leaders, is *Jones* rightly decided? Does the Court adequately deal with this history and explain why the blanket primary, among all other forms of candidate-selection regulations in the 20th century, violates the associational rights of parties?

3. Given this history of party regulation in the United States, there is a long-standing argument that the party nomination processes are public functions -- simply part of the electoral apparatus of the state. For an early form of this argument, see Alonzo H. Tuttle, *Limitations Upon the Power of the Legislature to Control Political Parties and Their Primaries,* 1 MICH. L. REV. 466, 468 (1903)("The right to nominate is as much a part of the franchise as the right to elect."). Justice Stevens dissent follows upon this analytic approach. Thus, according to Stevens, the reason that a state may impose a particular form of candidate selection, even recognizing that it is a "significant restriction on a party's associational freedoms" is that "both the general election and the primary are quintessential forms of state action . . . . " If this approach were to be followed, would there be any area of protection of the electoral activities of parties left protected from state regulation? For a challenge to the dissent's approach on this issue, see Samuel Issacharoff, *Private Parties With Public Purposes: Political Parties, Associational Freedoms, and Partisan Competition,* 101 COLUM. L. REV. ___ (forthcoming 2001).

4. Justice Scalia, the author of *Jones,* dissented from the Court's decisions holding patronage employment and contracting practices to violate First Amendment rights. *See Rutan v. Republican Party,* 497 U.S. 62 (1990) ("To the victor belong only those spoils that may be constitutionally obtained") (banning patronage decisions in transfer and promotion of public employees); *Board of County Comm'rs v. Umbehr,* 518 U.S. 668 (1996) (same for independent contractors). *See also Branti v. Finkel,* 445 U.S. 507 (1980) (banning patronge firing where party affiliation not required for effective performance of office) and *Elrod v. Burns,* 427 U.S. 347 (1976) (banning patronage firing). Justice Scalia argued that the constitutional ban on patronage "reflects a naive vision of politics and an inadequate appreciation of the systemic effects of patronage in promoting political stability and facilitating the social and political integration of previously powerless groups." *Rutan,* 497 U.S., at 107 (Scalia, J., dissenting). He asserted that the ban on patronage had contributed to a decline of party strength in the United States and therefore to the growth of interest-group politics over the last decade. *See* Michael Fitts, *The Vice of Virtue,* 136 U. PENN. L. REV. 1567, 1603-1607 (1988) (cited by Justice Scalia in support of this proposition). Justice Scalia

went on to argue:

> [P]atronage stabilizes political parties and prevents excessive
> political fragmentation – both of which are results in which States
> have a strong governmental interest. Party strength requires the
> efforts of the rank and file, especially in the "dull periods between
> elections," to perform such tasks as organizing precincts, registering
> new voters, and providing constituent services. Even the most
> enthusiastic supporter of a party's program will shrink before such
> drudgery, and it is folly to think that ideological conviction alone will
> motivate sufficient numbers to keep the party going through the off
> years. Here is the judgment of one such politician, Jacob Avery
> (best known as the promoter of Adlai Stevenson): Patronage is a
> "necessary evil if you want a strong organization, because the
> patronage system permits of discipline, and without discipline,
> there's no party organization. Id., at 104 [citations omitted].

How much does the Court's *Jones* opinion depend upon the same view of the
importance of strong, independent political parties reflected in Justice Scalia's
dissents in the patronage cases? Yet those were dissents, after all. Does that
suggest any fundamental inconsistency between the patronage decisions, which
deny party autonomy, and *Jones*, which upholds the importance of party
autonomy? For the view that the Court's decisions do indeed fail to offer any
consistent normative understanding of democratic practices across different
doctrinal problems in the law of politics, see Pamela S. Karlan, *Just Politics?
Five Not So Easy Pieces of the 1995 Term*, 34 HOUS. L. REV. 289 (1997).

5. Given the Court's sensitivity to the importance of party's being able
to have as their standard-bearer a candidate of its own choice, is there some
irony in the Court's endorsement of the Louisiana non-partisan blanket primary
as a constitutional safe harbor?. Under the Louisiana system, all candidates for
office run in a first round that is open to all voters. The two leading candidates
then survive to a second round in which the candidates run with no party
designation. While the Louisiana system does avoid allowing non-party
members to forcibly participate in selecting the party's standard-bearer, it does
so by denying the parties the right to ever select a standard-bearer at all. If the
justification for the Court's concern over the California blanket primary was
that "[I]n no area is the political association's right to exclude more important
than in the process of selecting its nominee," shouldn't the denial to the party
of all capacity to field a nominee in its own name be constitutionally suspect?

6. The *Jones* litigation sparked renewed attention to the legal
treatment of political parties. Consider the following summary of competing
models of how the law should treat political parties:

The Managerial Paradigm

> Drawing on the fears of faction so central to the Constitution's
> creation, the Manager enforces a worldview on the party and
> electoral system that has as its primary goal the preservation
> of political order. That order finds its purest expression in the
> maintenance of the traditional two-party system. . . Managers
> accord little importance to a political party's "freedom to
> associate." While there is something to be said for the
> Managerial paradigm, especially for its insight that parties

serve important functions for and derive valuable resources from the state, its major weaknesses lie in its reification of the state and deceptively simple treatment of party. . . it cannot effectively check the possible "tyranny" of the party as elected officials. It overlooks the fact that the party as elected officials controls the state, and hence, that actions the state takes can be manipulated to serve the interests of either elected officials generally or elected officials of the governing party specifically.

The Libertarian Paradigm

Libertarians take the direct opposite view of the Managers regarding the electoral and party system. Far from instruments to serve the state, parties are merely a species of private, organized interest groups, which should thus be accorded maximal rights of association, privacy, expression, and freedom from state discrimination. . . More specifically, parties should not receive any state benefits (e.g., public financing of party primaries) or be subject to state regulation (e.g., state law requiring parties to conduct primaries as the means of selecting general election candidates). However, like the Managerial paradigm, the Libertarian paradigm overlooks the heterogeneity of political parties: heterogeneity, that is, both in terms of type of party (i.e., major or minor) as well as the particular features of each state's laws that define and structure parties. . . [J]ust as the Managers go too far in the state interest direction, the Libertarian paradigm goes too far in the party rights direction. . . If the danger of the first paradigm can be called the "tyranny of the party as elected officials," then the corresponding problem raised by the Libertarian approach is the "tyranny of the party as organization."

The Progressive Paradigm

[Progressives exhibit a] generalized hostility to parties . . . [viewing them as] obstructive forces for the realization of the general will of the electorate. Progressives therefore tend to favor state regulations that vitiate party autonomy or freedom of association and make parties less relevant for electoral purposes. . . .[T]he real problem with the Progressive paradigm is that it does not recognize the essential role that parties play in brokering group interests and solving voters' collective action problems. A polity without parties places a greater cognitive burden on individual voters and weakens the collective responsibility of political agents.

Political Markets

Attempting to bring the virtues of law and economics and public choice analysis to the field of election law. . . [f]or the Political Marketeer, the primary purpose of political parties is to offer voter-consumers electoral choices. For it is through unfettered partisan competition that an invisible political hand will operate to supply voter-consumers with goods (in this case, candidates and/or policy positions) that are purchased with votes at the polls. While there is much to be said for a paradigm that promotes electoral competition, this approach suffers from some important weaknesses. To begin with, it overlooks the role of "voice" in politics and relies far too heavily on "exit.". . . Second, the Political Markets paradigm places its entire faith in the electorate. As consumers, they are sovereign. As such, it is a strongly populist approach that leaves little room for leadership, guidance, and assistance from the politically active. . . The Political Markets paradigm merely allows for the articulation of and response to consumer preferences. It does not allow for deliberation and the transmission of information within party networks, particularly in a two-party system.

The Pluralist Paradigm

Pluralism takes as its point of departure the importance of organized groups in the political process. . .American parties, according to the Pluralist, should be broader, decentralized coalitions of interest groups. . . [This] represents a normative preference for a party system that can aggregate and account for the intensity of group preferences in the most politically, economically, and ethnically diverse country in the world. . . . However, Pluralists may exaggerate the representativeness of the interest group system. They tend to downplay the potential for autonomous party organizations to ignore large interest groups with dispersed interests and small groups outside the mainstream or without the resources to make their voice heard. Finally, given their weak ideological cohesion, Pluralist parties at the legislative level often prove ineffective as policy making bodies and can blur accountability such that no party ever appears "responsible" for anything.

Nathaniel Persily & Bruce E. Cain, *The Legal Status of Political Parties: A Reassessment of Competing Paradigms,* 100 COLUM. L. REV. 775 (2000).

7. An alternative approach would situate political parties more broadly within the intermediary institutions that collectively may be referred to as "civil society." This is the more ambiguous area that is not as intimate as the family, but not as fully public as the state. For the exponents of the importance of civil society, these intermediary institutions are among the central promoters and transmitters of the values of the society. As expressed by political theorist Nancy L. Rosenblum, in *Law and Political Parties, Political Parties as Membership Groups,* 100 COLUM. L. REV. 813 (2000):

Parties are the groups people identify with, actively join, contribute to, work within, become officers of, and participate in - setting agendas, goals, and strategies. Both the large-scale, long-term effects of parties on the political system and political culture overall and their capacity to shape the democratic dispositions and practices of citizens personally and individually are a function of their vitality as membership groups. Civil society theorists should grant parties a central place, and should be at least as solicitous of political parties as the many other associations that are objects of concern today. The justification I propose for valuing political parties, and for their centrality to democratic civil society, is based on their distinctive characteristics and effects as membership groups.

In contrast to most interest and advocacy groups, parties must continuously seek to establish contact with the electorate in a fashion that elicits participation on a large scale. Parties do more than help recruit and support candidates for an extensive array of offices at every level of government. Indeed, the objective of contesting elections successfully involves more than campaign activities, registration drives, voter guides, and turn-out. It requires long-term development - establishing local presence, building cadres of activists, coordinating the support of social leaders, and seeking membership from every salient group. Parties raise and define public issues, engage in political education, choose officers, enact rules for process and representation, and decide on their purposes and policies as well as their strategies. They are distinctive sources of information and of experience in forming political judgments. They are forums for reasonably deliberative collective decision-making about public life. Potentially, they are the most important agenda-setting institution for the public interests of society as a whole. In all these respects, the value of parties is independent of particular electoral successes, but strongly dependent on the vitality of parties as membership groups.

For a more skeptical examination of the capacity of parties to instill broader civic values, see James A. Gardner, *Can Party Politics Be Virtuous?*, 100 COLUM. L. REV. 667 (2000).

8. In light of *Jones*, suppose a state party adopts a rule that no candidate can appear under its label on a primary ballot unless he or she receives at least 15% of the votes cast at a party convention (held, obviously, before the electoral primary). This would be a means of party leaders and activists seeking to recapture some of the control that the mandatory primary law otherwise transfers to those who state law permits to vote in the actual primary. The Massachusetts Democratic Party did precisely this in the 1980s with the adoption of such a 15 percent rule. Massachusetts's primary-election structure permitted previously unenrolled voters to enter a party primary and declare their affiliation with that party on election day (voters could change their enrollment or become unenrolled again the next day). In contrast to the party rule, State law required that to be listed as a party candidate in the primary, a candidate only had to be an enrolled party member and have gathered a specified number of signatures (which did not have to come from party members).

In a conflict between State law and party-imposed primary-candidate requirements, does the Constitution require that State law or the party prevail? The Massachusetts courts concluded that, because the Constitution protected "party autonomy," the State law would be unconstitutional unless it was construed to permit the party to supplement the state-law candidate requirements. The Supreme Court, in a 6-3 vote with a lengthy dissent, dismissed the appeal for want of jurisdiction. Justice Stevens, who along with

Justices Rehnquist and O'Connor dissented from the Court's refusal to hear the case on the merits, noted that the State Attorney General argued that the 15 percent rule and potentially similar internal party requirements "can permit the virtual nullification of the primary process." *Bellotti v. Connolly*, 460 U.S. 1057 (1983) (Stevens, J., dissenting).

Does *Jones* essentially also resolve the dispute within the Court over State-party conflicts such as that in *Connolly*? If so, why isn't the State right that *Jones* permits the "virtual nullification of the primary process?"

9. For a debate over the correctness of *Jones*, compare Richard L. Hasen, *Do The Parties or the People Own the Electoral Process*, 148 U. PENN. L. REV. ___ (2001) with Bruce Cain, *Party Autonomy and Two Party Electoral Competition* 148 U. PENN. L. REV. ___ (2001).

p. 264, insert new section:

3. THE INTERACTION OF ACCESS TO THE ELECTORAL ARENA AND THE PERPETUATION OF THE TWO PARTY SYSTEM.

Third parties can suffer from exclusion not simply by being denied formal access to the ballot. Consider the effects of exclusion from the public arena in which candidates are presented to the electorate:

ARKANSAS EDUCATIONAL TELEVISION COMMISSION, PETITIONER v. RALPH P. FORBES,
523 U.S. 666 (1998)

JUSTICE KENNEDY delivered the opinion of the Court.

* * *
   I

Petitioner, the Arkansas Educational Television Commission (AETC), is an Arkansas state agency owning and operating a network of five noncommercial television stations (Arkansas Educational Television Network or AETN). . .

In the spring of 1992, AETC staff began planning a series of debates between candidates for federal office in the November 1992 elections. AETC decided to televise a total of five debates, scheduling one for the Senate election and one for each of the four congressional elections in Arkansas. Working in close consultation with Bill Simmons, Arkansas Bureau Chief for the Associated Press, AETC staff developed a debate format allowing about 53 minutes during each 1-hour debate for questions to and answers by the candidates. Given the time constraint, the staff and Simmons "decided to limit participation in the debates to the major party candidates or any other candidate who had strong popular support."

On June 17, 1992, AETC invited the Republican and Democratic candidates for Arkansas' Third Congressional District to participate in the AETC debate for that seat. Two months later, after obtaining the 2,000 signatures required by Arkansas law, see Ark. Code Ann. § 7-7-103(c)(1) (1993), respondent Ralph Forbes was certified as an independent candidate qualified to appear on the ballot for the seat. Forbes was a perennial candidate who had sought, without success, a number of elected offices in Arkansas. On August 24, 1992, he wrote to AETC requesting permission to participate in the debate for his district, scheduled for October 22, 1992. On September 4, AETC Executive Director Susan Howarth denied Forbes' request, explaining that AETC had "made a bona fide journalistic judgement that our viewers would be best served by limiting the debate" to the candidates already invited.

On October 19, 1992, Forbes filed suit against AETC, seeking injunctive and declaratory relief as well as damages. Forbes claimed he was entitled to participate in the debate under both the First Amendment and *47 U.S.C. § 315,* which affords political candidates a limited right of access to television air time. Forbes requested a preliminary injunction mandating his inclusion in the debate. The District Court denied the request, as did the United States Court of Appeals for the Eighth Circuit. The District Court later dismissed Forbes' action for failure to state a claim.

Sitting en banc, the Court of Appeals affirmed the dismissal of Forbes' statutory claim, holding that he had failed to exhaust his administrative remedies. The court reversed, however, the dismissal of Forbes' First Amendment claim. Observing that AETC is a state actor, the court held Forbes had "a qualified right of access created by AETN's sponsorship of a debate, and that AETN must have [had] a legitimate reason to exclude him strong enough to survive First Amendment scrutiny."

On remand, the District Court found as a matter of law that the debate was a nonpublic forum, and the issue became whether Forbes' views were the reason for his exclusion. . . The District Court entered judgment for AETC. . .

The Court of Appeals again reversed. The court acknowledged that AETC's decision to exclude Forbes "was made in good faith" and was "exactly the kind of journalistic judgment routinely made by newspeople." The court asserted, nevertheless, that AETC had "opened its facilities to a particular group -- candidates running for the Third District Congressional seat." AETC's action, the court held, made the debate a public forum, to which all candidates "legally qualified to appear on the ballot" had a presumptive right of access. Applying strict scrutiny, the court determined that AETC's assessment of Forbes'"political viability" was neither a "compelling nor [a] narrowly tailored" reason for excluding him from the debate. . .

We now reverse.

II . . .

At the outset . . . it is instructive to ask whether public forum principles apply to the case at all.

Having first arisen in the context of streets and parks, the public forum doctrine should not be extended in a mechanical way to the very different context of public television broadcasting. In the case of streets and parks, the open access and viewpoint neutrality commanded by the doctrine is "compatible with the intended purpose of the property." In the case of television broadcasting, however, broad rights of access for outside speakers would be antithetical, as a general rule, to the discretion that stations and their editorial staff must exercise to fulfill their journalistic purpose and statutory obligations.

Congress has rejected the argument that "broadcast facilities should be open on a nonselective basis to all persons wishing to talk about public issues." . . . Public and private broadcasters alike are not only permitted, but indeed required, to exercise substantial editorial discretion in the selection and presentation of their programming. . .

Claims of access under our public forum precedents could obstruct the legitimate purposes of television broadcasters. Were the doctrine given sweeping application in this context, courts "would be required to oversee far more of the day-to-day operations of broadcasters' conduct, deciding such questions as whether a particular individual or group has had sufficient opportunity to present its viewpoint and whether a particular viewpoint has already been sufficiently aired." "The result would be a further erosion of the journalistic discretion of broadcasters," transferring "control over the treatment of public issues from the licensees who are accountable for broadcast performance to private individuals" who bring suit under our forum precedents. In effect, we would "exchange 'public trustee' broadcasting, with all its limitations, for a system of self-appointed editorial commentators."

. . . This is not to say the First Amendment would bar the legislative imposition of neutral rules for access to public broadcasting. Instead, we say that, in most cases, the First Amendment of its own force does not compel public broadcasters to allow third parties access to their programming.

Although public broadcasting as a general matter does not lend itself to scrutiny under the forum doctrine, candidate debates present the narrow exception to the rule. For two reasons, a candidate debate like the one at issue here is different from other programming. First, unlike AETC's other broadcasts, the debate was by design a forum for political speech by the candidates. Consistent with the long tradition of candidate debates, the implicit representation of the broadcaster was that the views expressed were those of the candidates, not its own. The very purpose of the debate was to allow the candidates to express their views with minimal intrusion by the broadcaster. In this respect the debate differed even from a political talk show, whose host can express partisan views and then limit the discussion to those ideas.

Second, in our tradition, candidate debates are of exceptional significance in the electoral process. "It is of particular importance that candidates have the opportunity to make their views known so that the electorate may intelligently evaluate the candidates' personal qualities and their positions on vital public issues before choosing among them on election day." Deliberation on the positions and qualifications of candidates is integral to our system of government, and electoral speech may have its most profound and widespread impact when it is disseminated through televised debates. A majority of the population cites television as its primary source of election information, and debates are regarded as the "only occasion during a campaign when the attention of a large portion of the American public is focused on the election, as well as the only campaign information format which potentially offers sufficient time to explore issues and policies in depth in a neutral forum."

The special characteristics of candidate debates support the conclusion that the AETC debate was a forum of some type. The question of what type must be answered by reference to our public forum precedents, to which we now turn.

III

Forbes argues, and the Court of Appeals held, that the debate was a public forum to which he had a First Amendment right of access. Under our precedents, however, the debate was a nonpublic forum, from which AETC could exclude Forbes in the reasonable, viewpoint-neutral exercise of its journalistic discretion.

A

. . . "The Court [has] identified three types of fora: the traditional public forum, the public forum created by government designation, and the nonpublic forum." Traditional public fora are defined by the objective characteristics of the property, such as whether, "by long tradition or by government fiat," the property has been "devoted to assembly and debate." The government can exclude a speaker from a traditional public forum "only when the exclusion is necessary to serve a compelling state interest and the exclusion is narrowly drawn to achieve that interest."

Designated public fora, in contrast, are created by purposeful governmental action. "The government does not create a [designated] public forum by inaction or by permitting limited discourse, but only by intentionally opening a nontraditional public forum for public discourse."

... "[T]he Court has looked to the policy and practice of the government to ascertain whether it intended to designate a place not traditionally open to assembly and debate as a public forum." If the government excludes a speaker who falls within the class to which a designated public forum is made generally available, its action is subject to strict scrutiny.

Other government properties are either nonpublic fora or not fora at all. The government can restrict access to a nonpublic forum "as long as the restrictions are reasonable and [are] not an effort to suppress expression merely because public officials oppose the speaker's view." . . .

B

The parties agree the AETC debate was not a traditional public forum. . . . The issue, then, is whether the debate was a designated public forum or a nonpublic forum.

Under our precedents, the AETC debate was not a designated public forum. To create a forum of this type, the government must intend to make the property "generally available," to a class of speakers. A designated public forum is not created when the government allows selective access for individual speakers rather than general access for a class of speakers. . .

[Our cases] illustrate the distinction between "general access," which indicates the property is a designated public forum, and "selective access," which indicates the property is a nonpublic forum. On one hand, the government creates a designated public forum when it makes its property generally available to a certain class of speakers. On the other hand, the government does not create a designated public forum when it does no more than reserve eligibility for access to the forum to a particular class of speakers, whose members must then, as individuals, "obtain permission." . . .

. . . That this distinction turns on governmental intent does not render it unprotective of speech. Rather, it reflects the reality that, with the exception of traditional public fora, the government retains the choice of whether to designate its property as a forum for specified classes of speakers.

Here, the debate did not have an open-microphone format. . . . AETC reserved eligibility for participation in the debate to candidates for the Third Congressional District seat (as opposed to some other seat). . . . AETC made candidate-by-candidate determinations as to which of the eligible candidates would participate in the debate. "Such selective access, unsupported by evidence of a purposeful designation for public use, does not create a public forum." Thus the debate was a nonpublic forum.

In addition to being a misapplication of our precedents, the Court of Appeals' holding would result in less speech, not more. In ruling that the debate was a public forum open to all ballot-qualified candidates, the Court of Appeals would place a severe burden upon public broadcasters who air candidates' views. . . . On logistical grounds alone, a public television editor might, with reason, decide that the inclusion of all ballot-qualified candidates would "actually undermine the educational value and quality of debates."

Were it faced with the prospect of cacophony, on the one hand, and First Amendment liability, on the other, a public television broadcaster might choose not to air candidates' views at all. A broadcaster might decide "'the safe course is to avoid controversy,' ... and by so doing diminish the free flow of information and ideas." In this circumstance, a "government-enforced right of access inescapably 'dampens the vigor and limits the variety of public debate.'". . .

C

The debate's status as a nonpublic forum, however, did not give AETC unfettered power to exclude any candidate it wished. . . . To be consistent with the First Amendment, the exclusion of a speaker from a nonpublic forum must not be based on the speaker's viewpoint and must otherwise be reasonable in light of the purpose of the property.

In this case, the jury found Forbes' exclusion was not based on "objections or opposition to his views." The record provides ample support for this finding, demonstrating as well that AETC's decision to exclude him was reasonable. . . . It is, in short, beyond dispute that Forbes was excluded not because of his viewpoint but because he had generated no appreciable public interest.

There is no substance to Forbes' suggestion that he was excluded because his views were unpopular or out of the mainstream. His own objective lack of support, not his platform, was the criterion. Indeed, the very premise of Forbes' contention is mistaken. A candidate with unconventional views might well enjoy broad support by virtue of a compelling personality or an exemplary campaign organization. By the same token, a candidate with a traditional platform might enjoy little support due to an inept campaign or any number of other reasons.

The broadcaster's decision to exclude Forbes was a reasonable, viewpoint-neutral exercise of journalistic discretion consistent with the First Amendment. The judgment of the Court of Appeals is

Reversed.

JUSTICE STEVENS, with whom JUSTICE SOUTER and JUSTICE

GINSBURG join, dissenting.

The judgment of the Court of Appeals should . . . be affirmed. The official action that led to the exclusion of respondent Forbes from a debate with the two major-party candidates for election to one of Arkansas' four seats in Congress does not adhere to well-settled constitutional principles. The ad hoc decision of the staff of the Arkansas Educational Television Commission (AETC) raises precisely the concerns addressed by "the many decisions of this Court over the last 30 years, holding that a law subjecting the exercise of First Amendment freedoms to the prior restraint of a license, without narrow, objective, and definite standards to guide the licensing authority, is unconstitutional."

* * *

I

Two months before Forbes was officially certified as an independent candidate qualified to appear on the ballot under Arkansas law, the AETC staff had already concluded that he "should not be invited" to participate in the televised debates because he was "not a serious candidate as determined by the voters of Arkansas." He had, however, been a serious contender for the Republican nomination for Lieutenant Governor in 1986 and again in 1990. Although he was defeated in a run-off election, in the three- way primary race conducted in 1990 -- just two years before the AETC staff decision -- he had received 46.88% of the statewide vote and had carried 15 of the 16 counties within the Third Congressional District by absolute majorities. Nevertheless, the staff concluded that Forbes did not have "strong popular support."

Given the fact that the Republican winner in the Third Congressional District race in 1992 received only 50.22% of the vote and the Democrat received 47.20%, it would have been necessary for Forbes, who had made a strong showing in recent Republican primaries, to divert only a handful of votes from the Republican candidate to cause his defeat. Thus, even though the AETC staff may have correctly concluded that Forbes was "not a serious candidate," their decision to exclude him from the debate may have determined the outcome of the election in the Third District. . .

The apparent flexibility of AETC's purported standard suggests the extent to which the staff had nearly limitless discretion to exclude Forbes from the debate based on ad hoc justifications. Thus, the Court of Appeals correctly concluded that the staff's appraisal of "political viability" was "so subjective, so arguable, so susceptible of variation in individual opinion, as to provide no secure basis for the exercise of governmental power consistent with the First Amendment."

II

AETC is a state agency whose actions "are fairly attributable to the State and subject to the Fourteenth Amendment, unlike the actions of privately owned broadcast licensees." . . . The Court implicitly acknowledges these facts by subjecting the decision to exclude Forbes to constitutional analysis. Yet the Court seriously underestimates the importance of the difference between private and public ownership of broadcast facilities, despite the fact that Congress and this Court have repeatedly recognized that difference.

* * *

. . . Because AETC is owned by the State, deference to its interest in making ad hoc decisions about the political content of its programs necessarily increases the risk of government censorship and propaganda in a way that protection of privately owned broadcasters does not.

III

The Court recognizes that the debates sponsored by AETC were "by design a forum for political speech by the candidates." The Court also acknowledges the central importance of candidate debates in the electoral process. Thus, there is no need to review our cases expounding on the public forum doctrine to conclude that the First Amendment will not tolerate a state agency's arbitrary exclusion from a debate forum based, for example, on an expectation that the speaker might be critical of the Governor, or might hold unpopular views about abortion or the death penalty. Indeed, the Court so holds today.

It seems equally clear, however, that the First Amendment will not tolerate arbitrary definitions of the scope of the forum. We have recognized that "once it has opened a limited forum, ... the State must respect the lawful boundaries it has itself set." It follows, of course, that a State's failure to set any meaningful boundaries at all cannot insulate the State's action from First Amendment challenge. The dispositive issue in this case, then, is not whether AETC created a designated public forum or a nonpublic forum, as the Court concludes, but whether AETC defined the contours of the debate forum with sufficient specificity to justify the exclusion of a ballot-qualified candidate.

AETC asks that we reject Forbes' constitutional claim on the basis of entirely subjective, ad hoc judgments about the dimensions of its forum. The First Amendment demands more, however, when a state government effectively wields the power to eliminate a political candidate from all consideration by the voters. All stations must act as editors, and when state-owned stations participate in the broadcasting arena, their editorial decisions may impact the constitutional interests of individual speakers. A state-owned broadcaster need not plan, sponsor, and conduct political debates, however. When it chooses to do so, the First Amendment imposes important limitations on its control over access to the debate forum.

* * *

The televised debate forum at issue in this case may not squarely fit within our public forum analysis, n16 but its importance cannot be denied. Given the special character of political speech, particularly during campaigns for elected office, the debate forum implicates constitutional concerns of the highest order, as the majority acknowledges. *Ante*, at 8. Indeed, the planning and management of political debates by state-owned broadcasters raise serious constitutional concerns that are seldom replicated when state-owned television networks engage in other types of programming. We have recognized that "speech concerning public affairs is ... the essence of self-government." The First Amendment therefore "has its fullest and most urgent application precisely to the conduct of campaigns for political office." Surely the Constitution demands at least as much from the Government when it takes action that necessarily impacts democratic elections as when local officials issue parade permits.

The reasons that support the need for narrow, objective, and definite standards to guide licensing decisions apply directly to the wholly subjective access decisions made by the staff of AETC. The importance of avoiding arbitrary or viewpoint-based exclusions from political debates militates strongly in favor of requiring the controlling state agency to use (and adhere to) pre-established, objective criteria to determine who among qualified candidates may participate. When the demand for speaking facilities exceeds supply, the State must "ration or allocate the scarce resources on some acceptable neutral principle." A constitutional duty to use objective standards -- *i.e.,* "neutral principles" -- for determining whether and when to adjust a debate format would impose only a modest requirement that would fall far short of a duty to grant every multiple-party request. Such standards would also have the benefit of providing the public with some assurance that state-owned broadcasters cannot select debate participants on arbitrary grounds.

Like the Court, I do not endorse the view of the Court of Appeals that all candidates who qualify for a position on the ballot are necessarily entitled to access to any state-sponsored debate. I am convinced, however, that the constitutional imperatives that motivated our decisions in [other] cases . . . command that access to political debates planned and managed by state-owned entities be governed by pre-established, objective criteria. Requiring government employees to set out objective criteria by which they choose which candidates will benefit from the significant media exposure that results from state-sponsored political debates would alleviate some of the risk inherent in allowing government agencies -- rather than private entities -- to stage candidate debates.

Accordingly, I would affirm the judgment of the Court of Appeals.

NOTES AND QUESTIONS

1. Consider the risk in circularity of reasoning about what is a legitimate candidate. For example, it may be argued that the single most important factor in gaining legitimacy for a candidate, particularly a third-party candidate is the ability to share the same stage with established candidates. Perhaps the clearest example of what that can mean to a third-party candidate is the gubernatorial election of Jesse Ventura in 1998 in Minnesota. By his own admission, Governor Ventura was not considered a serious candidate until "there were the three-way debates. Right at that point in the first debate, my numbers started rising very quickly . . . and they never changed." *ABC Good Morning America,* November 4, 1998. When asked about the possibility of having a minimum threshold of 15 percent in polls as a precondition for participating in the debates, Ventura opined, "I disagree with that 15 percent mark, because at the point in the primary here in Minnesota, which is six to seven weeks before the general election, I was only polling 10 percent. So if that criteria had been used here in Minnesota, I wouldn't be the governor today because I won the election because of debates and I don't think that that's a fair number to use. You should use the same number that you use to determine whether you have major party status." *Face The Nation,* April 2, 2000. How would Governor Ventura have fared under *Forbes* had he challenged exclusion from the Minnesota debates under a 15 percent threshold requirement for participation?

Moreover, unlike most other states, Minnesota's election laws also encouraged third-party candidacies like Ventura's. First, Minnesota is one of six states that permit same-day voter registration (post-election analyses indicate that Ventura would not have won without the votes of same-day registrants). Second, Minnesota has broad public financing of elections, including for third-party candidates; Ventura received a state contribution of $330,000, which was crucial because he raised little private money. Third, Minnesota has liberal ballot access laws for third parties. See Richard H. Pildes, *A Theory of Political Competition,* 85 VA. L. REV. 1605, 1617-18 (1999). As this commentary concludes: "Had the more common and more anticompetitive rules and practices in other states been in place – regarding registration, financing, ballot access, and participation in candidate debates – Minnesota would likely be as rigidly a two-party state as most others. Election laws, combined with the right circumstances, can indeed matter." *Id.,* at 1618.

2. What are the possible constitutional implications of *Forbes* for other areas of electoral regulation, such as campaign finance. Notice that *Forbes* holds that distinct constitutional rules apply to candidate-debates on public television because debates play a special role in the democratic process. What other aspects of electoral structures might be thought to play a similarly special role, thus justifying similar distinct constitutional treatment of regulation that would otherwise violate the Constitution were that regulation applied outside the electoral domain?

Notice the legal structure of the *Forbes* opinion: the Court first held that state-owned television programming was not subject to any of the First Amendment doctrines that would otherwise apply to what are known as public forums or even designated or limited public forums. Thus, the Court first held that state-owned television was akin to private journalism and immune from First Amendment constraints that would apply to state action, particularly those prohibiting viewpoint discrimination. But then, the Court went on to hold that because one specific kind of public-television programming – candidate debates – played a special role in the democratic process, this special role required candidate debates to be treated as a constitutional exception to the principle that state television was akin to private journalism. As a result, the Court held that state-sponsored candidate debates – alone among state-television programming – *did* indeed have to meet constitutional requirements of viewpoint neutrality.

If special constitutional rules are to apply to state-sponsored candidate debates because of the "special role" such debates play in the electoral domain, might *Forbes* suggest that other regulations of electoral politics can be similarly excepted from the First Amendment doctrines that would otherwise apply were those regulations to govern speech activity outside the domain of elections? Perhaps the central issue in the constitutional assessment of campaign-finance regulation, for example, is whether the First Amendment should recognize a distinction between the "general domain of public discourse" and what we might call "the electoral domain." Only if these two domains can be legally distinguished from each other is it possible to envision various kinds of proposed reforms of electoral processes. In assessing whether *Forbes* does support such a distinction, consider the following:

> [After *Forbes*], the question is whether regulation should be permissible to remedy various perceived pathologies of current electoral discourse, *even if* that same degree of government intervention would be impermissible to remedy the parallel pathologies of non-electoral discourse in roughly comparable situations. Even more specifically, the question is whether such regulation ought to be permissible against the perceived distortions resulting from the undue influence of wealth, even if doing so would leave an imbalance in other sources of political influence. Accepting that position would require accepting the idea that elections can be demarcated, for First Amendment purposes, from the general domain of public discourse. This is both a normative question in First Amendment theory and a functional question of whether any regulatory approach can enforce this boundary with sufficient integrity. Oddly, the Court in *Buckley* never confronted this issue in either of these terms . . .

Frederick Schauer and Richard H. Pildes, *Electoral Exceptionalism and the First Amendment,* 77 TEX. L. REV. 1803, 1825 (1999). Would "excepting" elections from First Amendment rules that apply in other domains be a radical intrusion on First Amendment principles? This article argues not, for even with respect to core political speech, all regulations under current law are "already measured by domain-specific, institution-specific, sometimes media-specific, and generally context-specific First Amendment principles." *Id.,* at 1824. Thus, it is not "essentially" inconsistent with the First Amendment to treat electoral politics as a distinct domain governed by its own First Amendment doctrines. For further elaboration, *see* Frederick Schauer, *Principles, Institutions, and the First Amendment,* 112 HARV. L. REV. 84 (1998); for a partial critique of this view, *see* Robert Post, *Regulating Election Speech Under the First Amendment,* 77 TEX. L. REV. 1337 (1999).

3. *Forbes* has generally been interpreted to allow state bodies to limit participation based on objective indicia of support, as opposed to a subjective assessment of the seriousness of the viewpoint being expressed. *See, e.g., Marcus v. Iowa Public Television*, 150 F.3d 924 (8th Cir. 1998)(approving the exclusion of third-party candidates since they were from minor parties and their exclusion was not based on their viewpoint); *Pryor v. Coats*, 2000 U.S. App. LEXIS 1805 (10th Cir. 2000)(approving law school policy providing bulletin board space only to registered student groups who qualified for such registration by submitting applications containing at least 10 student members; the court followed *Forbes* in finding that an individual speaker could be excluded because of his "own objective lack of support" not because of his platform.

4. The issue of how to choose "legitimate" candidates for purposes of candidate debates became a major one during the 2000 Presidential general election. Since 1988, the presidential debates have been overseen and structured by an entity called the Commission on Presidential Debates. This is established as an independent nonprofit group that is financially supported by corporate donations from major corporate entities. Although the Commission describes itself as "nonpartisan," its leadership is intentionally designed to have strong ties to the two major parties. One co-chair is a former Republican National Committee chairman; the other is a former Democratic National Committee chairman. In addition, various of the other members of the Commission's Board of Directors are heavily involved in traditional partisan politics, including Caroline Kennedy, former Sen. John C. Danforth (R-Missouri), and Rep. Jennifer Dunn (R-Washington). *See* Karen Branch-Brioso, *"Nonpartisan" Board has Failed to Tame Debates*, St. Louis Post-Dispatch, Sept. 17, 2000, at A9.

The Commission adopted formal rules for candidate eligibility for debate participation in 2000 that imposed quite high thresholds for third-party candidates: (1) they had to qualify for the ballots in enough states to theoretically be able to win a majority of the Electoral College and (2) they had to receive 15% or more in 5 national polls prior to the debates. The leading third-party candidates, Ralph Nader of the Green Party and Patrick Buchanan of the Reform Party were not able to meet both criteria, and as a result, all three Presidential debates involved only the two major-party candidates. Nader and Buchanan met the first requirement but did not meet the second. A main point of contention raised by Nader and Buchanan was the role of televised debates in boosting Ross Perot's candidacy in 1992. After Perot's relative success in 1992, the Commission did not invite Perot to the debates in 1996. Criticizing the high threshold for the 2000 elections, some experts in presidential politics suggested that a 15% threshold was unfairly high and recommended a 5% hurdle to bring about a more competitive election; as Bruce Cain, a Berkeley political scientist put it, "we're homogenizing [the political dialogue]; keeping it safe, narrow" by limiting the debates to two candidates. *See* Eric Bailey, *Shut out of the Debates, Nader and Buchanan Have Plenty of Company*, L.A. Times, Sept. 30, 2000, at A13. Compare this view with Cain's endorsement of the Supreme Court's decision in *Jones, supra*. Are Cain's demands for more competitive elections and his endorsement of *Jones* consistent? For more information on the Commission and its policies, go to its website: Commission on Presidential Debates, *Candidate Selection Process*, (visited Oct. 16, 2000) <http://www.debates.org/pages/candsel.html>.

CHAPTER FIVE

on page 285, add the following material at the end of Section A:

On the question of the constitutionality of § 5 in light of *Boerne* consider the Court's recent decision in Lopez v. Monterey County, 525 U.S. 255 (1999) (*Lopez II*).

LOPEZ v. MONTEREY COUNTY
525 U.S. 255 (1999)

JUSTICE O'CONNOR delivered the Opinion of the Court.

Under the Voting Rights Act of 1965, designated States and political subdivisions are required to obtain federal preclearance before giving effect to changes in their voting laws. Here, the State of California (California or State), which is not subject to the Act's preclearance requirements, has passed legislation altering the scheme for electing judges in Monterey County, California (Monterey County or County), a "covered" jurisdiction required to preclear its voting changes.... We hold that the Act's preclearance requirements apply to measures mandated by a noncovered State to the extent that these measures will effect a voting change in a covered county....

I

* * *

A

Congress enacted the Voting Rights Act under its authority to enforce the Fifteenth Amendment's proscription against voting discrimination....

In 1971, Monterey County was designated a covered jurisdiction based on findings that, as of November 1, 1968, the County maintained California's statewide literacy test as a prerequisite to voting and less than 50 percent of the County's voting age population participated in the November 1968 Presidential election....

In fact, over the last 30 years, there have been numerous changes in the structure of the County's trial court system and the scheme for electing judges....

Since 1972, ... the County's judicial system has undergone substantial change resulting in what is today a single, countywide municipal court ....

The County, although covered by § 5 of the Act, failed to seek federal preclearance for any of its six consolidation ordinances....

B

Appellants, Hispanic voters who reside in Monterey County, filed suit in the United States District Court for the Northern District of California on September 6, 1991, claiming that the County had failed to fulfill its § 5 obligation to preclear any of the consolidation ordinances passed between 1972 and 1983. A three-judge District Court concluded that the ordinances were voting changes requiring preclearance under § 5 and that the ordinances were unenforceable until they were precleared.

Accordingly, the County initiated proceedings before the United States District Court for the District of Columbia in an effort to preclear the ordinances. Ultimately, however, the County agreed to dismiss the suit without prejudice and to stipulate that its "Board of Supervisors is unable to establish that the [consolidation ordinances] adopted by the County between 1968 and 1983 did not have the effect of denying the right to vote to Latinos in Monterey County due to the retrogressive effect several of these ordinances had on Latino voting strength in Monterey County."

Back before the three-judge District Court in the Northern District of California, appellants and the County, working together, submitted alternatives to the districtwide voting scheme. Meanwhile, the State was allowed to intervene in the proceedings, and it opposed the proposed plans on the ground that they violated aspects of the California Constitution governing judicial elections....

.... [Ultimately, after a decision by this Court on a related issue the District Court on remand dismissed the complaint, holding that] preclearance was unnecessary because the countywide scheme was now mandated by California law....

In granting the motion to dismiss, the District Court reasoned that § 5, by its own terms, creates a preclearance obligation only for covered jurisdictions. Noncovered entities, like the State, bear no responsibility to preclear voting changes that they "enact or seek to administer."....

II

A

.... [T]he question before this Court is whether a covered jurisdiction "seeks to administer" a voting change when, without exercising any independent discretion, the jurisdiction implements a change required by the superior law of a noncovered State. Because we agree with appellants that a covered jurisdiction "seeks to administer" a voting change even where the jurisdiction exercises no discretion in giving effect to a state-mandated change, we conclude that the County is required to seek preclearance before implementing California laws that effect voting changes in the County.

The face of the Act itself provides the most compelling support for appellants' claim. The phrase "seek to administer" provides no indication that Congress intended to limit § 5's preclearance obligations to the discretionary actions of covered jurisdictions. To the contrary, "administer" is consistently defined in purely non-discretionary terms. *See, e.g.*, Webster's Third New International Dictionary 27 (1961) ("to manage the affairs of," "to direct or superintend the execution, use, or conduct of"); Random House Dictionary of the English Language 26 (2d ed. 1987) ("to manage (affairs, a government, etc.); have executive charge of"); Black's Law Dictionary 44 (6th ed. 1990) ("To manage or conduct"). The State's view that "administer" is intended to capture a covered jurisdiction's nonlegislative, executive initiatives is not to the contrary. Such a reading poses no barrier to the view that "administer" also encompasses nondiscretionary acts by covered jurisdictions endeavoring to comply with the superior law of the State....

We note, too, that this Court has elsewhere assumed that legislation from a partially covered State must be precleared to the extent that it affects covered counties. In *United Jewish Organizations of Williamsburgh, Inc. v. Carey*, 430 U.S. 144 (1977), we rejected a constitutional challenge brought by Hasidic residents of Kings County, New York, to a redistricting plan enacted by the state legislature. We assumed in that case that the state plan was subject to the Act's preclearance requirements, even though the State was not a covered jurisdiction, because Kings and other counties were themselves covered by the Act. We observed that, after the State's efforts to exempt its counties from the Act's coverage proved unsuccessful, see *New York ex rel. New York County v. United States*, 419 U.S. 888 (1974), "it became necessary for New York [State] to secure the approval of the Attorney General or of the United States District Court for the District of Columbia for its 1972 reapportionment statute insofar as that statute concerned [the covered] Counties." Moreover, the decision's constitutional analysis relies on the fact that the redistricting effort was meant to fulfill the State's obligations under the Act. [S]ee also *Shaw v. Hunt,* 517 U.S. 899 (1996) (evaluating whether partially covered State's § 5 obligations justified race-based districting without any consideration that State may not have been subject to preclearance requirement). These decisions reveal a clear assumption by this Court that § 5 preclearance is required where a noncovered State effects voting changes in covered counties.

Nor have we been alone in this assumption. The Department of Justice claims to have received more than 1,300 submissions seeking to preclear state laws from the seven States that are currently partially covered: California, Florida, Michigan, New Hampshire, New York, North Carolina, and South Dakota. In fact, cases before this and other federal courts reveal numerous instances in which interested parties have labored under the assumption that laws enacted by partially covered States require preclearance before they take effect in covered jurisdictions. *See, e.g., Shaw v. Reno*, 509 U.S. 630 (1993) ("Because the [North Carolina] General Assembly's reapportionment plan affected the covered counties, the parties agree that § 5 applied"); *Johnson v. De Grandy*, 512 U.S. 997 (1994) (Florida submitted statewide redistricting law for preclearance because five counties are covered) .... While this Court is not bound by its prior assumptions, the fact that courts and parties alike have routinely assumed a need for preclearance under the circumstances presented here supports our reading of § 5.

Finally, we find it especially relevant that the Attorney General also reads § 5 as we do. According to the Government, "The Attorney General has consistently construed Section 5 to require preclearance when a covered political subdivision 'seeks to administer' an enactment of a partially covered State." Subject to certain limitations not implicated here, *see, e.g., Presley v. Etowah County Comm'n*, 502 U.S. 491 (1992), we traditionally afford substantial deference to the Attorney General's interpretation of § 5 in light of her "central role . . . in formulating and implementing" that section....

B

The State also urges that requiring preclearance here would tread on rights constitutionally reserved to the States. The State contends, specifically, that § 5 could not withstand constitutional scrutiny if it were interpreted to apply to voting measures enacted by States that have not been designated as historical wrongdoers in the voting rights sphere. In the State's view, because California has not been designated as a covered jurisdiction, its laws are not subject to § 5 preclearance.

We have recognized that the Act, which authorizes federal intrusion into sensitive areas of state and local policymaking, imposes substantial "federalism costs." The Act was passed pursuant to Congress' authority under the Fifteenth Amendment, however, and we have likewise acknowledged that the Reconstruction Amendments by their nature contemplate some intrusion into areas traditionally reserved to the States. As the Court recently observed with respect to Congress' power to legislate under the Fourteenth Amendment, "legislation which deters or remedies constitutional violations can fall within the sweep of Congress' enforcement power even if in the process it prohibits conduct which is not itself unconstitutional and intrudes into legislative spheres of autonomy previously reserved to the States." *City of Boerne v. Flores*, 521 U.S. 507 (1997).

Moreover, we have specifically upheld the constitutionality of § 5 of the Act against a challenge that this provision usurps powers reserved to the States. Nor does *Katzenbach* require a different result where, as here, § 5 is held to cover acts initiated by noncovered States. The Court in *Katzenbach* recognized that, once a jurisdiction has been designated, the Act may guard against both discriminatory animus and the potentially harmful effect of neutral laws in that jurisdiction. In *City of Rome [v. United States]*, we thus expressly reaffirmed that, "under the Fifteenth Amendment, Congress may prohibit voting practices that have only a discriminatory effect."

Recognizing that Congress has the constitutional authority to designate covered jurisdictions and to guard against changes that give rise to a discriminatory effect in those jurisdictions, we find no merit in the claim that Congress lacks Fifteenth Amendment authority to require federal approval before the implementation of a state law that may have just such an effect in a covered county. Section 5, as we interpret it today, burdens state law only to the extent that that law affects voting in jurisdictions properly designated for coverage. With respect to literacy tests, in fact, the Act already allows for the very action that the State claims would be unconstitutional here. At least until a 1970 amendment to the Act barring literacy tests nationwide, § 4 had been used to ban these tests in covered jurisdictions even where the tests had been enacted by a noncovered State. *See Gaston County v. United States*, 395 U.S. 285 (1969) (although State was not covered, "use of the State's literacy test within the county was . . . suspended" when the county was designated a covered jurisdiction). Moreover, under § 4(b), a state-imposed literacy test may, as it did here, provide grounds for designating a county as a covered jurisdiction, notwithstanding the fact that the State as a whole is not covered.

The State seeks to bolster its constitutional argument by noting that partially covered States, like California, have no statutory ability to seek an exemption from the Act's coverage. Section 4(a) permits a covered jurisdiction to seek declaratory relief exempting the jurisdiction from further coverage if it meets certain criteria. 42 U.S.C. § 1973b(a). Even if California were unable to use this "bailout" provision on behalf of its covered counties, this would not advance the State's constitutional claim. Partially covered States facing suspension of their literacy tests in covered counties would have faced the same dilemma. In any event, there is no question that the County may avail itself of § 4(a)'s bailout procedures.

In short, the Voting Rights Act, by its nature, intrudes on state sovereignty. The Fifteenth Amendment permits this intrusion, however, and our holding today adds nothing of constitutional moment to the burdens that the Act imposes....

Finally, we note that this Court has created an exception to the preclearance requirement in certain cases involving federally court-ordered voting changes. As a general rule, voting changes crafted wholly by a federal district court in the first instance do not require preclearance.... This narrow exception to the preclearance requirement, however, is not grounded in the fact that a voting change is mandated by a noncovered entity, without room for discretion on the part of a covered jurisdiction. Rather, the exception grows largely from separation-of-powers concerns arising where a voting measure is the product of a federal court, specifically....

JUSTICE KENNEDY, with whom THE CHIEF JUSTICE joins, concurring in the judgment.

.... I concur in the majority's disposition of this case ... because it is clear that the state enactments requiring the voting changes at issue in fact embodied the policy preferences and determinations of the county itself. For example, the 1979 state law which codified the county's merger of its municipal court districts stated on its face that it was enacted at the county's behest. 1979 Cal. Stats., ch. 694, § 4 ("This act is in accordance with the request of a local governmental entity or entities which desired legislative authority to carry out the program specified in this act"). In these circumstances, the county was required to seek preclearance of the voting changes codified by the state enactments.

JUSTICE THOMAS, dissenting.

***

II

.... Section 5 is a unique requirement that exacts significant federalism costs, as we have recognized on more than one occasion. The section's interference with state sovereignty is quite drastic -- covered States and political subdivisions may not give effect to their policy choices affecting voting without first obtaining the Federal Government's approval. As Justice Powell wrote in City of Rome, the section's "encroachment is especially troubling because it destroys local control of the means of self-government, one of the central values of our polity."

Despite these serious and undeniable costs, we have twice upheld the preclearance requirement as a constitutional exercise of Congress' Fifteenth Amendment enforcement power, first in Katzenbach and again in City of Rome. In those cases, we compared Congress' Fifteenth

Amendment enforcement power to its broad authority under the Necessary and Proper Clause. But we have taken great care to emphasize that Congress' enforcement power is remedial in nature. *See City of Boerne v. Flores*, 521 U.S. 507 (1997) ....

There can be no remedy without a wrong. Essential to our holdings in *Katzenbach* and *City of Rome* was our conclusion that Congress was remedying the effects of prior intentional racial discrimination. In both cases we required Congress to have some evidence that the jurisdiction burdened with preclearance obligations had actually engaged in such intentional discrimination. In *Katzenbach*, we recognized that Congress had "evidence of actual voting discrimination" in some jurisdictions. In each of those jurisdictions, two characteristics were present -- depressed voter turnout and the use of a test or device. We concluded that it was permissible for Congress to impose § 5 preclearance requirements on the States and political subdivisions for which Congress had "more fragmentary evidence" of voting discrimination, where those two conditions (incorporated into the Act's coverage formula) could be found to exist, "at least in the absence of proof that [such jurisdictions] have been free of substantial voting discrimination in recent years." We also thought it quite important that "the Act provided for termination of special statutory coverage at the behest of States and political subdivisions in which the danger of substantial voting discrimination had not materialized during the preceding five years." In *City of Rome*, we rejected the city's argument that, because it had not employed any discriminatory practices over the relevant period, § 5 was unconstitutional as applied. We thought that "because electoral changes by jurisdictions with a demonstrable history of intentional racial discrimination in voting create the risk of purposeful discrimination, it was proper [for Congress] to prohibit changes that have a discriminatory impact."

.... There has been no legislative finding that the State of California has ever intentionally discriminated on the basis of race, color, or ethnicity with respect to voting. Nor has the State been found to run afoul of the Act's overbroad coverage formula. We recognized in *City of Boerne* that "preventive measures prohibiting certain types of laws may be appropriate when there is reason to believe that many of the laws affected by the congressional enactment have a significant likelihood of being unconstitutional." But I do not see any reason to think that California's laws discriminate in any way against voting or that the State's laws will be anything but constitutional. I therefore doubt that § 5 can be extended to require preclearance of the State's enactments and remain consistent with the Constitution.

Moreover, it is plain that the majority's reading of § 5 raises to new levels the federalism costs that the statute imposes. If preclearance of a State's voting law is denied when sought by a covered political subdivision, the State will be unable to develop a consistent statewide voting policy; its laws will be enforceable in noncovered subdivisions, but not in the covered subdivision. And under the majority's reading of § 5, noncovered States are forced to rely upon their covered political subdivisions to defend their interests before the Federal Government. The subdivision may not know the State's interest, or may simply disagree with the State and therefore choose not to defend vigorously the State's policy choices before the Federal Government. Indeed, in this case, the County represented that it "concurs with the essential arguments of the Appellants that state law affecting voting insofar as such law may affect elections within a covered jurisdiction, must be precleared . . . ."

.... I do not think ... that the suspension of tests and the preclearance remedy can be compared. The literacy test had a history as a "notorious means to deny and abridge voting rights on racial grounds." Literacy tests were unfairly administered; whites were given easy questions, blacks were given more difficult questions, such as "the number of bubbles in a soap bar, the news contained in a copy of the Peking Daily, the meaning of obscure passages in state constitutions, and the definition of terms such as habeas corpus." When we upheld the constitutionality of the suspension provision of the Voting Rights Act in *Katzenbach*, we indicated that the tests had actually been employed to disenfranchise black voters. Later in *Oregon v. Mitchell*, 400 U.S. 112 (1970), we upheld the national ban on the use of such tests -- even though we recognized that they were not facially unconstitutional -- as a proper means of preventing purposeful discrimination in the application of the tests and remedying prior constitutional violations by state and local governments in the education of minorities. Congress' suspension of tests, then, was a focused remedy directed at one particular prerequisite to voting. In contrast, the preclearance requirement presumes that a voting change -- no matter how innocuous -- is invalid, and prevents its enforcement until the Federal Government gives its approval....

NOTES AND QUESTIONS

1. Does the Court's decision completely resolve the question of § 5's continuing constitutionality? Does the fact that the Court extends § 5's coverage to acts that reflect the policy choices of uncovered entities, if those choices are ultimately implemented or enforced by covered jurisdictions, represent an expansion of the original rationale for § 5 in *South Carolina v. Katzenbach*, which focused on Congress' narrow tailoring of § 5's coverage? The constitutionality of impact tests under the Voting Rights Act is treated at greater length later in the Supplement, in Chapter 7, but you might want to consider those materials here as well.

2. In *Young v. Fordice*, 520 U.S. 273 (1997), the Court required Mississippi to seek preclearance of its system for registering voters even though the changes were made in an effort to comply with federal law, since the precise changes reflected policy choices made by state or local officials from covered jurisdictions. Unless the federal government essentially pre-empts the field, are

there any changes that fall clearly outside the "policy choice" trigger for § 5 preclearance?

3. Note the practical problem created by *Lopez*: the appropriate remedy in a section 5 coverage action is to enjoin use of a new plan unless and until it receives preclearance. If the County's stipulation is correct, and the change from districted to at-large elections "ha[s] it the effect of denying the right to vote to Latinos in Monterey County due to the retrogressive effect several of these ordinances had on Latino voting strength in Monterey County," then the District Court should order the County to keep using the last precleared plan. But the State of California has consolidated the court system, so those positions no longer exist. And Monterey County lacks the power, under California law, to establish its own court system.

on page 312, after the existing material, add the following:

3. One of the explanations for the exemption of court-ordered plans from preclearance is separation of powers: neither the Department of Justice nor the United States District Court for the District of Columbia ought to be reviewing the decisions of a federal court. This points to a more general issue, explicit in *South Carolina v. Katzenbach* and *Katzenbach v. Morgan*, and implicit, perhaps in the Court's decision about what changes are covered and when a covered change ought to be precleared (the subject of Section C of this Chapter): the interaction of constitutional concerns with statuory interpretation.

For recent examples of this point, consider the District Court's decision in *LaRouche v. Fowler*, 77 F. Supp. 2d 80 (D.D.C. 1999) (three-judge court) (per curiam). Recall that the Supreme Court had held in *Morse v. Republican Party of Virginia*, 517 U.S. 186 (1995), that state political parties might be "covered jurisdictions" for purposes of requiring them to preclear changes in the eligibility rules for participating in state nominating conventions. (*Morse* is discussed on page 276 of the casebook.)

In *LaRouche*, the district court confronted the question of the scope of § 5's applicability to the activities of political parties.

The Democratic Party passed several rules governing its 1996 presidential nomination process that provided, in pertinent part, that a Democratic candidate for President have a "record of public service, accomplishment, public writings and/or public statements" that affirmatively showed his or her commitment to "the interests, welfare and success of the Democratic Party."

Lyndon LaRouche qualified for a position on the Democratic Party primary ballot in several states. But in January 1996, the chairman of the Democratic National Committee, Donald Fowler, sent a letter to the chairpersons of all state Democratic Party organizations stating that LaRouche was "not a bona fide Democrat," as shown by his "beliefs which are explicitly racist and anti-Semitic, and otherwise utterly contrary to the fundamental beliefs ... of the Democratic Party ...." Thus, LaRouche was "not to be considered a qualified candidate," and state parties were instructed to "disregard any votes that might be cast for Mr. Larouche, ... not allocate delegate positions to Mr. Larouche and ... not recognize the selection of delegates pledged to him at any stage of the Delegate Selection Process."

LaRouche alleged that he had received enough votes to receive representation in Democratic nominating activities in Louisiana, Virginia, Texas, and Arizona, and the District of Columbia. Due to the Fowler letter, however, each of these jurisdictions denied LaRouche such representation.

LaRouche and his supporters filed a § 5 coverage suit alleging that the Democratic Party nominating procedures which undermined his campaign had been adopted unlawfully because they had not been precleared.

The three-judge court held, first, that the National Party was not a covered jurisdiction, and therefore was not itself required to seek preclearance. It distinguished *Morse* by finding that the national Democratic Party was neither itself a covered jurisdiction nor, within the terms of Justice Stevens' opinion in Morse (there was no opinion for the Court in that case), had it "exercise[d] delegated power over the electoral process" conferred by a covered jurisdiction.   Relying on *Lopez v. Monterey County*, 525 U.S. 266 (1999) (discussed in this supplement *supra*), the district court held that the National Party was not a "delegatee of power from any of its covered political subunits." Under *Lopez*, "it is logical to require preclearance of the organization that is resident in the covered jurisdiction, but absolve the parent entity."

With respect to the local parties in Arizona, Louisiana, Texas, and Virginia (the District of Columbia Democratic Party was dismissed as a defendant since the District was not itself a covered jurisdiction), the district court recognized that some state party rules in covered states would require preclearance. (The rule in *Morse* concerned payment of a fee to participate in nominating activities.) But it held that application of the Act to the decisions at issue in La Rouche's case would trench on the parties' First Amendment associational rights to an impermissible extent:

> [T]he Supreme Court has consistently held that political party membership and governance implicate "core associational activities" constitutionally protected from government interference absent sufficient justification. Here, we have the state parties administering internal national party rules governing who, as a Democrat, can be a candidate for president. This would appear to fall within the core associational rights of a political party. *See, e.g, Democratic Party of the United States [v. Wisconsin]*, 450 U.S. [107 (1981)] (stating that the freedom to associate "necessarily presupposes the freedom to identify the people who constitute the association, and to limit the association to those people only").... Indeed, Justice Breyer intimated in his opinion in *Morse* that party activities such as the adoption of resolutions or platforms regarding party philosophy and rules governing internal operation, "are very likely not subject to preclearance."

> Pitted against this core constitutional right is the Voting Rights Act preclearance requirement, intended to enforce the guarantees of the Fifteenth Amendment. In a normal case, § 5 can cover candidacy requirements and qualifications. But while the Act is unarguably a statute of importance, it should not be read to extend coverage that would interfere with core associational rights; specifically here, internal national party rules as followed by state parties in a covered jurisdiction.

In reaching this conclusion, we are guided by the principle that we should construe statutes so as to avoid constitutional questions. To hold as LaRouche seeks would unnecessarily implicate First Amendment rights. By holding that the preclearance requirement does not apply to the political party rules at issue here, we avoid the implication of the First Amendment rights of association.... The prevailing Justices in Morse did not find this rule of construction implicated on the facts of that case, but held that the practice challenged was "well outside the area of greatest 'associational' concern." *Morse*, 517 U.S. at 239 (Breyer, J.). Here, however, we have a core right before us. We must invoke the rule.

We point out that this case does not present the direct clash of a Fifteenth Amendment violation and a First Amendment right. LaRouche's constitutional claim under the Fifteenth Amendment was dismissed by the one-judge district court and affirmed by the court of appeals.... Thus, this case is not governed by *The White Primary Cases*, in which the Court struck down practices excluding minority voters from the Texas Democratic Party nomination process as violative of the Fifteenth and Fourteenth Amendments. The history of the White Primary Cases supports the proposition that Congress intended the Voting Rights Act to have a broad scope, but we cannot "lightly assume that Congress intended to infringe constitutionally protected liberties or usurp power constitutionally forbidden it." The Court of Appeals observed that nothing in the historical context of the Voting Rights Act evidences "a concern that a covered jurisdiction would to try achieve [unconstitutional] end[s] by delegating authority to a national party, or that a national party would attempt to impose racially discriminatory rules on a covered jurisdiction." Although it may be true that "the right of associative freedom would not provide a defense to many practices condemned by § 5," we only consider a national party rule concerning core associational freedoms formulated by an uncovered entity, which does not implicate suspect classifications, and which is administered without alteration by covered jurisdictions. Heeding Justice Breyer's concerns in Morse, we need not go further....

To what extent is *LaRouche* a straightforward application of the First Amendment principles regarding political parties' ideological autonomy described in Chapter Four? To what extent is the court's interpretation here driven by the idea that section 5's core purpose -- to protect the voting rights of minority citizens -- is not apparently implicated by the Democratic Party's decision? Consider historical context here: following the decision in *Terry v. Adams* (the final white primary case, discussed in Chapter 2, pages 85-95), the South Carolina Democratic Party in the mid-1950's enacted a rule that permitted anyone (including African Americans) to participate in the party's primary, but only if the individual swore that he or she "believe[d] in and will support the social (religious) and educational separation of the races." Would such a rule require preclearance? How would the *LaRouche* Court analyze this question?

on page 323, replace the final paragraph of note 6 with the following:

The Court's opinion "le[ft] open for another day the question whether the § 5 purpose inquiry ever extends beyondthe search for retrogressive intent" and remanded the case to the district court for further proceedings. Two years later, the Court itself answered that question.

RENO v. BOSSIER PARISH SCHOOL BOARD
528 U.S. 320 (1999)

JUSTICE SCALIA delivered the opinion of the Court.

These cases present the question whether § 5 of the Voting Rights Act of 1965 prohibits preclearance of a redistricting plan enacted with a discriminatory but nonretrogressive purpose.

I.

This is the second time the present cases are before us, and we thus recite the facts and procedural history only in brief. Like every other political subdivision of the State of Louisiana, Bossier Parish, because of its history of discriminatory voting practices, is a jurisdiction covered by § 5 of the Voting Rights Act....

Bossier Parish is governed by a 12-member Police Jury elected from single-member districts for 4-year terms. In the early 1990s, the Police Jury set out to redraw its electoral districts in order to account for demographic changes reflected in the decennial census. In 1991, it adopted a redistricting plan which, like the plan then in effect, contained no majority-black districts, although blacks made up approximately 20% of the parish's population. On May 28, 1991, the Police Jury submitted its new districting plan to the Attorney General; two months later, the Attorney General granted preclearance.

The Bossier Parish School Board (Board) is constituted in the same fashion as the Police Jury, and it too undertook to redraw its districts after the 1990 census. During the course of that redistricting, appellant-intervenor George Price, president of the local chapter of the National Association for the Advancement of Colored People (NAACP), proposed that the Board adopt a plan with majority-black districts. In the fall of 1992, amid some controversy, the Board rejected Price's suggestion and adopted the Police Jury's 1991 redistricting plan as its own.

On January 4, 1993, the Board submitted its redistricting plan to the Attorney General for preclearance. Although the Attorney General had precleared the identical plan when submitted by the Police Jury, she interposed a formal objection to the Board's plan, asserting that "new information" -- specifically, the NAACP plan proposed by appellant-intervenor Price -- demonstrated that "black residents are sufficiently numerous and geographically compact so as to constitute a majority in two single-member districts." The Attorney General disclaimed any attempt to compel the Board to "adopt any particular plan," but maintained that the Board was "not free to adopt a plan that unnecessarily limits the opportunity for minority voters to elect their candidates of choice."

After the Attorney General denied the Board's request for reconsideration, the Board filed the present action for judicial preclearance of the 1992 plan in the United States District Court for the District of Columbia.... Before the District Court, appellants conceded that the Board's plan did not have a prohibited "effect" under § 5, since it did not worsen the position of minority voters. (In *Beer v. United States*, 425 U.S. 130 (1976), we held that a plan has a prohibited "effect" only if it is retrogressive.) Instead, appellants made two distinct claims. First, they argued that preclearance should be denied because the Board's plan, by not creating as many majority-black districts as it should create, violated § 2 of the Voting Rights Act, which bars discriminatory voting practices. Second, they contended that, although the Board's plan would have no retrogressive effect, it nonetheless violated § 5 because it was enacted for a discriminatory "purpose."

The District Court granted preclearance. As to the first of appellants' two claims, the District Court held that it could not deny preclearance of a proposed voting change under § 5 simply because the change violated § 2. Moreover, in order to prevent the Government "[from doing] indirectly what it cannot do directly," the District Court stated that it would "not permit section 2 evidence to prove discriminatory purpose under section 5." As to the second of appellants' claims, the District Court concluded that the Board had borne its burden of proving that the 1992 plan was adopted for two legitimate, nondiscriminatory purposes: to assure prompt preclearance (since the identical plan had been precleared for the Police Jury), and to enable easy implementation (since the adopted plan, unlike the NAACP's proposed plan, required no redrawing of precinct lines).

On appeal, we agreed with the District Court that a proposed voting change cannot be denied preclearance simply because it violates § 2, but disagreed with the proposition that all evidence of a dilutive (but nonretrogressive) effect forbidden by § 2 was irrelevant to whether the Board enacted the plan with a retrogressive purpose forbidden by § 5. *Reno v. Bossier Parish School Bd.*, 520 U.S. 471 (1997) (*Bossier Parish I*).... [W]e left open the additional question of "whether the § 5 purpose inquiry ever extends beyond the search for retrogressive intent."....

II

Before proceeding to the merits, we must dispose of a challenge to our jurisdiction. The Board contends that these cases are now moot, since its 1992 plan "will never again be used for any purpose." Under Louisiana law, school board members are elected to serve 4-year terms.

One month after appellants filed the jurisdictional statements for this appeal, the scheduled 1998 election for the Board took place. The next scheduled election will not occur until 2002, by which time, as appellants concede, the data from the upcoming decennial census will be available and the Board will be required by our "one-man-one-vote" precedents to have a new apportionment plan in place. Accordingly, appellee argues, the District Court's declaratory judgment with respect to the 1992 plan is no longer of any moment and the dispute no longer presents a live "case or controversy" for purposes of Article III of the Constitution....

[I]n at least one respect the 1992 plan will have probable continuing effect: Absent a successful subsequent challenge under § 2, it, rather than the 1980 predecessor plan -- which contains quite different voting districts -- will serve as the baseline against which appellee's next voting plan will be evaluated for the purposes of preclearance. Whether (and precisely how) that future plan represents a change from the baseline, and, if so, whether it is retrogressive in effect, will depend on whether preclearance of the 1992 plan was proper....

III

.... When considered in light of our longstanding interpretation of the "effect" prong of § 5 in its application to vote dilution claims, the language of § 5 leads to the conclusion that the "purpose" prong of § 5 covers only retrogressive dilution.

As noted earlier, in order to obtain preclearance under § 5, a covered jurisdiction must demonstrate that the proposed change "does not have the purpose and will not have the effect of denying or abridging the right to vote on account of race or color." A covered jurisdiction, therefore, must make two distinct showings: first, that the proposed change "does not have the purpose . . . of denying or abridging the right to vote on account of race or color," and second, that the proposed change "will not have the effect of denying or abridging the right to vote on account of race or color." The covered jurisdiction bears the burden of persuasion on both points.

In *Beer v. United States*, 425 U.S. 130 (1976), this Court addressed the meaning of the no-effect requirement in the context of an allegation of vote dilution. The case presented the question whether a reapportionment plan that would have a discriminatory but nonretrogressive effect on the rights of black voters should be denied preclearance.... [W]e held that "a legislative reapportionment that enhances the position of racial minorities with respect to their effective exercise of the electoral franchise can hardly have the 'effect' of diluting or abridging the right to vote on account of race within the meaning of § 5." In other words, we concluded that, in the context of a § 5 challenge, the phrase "denying or abridging the right to vote on account of race or color" ... limited the term it qualified, "effect," to retrogressive effects.

Appellants contend that in qualifying the term "purpose," the very same phrase does not impose a limitation to retrogression -- i.e., that the phrase "abridging the right to vote on account of race or color" means retrogression when it modifies "effect," but means discrimination more generally when it modifies "purpose." We think this is simply an untenable construction of the text, in effect recasting the phrase "does not have the purpose and will not have the effect of x" to read "does not have the purpose of y and will not have the effect of x." As we have in the past, we refuse to adopt a construction that would attribute different meanings to the same phrase in the same sentence, depending on which object it is modifying.

Appellants point out that we did give the purpose prong of § 5 a broader meaning than the effect prong in *Richmond v. United States,* 422 U.S. 358 (1975). That case involved requested preclearance for a proposed annexation that would have reduced the black population of the city of Richmond, Virginia, from 52% to 42%. We concluded that, although the annexation may have had the effect of creating a political unit with a lower percentage of blacks, so long as it "fairly reflected the strength of the Negro community as it existed after the annexation" it did not violate § 5....

We refused, however, to impose a similar limitation on § 5's purpose prong, stating that preclearance could be denied when the jurisdiction was acting with the purpose of effecting a percentage reduction in the black population, even though it could not be denied when the jurisdiction's action merely had that effect.

It must be acknowledged that Richmond created a discontinuity between the effect and purpose prongs of § 5. We regard that, however, as nothing more than an ex necessitate limitation upon the effect prong in the particular context of annexation -- to avoid the invalidation of all annexations of areas with a lower proportion of minority voters than the annexing unit. The case certainly does not stand for the proposition that the purpose and effect prongs have fundamentally different meanings -- the latter requiring retrogression, and the former not -- which is what is urged here. The approved effect of the redistricting in Richmond, and the hypothetically disapproved purpose, were both retrogressive. We found it necessary to make an exception to normal retrogressive-effect principles, but not to normal retrogressive-purpose principles, in order to permit routine annexation. That sheds little light upon the issue before us here.

Appellants' only textual justification for giving the purpose and effect prongs different meanings is that to do otherwise "would reduce the purpose prong of Section 5 to a trivial matter" ....

It is true enough that, whenever Congress enacts a statute that bars conduct having "the purpose or effect of x," the purpose prong has application entirely separate from that of the effect prong only with regard to unlikely conduct that has "the purpose of x" but fails to have "the effect of x" -- in the present context, the conduct of a so-called "incompetent retrogressor." The purpose prong has value and effect, however, even when it does not cover additional conduct. With regard to conduct that has both "the purpose of x" and "the effect of x," the Government need only prove that the conduct at issue has "the purpose of x" in order to prevail. In the specific context of § 5, where the covered jurisdiction has the burden of persuasion, the Government need only refute the covered jurisdiction's prima facie showing that a proposed voting change does not have a retrogressive purpose in order for preclearance to be denied. When it can do so, it is spared the necessity of countering the jurisdiction's evidence regarding actual retrogressive effect -- which, in vote-dilution cases, is often a complex undertaking. This advantage, plus the ability to reach malevolent incompetence, may not represent a massive addition to the effect prong, but it is enough to justify the separate existence of the purpose prong in this statute, and is no less than what justifies the separate existence of such a provision in many other laws.

At bottom, appellants' disagreement with our reading of § 5 rests not upon textual analysis, but upon their opposition to our holding in *Beer*. Although they do not explicitly contend that *Beer* should be overruled, they all but do so by arguing that it would be "untenable" to conclude (as we did in *Beer*) that the phrase "abridging the right to vote on account of race or color" refers only to retrogression in § 5, in light of the fact that virtually identical language elsewhere in the voting Rights Act -- and indeed, in the Fifteenth Amendment -- has never been read to refer only to retrogression. See § 2(a) of the Voting Rights Act ("No voting [practice] shall be imposed or applied by any State or political subdivision in a manner which results in a denial or abridgement of the right of any citizen of the United States to vote on account of race or color . . . "); U.S. Const., Amdt. 15, § 1 ("The right of citizens of the United States to vote shall not be denied or abridged by the United States or by any State on account of race, color, or previous condition of servitude"). The term "abridge," however -- whose core meaning is "shorten," see Webster's New International Dictionary 7 (2d ed. 1950); American Heritage Dictionary 6 (3d ed. 1992) -- necessarily entails a comparison. It makes no sense to suggest that a voting practice "abridges" the right to vote without some baseline with which to compare the practice. In § 5 preclearance proceedings -- which uniquely deal only and specifically with changes in voting procedures -- the baseline is the status quo that is proposed to be changed: If the change "abridges the right to vote" relative to the status quo, preclearance is denied, and the status quo (however discriminatory it may be) remains in effect. In § 2 or Fifteenth Amendment proceedings, by contrast, which involve not only changes but (much more commonly) the status quo itself, the comparison must be made with an hypothetical alternative: If the status quo "results in [an] abridgement of the right to vote" or "abridges [the right to vote]" relative to what the right to vote ought to be, the status quo itself must be changed. Our reading of "abridging" as referring only to retrogression in § 5, but to discrimination more generally in § 2 and the Fifteenth Amendment, is faithful to the differing contexts in which the term is used.[1]

In another argument that applies equally to our holding in *Beer*, appellants object that our reading of § 5 would require the District Court or Attorney General to preclear proposed voting changes with a discriminatory effect or purpose, or even with both. That strikes appellants as an inconceivable prospect only because they refuse to accept the limited meaning that we have said preclearance has in the vote-dilution context. It does not represent approval of the voting change; it is nothing more than a determination that the voting change is no more dilutive than what it replaces, and therefore cannot be stopped in advance under the extraordinary burden-shifting procedures of § 5, but must be attacked through the normal means of a § 2 action. As we have repeatedly noted, in vote-dilution cases § 5 prevents nothing but backsliding, and preclearance under § 5 affirms nothing but the absence of backsliding.[2] This explains why the sole consequence of failing to obtain preclearance is continuation of the status quo. To deny preclearance to a plan that is not retrogressive -- no matter how unconstitutional it may be -- would risk leaving in effect a status quo that is even worse. For example, in the case of a voting change with a discriminatory but nonretrogressive purpose and a discriminatory but ameliorative effect, the result of denying preclearance would be to preserve a status quo with more discriminatory effect than the proposed change.

---

[1] Even if § 5 did not have a different baseline than the Fifteenth Amendment, appellants' argument that § 5 should be read in parallel with the Fifteenth Amendment would fail for the simple reason that we have never held that vote dilution violates the Fifteenth Amendment. See Voinovich v. Quilter, 507 U.S. 146 (1993) (citing Beer v. United States, 425 U.S. 130 (1976)). Indeed, contrary to JUSTICE SOUTER'S assertion, we have never even "suggested" as much. Gomillion v. Lightfoot, 364 U.S. 339 (1960), involved a proposal to redraw the boundaries of Tuskegee, Alabama, so as to exclude all but 4 or 5 of its 400 black voters without excluding a single white voter. Our conclusion that the proposal would deny black voters the right to vote in municipal elections, and therefore violated the Fifteenth Amendment, had nothing to do with racial vote-dilution, a concept that does not appear in our voting-rights opinions until nine years later. See Allen v. State Bd. of Elections, 393 U.S. 544 (1969). As for the other case relied upon by JUSTICE SOUTER, the plurality opinion in Mobile v. Bolden, 446 U.S. 55 (1980), not only does that not suggest that the Fifteenth Amendment covers vote dilution, it suggests the opposite, rejecting the appellees' vote-dilution claim in the following terms: "The answer to the appellees' argument is that . . . their freedom to vote has not been denied or abridged by anyone. The Fifteenth Amendment does not entail the right to have Negro candidates elected . . . . Having found that Negroes in Mobile 'register and vote without hindrance,' the District Court and Court of Appeals were in error in believing that the appellants invaded the protection of that Amendment in the present case."

[2] In search of support for the argument that § 5 prevents not just backsliding on vote dilution but all forms of vote dilution, JUSTICE SOUTER embarks upon a lengthy expedition into legislative history. He returns empty-handed, since he can point to nothing suggesting that the Congress thought § 5 covered both retrogressive and nonretrogressive dilution. Indeed, it is doubtful whether the Congress that passed the 1965 voting Rights Act even had the practice of racial vote-dilution in mind. As JUSTICE SOUTER acknowledges, this Court did not address the concept until 1969, and the legislative history of the 1969 extension of the Act, quoted by JUSTICE SOUTER, refers to at-large elections and consolidation of counties as "new, unlawful ways to diminish the Negroes' franchise" developed since passage of the Act.

... [B]y suggesting that § 5 extends to discriminatory but nonretrogressive vote-dilutive purposes, appellants ... would also exacerbate the "substantial" federalism costs that the preclearance procedure already exacts, *Lopez v. Monterey County*, 525 U.S. 266 (1999), perhaps to the extent of raising concerns about § 5's constitutionality. Most importantly, however, in light of our holding in Beer, appellants' reading finds no support in the language of § 5.

IV

Notwithstanding the fact that *Bossier Parish I* explicitly "left open for another day" the question whether § 5 extends to discriminatory but nonretrogressive intent, appellants contend that two of this Court's prior decisions have already reached the conclusion that it does. First, appellants note that, in *Beer*, this Court stated that "an ameliorative new legislative apportionment cannot violate § 5 unless the apportionment itself so discriminates on the basis of race or color as to violate the Constitution." Appellants contend that this suggests that, at least in some cases in which the covered jurisdiction acts with a discriminatory but nonretrogressive dilutive purpose, the covered jurisdiction should be denied preclearance because it is acting unconstitutionally.

We think that a most implausible interpretation. At the time *Beer* was decided, it had not been established that discriminatory purpose as well as discriminatory effect was necessary for a constitutional violation, compare *White v. Regester*, 412 U.S. 755 (1973), with *Washington v. Davis*, 426 U.S. 229 (1976). If the statement in *Beer* had meant what appellants suggest, it would either have been anticipating (without argument) that later holding, or else would have been gutting *Beer's* holding (since a showing of discriminatory but nonretrogressive effect would have been a constitutional violation and would, despite the holding of *Beer*, have sufficed to deny preclearance). A much more plausible explanation of the statement is that it referred to a constitutional violation other than vote dilution -- and, more specifically, a violation consisting of a "denial" of the right to vote, rather than an "abridgement." Although in the context of denial claims, no less than in the context of abridgement claims, the antibacksliding rationale for § 5 (and its effect of avoiding preservation of an even worse status quo) suggests that retrogression should again be the criterion, arguably in that context the word "deny" (unlike the word "abridge") does not import a comparison with the status quo.[3]

---

[3]

    JUSTICE BREYER suggests that "it seems obvious . . . that if Mississippi had enacted its 'moral character' requirement in 1966 (after enactment of the Voting Rights Act), a court applying § 5 would have found 'the purpose . . . of denying or abridging the right to vote on account of race,' even if Mississippi had intended to permit, say, 0.4%, rather than 0.3%, of the black voting age population of Forrest County to register." As we note above, however, our holding today does not extend to violations consisting of an outright "denial" of an individual's right to vote, as opposed to an "abridgement" as in dilution cases. In any event, if Mississippi had attempted to enact a "moral character" requirement in 1966, it would have been precluded from doing so under § 4, which bars certain types of voting tests and devices altogether, and the

In any event, it is entirely clear that the statement in *Beer* was pure dictum: The Government had made no contention that the proposed reapportionment at issue was unconstitutional. And though we have quoted the dictum in subsequent cases, we have never actually applied it to deny preclearance. We have made clear, on the other hand, what we reaffirm today: that proceedings to preclear apportionment schemes and proceedings to consider the constitutionality of apportionment schemes are entirely distinct....

Second, appellants contend that we denied preclearance on the basis of a discriminatory but nonretrogressive purpose in *Pleasant Grove v. United States*, 479 U.S. 462 (1987). That case involved an unusual fact pattern. The city of Pleasant Grove, Alabama -- which, at the time of the District Court's decision, had 32 black inhabitants, none of whom was registered to vote and of whose existence city officials appear to have been unaware -- sought to annex two parcels of land, one inhabited by a few whites, and the other vacant but likely to be inhabited by whites in the near future. We upheld the District Court's conclusion that the city acted with a discriminatory purpose in annexing the land, rejecting the city's contention that it could not have done so because it was unaware of the existence of any black voters against whom it could have intended to discriminate:

> '[The city's] argument is based on the incorrect assumption that an impermissible purpose under § 5 can relate only to present circumstances. Section 5 looks not only to the present effects of changes, but to their future effects as well . . . . Likewise, an impermissible purpose under § 5 may relate to anticipated as well as present circumstances.
>
> "It is quite plausible to see [the annexation] as motivated, in part, by the impermissible purpose of minimizing future black voting strength . . . . This is just as impermissible a purpose as the dilution of present black voting strength."

Appellants assert that we must have viewed the city's purpose as discriminatory but nonretrogressive because, as the city noted in contending that it lacked even a discriminatory purpose, the city could not have been acting to worsen the voting strength of any present black residents, since there were no black voters at the time. However, as the above quoted passage suggests, we did not hold that the purpose prong of § 5 extends beyond retrogression, but rather held that a jurisdiction with no minority voters can have a retrogressive purpose, at the present time, by intending to worsen the voting strength of future minority voters. Put another way, our holding in *Pleasant Grove* had nothing to do with the question whether, to justify the denial of preclearance on the basis of the purpose prong, the purpose must be retrogressive; instead,

---

issue of § 5 preclearance would therefore never have arisen. See 42 U.S.C. §§ 1973b(a)(1), (c).

it involved the question whether the purpose must be to achieve retrogression at once or could include, in the case of a jurisdiction with no present minority voters, retrogression with regard to operation of the proposed plan (as compared with operation of the status quo) against new minority voters in the future....

JUSTICE THOMAS, concurring.

The Bossier Parish School Board first sought preclearance of the redistricting plan at issue in this case almost seven years ago. The Justice Department and private appellants opposed that effort, arguing throughout this litigation that a "safe" majority-minority district is necessary to ensure the election of a black school board member. Ironically, while this litigation was pending, three blacks were elected from majority-white districts to serve on the Bossier Parish School Board. Although these election results are not part of the record, they vividly illustrate the fact that the federal intervention that spawned this litigation was unnecessary.

JUSTICE STEVENS, with whom JUSTICE GINSBURG joins, dissenting.

In its administration of the voting rights statute for the past quarter century, the Department of Justice has consistently employed a construction of the Voting Rights Act of 1965 contrary to that imposed upon the Act by the Court today. Apart from the deference such constructions are always afforded, the Department's reading points us directly to the necessary starting point of any exercise in statutory interpretation -- the plain language of the statute.

.... [T]here is simply nothing in the word "purpose" or the entire phrase "does not have the purpose" that would lead anyone to think that Congress had anything in mind but a present-tense, intentional effort to "deny or abridge the right to vote on account of race." Ergo, if a municipality intends to deny or abridge voting rights because of race, it may not obtain preclearance.

Like JUSTICE SOUTER, I am persuaded that the dissenting opinions of Justices White and Marshall were more faithful to the intent of the Congress that enacted the voting Rights Act of 1965 than that of the majority in *Beer v. United States*, 425 U.S. 130 (1976). One need not, however, disavow that precedent in order to explain my profound disagreement with the Court's holding today. The reading above makes clear that there is no necessary tension between the Beer majority's interpretation of the word "effect" in § 5 and the Department's consistent interpretation of the word "purpose."...

JUSTICE BREYER, dissenting.

I agree with JUSTICE SOUTER, with one qualification. I would not reconsider the correctness of the Court's decision in *Beer v. United States* 425 U.S. 130 (1976) -- an "effects" case -- because, regardless, § 5 of the Voting Rights Act prohibits preclearance of a voting change that has the purpose of unconstitutionally depriving minorities of the right to vote.

As JUSTICE SOUTER points out, Congress enacted § 5 in 1965 in part to prevent certain jurisdictions from limiting the number of black voters through "the extraordinary stratagem of contriving new rules of various kinds for the sole purpose of perpetuating voting discrimination in the face of adverse federal court decrees." *South Carolina v. Katzenbach*, 383 U.S. 301, (1966). This "stratagem" created a moving target with a consequent risk of judicial runaround.... [S]ince at the time, in certain places, historical discrimination had left the number of black voters at close to zero, retrogression would have proved virtually impossible where § 5 was needed most.

An example drawn from history makes the point clear. In Forrest County, Mississippi, as of 1962, precisely three-tenths of 1% of the voting age black population was registered to vote. This number was due in large part to the county registrar's discriminatory application of the State's voter registration requirements. Prior to 1961, the registrar had simply refused to accept voter registration forms from black citizens. After 1961, those blacks who were allowed to apply to register had been subjected to a more difficult test than whites, while whites had been offered assistance with their less taxing applications. And the registrar, upon denying the applications of black citizens, had refused to supply them with an explanation. The Government attacked these practices, and the Fifth Circuit enjoined the registrar from "failing to process applications for registrations submitted by Negro applicants on the same basis as applications submitted by white applicants."

Mississippi's "immediate response" to this injunction was to impose a "good moral character requirement," a standard this Court has characterized as "an open invitation to abuse at the hands of voting officials."... Such defiance would result in maintaining -- though not, in light of the absence of blacks from the Forrest County voting rolls, in increasing -- white political supremacy.

This is precisely the kind of activity for which § 5 was designed, and the purpose of § 5 would have demanded its application in such a case.

And nothing in the Act's language or its history suggests the contrary. See, e.g., H.R. Rep. No. 439, 89th Cong., 1st Sess., 10 (1965) ("Barring one contrivance too often has caused no change in result, only in methods") ...; Hearings on H. R. 6400 before Subcommittee No. 5 of the House Committee on the Judiciary, 89th Cong., 1st Sess., 5 (1965) (testimony of Attorney General Katzenbach) (discussing those jurisdictions that are "able, even after apparent defeat in the courts, to devise whole new methods of discrimination").

It seems obvious, then, that if Mississippi had enacted its "moral character" requirement in 1966 (after enactment of the Voting Rights Act), a court applying § 5 would have found "the purpose . . . of denying or abridging the right to vote on account of race," even if Mississippi had intended to permit, say, 0.4%, rather than 0.3%, of the black voting age population of Forrest County to register. And if so, then irrespective of the complexity surrounding the administration of an "effects" test, the answer to today's purpose question is "yes."

JUSTICE SOUTER, with whom JUSTICE STEVENS, JUSTICE GINSBURG, and JUSTICE BREYER join, concurring in part and dissenting in part.

.... It is true that today's decision has a precursor of sorts in *Beer v. United States*, 425 U.S. 130 (1976), which holds that the only anticipated redistricting effect sufficient to bar preclearance is retrogression in minority voting strength, however dilutive of minority voting power a redistricting plan may otherwise be. But if today's decision achieves a symmetry with Beer, the achievement is merely one of well-matched error. The Court was mistaken in Beer when it restricted the effect prong of § 5 to retrogression, and the Court is even more wrong today when it limits the clear text of § 5 to the corresponding retrogressive purpose. Although I adhere to the strong policy of respecting precedent in statutory interpretation and so would not reexamine Beer, that policy does not demand that recognized error be compounded indefinitely, and the Court's prior mistake about the meaning of the effects requirement of § 5 should not be expanded by an even more erroneous interpretation of the scope of the section's purpose prong.

.... The evidence in these very cases shows that the Bossier Parish School Board (School Board or Board) acted with intent to dilute the black vote, just as it acted with that same intent through decades of resistance to a judicial desegregation order. The record illustrates exactly the sort of relentless bad faith on the part of majority-white voters in covered jurisdictions that led to the enactment of § 5. The evidence all but poses the question why Congress would ever have meant to permit preclearance of such a plan, and it all but invites the answer that Congress could hardly have intended any such thing. While the evidence goes substantially unnoticed on the Court's narrow reading of the purpose prong of § 5, it is not only crucial to my resolution of these cases, but insistent in the way it points up the implausibility of the Court's reading of purpose under § 5.

I

.... As the parties have stipulated, the School Board had applied its energies for decades in an effort to "limit or evade" its obligation to desegregate the Parish schools. When the Board first received a court order to desegregate the parish's schools in the mid-1960's, it responded with the flagrantly defiant tactics of that era, and the record discloses the Board's continuing obstructiveness down to the time covered by these cases. During the 1980's, the degree of racial polarization in the makeup of the parish's schools rose, and the disproportionate assignment of black faculty to predominantly black schools increased....

[T]he Board has not achieved a unitary school system and remains under court order to this day....

The course of the Board's redistricting efforts tell us much about what it had in mind when it proposed its plan.... While the Board could simply have adopted the Police Jury plan once the Attorney General had precleared it, the Board did not do so .... [I]t is noteworthy that the jury plan ignored some of the Board's customary districting concerns.... [T]he jury plan would have pitted two pairs of incumbents against each other and created two districts in which no incumbent resided. The jury plan disregarded school attendance zones, and even included two districts containing no schools. The jury plan, moreover, called for a total variation in district populations exceeding the standard normally used to gauge satisfaction of the "one person, one vote" principle, four of its districts failed the standard measure of compactness used by the Board's own cartographer, and one of its districts contained noncontiguous elements.

In addressing the need to devise a plan of its own, the Board hired the same redistricting consultant who had advised the Police Jury, Gary Joiner. Joiner and the Board members (according to Joiner's testimony) were perfectly aware of their responsibility to avoid vote dilution in accordance with the Voting Rights Act .... In March 1992, George Price, president of the parish's branch of the National Association for the Advancement of Colored People (NAACP), wrote to the superintendent of parish schools asking for a chance to play some role in the redistricting process. Although the superintendent passed the letter on to the Board, the Board took no action, and neither the superintendent nor the Board even responded to Price's request. In August, Price wrote again, this time in concert with a number of leaders of black community organizations, again seeking an opportunity to express views about the redistricting process, as well as about a number of Board policies bearing on school desegregation. Once again the Board made no response.

Being frustrated by the Board's lack of responsiveness, Price then asked for help from the national NAACP's Redistricting Project, which sent him a map showing how two compact black-majority districts might be drawn in the parish. When Price showed the map to a school district official, he was told it was unacceptable because it failed to show all 12 districts. At Price's request, the Redistricting Project then provided a plan showing all 12 districts, which Price presented to the Board at its September 3, 1991, meeting, explaining that it showed the possibility of drawing black-majority districts. Several Board members said they could not consider the NAACP plan unless it was presented on a larger map, and both the Board's cartographer and their legal advisor, the parish district attorney, dismissed the plan out of hand because it required precinct splits.

There is evidence that other implications of the NAACP proposal were objectionable to the Board. According to one black leader, Board member Henry Burns told him that while he personally favored black representation on the Board, a number of other Board members opposed the idea.[4] ....

Although the NAACP plan received no further public consideration, the pace of public redistricting activity suddenly speeded up. At the Board's September 17, 1992, meeting, without asking Joiner to address the possibility of creating any majority-black district, the Board abruptly passed a statement of intent to adopt the Police Jury plan. At a public hearing on the plan one week later, attended by an overflow crowd, a number of black voters spoke against the plan, and Price presented the Board with a petition bearing over 500 signatures urging consideration of minority concerns. No one spoke in favor of the plan, and Price explained to the Board that preclearance of the jury plan for use by the Police Jury was no guarantee of preclearance of the same plan for the Board. Nonetheless, at its October 1 meeting, the voting members of the Board unanimously adopted the Police Jury plan, with one member absent and the Board's only black member (who had been appointed just two weeks earlier to fill a vacancy) abstaining. The Board did not submit the plan for preclearance by the Attorney General until January 4, 1993.

II

.... The parties stipulate that for decades before this redistricting the Board had sought to "limit or evade" its obligation to end segregation in its schools, an obligation specifically imposed by Court order nearly 35 years ago and not yet fulfilled. The Board has also conceded the discriminatory impact of the Police Jury plan in falling "more heavily on blacks than on whites," and in diluting "black voting strength." Even without the stipulated history, the conceded dilution would be evidence of a correspondingly discriminatory intent. With the history, the

---

[4] One other Board member, Marguerite Hudson, when asked to explain why two of the schools in Plain Dealing, one of the parish's towns, were predominantly black, stated: "Those people love to live in Plain Dealing . . . . And most of them don't want to get a big job, they would just rather stay out there in the country, and stay on Welfare, and stay in Plain Dealing."

implication of intent speaks louder, and it grows more forceful still after a closer look at two aspects of the dilutive impact of the Police Jury plan.

First, the plan includes no black-majority districts even though residential and voting patterns in Bossier Parish meet the three conditions we identified in *Thornburg v. Gingles,* as opening the door to drawing majority-minority districts to put minority voters on an equal footing with others. The first *Gingles* condition is that "the minority group must be able to demonstrate that it is sufficiently large and geographically compact to constitute a majority in a single-member district." The Board does not dispute that black voters in Bossier Parish satisfy this criterion. The Board joined in a stipulation of the parties that in 1991, "it was obvious that a reasonably compact black-majority district could be drawn within Bossier City," and that the NAACP plan demonstrated that two such districts could have been drawn in the parish. As to the second and third Gingles conditions, that the minority population be politically cohesive and that the white-majority block voting be enough to defeat the minority's preferred candidate, the Government introduced expert testimony showing such polarization in Bossier Parish's voting patterns....[5]

Second, the Police Jury plan diluted black votes by dividing neighboring black communities with common interests in and around at least two of the Parish's municipalities, thereby avoiding the creation of a black-majority district....

Despite its stated view that the record would not support a conclusion of nonretrogressive discriminatory intent, the District Court majority listed a series of "allegedly dilutive impacts" said to point to discriminatory intent: "that some of the new districts have no schools, that the plan ignores attendance boundaries, that it does not respect communities of interest, that there is one outlandishly large district, that several of them are not compact, that there is a lack of contiguity, and that the population deviations resulting from the jury plan are greater than the limits (+ 5%) imposed by Louisiana law." The District Court found this evidence "too theoretical, and too attenuated" to be probative of retrogressive intent in the absence of corroborating evidence of a "deliberate attempt." But whatever the force of such evidence may be on the issue of intent to cause retrogression, there is nothing "theoretical" or "attenuated" in its significance as showing intent to dilute generally....

---

[5]

The parties agreed that black candidates for other offices have been able to win from white-majority districts in the parish, but those instances all involved districts in which the presence of an Air Force base, meant both that the effective percentage of black voters was considerably higher than the raw figures suggested and, in the view of all the successful black candidates, that the degree of hostility to black candidates among white voters was lower than in the rest of the parish.

III

A

The legal issue here is the meaning of "abridging" in the provision of § 5 that preclearance of a districting change in a covered jurisdiction requires a showing that the new plan does not "have the purpose . . . of denying or abridging the right to vote on account of race or color . . . ." The language tracks that of the Fifteenth Amendment's guarantee that "the right of citizens . . . to vote shall not be denied or abridged . . . on account of race [or] color . . . ." Since the Act is an exercise of congressional power under § 2 of that Amendment, *South Carolina v. Katzenbach*, the choice to follow the Amendment's terminology is most naturally read as carrying the meaning of the constitutional terms into the statute. Any construction of the statute, therefore, carries an implication about the meaning of the Amendment, absent some good reason to treat the parallel texts differently on some particular point, and a reading of the statute that would not fit the Constitution is presumptively wrong.[6]

In each context, it is clear that abridgment necessarily means something more subtle and less drastic than the complete denial of the right to cast a ballot, denial being separately forbidden. Abridgment therefore must be a condition in between complete denial, on the one hand, and complete enjoyment of voting power, on the other. The principal concept of diminished voting strength recognized as actionable under our cases is vote dilution, defined as a regime that denies to minority voters the same opportunity to participate in the political process and to elect representatives of their choice that majority voters enjoy. The benchmark of dilution pure and simple is thus a system in which every minority voter has as good a chance at political participation and voting effectiveness as any other voter. Our cases have also recognized retrogression as a subspecies of dilution, the consequence of a scheme that not only gives a minority voter a lesser practical chance to participate and elect than a majority voter enjoys, but even reduces the minority voter's practical power from what a preceding scheme of electoral law provided. Although our cases have dealt with vote dilution only under the Fourteenth Amendment, I know of no reason in text or history that dilution is not equally violative of the Fifteenth Amendment guarantee against abridgement....

The Court has never held (save in *Beer*) that the concept of voting abridgment covers only retrogressive dilution, and any such reading of the Fifteenth Amendment would be outlandish. The Amendment contains no textual limitation on abridgement, and when it was adopted,

---

[6]

.... The majority limits the purpose prong to the few cases in which attempted retrogression fails of its goal, a rather paltry coverage given that it is discriminatory purpose, not discriminatory effect, that is at the heart of the Fifteenth Amendment.

the newly emancipated citizens would have obtained practically nothing from a mere guarantee that their electoral power would not be further reduced. Since § 5 of the Act is likewise free of any language qualifying or limiting the terms of abridgment which it shares with the Amendment, abridgement under § 5 presumably covers any vote dilution, not retrogression alone, and no redistricting scheme should receive preclearance without a showing that it is nondilutive....

[The] evil in Congress's sights [when it enacted § 5] was discrimination, abridgment of the right to vote, not merely discrimination that happens to cause retrogression, and Congress's intent to frustrate the unconstitutional evil by barring a replacement scheme of discrimination from being put into effect was not confined to any one subset of discriminatory schemes. The Bossier Parish School Board's purpose thus seems to lie at the very center of what Congress meant to counter by requiring preclearance, and the Court's holding that any nonretrogressive purpose survives § 5 is an exceedingly odd conclusion.

B

The majority purports to shoulder its burden to justify a limited reading of "abridging" by offering an argument from the "context" of § 5. Since § 5 covers only changes in voting practices, this fact is said to be a reason to think that "abridging" as used in the statute is narrower than its cognate in the Fifteenth Amendment, which covers both changes and continuing systems. In other words, on the majority's reading, the baseline in a § 5 challenge is the status quo that is to be changed, while the baseline in a Fifteenth Amendment challenge (or one under § 2 of the voting Rights Act) is a nondiscriminatory regime, whether extant or not. From the fact that § 5 applies only when a voting change is proposed, however, it does not follow that the baseline of abridgment is the status quo; Congress could perfectly well have decided that when a jurisdiction is forced to change its voting scheme (because of malapportionment shown by a new census, say), it ought to show that the replacement is constitutional. This, of course, is just what the unqualified language and its Fifteenth Amendment parallel would suggest.

In fact, the majority's principal reason for reading intent to abridge as covering only intent to cause retrogression is not the peculiar context of changes in the law, but *Beer v. United States*, 425 U.S. 130 (1976), which limited the sort of "effect" that would be an abridgment to retrogressive effect. The strength of the majority's position, then, depends on the need for parallel limitations on the purpose and effect prongs of § 5. The need, however, is very much to the contrary.

1

Insofar as *Beer* is authority for defining the "effect" of a redistricting plan that would bar preclearance under § 5, I will of course respect it as precedent. The policy of stare decisis is at its most powerful in statutory interpretation (which Congress is always free to supersede with new legislation), and § 5 presents no exception to the rule that when statutory language is construed it should stay construed. But it is another thing entirely to ignore error in extending discredited reasoning to previously unspoiled statutory provisions. That, however, is just what the Court does in extending *Beer* from § 5 effects to § 5 purpose.

Beer was wrongly decided, and its error should not be compounded in derogation of clear text and equally clear congressional purpose. The provision in § 5 barring preclearance of a districting plan portending an abridging effect is unconditional (and just as uncompromising as the bar to plans resting on a purpose to abridge). The *Beer* Court nonetheless sought to justify the imposition of a nontextual limitation on the forbidden abridging effect to retrogression by relying on a single fragment of legislative history, a statement from a House Report that § 5 would prevent covered jurisdictions from "'undoing or defeating the rights recently won'" by blacks. Relying on this one statement, however, was an act of distorting selectivity, for the legislative history is replete with references to the need to block changes in voting practices that would perpetuate existing discrimination and stand in the way of truly nondiscriminatory alternatives. In the House of Representatives, the Judiciary Committee noted that "even after apparent defeats resisters seek new ways and means of discriminating. Barring one contrivance too often has caused no change in result, only in methods," and the House Report described how jurisdictions had used changes in voting practices to stave off reform. By making trifling changes in registration requirements, for example, Dallas County, Alabama, was able to terminate litigation against it without registering more than a handful of minority voters, and new practices were similarly effective devices for perpetuating discrimination in other jurisdictions as well. After losing voting rights cases, jurisdictions would adopt new voting requirements "'as a means for continuing the rejection of qualified Negro applicants.'" Thanks to the discriminatory traditions of the jurisdictions covered by § 5, these new practices often avoided retrogression[7] even as they stymied improvements. In the days before § 5, the ongoing litigation would become moot and minority litigants would be back at square one, shouldering the burden of new challenges with the prospect of further dodges to come...

In fine, the full legislative history shows beyond any doubt just what the unqualified text of § 5 provides. The statute contains no reservation in favor of customary abridgment grown familiar after years of relentless discrimination, and the preclearance requirement was not

---

[7] The legislative history did not use the terms "retrogression" and "dilution" to describe discriminatory regimes. In the voting Rights Act context, the former appears for the first time in a federal case in *Beer*; the latter made its first appearance in Allen v. State Bd. of Elections, 393 U.S. 544 (1969).

enacted to authorize covered jurisdictions to pour old poison into new bottles....

2

Giving purpose-to-abridge the broader, intended reading while preserving the erroneously truncated interpretation of effect would not even result in a facially irrational scheme. This is so because intent to dilute is conceptually simple, whereas a dilutive abridgment-in-fact is not readily defined and identified independently of dilutive intent. A purpose to dilute simply means to subordinate minority voting power; exact calibration is unnecessary to identify what is intended. Any purpose to give less weight to minority participation in the electoral process than to majority participation is a purpose to discriminate and thus to "abridge" the right to vote. No further baseline is needed because the enquiry goes to the direction of the majority's aim, without reference to details of the existing system.

Dilutive effect, for the reason the majority points out, is different. Dilutive effect requires a baseline against which to compare a proposed change. While the baseline is in theory the electoral effectiveness of majority voters, dilution is not merely a lack of proportional representation, and we have held that the maximum number of possible majority-minority districts cannot be the standard. Thus we have held that an enquiry into dilutive effect must rest on some idea of a reasonable allocation of power between minority and majority voters; this requires a court to compare a challenged voting practice with a reasonable alternative practice. Looking only to retrogression in effect, while looking to any dilutive or other abridgment in purpose, avoids the difficulty of baseline derivation. The distinction was not intended by Congress, but such a distinction is not irrational.

Indeed, the Justice Department has always taken the position that *Beer* is limited to the effect prong and puts no limitation on discriminatory purpose in § 5. The Justice Department's longstanding practice ... is entitled to "particular deference" in light of the Department's "central role" in administering § 5. Most significant here, the fact that the Justice Department has for decades understood Beer to be limited to effect demonstrates that such a position is entirely consistent and coherent with the law as declared in Beer, even though it may not have been what Congress intended.

3

Giving wider scope to purpose than to effect under § 5 would not only preserve the capacity of § 5 to bar preclearance to all intended violations of the Fifteenth Amendment, it would also enjoy the virtue of consistency with prior decisions apart from *Beer*. In *Richmond v. United States*, 422 U.S. 358 (1975), the Court held that a city's territorial annexation reducing the percentage of black voters could not be recognized as a legal wrong under the effect prong of § 5, but remanded for further consideration of discriminatory purpose. The majority distinguishes Richmond as "nothing more than an ex necessitate limitation upon the effect prong in the particular context of annexation." But in fact, Richmond laid down no eccentric effect rule and is squarely at odds with the majority's position that only an act taken with intent to produce a forbidden effect is forbidden under the intent prong....

> "It may be asked how it could be forbidden by § 5 to have the purpose and intent of achieving only what is a perfectly legal result under that section .... The answer is plain, and we need not labor it. An official action, whether an annexation or otherwise, taken for the purpose of discriminating against Negroes on account of their race has no legitimacy at all under our Constitution or under the statute. Section 5 forbids voting changes taken with the purpose of denying the vote on the grounds of race or color."

    .... The majority's attempt to distinguish *Pleasant Grove v. United States*, 479 U.S. 462 (1987), is equally vain.... One thing is clear beyond peradventure: the annexation in that case could not have been intended to cause retrogression. No one could have intended to cause retrogression because no one knew of any minority voting strength from which retrogression was possible. The fact that the annexation was nonetheless barred under the purpose prong of § 5, 11 years after *Beer*, means that today's majority cannot hold as they do without overruling *Pleasant Grove*.

The majority seeks to avoid *Pleasant Grove* by describing it as barring "future retrogression" by nipping any such future contingency even before the bud had formed. This gymnastic, however, not only overlooks the contradiction between *Pleasant Grove's* holding that a voting change without possible retrogressive intent could fail under the purpose prong and the majority's reasoning today that the baseline for the purpose prong is the status quo; it even ignores what the Court actually said. While the *Pleasant Grove* Court said that impermissible purpose could relate to anticipated circumstances, it said nothing about anticipated retrogression (a concept familiar to the Court since the time of *Beer*). The Court found it "plausible" that the city had simply acted with "the impermissible purpose of minimizing future black voting strength." The Court spoke of "minimizing," not "causing retrogression to." But there is more:

> One means of thwarting [integration] is to provide for the growth of a monolithic white voting block, thereby effectively diluting the black vote in advance. This is just as impermissible a purpose as the dilution of present black voting strength.

That is, a nonretrogressive dilutive purpose is just as impermissible under § 5 as a retrogressive one. Today's holding contradicts that. The majority is overruling Pleasant Grove....

NOTES AND QUESTIONS

1. There may be considerable importance to the Court's mootness determination. The Court held that the case was not moot because, "[a]bsent a successful subsequent challenge under § 2, it ... will serve as the baseline against which appellee's next voting plan will be evaluated for the purposes of preclearance." In the post-1990 round of reapportionment, many covered jurisdictions were required to draw plans with new majority-minority districts. These plans may be vulnerable to attack under *Shaw v. Reno*, 509 U.S. 630 (1993), and its progeny (discussed in Chapter 8 of the casebook and supplement.) If a plan is not successfully challenged under *Shaw*, then presumably it constitutes the "benchmark" for any subsequent apportionment, even if the plan did impermissibly subordinate traditional districting factors in favor of creating unusually shaped majority-minority districts. Does *Bossier Parish II* suggest that we may see challenges to redistricting plans that survive the end of a decennial cycle.

Moreover, as a substantive matter, does the Court's holding that neither the Justice Department nor the District Court should deny preclearance to an intentionally discriminatory plan as long as it is not retrogressive mean that the preclearance process should not take into account the Court's holding in *Shaw*? Does this mean that the Justice Department, for example, is required to object to a plan as retrogressive in either purpose or effect even if there is no less retrogressive plan that complies with *Shaw*? Consider 28 C.F.R. § 51.54(b), in the statutory supplement, on the question of how the Department defines the appropriate benchmark.

2. Is the outcome in *Bossier II* in fact compelled by *Beer*? If so, how does the Court explain the continued vitality of *Pleasant Grove*? What is the difference between a present discriminatory (but nonretrogressive purpose) and a future purpose to retrogress?

3. Why does the Court's opinion suggest that "extend[ing § 5] to discriminatory but nonretrogressive vote-dilutive purposes, ... would also exacerbate the 'substantial' federalism costs that the preclearance procedure already exacts ... perhaps to the extent of raising concerns about § 5's constitutionality"? Isn't such activity precisely within the core of what the Fourteenth and Fifteenth Amendments prohibit, namely, purposeful discrimination on the basis of race? Does this suggest a majority of the Court may think that the preclearance requirement itself comes close to exceeding congressional enforcement power?

4. The current administrative guidelines for § 5 preclearance provide, in pertinent part, that

> In making a determination the Attorney General will consider whether the change is free of discriminatory purpose and retrogressive effect in light of, and with particular attention being given to, the requirements of the 14th, 15th, and 24th amendments to the Constitution, 42 U.S.C. 1971(a) and (b), sections 2, 4(a), 4(f)(2), 4(f)(4), 201, 203(c), and 208 of the Act, and

other constitutional and statutory provisions designed to safeguard the right to vote from denial or abridgment on account of race, color, or membership in a language minority group.

28 C.F.R. § 51.55(a). (See the Statutory Supplement for the entire set of administrative regulations.) In light of the Court's opinion, must this regulation be rewritten? How, if at all, ought evidence of discriminatory purpose as that concept is understood in Fourteenth or Fifteenth Amendment cases inform a preclearance authority's decisions?

CHAPTER SEVEN

on page 472, after note 4:

In recent years, the social-scientific tools on which voting-rights litigation depends have grown substantially more sophisticated. A major development was the technical advances offered in GARY KING, A SOLUTION TO THE ECOLOGICAL INFERENCE PROBLEM (1997). As one of the leading expert witnesses and social scientists concerning voting-rights litigation writes, the new tools reflected in King's work and others is "in the process of revolutionizing the analysis of [racial bloc voting] . . . ." Bernard Grofman, *A Primer on Racial Bloc Voting Analysis*, in THE REAL Y2K PROBLEM CENSUS 2000 DATA AND REDISTRICTING TECHNOLOGY 43-80 (N. Persily ed. 2000). Grofman's article is an excellent, accessible synthesis of the different methods of assessing racial voting patterns, the approaches reflected in the latest techniques, and the extent to which different methods do or do not tend to converge on similar legal conclusions regarding racial-polarization patterns. The article is a must read for those in the coming round of redistricting litigation who will be working with experts on measurements of racial polarization in specific jurisidictions.

on page 478, replace the second paragraph of note 1 with the following:

Does the court's analysis of the need for seven rather than five districts survive *Holder v. Hall*, where the Court held that the size of a governing authority is not subject to a vote dilution challenge under § 2? (*Holder* is treated in the casebook on pages 519-35.) In *Dillard v. Baldwin County Commissioners*, 225 F.3d 1271 (11th Cir. 2000), four voters intervened to challenge the district court's approval of a remedy for vote dilution in elections for the Baldwin County Commission that increased the membership of the Commission from four to seven members. In their complaint, the intervenors alleged increasing the size of the Commission exceeeded the district court's authority and "violated the Tenth and Eleventh Amendments." The intervenors asked the court to enter an order modifying the injunction and providing for the establishment of a districting plan composed of four single-member districts. The original plaintiffs in *Dillard* and the defendant (the incumbent county commission) opposed the motion.

The court of appeals held, first, that the intervenors had standing to seek modification of the injunction: "The intervenors sought to vindicate important personal interests in maintaining the election system that governed their exercise of political power, a democratically established system that the district court's order had altered," and this gave them the particularized, individual stake necessary to confer standing. To what extent is this notion of standing an outgrowth of the relaxed notion of standing offered in the *Shaw* cases (discussed in Chapter 8 of the casebook and supplement)? That is, is there anything that separates these voters from every other citizen of Baldwin County? Should their remedy be a political, rather than a judicial, one?

On the merits, the court of appeals held that the intervenors had stated claims under § 2 as well as under the Tenth Amendment. With regard to the § 2 claim:

> The intervenors' complaint ... allege[s] that the district court intentionally increased the size of the Baldwin County Commission and redrew the district lines specifically in order to create a majority black district....Moreover, the Complaint alleges that the Intervenors have been hurt by this racially-based increase in the size of the County Commission. See Complaint, P 14 (alleging that "Plaintiff-Intervenors ... are residents, citizens, and qualified electors of Baldwin County, Alabama. Each is adversely affected by the increase in the number of members of the Commission").... By alleging that they are being subjected to, and their voting power is being affected by, an illegal election scheme that was plainly created because of or on account of race, the Intervenors have adequately stated a claim for a section 2 violation of the Voting Rights Act.

Does the Court of Appeals decision create a new cause of action under § 2? What will the plaintiffs have to show -- some dilution in their voting strength on account of race or simply the fact that race was taken into account in creating the new plan? If the latter, is the intent requirement less stringent here than it would be in a *Shaw* case?

As for the Tenth Amendment claim -- which presumably consisted in the federal court's having overridden the state's policy preferences on the seize of governing commissions (the court of appeals never actually described the content of the Tenth Amendment claim) -- the court of appeals held that the fact that the commission had adopted the plan in settlement of a § 2 lawsuit did not immunize it: "What is being challenged here is the allegedly unconstitutional decision by a federal district court to alter the size of a local governing body.... We cannot shield federal court orders from constitutional challenge simply because the federal court's orders are being implemented by local officials."

The court of appeals remanded the case for further proceedings on the question whether the existing remedy violated either § 2 of the Tenth Amendment. In addition, it left open the question whether such a remedy might have been appropriate to remedy a violation of the Fourteenth Amendment, an issue not decided by *Holder*. Consider the effects that different rules about the scope of permissible remedies in § 2 and constitutional cases may have on litigation strategy and settlement negotiations. That is, the district court in the original *Dillard* litigation found purposeful discrimination by the State of Alabama in the maintenance and alteration of rules governing local elections, but found liability on a statutory, rather than a constitutional, theory. If the case were being decided today, would the rule from *Dillard II* create pressure for the court to reach the constitutional question?

on page 496, add the following after note 2:

The Second Circuit took a somewhat different tack on the question of the relationship among discriminatory purpose, partisan voting patterns, racial polarization, and § 2. *Goosby v. Town of Hempstead*, 180 F.3d 476 (2d Cir. 1999) involved a challenge to at-large elections for the Town Council, which has six members. (The Town has a population of over 725,000 people, making it more populous than six states and all but thirteen cities.) Since the inception of Town government in 1907, a member of the Republican Party had won every Town-wide election.

African Americans constituted 12.1% of the Town's 725,639 residents, and lived for the most part in a set of relatively segregated neighborhoods. Among white registered voters, 51% registered as Republicans, 26% as Democrats and 23% in another party or in no party. Among black registered voters, however, only 22% registered as Republicans, while 68% registered as Democrats and 10% in another party or expressed no party affiliation.

At trial, the plaintiffs concededly met the first two prongs of *Gingles*. And they also concededly showed that white voters and black voters preferred different candidates and that the candidates preferred by white voters invariably one. The district court rejected the Town's contention that the strong correlation between race and party precluded it from finding "legally significant white bloc voting" unless it first found that partisan politics was a proxy for racial animus, and instead considered the evidence of partisanship under the "totality of the circumstances" test. Ultimately, it found a violation of § 2 and ordered a single-member district remedy.

On appeal, the court of appeals affirmed. It agreed with the Fourth Circuit's decision in *Lewis v. Alamance County*, 99 F.3d 600 (4th Cir. 1996), that causation, that is, the reason for divergent voting patterns, is irrelevant in the inquiry into the three Gingles preconditions, but relevant in the totality of circumstances inquiry, a position that had been taken by several other circuits as well.

The court of appeals rejected the Town's argument that "blacks have lost as Democrats, not as 'blacks'":

> The Town's argument implies that if blacks registered and voted as Republicans, they would be able to elect the candidates they prefer. But they are not able to elect preferred candidates under the Republican Party regime that rules in the Town. Moreover, blacks should not be constrained to vote for Republicans who are not their preferred candidates.

> The Supreme Court instructs that a Voting Rights Act violation occurs when "a certain electoral law, practice, or structure interacts with social and historical conditions to cause an inequality in the opportunities enjoyed by black and white voters to elect their preferred representatives." *Gingles*, 478 U.S. at 47. The electoral law at issue provides for at-large voting for Town Board members. The historical conditions implicated are the Republican Party's hegemony over the Town of Hempstead since the Town's inception over 90 years ago, the slating process by which candidates are selected by the Republican Party, and the predilection of the great majority of blacks to vote for Democrat candidates. The concatenation of these conditions has resulted in the vote dilution of which the plaintiff class complains and the consequent inability of blacks to elect their preferred candidates.

The Republican slating process in the Town is unique. Although the Republican Committee members in the Town of Hempstead theoretically are empowered to choose a slate of candidates for the Town Board, the actual selection process has been much different. The Committee members have ceded their authority to the County Chairman, who designates the Town slate. The choice of candidates is his alone, although any number of people may suggest potential candidates. The present Nassau County Chairman, Joseph Mondello, has served in that capacity for some fifteen years. While black Republicans could mount a primary campaign to secure the Republican nomination for Town Board for a preferred candidate, it would be futile to do so. The Chairman-preferred candidate would always win in a Town-wide primary election, due to the overwhelming strength of the monolithic Republican organization.... [O]ne-man, no-vote ... prevails in the Republican Party in the Town of Hempstead and in the County of Nassau....

180 F.3d at 495-97. To what extent is the unique slating process relevant given that the overwhelming majority of black voters in Hempstead do not participate in Republican politics in the first place?

Judge Leval filed a thought-provoking concurrence on the question of the role of discriminatory intent or racial animus in § 2 cases. He offered a hypothetical jurisdiction, one in which the election rules were set many years ago, before members of a protected class moved into the area. In Judge Leval's view, "the more deeply judicial intervention would intrude into the political process, the more reluctant courts should be to find a violation without a finding of racial motivation." *Id.* at 501-02. So, for example, § 2 "might require the establishment of a polling place near a new concentration of protected class members, even though the location of polling places had not been racially motivated, if the inaccessibility of the polling place lessened the opportunity of class members to cast ballots. Such a remedy involves little judicial intrusion into the political process." But, he felt very differently about the question of districting. Suppose an electoral district's boundaries were

set long ago and ha[ve] since been maintained without any racial motivation. In recent years, a cluster of members of a protected class develops around the dividing line, with a substantial percentage of the cluster falling on both sides of the line. If the members of that class could not elect their preferred representative in the districts on either side of the line, but could elect a representative if the line were shifted so that the entire community fell into one district, then plaintiffs from that class could argue that the maintenance of the line deprived them of the opportunity to elect a representative of their choice. In such a circumstance, the notion that courts could invalidate an election and require revision of election districts, without any showing of discriminatory intent, seems to me alarming and far beyond the probable contemplation of Congress. *Id.* at 501 n.3.

Judge Leval also suggested that

In deciding whether or not discriminatory intent is necessary to a section 2 violation, another factor that may be relevant is whether the alleged violation appears more concerned with process or outcomes. The accessible location of polling places, for example, is necessary to a fair process in which all persons can cast a vote. The law may plausibly guarantee a fair process regardless whether the unfairness to be remedied is the product of discriminatory intent. But where plaintiffs allege that they are unable to elect representatives of their choice, their complaint, at least on its face, is that the outcome is unfavorable to them. Ordinarily, American law guarantees equal electoral opportunity, not equal electoral results. *See Davis v. Bandemer*, 478 U.S. 109 (1986). If courts are to police electoral outcomes, it is reasonable that they first require that discrimination, within the electorate if not the state, have infected the election. When discrimination is present, it can be said that the process also was not fair, in the sense that it was marred by illegitimate animus.

Id. at 502 n.4. Is there any warrant for Judge Leval's proposal in the text or structure of § 2?

Despite his disagreement with the majority's framework, Judge Leval agreed with the result. In his view, proof of the three *Gingles* factors "sufficiently supports an inference that race may have been a factor" to shift the burden to defendants to disprove the presumption of discriminatory purpose by government officials or the electorate. *Id.* at 502-03. In this case, based on the district court's factual findings, Judge Leval did not think the Town had carried its burden of disproving racial motivation. In reaching this conclusion, Judge Leval pointed to the fact that "[r]acial appeals have been features of Town elections on more than one occasion, [t]own law enforcement officers have engaged in race-conscious policing, ... [a]gencies of the Town government have committed acts of racial discrimination to which the Town has made no response, ... [and] has a history of indifference to the economic and social needs of the black communities within Hempstead...." Moreover, until "litigation began, the Republican Party in Hempstead had never recruited an African-American candidate for the Town Board" and "a majority of white voters in Hempstead had never supported a black candidate for the Board." *Id.* at 503.

As a policy matter, is Judge Leval's approach actually less intrusive? Moreover, on whose discriminatory intent is he relying?

on page 499, add the following after note 6:

7. Several recent court of appeals decisions have given additional consideration to the third *Gingles* factor. In *Old Person v. Cooney*, ___ F.3d ___ (9th Cir. 2000), American Indians challenged Montana's state house apportionment under section 2. In remanding the case for further proceedings, the Ninth Circuit held that the district court had erred in relying on white voting behavior within majority-Indian electoral districts to conclude that white voters did not usually (that is, more often than not) vote to defeat the preferred candidate of Indian voters. The Court of Appeals relied in part on the Court's decision in *Johnson v. DeGrandy*, 512 U.S. 997 (1994) (casebook pages 500-06), which reflected "a post-Gingles phenomenon, a § 2 challenge to a plan that already included some majority-minority districts." *DeGrandy* had found racial bloc voting in the "tendency of non-Hispanic whites to vote as a bloc to bar minority groups from electing their chosen candidates *except in a district where a given minority makes up a voting majority.*" *Id.* at 1003-04 (emphasis added). Thus, the Ninth Circuit concluded that it should "consider Indian electoral

success in majority-Indian districts only in the inquiry into the totality of the circumstances," but not in deciding whether Indian voters had satisfied the third prong of *Gingles*. "To do otherwise would permit white bloc voting in a majority-white district to be washed clean by electoral success in neighboring majority-Indian districts. Such an approach would be antithetical to the directive in *Gingles* that legally significant white bloc voting be determined on a fact-specific 'district to district' basis." What is the underlying rationale for excluding white voting behavior in majority-minority districts? Is it that white voters' behavior under these circumstances may be colored by the knowledge that they are the numerical minority and thus they may be more willing to support coalitions with nonwhite voters? The Ninth Circuit also rejected the state's argument that whatever white bloc voting existed was not legally significant somewhere between 22 and 38 percent of white voters crossed over to vote for Indian preferred candidates.

Finally, the Court of Appeals rejected the state's alternative rationale for the observed behavior of white voters, namely partisan politics. The state argued that losses by Indian candidates could fairly be ascribed to partisan politics and not race when Democratic Indian candidates lose in majority Republican districts. But the court of appeals found that Indian (Indian-preferred) candidates generally received a lower percentage of white votes than did white Indian-preferred candidates in the same district and thus refused to attribute white bloc voting to "mere" partisan politics.

In *Rural West Tennessee African-American Affairs Council v. Sundquist*, 209 F.3d 835 (6th Cir. 2000), the court of appeals confronted the question of the weight to give so-called white-on-white elections in addressing the third *Gingles* factor. It held that while courts could consider electoral contests involving only white candidates, those elections might be less probative than contests that involved black candidates as well. See also *Nipper v. Smith*, 39 F.3d 1494, 1540 (11th Cir. 1994) (en banc) (holding that white-white elections may be considered, but are less probative than those involving black candidates); *Smith v. Clinton*, 687 F. Supp. 1310, 1318 (E.D. Ark.) (three judge court) (observing that § 2's guarantee of equal opportunity is not met when "candidates favored by blacks can win, but only if the candidates are white"), *aff'd*, 488 U.S. 988 (1988). In *Rural West*, the court of appeals noted that white voter cohesion in rural west Tennessee increased from 59% in white-white elections to 86% in black-white elections: "In view of such evidence that a white voting bloc coalesces to frustrate African-American candidacies, the district court properly considered the race of candidates in its § 2 analysis, and accorded greater weight to the results of black-white elections." 209 F.3d at 840-41.

on page 518, after note 2, add the following:

2a.   In *Rural West Tennessee African-American Affairs Council v. Sundquist*, 209 F.3d 835 (6th Cir. 2000), which challenged the Tennessee state house districts (the principal case involved state senate districts), the court of appeals considered the relationship between *DeGrandy* and the Supreme Court's decisions in *Shaw v. Reno* and its progeny and their effect on the question of the relevant geographic area in which to measure dilution. Recall that in *DeGrandy*, the Court had rejected Florida's argument that, as a matter of law, there is no dilution when the percentage of single-member districts in which minority voters form an effective majority mirrors the their percentage of the relevant population. The *Rural West* court noted that *Shaw* had taken a similar tack:

If a § 2 violation is proved for a particular area, it flows from the fact that individuals in this area "have less opportunity than other members of the electorate to participate in the political process and to elect representatives of their choice." 42 U.S.C. § 1973(b). The vote-dilution injuries suffered by these persons are not remedied by creating a safe majority-black district somewhere else in the State . . . .

. . . To accept that the district may be placed anywhere implies that the claim, and hence the coordinate right to an undiluted vote (to cast a ballot equal among voters), belongs to the minority as a group and not to its individual members. It does not.

Thus, the *Rural West* court accepted the relatively narrow "geographical frame of reference that the plaintiffs have selected":

The State complains that by allowing the plaintiffs to define the frame of reference for their § 2 claim, we will enable future litigants to carve up successively smaller areas of the State until they are able to maximize the number of majority-minority legislative districts--a result not countenanced by the Voting Rights Act. *See De Grandy*, 512 U.S. at 1017 ("Failure to maximize cannot be the measure of § 2."). As the district court pointed out, however, the *Gingles* preconditions operate to prevent just the sort of limitlessly small "reverse gerrymander" whose specter the State raises here. *See, e.g., Campos v. City of Houston*, 113 F.3d 544, 547-48 (5th Cir. 1997) (holding that minority group was not sufficiently large and geographically compact to sustain a § 2 claim). In this regard, we note that the region selected by the plaintiffs in this case is a sensible one-- indeed, more sensible than the seven-county area including Shelby County urged by the State. While Shelby County is the southernmost and westernmost county in the State, and, like the six neighboring counties of rural west Tennessee, has a large African-American population, the seven counties do not form a coherent demographic unit. The African-American population in Shelby County is concentrated in inner-city Memphis, and is largely set off from rural west Tennessee by a "buffer zone" of white suburbs. As a result, the African-American populations in these two areas are not likely to be particularly cohesive. For this reason, the district court properly restricted the geographic scope of relevant statistical data to the six counties of rural west Tennessee. 209 F.3d at 844.

on page 545, add the following new section:

D.   THE CONSTITUTIONALITY OF AMENDED SECTION 2

As the cases in this chapter show, amended § 2 has spawned a torrent of litigation that has dramatically reshaped the American electoral landscape. As late as 1982, a sizeable majority of municipal elections were conducted at large and most southern states elected at least some state legislators from multimember districts. But by the mid-1990's, most jurisdictions with substantial minority populations had switched to using at least some single-member districts, and state legislatures were elected entirely from single-member districts, at least some of which were majority nonwhite. *See generally* QUIET REVOLUTION IN THE SOUTH: THE IMPACT OF THE VOTING RIGHTS ACT, 1965-1900 (Chandler Davidson & Bernard Grofman eds., 1994); Pamela S. Karlan, *The Future of Voting Rights Litigation*, in CENSUS 2000: CONSIDERATIONS AND STRATEGIES FOR STATE AND LOCAL GOVERNMENT (Benjamin E. Griffith ed. 2000).

As we saw in Chapter 6 and in the Supreme Court's decision in *Gingles*, Congress amended § 2 in substantial part because it disagreed with the Court's decision in *City of Mobile v. Bolden*. Section 2 forbids voting practices and procedures that have a discriminatory result, even if the state or political subdivision behaved without a discriminatory purpose. By contrast, the Court has interpreted both the Fourteenth and the Fifteenth Amendments to prohibit only purposefully discriminatory actions. It is therefore striking that the Court has never squarely addressed the question of the constitutionality of amended § 2's results test.

In *Mississippi Republican Executive Committee v. Brooks*, 469 U.S. 1002 (1984) , the Court summarily affirmed an appeal from a district court's order redrawing Mississippi's congressional districts to create draw a majority-black congressional district. The questions presented in the jurisdictional statement included "Whether Section 2 as amended prohibits only those electoral schemes intentionally designed or maintained to discriminate on the basis of race" and "Whether Section 2, if construed to prohibit anything other than intentional discrimination on the basis of race in registration and voting, exceeds the power vested in Congress by the Fifteenth Amendment." Then-Justice Rehnquist and Chief Justice Burger dissented from the summary affirmance, arguing that plenary review of the scope of § 2 was required.

As a general matter, "[s]ummary affirmances ... without doubt reject the specific challenges presented in the statement of jurisdiction," *Mandel v. Bradley*, 432 U.S. 173, 176 (1977); see also *Illinois State Bd. v. Socialist Workers Party*, 440 U.S. 173, 182-83 (1979). While the Supreme Court itself gives less precedential weight to its own prior summary affirmances, lower courts are required to grant summary affirmances the same binding weight they give to other Supreme Court judgments. *See generally* ROBERT L. STERN ET AL., SUPREME COURT PRACTICE § 4.29 (7th ed. 1993). In part, then, as a result of the Supreme Court's decision in *Brooks*, the lower courts have unanimously upheld amended § 2 against constitutional attack.

At the same time, several Justices have indicated the view that the question of amended § 2's constitutionality remains open. *See, e.g., Chisom v. Roemer*, 501 U.S. 380, 418 (1990) (Kennedy, J., dissenting); *Johnson v. DeGrandy*, 512 U.S. 997, 1028-29 (1994) (Kennedy, J., concurring); *cf. Bush v. Vera*, 517 U.S. 952, 990 (1996) (O'Connor, J., concurring) (noting that "[i]In the 14 years since the enactment of § 2(b), we have interpreted and enforced the obligations that it places on States in a succession of cases, assuming but never directly addressing its constitutionality").

The Court's decision in *City of Boerne v. Flores*, 521 U.S. 507 (1997), potentially affects the question. In *Boerne*, the Court struck down a provision of the Religious Freedom Restoration Act of 1993 (RFRA) that prohibited state and local governments from "substantially burdening" a person's exercise of religion even if the burden resulted from a rule of general applicability -- that is a rule that was not intended to burden religious free exercise -- unless the government could demonstrate that the burden "(1) is in furtherance of a compelling governmental interest; and (2) is the least restrictive means of furthering that . . . interest." 42 U.S.C. § 2000bb-1.

The Federal Government defended RFRA as an appropriate use of Congress' enforcement power under § 5 of the Fourteenth Amendment. It argued that Congress' "decision to dispense with proof of deliberate or overt discrimination and instead concentrate on a law's effects accords with the settled understanding that § 5 includes the power to enact legislation designed to prevent as well as remedy constitutional violations." 521 U.S. at 517.

The Court, in an opinion by Justice Kennedy, disagreed. While it acknowledged that "[l]egislation which deters or remedies constitutional violations can fall within sweep of Congress' enforcement power even if in the process it prohibits conduct which is not itself unconstitutional and intrudes into legislative spheres of autonomy previously reserved to the States," it declared that "[t]here must be a congruence and proportionality between the injury to be prevented or remedied and the means adopted to that end." 521 U.S. at 518, 520.

With respect to RFRA, the Court found no such congruity: the record before Congress did not indicate a pervasive practice of intentional discrimination against religious free exercise that would justify the prophylactic step of prohibiting conduct with a discriminatory impact absent a finding of purposeful discrimination. Given that failure, the Court saw Congress' action as an attempt to redefine the substantive scope of First/Fourteenth Amendment protections, rather than an appropriate remedial response.

For present purposes, perhaps the most significant aspects of *Boerne* were, first, its overruling of the so-called "ratchet" theory of congressional enforcement powers advanced by the Court in *Katzenbach v. Morgan*, 384 U.S. 641 (1966) (discussed in the casebook at pages 278 and 280), and second, its explicit contrast between the impermissible use of the enforcement power to enact RFRA and Congress' appropriate use of that power to ban literacy tests and impose the preclearance requirement of § 5 of the Voting Rights Act.

[T]he Court upheld a suspension of literacy tests and similar voting requirements under Congress' parallel power to enforce the provisions of the Fifteenth Amendment, see U.S. Const., Amdt. 15 § 2, as a measure to combat racial discrimination in voting, *South Carolina v. Katzenbach*, 383 U.S. 301 (1966), despite the facial constitutionality of the tests under *Lassiter v. Northampton County Bd. of Elections*, 360 U.S. 45 (1959) We have also concluded that other measures protecting voting rights are within Congress' power to enforce the Fourteenth and Fifteenth Amendments, despite the burdens those measures placed on the States. *South Carolina v. Katzenbach, supra* (upholding several provisions of the Voting Rights Act of 1965); *Katzenbach v. Morgan, supra* (upholding ban on literacy tests that prohibited certain people schooled in Puerto Rico from voting); *Oregon v. Mitchell*, 400 U.S. 112 (1970) (upholding 5-year nationwide ban on literacy tests and similar voting requirements for registering to vote); *City of Rome v. United States*, 446 U.S. 156 (1980) (upholding 7-year extension of the Voting Rights Act's requirement that certain jurisdictions preclear any change to a "standard, practice, or procedure with respect to voting") ....

521 U.S. at 519. Notably, the Court's opinion did not mention the results test of amended § 2 of the Voting Rights Act.

One commentator has identified three potential explanations within *Boerne* and the four Voting Rights Act cases for why Congress could reach nonpurposeful discrimination:

> First, under the internal model, literacy tests themselves might be the source of invidious discrimination; that is, the unconstitutional discrimination might occur within the electoral system. Congress and the Court had substantial evidence that literacy tests were administered in deliberately discriminatory ways for the purpose of excluding black citizens who possessed the same abilities as white individuals who were permitted to register. Under this view, Congress could ban literacy tests because the available evidence gave it "reason to believe that many of the laws affected by the congressional enactment have a significant likelihood of being unconstitutional." The congressional ban might-and in fact did-reach some literacy tests that could not be proven to be purposefully discriminatory. But as long as there was "congruence and proportionality between the [unconstitutional] injury to be prevented or remedied and the means adopted to that end," the Constitution does not require a perfect fit.

> Second, in the external model, purposeful governmental discrimination outside the electoral system might play out within the electoral system, where it would be observed in the disparate impact of otherwise acceptable policies. For example, the inability of minority voters to pass even a fairly administered literacy test might be "the direct consequence of previous governmental discrimination in education." Under this view, Congress could ban literacy tests to reach and remedy the effects of that impermissible prior discrimination. Again, even though some of the beneficiaries of the ban on literacy tests might not be actual victims of the government's unconstitutional provision of an inferior and inadequate education, there was a sufficient connection to justify some level of overbreadth.

> Third, under the prospective model, literacy tests might be seen as enabling future invidious action. For example, if literacy tests eliminate a disproportionate number of minority citizens from the electorate, then their diminished voting power might leave minorities vulnerable to discrimination in a wide range of government programs by officials who would be relieved of any practical need to be responsive to the minority's concerns. Under this expansive view, Congress might ban literacy tests "as a remedial measure to deal with . . . discrimination in the provision of public services."

Pamela S. Karlan, *Two Section Twos and Two Section Fives: Voting Rights and Remedies After* Boerne, 39 WM. & MARY L. REV. 725, 728-29 (1998).

Karlan argues that amended § 2 can be sustained under all three models: the internal, the external, and the prospective. With respect to the internal model, she argued that:

> The record before Congress in 1982 revealed numerous "modern instances of generally applicable laws passed because of [racial] bigotry." As the Senate Report accompanying the 1982 amendments explained, the very passage of the 1965 Act seems to have prompted a new wave of purposeful discrimination within the electoral system: "a broad array of dilution schemes were employed to cancel the impact of the new black vote." Of particular salience to the question whether the Act's treatment of racial vote dilution represents appropriate congressional action, "election boundaries were gerrymandered" and "at-large elections were substituted for election by single-member districts, or combined with other sophisticated rules to prevent an effective minority vote." Extensive hearings and the record of preclearance objections during the period from 1975 to 1980 showed repeated problems with apparently purposeful racial vote dilution.

Id. at 733-34. In light of this record, she argued that Congress might reasonably prohibit practices with a discriminatory result on the theory that a broader prophylactic rule was necessary to reach all the cases where purposeful discrimination had occurred.

With respect to the external and prospective models, Karlan argued that racial bloc voting -- the *sine qua non* of § 2 vote dilition cases -- is partially a contemporary manifestation of external discrimination:

> To the extent that racially correlated differences in political preferences are the product of socioeconomic disparities produced by inferior access to schools, government services, and the like, state action has caused polarized voting.... Even beyond the material reasons why past discrimination might cause differences in voting behavior, there may be an attitudinal effect too. The broad range of purposeful past governmental discrimination "is likely to have affected white voters' attitudes by communicating the idea that black voters' attempts to gain political power should be resisted."

Id. at 739. Creating single-member districts might be an appropriate remedy to dampen the present effects of past external discrimination, since it would enable black voters to elect candidates despite them.

Finally, the results test might be an appropriate response to the post-electoral nonresponsiveness that racial bloc voting might produce. Submergence in a racially polarized electorate might produce elected officials with no incentive to be responsive to the minority community's distinctive needs. Given the connection between minority political powerlessness and the unequal provision of government services, "Congress might reasonably conclude that such inequality is better combatted on the wholesale level, by providing all citizens with an equal opportunity to participate in the political process and to elect representatives of their choice, than on only the retail level, by laws that impose equal treatment obligations in discrete areas of state government activity such as schools, public employment, or housing." *Id.* at 740.

By contrast, Professor Douglas Laycock argues that *Boerne* casts a serious shadow over § 2's constitutionality:

> The political history of the 1982 Act, and the structural relationship of the statutory and constitutional standards, are indistinguishable from RFRA. RFRA was a direct congressional response to *Smith*; the 1982 Voting Rights Act was a direct congressional response to *City of Mobile v. Bolden*. The legislative history of the 1982 Act denounced *Bolden* as often and as vigorously as the legislative history of RFRA denounced *Smith*. RFRA covered nearly the whole scope of the Free Exercise Clause, and the 1982 Act covers the whole scope of the Fifteenth Amendment. Both RFRA and the 1982 Act enacted a broad standard drawn from prior constitutional interpretation. In each case, the Court's new constitutional standard required discrimination that was either deliberate (in the sense of unconstitutional motive) or overt (in the sense of disparate treatment, whatever the motive) and the statutory standard that Congress enacted in response dispensed with that requirement. In each case, there was some evidence that the new statutory standard simplified proof of constitutional violations, and substantial evidence that Congress disagreed with the new court-defined constitutional standard. The Senate Report on the 1982 Act was explicit about which consideration was more important: "During the hearings, there was considerable discussion of the difficulty often encountered in meeting the intent test, but that is not the principal reason why we have rejected it. The main reason is that, simply put, the test asks the wrong question."

> The 1982 Voting Rights Act was not aimed at efforts to prevent blacks from voting; those efforts had largely ended by 1982. Instead, it was aimed at second and third generation voting rights problems, especially the inability of minority groups to elect representatives either in at-large elections or in elections in which the minority vote was dispersed across a number of single-member districts. The 1982 Act requires the creation of minority-controlled districts where there is a history of racially polarized voting and where such districts can be drawn without gross racial gerrymandering. Neither element of this threshold showing is plausibly a violation of the Constitution as the Court interprets it. Plaintiffs seem to be able to prove racially polarized voting almost everywhere, but it is hard to imagine the Court holding that the electoral choices of individual voters are unconstitutional, even when cumulated into racial patterns.

> The failure to draw minority-controlled districts is not unconstitutional either, nor is it sufficient evidence of likely unconstitutional motive. The Constitution permits any districting scheme not deliberately designed to reduce minority voting strength. State and local governments have myriad legitimate reasons, and also a range of dubious, but clearly nonracial reasons-especially party gerrymanders and incumbent protection-for at-large elections and for drawing single-member districts one way instead of another. It seems unlikely that color-blind districting would reliably create minority-controlled seats outside the largest concentrations of minority population. As with RFRA,

the number of statutory violations appears disproportionately large in relation to the number of constitutional violations. The Court summarily upheld the 1982 Act in 1984, but *Flores* implied the opposite result.

Douglas Laycock, *Conceptual Gulfs in City of Boerne v. Flores*, 39 WM. & MARY L. REV. 743, 749-52 (1998). *See also* John Matthew Guard, Comment, *"Impotent Figureheads"? State Sovereignty, Federalism, and the Constitutionality of Section 2 of the Voting Rights Act After Lopez v. Monterey County and City of Boerne v. Flores*, 74 TUL. L. REV. 329 (1999) (distinguishing amended § 2's results test from the practices at issue in *South Carolina v. Katzenbach, Katzenbach v. Morgan, Oregon v. Mitchell*, and *City of Rome v. United States*, and suggesting that *Boerne* therefore casts serious doubt on the Act's constitutionality).

To what extent is the difference in Professor Karlan and Professor Laycock's assessment dependent on different empirical predicates about the record before Congress in 1982?

In addition to the specific decision in *Boerne*, consider the potential implications of the Court's recent revival of federalism (and corresponding mistrust of congressional legislation) across the board in cases such as *Alden v. Maine*, 119 S.Ct. 2240 (1999*), Florida Prepaid Postsecondary Education Expense Board v. College Savings Bank*, 120 S.Ct. 2199 (2000), and *Kimel v. Florida Board of Regents*, 120 S.Ct. 621 (2000). Over the past few Terms, the Supreme Court has struck down a number of congressional attempts to regulate state activities. In both *Florida Prepaid* and *Kimel*, the Court thought Congress had exceeded its Fourteenth Amendment enforcement powers because of the incongruity between the sweeping prohibition and the likely set of constitutional violations.

CHAPTER EIGHT

Page 582, at the end of note 1:

The Court's decision in *Shaw v. Reno* precipitated litigation challenging congressional or state legislative reapportionments in at least a dozen states. And *Shaw* lawsuits have occupied a significant fraction of the Supreme Court's docket over the last seven years. In part, this is due to a technical question of appellate jurisdiction. Most of the time, the Supreme Court has discretion to decide whether to hear a case; if it thinks that an issue is not very important, or that the lower courts have properly applied the law, or even that the case would simply be too time consuming because of an intricate factual record, the Court can deny the petition for a writ of certiorari, leaving in place the ruling of the lower courts. But the Supreme Court has mandatory appellate jurisdiction over cases heard by three-judge (rather than single-judge) district courts. What this means is that if a party seeks appellate review of a case tried before a three-judge district court, the case bypasses the courts of appeals and the Supreme Court must decide the merits. There are very few cases that are tried by these special district courts anymore, but federal statutes require them both for cases brought under section 5 of the Voting Rights Act (the preclearance provision discussed in Chapter 5), see 42 U.S.C. § 1973c, and for cases challenging statewide legislative reapportionments, see 28 U.S.C. § 2284. The conventional explanation for why Congress retained three-judge district courts in statewide apportionment cases is that respect for values of federalism in the area of redistricting militated against letting a single district judge overturn a state's decisions. For an extensive discussion of the issues raised by the use of three-judge court, see Michael E. Solimine, *The Three-Judge District Court in Voting Rights Litigation,* 30 U. MICH. J.L. REF. 79 (1996).

Although the Court thus has mandatory appellate jurisdiction over many *Shaw* challenges – all those involving congressional and state legislative apportionments – it *could* dispose of these cases summarily, by affirming or reversing without oral argument. It has done so occasionally. *See, e.g., King v. Illinois Board of Elections,* 522 U.S. 1087 (1998) (affirming three-judge court's judgment that Illinois' majority-Hispanic Fourth Congressional District was created to satisfy the state's compelling interest in compliance with § 2 of the Voting Rights Act); *Meadows v. Moon,* 521 U.S. 1113 (1997) (affirming a three-judge court's invalidation of Virginia's majority-black Third Congressional District). But more often, it has noted probable jurisdiction and decided cases after briefing and oral argument. As the following notes and cases show, the Court remains deeply divided on the scope and interpretation of *Shaw,* and it seems that there are always four Justices dissatisfied with the approach taken by the lower courts.

In addition to spurring a deluge of litigation, *Shaw* and its progeny have generated a wealth of scholarship. See, e.g., J. MORGAN KOUSSER, COLORBLIND Injustice: MINORITY VOTING RIGHTS AND THE UNDOING OF THE SECOND RECONSTRUCTION 366-455 (1999); T. Alexander Aleinikoff & Samuel Issacharoff, *Race and Redistricting: Drawing Constitutional Lines After Shaw v. Reno*, 92 MICH. L. REV. 588 (1993); Andrea Bierstein, *Millennium Approaches: The Future of the Voting Rights Act After Shaw, DeGrandy, and Holder*, 46 HASTINGS L.J. 1457 (1995); James U. Blacksher, *Dred Scott's Unwon Freedom: The Redistricting Cases As Badges of Slavery*, 39 HOW. L.J. 633 (1996); James U. Blacksher, *Majority Black Districts, Kiryas Joel, and Other Challenges to American Nationalism*, 26 CUMB. L. REV. 407 (1996); James F. Blumstein, *Shaw v. Reno in Doctrinal Context*, 26 RUTGERS L.J. 517 (1995); James F. Blumstein, *Shaw v. Reno and Miller v. Johnson: Where We Are and Where We Are Headed*, 26 CUMB. L. REV. 503 (1996); Katherine Inglis Butler, *Affirmative Racial Gerrymandering: Rhetoric and Reality*, 26 CUMB. L. REV. 313 (1996); David R. Dow, *The Equal Protection Clause and the Legislative Redistricting Cases - Some Notes Concerning the Standing of White Plaintiffs*, 81 MINN. L. REV. 1123 (1997); John Hart Ely, *Gerrymanders: The Good, the Bad, and the Ugly*, 50 STAN. L. REV. 607 (1998); John Hart Ely, *Standing to Challenge Pro-Minority Gerrymanders*, 111 HARV. L. REV. 576 (1997); Benjamin E. Griffith, *Proactive Defense Strategies in Voting Rights Litigation after Miller v. Johnson*, 65 MISS. L.J. 315 (1995); Benjamin E. Griffith, *Implementing the Race-Predominant Standard for State and Local Government Redistricting Plans*, 27 STETSON L. REV. 835 (1998); Bernard Grofman & Lisa Handley, *1990s Issues in Voting Rights*, 65 MISS. L.J. 205 (1995); Samuel Issacharoff and Thomas C. Goldstein, *Identifying the Harm in Racial Gerrymandering Cases*, 1 MICH. J. RACE & L. 47 (1996); Samuel Issacharoff, *Racial Gerrymandering in a Complex World*, 45 CATH. U.L. REV. 1257 (1996); Samuel Issacharoff and Pamela S. Karlan, *Standing and Misunderstanding in Voting Rights Law*, 111 HARV. L. REV. 2276 (1998); Samuel Issacharoff, *The Constitutional Contours of Race and Politics*, 1995 SUF. CT. REV. 45. Pamela S. Karlan, *The Fire Next Time: Reapportionment After the 2000 Census*, 50 STAN. L. REV. 731 (1998); Pamela S. Karlan, *Just Politics? Five Not So Easy Pieces of the 1995 Term*, 34 HOUS. L. REV. 289 (1997); Pamela S. Karlan, *Still Hazy After All These Years: Voting Rights in the Post-Shaw Era*, 26 CUMB. L. REV. 287 (1996); Pamela S. Karlan & Daryl J. Levinson, *Why Voting Is Different*, 84 CALIF. L. REV. 1201 (1996); Daniel Hays Lowenstein, *You Don't Have to Be Liberal to Hate the Racial Gerrymandering Cases*, 50 STAN. L. REV. 779 (1998); Earl M. Maltz, *Political Questions and Representational Politics: A Comment on Shaw v. Reno*, 26 RUTGERS L. J. 711 (1995); Paul L. McKaskle, *The Voting Rights Act and the "Conscientious Redistricter,"* 30 U.S.F.L. REV. 1 (1995); Richard H. Pildes & Richard G. Niemi, *Expressive Harms, "Bizarre Districts," and Voting Rights: Evaluating Election-District Appearances After Shaw v. Reno*, 92 MICH. L. REV. 483 (1993); Richard H. Pildes, *The Politics of Race*, 108 HARV. L. REV. 1359 (1995); Richard H. Pildes, *Principled Limitations on Racial and Partisan Redistricting*, 106 Yale L.J. 2505 (1997); Judith Reed, *Sense and Nonsense: Standing in the Racial Districting Cases as a Window on the Supreme Court's View of the Right to Vote*, 4 Mich. J. Race & L. 389 (1999); Melissa L. Saunders, *Reconsidering Shaw: The Miranda of Race-Conscious Districting*, 109 YALE L.J. 1603 (2000); Symposium, The American Bar Association Presidential Showcase Program, *The Geography of Race in Elections: Color-blindness and Redistricting*, 14 J. L. & POL. 109 (1998); Symposium, *The Supreme Court, Racial Politics, and the Right to Vote: Shaw v. Reno and the Future of the Voting Rights Act*, 44 AM. U.L. REV. 1 (1994); Symposium: *Voting Rights After Shaw v. Reno*, 26 RUTGERS L.J. 517 (1995).

The scholarship tends to focus on a set of issues: What is the Court's conception of *Shaw*-type injury?, and, in part as a consequence of how injury is defined, who can be a plaintiff in a *Shaw* challenge? What is the relationship between *Shaw* claims and traditional equal protection claims that involve allegations of purposeful racial discrimination or vote dilution against minority voters? Are *Shaw* claims claims about voting and participation in the political process or are they about something else? What triggers strict scrutiny and what serves as a compelling government interest sufficient to justify race-conscious redistricting? What is the relationship between *Shaw* claims and the Voting Rights Act of 1965, which seems to require some level of race consciousness in redistricting? How can local governments comply with both *Shaw* and the Act?

The following notes examine these issues, and the Court's response to these questions in greater depth.

Page 585:

Change the caption under this map to "Texas Congressional District 6"

Page 598, at the end of note 9, add:

In John Hart Ely, *Standing to Challenge Pro-Minority Gerrymanders*, 111 HARV. L. REV. 576 (1997), Professor Ely argued that the basis for finding standing in the *Shaw* cases was obvious. "White filler people" - that is, white voters placed within majority-nonwhite districts in order to top off those districts' populations in compliance with the requirements of one person, one vote - "have standing basically because they've been deprived of a meaningful shot at helping to elect a representative whose race is the same as theirs." *Id*. At 594. In response, two of the co-authors of this casebook argued that *Shaw* standing was simply an incoherent doctrine. Samuel Issacharoff and Pamela S. Karlan, *Standing and Misunderstanding in Voting Rights Law*, 111 HARV. L. REV. 2276 (1998):

A core question of the *Shaw* cases concerns how the use of race in the apportionment process might injure a particular voter in a constitutionally cognizable way. To understand the array of potential injuries, consider the following schematic representation of the relationship between voters and a given district in a particular plan.

	Voter Lives in District X	Voter Lives Outside District X
Voter Is White	A	B
Voter Is Nonwhite	C	D

The main thrust of the *Shaw* cases has been to assume that voters in boxes A and C, but not voters in boxes B and D, have standing to raise the claim that District X "rationally cannot be understood as anything other than an effort to segregate citizens into separate voting districts on the basis of race without sufficient justification." By contrast, Ely would confine standing to voters in boxes A and C, but members of each group would have standing only if the group were a numerical minority within the challenged district. Thus, only white voters (voters in box A) would have standing to challenge a majority-nonwhite District X, and only nonwhite voters (voters in box C) would have standing to challenge a majority-white District X....

The clearest voting injury is denial of the right altogether. Voters in boxes B and D have been denied the right to vote in District X's elections. For example, the plaintiffs in the classic case of *Gomillion v. Lightfoot*, on which the Court heavily relied in *Shaw*, fell in box D. They were black citizens whose houses were removed from within the municipal boundaries of Tuskegee, Alabama, when those boundaries were redrawn. The injury that they suffered was quite concrete: because of their race, they were denied the right to vote and "the consequent advantages that the ballot affords."

In the *Shaw* cases ... the "X Districts" are majority nonwhite, usually majority black or majority Hispanic. Thus, the group of voters most nearly analogous to the *Gomillion* plaintiffs fall in box B: they are white voters who allege they were purposefully excluded from District X in order to ensure that the district's electorate would be majority nonwhite.

If *Gomillion* is the template for a *Shaw* claim, one might plausibly assume that voters who allege assignment to box B because of their race would have standing to challenge the apportionment plan that put them there, even if the government ultimately could show that their placement was not in fact based on race or was justified by a compelling government interest. But this is precisely the group the Supreme Court has held does not have standing to bring a *Shaw* claim. In *Hays*, the Court unanimously denied standing to both white and black voters; although they had lived in the challenged district as originally drawn, by the time the case reached the Supreme Court they had been relocated into the nearby Fifth District.... So, wherever *Shaw*'s notion of constitutionally cognizable injury comes from, it's not a straightforward lineal descendant of *Gomillion*....

[As for relying on precedents involving claims of racial vote dilution, as] an abstract matter, voters in all four boxes might have dilution claims. The modern paradigmatic case involves a claim by minority voters of racial vote dilution. First, suppose that the minority community were large enough to form a majority in a fairly drawn single-member district but that no such district had been drawn. Voters in boxes C and D might jointly sue to force the state to draw a new district, District Y, in which they would form a majority of the electorate. Clearly, if the claim is dilution through cracking, voters in boxes C and D are identically situated and thus have identical claims to standing.

Suppose, instead, that the state created a 100% black District X, leaving an adjoining district only 30% black; by reallocating voters among the two districts, the state could have created two 65% black districts instead. Voters in box C would now not have their votes directly diluted: they are, by hypothesis, in a district that allows the group to which they belong to elect its representative of choice. Still, one might argue that they have suffered a concrete, constitutionally cognizable injury in that the group of which they are members has less "influence on the political process as a whole" than it could have. It elects fewer representatives, and thus has less power within the legislature, than it would under an alternative apportionment. In any event, voters in box D surely suffer a direct and concrete injury: if the lines were redrawn, they would find themselves within a district that gave them the power to elect the candidate of their choice. Under the present system, by contrast, they find themselves in a district where they lack that ability. *Wright v. Rockefeller*, the other voting rights precedent on which *Shaw* relied, illustrates the situation of voters in boxes C and D. *Wright* involved a claim by plaintiffs from both within and outside New York City's overwhelmingly nonwhite Eighteenth District that nonwhites had been deliberately packed into a single congressional district, thereby leaving the adjoining districts between 71% and 95% white.... [B]oth the district court and the Supreme Court apparently assumed that voters in both boxes shared similar claims of injury.

Of course, white voters also have standing to bring vote dilution claims. Voters in boxes A or B could conceivably allege that the state's decision to draw a majority-nonwhite District X diluted their voting strength by denying white voters the ability to elect the candidates of their choice.... But the *Shaw* plaintiffs deliberately declined to claim racial vote dilution, and thus their standing cannot rest on the injury of having "less opportunity than did other residents in the district to participate in the political processes and to elect legislators of their choice."...

[T]he injury that the Court has identified must rest not on the direct, practical consequences of segregation, but on the fact of segregation itself. This is why our colleague Richard Pildes has labeled the *Shaw* injury "expressive...."

Returning to our schematic diagram, which voters have suffered this expressive, noninstrumental injury? The most logical answer is that all of them have. Every citizen who looks at the map, or reflects on the process that produced it, presumably gets the message: the government deliberately ignored the "central mandate" of the equal protection clause, "racial neutrality in governmental decisionmaking." When the government uses race to assign some voters to District X, it tells all voters that race matters.

Even if we try to particularize the injury, there is nothing distinctive about the injury to the voters assigned to District X (boxes A and C). Minority citizens within the challenged district (box C) are victims of the same offensive, demeaning, or reductionist assumptions as white citizens outside the district (box B): the minority citizens were put inside the district because the government assumed they would "think alike, share the same political interests, and ... prefer the same candidates at the polls," and the white citizens were excluded because the government assumed they would not make common cause with their minority neighbors. If voters in box B lack standing - the holding in *Hays* - then it is unclear how voters in box C would possess it; yet the Supreme Court could not deny standing to box C voters and hold that only white voters (box A) could bring a challenge. The only possible distinction between the white voters in box A and the minority voters in box C would be that the former would likely have a representative not of their own race, unlike the latter. Such a rule could not possibly be reconciled with *Shaw*'s adamant conclusion that voting rights law must not presume political identity from the fact of race alone....

More pointedly, most *Shaw* plaintiffs are now located in box A - that is, they are white voters who live in the majority-black or majority-Hispanic district they challenge; whatever injuries this group suffers do not involve any expressly offensive, demeaning, or reductionist assumptions about *them*. They are the "filler people," put inside the district to top off its population in compliance with one-person, one-vote. The government is indifferent to how they vote within that district. Ironically, whatever injury they suffer stems from the government's *failure* to acknowledge the concrete influence of race in the electoral process: only if race matters have they been relegated to a district where their interests will be disregarded.

Id. at 2279-87.

With respect to the nature of *Shaw* standing, consider the opinion of the three-judge court in *Kelley v. Bennett*, 96 F. Supp. 2d 1301 (M.D. Ala. 2000), *rev'd*, 531 U.S. ___ (2000) (per curiam). The plaintiffs lived in several majority-white state legislative districts that were adjacent to deliberately-created majority black legislative districts. The defendants – the state of Alabama and black voters who lived in the adjacent districts and who had been plaintiffs in a prior state-court proceeding that had imposed the challenged plan as part of a consent decree – argued that the plaintiffs lacked standing. A majority of the three-judge court disagreed:

The defendants first argue ... that the plaintiffs lack standing. The reason, according to the defendants, is that the plaintiffs' real goal is to eliminate the majority-minority districts in Alabama, and that the "primary focus" of their case is therefore not on the districts they inhabit (all of which are majority white), but the adjacent majority-black districts. Thus, in applying the analysis of *United States v. Hays*, which controls on the issue of standing, the court must first determine which districts the plaintiffs are really challenging.

The Court in *Hays* was confronted as we are with the issue of what district the plaintiffs were challenging. The *Hays* plaintiffs challenged the entire legislative act that created

Louisiana's congressional districts. Applying any district-limited concept of standing required the Court, therefore, to infer from other indicia in the case -- the evidence presented at trial, for instance, and the district court's fact-findings -- what district at bottom was actually under challenge. The plaintiffs here, by contrast, had the benefit of *Hays*'s district-limited standing rule and were able to particularize their claims by district. We can therefore thank them, and the drafters of the Federal Rules of Civil Procedure, for saving us from floundering in the vagueness of the infinitely manipulable term "primary focus." Instead, we can look to the complaint.... And there, plain as day, the plaintiffs challenge the districts in which they vote. They do not challenge the majority-black districts next door, as the defendants contend. They would perhaps have stronger claims if they did challenge the next-door districts, but that does not mean they must be deemed to challenge those rather than the ones they say they challenge.

That decided, we can turn to the question of whether they have standing to attack their districts of residence under *Hays*'s interpretation of the Case or Controversy Clause. Many trees have perished in the academic pursuit of an understanding of *Hays*'s theories of constitutional harm. See, e.g., Judith Reed, *Sense and Nonsense: Standing in the Racial Districting Cases as a Window on the Supreme Court's View of the Right to Vote*, 4 MICH. J. RACE & L. 389 (1999); Samuel Issacharoff & Pamela S. Karlan, *Standing and Misunderstanding in Voting Rights Law*, 111 HARV. L. REV. 2276 (1998); Melvyn R. Durchslag, *United States v. Hays: An Essay on Standing to Challenge Majority-Minority Districts*, 65 U. CIN. L. REV. 341 (1997); John Hart Ely, Standing to Challenge Pro-Minority Gerrymanders, 111 HARV. L. REV. 576 (1997); Pamela S. Karlan, *Still Hazy After All These Years: Voting Rights in the Post-Shaw Era*, 26 CUMB. L. REV. 287 (1995-96). This academic wisdom suggests that applying *Hays*'s theory of standing in a principled way to our case, which is apparently unique among the *Shaw* cases in that we have white plaintiffs challenging majority-white districts that are next door to engineered minority "safe seats," may be difficult.

But we are charged with applying the law as it is. Consequently, we read *Hays* in its simplest terms, arbitrary as that may seem to academia: a *Shaw* plaintiff can satisfy the first element of Article III standing, injury-in-fact, by showing (1) that he lives in the district he challenges and (2) that the district is "racially gerrymandered." This is indeed how simply the Supreme Court has applied *Hays* in later cases. The second prong, as we read *Hays*, admittedly conflates Article III jurisdiction with the merits, a situation not often encountered. But that is what *Hays* strongly implies when it speaks of the necessity that the plaintiff reside in a "gerrymandered district." The upshot here is that we must dismiss for want of jurisdiction all claims in which the plaintiffs have failed to prove that the district is "racially gerrymandered." That second prong of the *Hays* test, moreover, will have to wait until we finish discussing the merits, below. At the outset, we note simply that all the plaintiffs undisputedly inhabit their challenged district or districts, and that they are therefore halfway there on their standing showing.

The Sinkfield defendants .... point to the two constitutional harms that *Hays* identified -- representational (poor representation because representatives of racially gerrymandered districts will see their constituency monochromatically) and stigmatic (the emotional harm from being racially classified) -- and then argue that none of these plaintiffs has testified to suffering either one of these harms. Thus, for example, they argue that the plaintiff Karen Outlaw's satisfaction with her present state senator defeats any assertion of representational harm, and that the fact that she does not live near a part of the district where borders are racial makes impossible any stigmatic harm.

The Supreme Court has never demanded that a resident of a "gerrymandered district" prove with evidence that either one of these two constitutionally cognizable harms has afflicted him specifically. See *Bush [v. Vera]* ("Plaintiffs Blum and Powers are residents of District 18, plaintiffs Thomas and Vera are residents of District 29, and plaintiff Orcutt is a resident of District 30. We stated in *Hays* that 'where a plaintiff resides in a racially gerrymandered district, . . . the plaintiff has been denied equal treatment because of the legislature's reliance on racial criteria, and therefore has standing to challenge the legislature's action.' . . . . Under this rule, these plaintiffs have standing to challenge Districts 18, 29, and 30."); *Shaw II* ("[A] plaintiff who resides in a district which is the subject of a racial-gerrymander claim has standing to challenge the legislation which created that district, but . . . a plaintiff from outside that district lacks standing absent specific evidence that he personally has been subjected to a racial classification."). The Supreme Court has, moreover, found standing to exist for a Hispanic-surnamed plaintiff challenging a Hispanic-majority district, in which case it would be difficult to conclude (under the defendants' version of the standing rule) that the plaintiff suffered representational harm. The defendants have cited no case that applies *Hays*'s standing rule to require harm to be subjectively felt by the plaintiff. We therefore conclude that in the present state of the law it appears that injury-in-fact is conclusively presumed from the mere fact of residence in a gerrymandered district, independent of the plaintiff's subjective assessment of harm.

Does the majority's opinion reduce *Hays* to simply an exercise in pleading?

In dissent, Judge Thompson argued that the posture of the plaintiffs in *Hays* was 'identical" to that of the *Kelley* plaintiffs:

In both cases, the drawing of new state-wide districting plans led to the creation of new districts whose populations were majority African-American. In both, the evidence demonstrates that the new majority-black districts were drawn primarily to increase representation for the black population in the State.

Indeed, no evidence in either case suggests that the racial composition of the neighboring majority-white districts was of any interest or import to the drafters. Finally, the plaintiffs in both cases live not in the new majority-black districts, but rather in the neighboring districts that are majority white....

[T]hat the primary focus of this litigation is the majority-black districts is revealed by the very words the majority uses to explain and examine the plaintiffs' claims. The majority admits that the majority-black districts are the "targeted districts" of the alleged racial gerrymander, and the plaintiffs' districts are the "next door districts." It admits that the purpose of the state-wide redistricting plan was to create safe majority-black, and not safe majority-white, districts....

Th[e majority's position] boils down to the contention (and a superficially attractive one at that I must admit) that you cannot segregate on one side of the line without segregating on other side--that is, you cannot segregate blacks into majority-black districts without segregating whites into neighboring districts. Or, to put it more figuratively, you cannot separate the goats from the sheep without separating the sheep from the goats as well.

But, for two reasons, this approach to standing in *Shaw* cases is inappropriate in light of *Hays*. First, this approach is not the approach imposed in *Hays*, and, second, *Hays* expressly rejects it. In *Hays*, the Supreme Court sought to draw a legal bright line between those who live in and are challenging the district that is the primary focus or target of the racial gerrymander (and who thus enjoy an injury-in-fact presumption) and all others in the State who do not live in and are not challenging that district (and who thus must demonstrate personal, individualized harm). It is therefore true that "next door districts are not necessarily just leftovers," but rather, for these districts' residents to establish standing, they must present specific evidence of personal harm resulting from the racial gerrymander....

The Supreme Court, in a per curiam opinion, agreed with Judge Thompson and summarily reversed the district court, directing it to dismiss the complaint:

Appellees' position here is essentially indistinguishable from that of the appellees in *Hays*. Appellees are challenging their own majority-white districts as the product of unconstitutional racial gerrymandering under a redistricting plan whose purpose was the creation of majority-minority districts, some of which border appellees' districts. Like the appellees in *Hays*, they have neither alleged nor produced any evidence that any of them was assigned to his or her district as a direct result of having "personally been subjected to a racial classification." Rather, appellees suggest that they are entitled to a presumption of injury-in-fact because the bizarre shapes of their districts reveal that the districts were the product of an unconstitutional racial gerrymander.

The shapes of appellees' districts, however, were necessarily influenced by the shapes of the majority-minority districts upon which they border, and appellees have produced no evidence that anything other than the deliberate creation of those majority-minority districts is responsible for the districting lines of which they complain. Appellees' suggestion thus boils down to the claim that an unconstitutional use of race in drawing the boundaries of majority-minority districts necessarily involves an unconstitutional use of race in drawing the boundaries of neighboring majority-white districts. We rejected that argument in *Hays*, explaining that evidence sufficient to support a *Shaw* claim with respect to a majority-minority district did "not prove anything" with respect to a neighboring majority-white district in which the appellees resided. Accordingly, "an allegation to that effect does not allege a cognizable injury under the Fourteenth Amendment."

Does the Supreme Court's opinion reflect any coherent theory of a plaintiff's injury in a *Shaw* case or has the Court simply chosen a formalistic rule with no real substantive content?

Kelley also illustrates another complex procedural aspect of *Shaw* litigation: the interaction of state and federal courts. Consider the following account of the litigation leading up to the federal court's decision in *Kelley*:

In 1992, two groups of plaintiffs - one black (the "Brooks" plaintiffs), the other Republican (the "Peters" plaintiffs) - brought separate lawsuits in federal district court "challenging, under federal law, the way district lines are currently drawn for the Alabama State Legislature." The cases were consolidated and the federal court stayed the proceedings "on the ground that the Alabama legislative process had not run its course." After the Supreme Court announced its decision in *Growe [v. Emison*, which required federal courts to defer to ongoing state reapportionment proceedings] - and still before the legislature had enacted a plan - the Brooks plaintiffs, along with other black voters, filed a lawsuit in the Montgomery County Circuit Court (the "*Sinkfield*" litigation) in which they challenged the existing state legislative district lines under both federal and state law. In 1993, the state circuit court approved a consent judgment among all the parties in *Sinkfield*. The parties sought preclearance of the proposed plan from the Attorney General because, under *McDaniel v. Sanchez,* court-implemented plans that reflect a "legislative" judgment require pre- clearance.

After the plan was precleared, the circuit court entered a final judgment on August 13, 1993, implementing the plan, but as a matter of course, retaining jurisdiction.

The defendants in *Brooks* and *Peters*, as well as the *Brooks* plaintiffs (who were, after all, virtually identical to the *Sinkfield* plaintiffs), successfully moved to dismiss the two federal cases on the grounds that the federal court should defer to the final judgment of the state circuit court.

Three years later, a disappointed white aspirant for office who lived in one of the majority-black districts filed a new lawsuit in federal court claiming that the *Sinkfield* plan was invalid in light of *Shaw* and *Miller* (the "*Rice*" litigation). The *Sinkfield* plaintiffs intervened as defendants in *Rice* and moved to dismiss the lawsuit on the grounds that the *Rice* plaintiffs should first present their claims to the *Sinkfield* court. The *Rice* court, recognizing that the *Sinkfield* court had retained jurisdiction over the consent decree embodying the apportionment and relying on *Growe* and "principles of federalism, deem[ed] it prudent to defer acting until the plaintiffs first [had] an opportunity to intervene in the state court action." In the event the *Sinkfield* court denied the motion to intervene or declined to act within thirty days, the *Rice* court indicated its willingness to revisit the matter.

In light of the federal court's directive, the *Rice* plaintiffs filed a complaint in intervention in *Sinkfield*. After a three-day trial, the Montgomery County Circuit Court upheld its original plan against the *Rice* plaintiffs' *Shaw* challenge. The Circuit Court described its original plan as "the result of political negotiation and compromise" among the Speaker of the State House of Representatives, several affected state legislators, the Secretary of State, the State Attorney General - all of whom were white - and several black political leaders. The negotiations, it concluded, reflected black citizens' exercise of "their right of free political association under the First, Thirteenth and Fifteenth Amendments, to form and support political organizations who support their political interests so that they have an equal opportunity to elect candidates of their choice." Their successful participation did not trigger strict scrutiny since that would "hold black political negotiators to a different standard"; the districts they drew reflected traditional political criteria.

Pamela S. Karlan, *The Fire Next Time: Reapportionment After the 2000 Census*, 50 Stan. L. Rev. 731, 760-62 (1998). On appeal, the Alabama Supreme Court dismissed the *Rice* plaintiffs' appeal as moot, because there were no more scheduled elections before the next reapportionment, *Rice v. Sinkfield*, 732 So, 2d 993 (1998). At that point, the *Rice* plaintiffs returned to federal court, where several other voters, represented by the same counsel, intervened as plaintiffs to challenge the districts in which they lived. The federal court held that plaintiffs' claims against the districts in which the Rices lived were now precluded, but because the Rices lacked standing under *Hays* to challenge districts in which they did not live, it then entertained the remaining plaintiffs' claims and struck down a number of the districts. Because the Supreme Court disposed of the case solely on the question of standing, it did not reach the contentions raised by the black voters and the state defendants about the proper relationship between federal and state court judgments.

On page 611, add the following new material after note 15:

16a. The tortuous history of North Carolina's post 1990-reapportionment, which as this supplement went to press is back before the United States Supreme Court for the fourth time (including the summary affirmance on the claim of political gerrymandering, in *Pope v. Blue*, 506 U.S. 801 (1992)), illustrates several of the theoretical, practical, and doctrinal difficulties with the Court's approach.

Hunt v. Cromartie
526 U.S. 541 (1999)

JUSTICE THOMAS delivered the Opinion of the Court.

In this appeal, we must decide whether appellees were entitled to summary judgment on their claim that North Carolina's Twelfth Congressional District, as established by the State's 1997 congressional redistricting plan, constituted an unconstitutional racial gerrymander in violation of the Equal Protection Clause of the Fourteenth Amendment.

I

This is the third time in six years that litigation over North Carolina's Twelfth Congressional District has come before this Court. The first time around, we held that plaintiffs whose complaint alleged that the State had deliberately segregated voters into districts on the basis of race without compelling justification stated a claim for relief under the Equal Protection Clause of the Fourteenth Amendment. *Shaw v. Reno*, 509 U.S. 630 (1993) (*Shaw I*). After remand, we affirmed the District Court's finding that North Carolina's District 12 classified voters by race and further held that the State's reapportionment scheme was not narrowly tailored to serve a compelling interest. *Shaw v. Hunt*, 517 U.S. 899 (1996) (*Shaw II*).

In response to our decision in *Shaw II*, the State enacted a new districting plan. See 1997 N. C. Sess. Laws, ch. 11. A map of the unconstitutional District 12 was set forth in the Appendix to the opinion of the Court in *Shaw I*, and we described it as follows:

> "The second majority-black district, District 12, is . . . unusually shaped. It is approximately 160 miles long and, for much of its length, no wider than the [Interstate]-85 corridor. It winds in snakelike fashion through tobacco country, financial centers, and manufacturing areas 'until it gobbles in enough enclaves of black neighborhoods.' Northbound and southbound drivers on [Interstate]-85 sometimes find themselves in separate districts in one county, only to 'trade' districts when they enter the next county. Of the 10 counties through which District 12 passes, 5 are cut into 3 different districts; even towns are divided. At one point the district remains contiguous only because it intersects at a single point with two other districts before crossing over them."

The State's 1997 plan altered District 12 in several respects. By any measure, blacks no longer constitute a majority of District 12: blacks now account for approximately 47% of the district's total population, 43% of its voting age population, and 46% of registered voters. The new District 12 splits 6 counties as opposed to 10; beginning with Guilford County, the district runs in a southwestern direction through parts of Forsyth, Davidson, Rowan, Iredell, and Mecklenburg Counties, picking up concentrations of urban populations in Greensboro and High Point (both in Guilford), Winston-Salem (Forsyth), and Charlotte (Mecklenburg). (The old District 12 went through the same six counties but also included portions of Durham, Orange, and Alamance Counties east of Guilford, and parts of Gaston County west of Mecklenburg.) With these changes, the district retains only 41.6% of its previous area, and the distance between its farthest points has been reduced to approximately 95 miles. But while District 12 is wider and shorter than it was before, it retains its basic "snakelike" shape and continues to track Interstate-85.

Appellees believed the new District 12, like the old one, to be the product of an unconstitutional racial gerrymander. They filed suit in the United States District Court for the Eastern District of North Carolina against several state officials in their official capacities seeking to enjoin elections under the State's 1997 plan. The parties filed competing motions for summary judgment and supporting materials, and the three-judge District Court heard argument on the pending motions, but before either party had conducted discovery and without an evidentiary hearing. Over one judge's dissent, the District Court granted appellees' motion and entered the injunction they sought. The majority of the Court explained that "the uncontroverted material facts" showed that "District 12 was drawn to collect precincts with high racial identification rather than political identification," that "more heavily Democratic precincts . . . were bypassed in the drawing of District 12 and included in the surrounding congressional districts," and that "the legislature disregarded traditional districting criteria." From these "uncontroverted material facts," the District Court concluded "the General Assembly, in redistricting, used criteria with respect to District 12 that are facially race driven," and thereby violated the Equal Protection Clause of the Fourteenth Amendment. (Apparently because the issue was not litigated, the District Court did not consider whether District 12 was narrowly tailored to serve a compelling interest.)....

II

Our decisions have established that all laws that classify citizens on the basis of race, including racially gerrymandered districting schemes, are constitutionally suspect and must be strictly scrutinized. When racial classifications are explicit, no inquiry into legislative purpose is necessary. A facially neutral law, on the other hand, warrants strict scrutiny only if it can be proved that the law was "motivated by a racial purpose or object," *Miller [v. Johnson]*, or if it is "'unexplainable on grounds other than race,'" *Shaw I....* The task of assessing a jurisdiction's motivation, however, is not a simple matter; on the contrary, it is an inherently complex endeavor, one requiring the trial court to perform a "sensitive inquiry into such circumstantial and direct evidence of intent as may be available."

Districting legislation ordinarily, if not always, classifies tracts of land, precincts, or census blocks, and is race-neutral on its face. North Carolina's 1997 plan was not atypical; appellees, therefore, were required to prove that District 12 was drawn with an impermissible racial motive -- in this context, strict scrutiny applies if race was the "predominant factor" motivating the legislature's districting decision. To carry their burden, appellees were obliged to show -- using direct or circumstantial evidence, or a combination of both -- that "the legislature subordinated traditional race-neutral districting principles, including but not limited to compactness, contiguity, and respect for political subdivisions or communities defined by actual shared interests, to racial considerations."

Appellees offered only circumstantial evidence in support of their claim. Their evidence included maps of District 12, showing its size, shape,[1] and alleged lack of continuity. They also submitted evidence of the district's low scores with respect to traditional measures of compactness and expert affidavit testimony explaining that this statistical evidence proved the State had ignored traditional districting criteria in crafting the new Twelfth District. Appellees further claimed that the State had disrespected political subdivisions and communities of interest. In support, they pointed out that under the 1997 plan, District 12 was the only one statewide to contain no undivided county and offered figures showing that District 12 gathered almost 75% of its population from Mecklenburg County, at the southern tip of the district, and from Forsyth and Guilford Counties at the northernmost part of the district.

Appellees also presented statistical and demographic evidence with respect to the precincts that were included within District 12 and those that were placed in neighboring districts. For the six subdivided counties included within District 12, the proportion of black residents was higher in the portion of the county within District 12 than the portion of the county in a neighboring district.[2] Other maps and

---

[1] JUSTICE STEVENS asserts that proof of a district's "bizarre configuration" gives rise equally to an inference that its architects were motivated by politics or race. We do not necessarily quarrel with the proposition that a district's unusual shape can give rise to an inference of political motivation. But we doubt that a bizarre shape equally supports a political inference and a racial one. Some districts, we have said, are "so highly irregular that [they] rationally cannot be understood as anything other than an effort to 'segregate . . . voters' on the basis of race.' *Shaw I* (quoting *Gomillion v. Lightfoot*, 364 U.S. 339 (1960)).

[2] In the portion of Guilford County in District 12, black residents constituted 51.5% of the population, while in the District 6 portion, only 10.2% of the population was black. Appellees' evidence as to the other counties showed: Forsyth District 12 was 72.9% black while

supporting data submitted by appellees compared the demographics of several so-called "boundary segments."[3] This evidence tended to show that, in several instances, the State had excluded precincts that had a lower percentage of black population but were as Democratic (in terms of registered voters) as the precinct inside District 12.

Viewed in toto, appellees' evidence tends to support an inference that the State drew its district lines with an impermissible racial motive -- even though they presented no direct evidence of intent. Summary judgment, however, is appropriate only where there is no genuine issue of material fact and the moving party is entitled to judgment as a matter of law. To be sure, appellants did not contest the evidence of District 12's shape (which hardly could be contested), nor did they claim that appellees' statistical and demographic evidence, most if not all of which appears to have been obtained from the State's own data banks, was untrue.

The District Court nevertheless was only partially correct in stating that the material facts before it were uncontroverted. The legislature's motivation is itself a factual question. See *Shaw II*; *Miller*. Appellants asserted that the General Assembly drew its district lines with the intent to make District 12 a strong Democratic district. In support, they presented the after-the-fact affidavit testimony of the two members of the General Assembly responsible for developing the State's 1997 plan. Those legislators further stated that, in crafting their districting law, they attempted to protect incumbents, to adhere to traditional districting criteria, and to preserve the existing partisan balance in the State's congressional delegation, which in 1997 was composed of six Republicans and six Democrats.

More important, we think, was the affidavit of an expert, Dr. David W. Peterson. He reviewed racial demographics, party registration, and election result data (the number of people voting for Democratic candidates) gleaned from the State's 1998 Court of Appeals election, 1998 Lieutenant Governor election, and 1990 United States Senate election for the precincts included within District 12 and those surrounding it. Unlike appellees' evidence, which highlighted select boundary segments, appellants' expert examined the district's entire border -- all 234 boundary segments. He recognized "a strong correlation between racial composition and party preference" so that "in precincts with high black representation, there is a correspondingly high tendency for voters to favor the Democratic Party" but that "in precincts with low

_____

Forsyth District 5 was 11.1% black; Davidson District 12 was 14.8% black while Davidson District 6 was 4.1% black; Rowan District 12 was 35.6% black and Rowan District 6 was 7.7% black; Iredell District 12 was 24.3% black while Iredell District 10 was 10.1% black; Mecklenburg District 12 was 51.9% black but Mecklenburg District 9 was only 7.2% black.

[3] Boundary segments, we are told, are those sections along the district's perimeter that separate outside precincts from inside precincts. In other words, the boundary segment is the district borderline itself; for each segment, the relevant comparison is between the inside precinct that touches the segment and the corresponding outside precinct.

black representation, there is much more variation in party preference, and the fraction of registered voters favoring Democrats is substantially lower." Because of this significant correlation, the data tended to support both a political and racial hypothesis. Therefore, Peterson focused on "divergent boundary segments," those where blacks were greater inside District 12 but Democrats were greater outside and those where blacks were greater outside the district but Democrats were greater inside. He concluded that the State included the more heavily Democratic precinct much more often than the more heavily black precinct, and therefore, that the data as a whole supported a political explanation at least as well as, and somewhat better than, a racial explanation. ("There is at least one other explanation that fits the data as well as or better than race, and that explanation is political identification").

Peterson's analysis of District 12's divergent boundary segments and his affidavit testimony that District 12 displays a high correlation between race and partisanship support an inference that the General Assembly did no more than create a district of strong partisan Democrats. His affidavit is also significant in that it weakens the probative value of appellees' boundary segment evidence, which the District Court appeared to give significant weight. Appellees' evidence was limited to a few select precincts, whereas Peterson analyzed all 234 boundary segments. Moreover, appellees' maps reported only party registration figures. Peterson again was more thorough, looking also atactual voting results. Peterson's more complete analysis was significant because it showed that in North Carolina, party registration and party preference do not always correspond.

Accepting appellants' political motivation explanation as true, as the District Court was required to do in ruling on appellees' motion for summary judgment, appellees were not entitled to judgment as a matter of law. Our prior decisions have made clear that a jurisdiction may engage in constitutional political gerrymandering, even if it so happens that the most loyal Democrats happen to be black Democrats and even if the State were conscious of that fact. *See Bush v. Vera*, 517 U.S. 952 (1996); *Shaw II; Miller; Shaw I.*[4] Evidence that blacks constitute even a supermajority in one congressional district while amounting to less than a plurality in a neighboring district will not, by itself, suffice to prove that a jurisdiction was motivated by race in drawing its district lines when the evidence also shows a high correlation between race and party preference.

Of course, neither appellees nor the District Court relied exclusively on appellees' boundary segment evidence, and appellees submitted other evidence tending to show that the General Assembly

---

[4]   This Court has recognized, however, that political gerrymandering claims are justiciable under the Equal Protection Clause although we were not in agreement as to the standards that would govern such a claim. See *Davis v. Bandemer*, 478 U.S. 109 (1986).

was motivated by racial considerations in drawing District 12 -- most notably, District 12's shape and its lack of compactness. But in ruling on a motion for summary judgment, the nonmoving party's evidence "is to be believed, and all justifiable inferences are to be drawn in [that party's] favor." While appellees' evidence might allow the District Court to find that the State acted with an impermissible racial motivation, despite the State's explanation as supported by the Peterson affidavit, it does not require that the court do so. All that can be said on the record before us is that motivation was in dispute. Reasonable inferences from the undisputed facts can be drawn in favor of a racial motivation finding or in favor of a political motivation finding. The District Court nevertheless concluded that race was the "predominant factor" in the drawing of the district. In doing so, it either credited appellees' asserted inferences over those advanced and supported by appellants or did not give appellants the inference they were due. In any event, it was error in this case for the District Court to resolve the disputed fact of motivation at the summary judgment stage.

Outright admissions of impermissible racial motivation are infrequent and plaintiffs often must rely upon other evidence. Summary judgment in favor of the party with the burden of persuasion, however, is inappropriate when the evidence is susceptible of different interpretations or inferences by the trier of fact.[5] That is not to say that summary judgment in a plaintiff's favor will never be appropriate in a racial gerrymandering case sought to be proved exclusively by circumstantial evidence. We can imagine an instance where the uncontroverted evidence and the reasonable inferences to be drawn in the nonmoving party's favor would not be "significantly probative" so as to create a genuine issue of fact for trial. But this is not that case. And even if the question whether appellants had created a material dispute of fact was a close one, we think that "the sensitive nature of redistricting and the presumption of good faith that must be accorded legislative enactments," would tip the balance in favor of the District Court making findings of fact.... "Courts must also recognize . . . the intrusive potential of judicial intervention into the legislative realm, when assessing . . . the adequacy of a plaintiff's showing at the various stages of litigation and determining whether to permit discovery or trial to proceed."

In reaching our decision, we are fully aware that the District Court is more familiar with the evidence than this Court, and is likewise better suited to assess the General Assembly's motivations. Perhaps, after trial, the evidence will support a finding that race was the State's predominant motive, but we express no position as to that question. We

---

5

Just as summary judgment is rarely granted in a plaintiff's favor in cases where the issue is a defendant's racial motivation, such as disparate treatment suits under Title VII or racial discrimination claims under 42 U.S.C. § 1981, the same holds true for racial gerrymandering claims of the sort brought here.

decide only that this case was not suited for summary disposition. The judgment of the District Court is reversed.

JUSTICE STEVENS, with whom JUSTICE SOUTER, JUSTICE GINSBURG and JUSTICE BREYER join, concurring in the judgment.

The disputed issue of fact in this case is whether political considerations or racial considerations provide the "primary" explanation for the seemingly irregular configuration of North Carolina's Twelfth Congressional District. The Court concludes that evidence submitted to the District Court on behalf of the State made it inappropriate for that Court to grant appellees' motion for summary judgment. I agree with that conclusion, but write separately to emphasize the importance of two undisputed matters of fact that are firmly established by the historical record and confirmed by the record in this case.

First, bizarre configuration is the traditional hallmark of the political gerrymander. This obvious proposition is supported by the work product of Elbridge Gerry, by the "swan" designed by New Jersey Republicans in 1982, see *Karcher v. Daggett*, 462 U.S. 725 (1983), and by the Indiana plan reviewed in *Davis v. Bandemer*, 478 U.S. 109 (1986). As we learned in *Gomillion v. Lightfoot*, 364 U.S. 339 (1960), a racial gerrymander may have an equally "uncouth" shape. Thus, the shape of the congressional district at issue in this case provides strong evidence that either political or racial factors motivated its architects, but sheds no light on the question of which set of factors was more responsible for subordinating any of the State's "traditional" districting principles.

Second, as the Presidential campaigns conducted by Strom Thurmond in 1948 and by George Wallace in 1968, and the Senate campaigns conducted more recently by Jesse Helms, have demonstrated, a great many registered Democrats in the South do not always vote for Democratic candidates in federal elections. The Congressional Quarterly recently recorded the fact that in North Carolina "Democratic voter registration edges . . . no longer translate into success in statewide or national races. In recent years, conservative white Democrats have gravitated toward Republican candidates."[6] This voting pattern has

---

[6]

The Congressional Quarterly's publication, which is largely seen as the authoritative source regarding the political and demographic makeup of the congressional districts resulting from each decennial census, is even more revealing when one examines its district-by-district analysis of North Carolina's partisan voting patterns. With regard to the original First District, which was just over 50 percent black, the book remarks: "The white voters of the 1st claim the Democratic roots of their forefathers, but often support GOP candidates at the state and national level. A fair number are 'Jessecrats,' conservative Democratic supporters of GOP Sen. Jesse Helms." The book shows that while the Second and Third Districts have "significant Democratic voter registration edges," Republican candidates actually won substantial victories in four of five recent elections. Statistics also demonstrate that a majority of voters in the Eleventh District consistently vote for Republicans "despite a wide Democratic registration advantage."....

proven to be particularly pronounced in voting districts that contain more than about one-third African-American residents. There was no need for expert testimony to establish the proposition that "in North Carolina, party registration and party preference do not always correspond."

Indeed, for me the most remarkable feature of the District Court's erroneous decision is that it relied entirely on data concerning the location of registered Democrats and ignored the more probative evidence of how the people who live near the borders of District 12 actually voted in recent elections. That evidence not only undermines and rebuts the inferences the District Court drew from the party registration data, but also provides strong affirmative evidence that is thoroughly consistent with the sworn testimony of the two members of the state legislature who were most active in drawing the boundaries of District 12. The affidavits of those members, stating that district lines were drawn according to election results, not voter registration, are uncontradicted. And almost all of the majority-Democrat registered precincts that the state legislature excluded from District 12 in favor of precincts with higher black populations produced significantly less dependable Democratic results and actually voted for one or more Republicans in recent elections.

The record supports the conclusion that the most loyal Democrats living near the borders of District 12 "happen to be black Democrats," and I have no doubt that the legislature was conscious of that fact when it enacted this apportionment plan. But everyone agrees that that fact is not sufficient to invalidate the district. That fact would not even be enough, under this Court's decisions, to invalidate a governmental action, that, unlike the action at issue here, actually has an adverse impact on a particular racial group. See, e.g., *Personnel Administrator of Mass. v. Feeney*, 442 U.S. 256, 279 (1979) (holding that the Equal Protection Clause is implicated only when "a state legislature selected or reaffirmed a particular course of action at least in part 'because of,' not merely 'in spite of,' its adverse effects upon an identifiable group")
....

Accordingly, appellees' evidence may include nothing more than (i) a bizarre shape, which is equally consistent with either political or racial motivation, (ii) registration data, which are virtually irrelevant when actual voting results were available and which point in a different direction, and (iii) knowledge of the racial composition of the district. Because we do not have before us the question whether the District Court erred in denying the State's motion for summary judgment, I need not decide whether that circumstantial evidence even raises an inference of improper motive. It is sufficient at this stage of the proceedings to join in the Court's judgment of reversal, which I do.

NOTES AND QUESTIONS

1. On remand, the district court allowed additional discovery, held a trial, and reached essentially the same conclusion with regard to the Twelfth Congressional District. Note that although it found that race was also the predominant motivation in the creation of the First Congressional District, it upheld that district as necessary to achieve the state's compelling interest in complying with section 2 of the Voting Rights Act. Cf. King v. State Board of Elections, 979 F. Supp. 619 (N.D. Ill. 1997) (finding that Illinois' majority-Hispanic Fourth Congressional District survived strict scrutiny because it was necessary to create a majority-Hispanic district for the state to avoid § 2 liability), aff'd, 522 U.S. 1087 (1998). Consider whether the district court's explanation for the difference between the First and the Twelfth Districts is coherent. Does district shape turn out to be the critical factor, after all, in triggering *Shaw*'s constitutional constraints?

2. Consider also the role that the previously existing, invalidated districts play in the court's analysis. This issue may assume great significance in the post-2000 reapportionment. If a plan has *not* been invalidated under *Shaw*, then it serves as the existing benchmark for section 5 purposes in a covered jurisdiction. Moreover, if the legislature then draws new districts that are designed to preserve the incumbents' advantage, does this vitiate any excessive race-consciousness in the predecessor district's creation? Is the primary motive now political rather than racial?

3. As this supplement went to press, the Supreme Court was about to hear oral argument on an appeal from the decision reprinted below.

Hunt v. Cromartie
unreported district court decision, Mar. 7, 2000 (E.D.N.C.) (three-judge court)

BOYLE, Chief District Judge:

This matter is before the Court on remand from the United States Supreme Court's order holding that the underlying case was not suited for summary disposition and ordering this Court to conduct further proceedings. *Hunt v. Cromartie*, 526 U.S. 541 (1999)....

BACKGROUND

In *Shaw II* the United States Supreme Court held that the Twelfth Congressional District created by the 1992 Congressional Redistricting Plan (hereinafter, the" 1992 Plan") was race based and could not survive the required "strict scrutiny." The five plaintiffs in *Shaw* lacked standing to attack the other majority-minority district (the First Congressional District under the 1992 Plan) because they were not registered voters in the district.

Soon after the Supreme Court ruled in *Shaw II*, three residents of Tarboro, North Carolina, filed the original Complaint in this action on July 3, 1996. These original Plaintiffs resided in the First Congressional

District (alternatively, "District 1") as it existed under North Carolina's 1992 Plan. The Plaintiffs charged that the First Congressional District violated their rights to equal protection under the United States Constitution because race predominated in the drawing of the District. The action was stayed pending resolution of remand proceedings in *Shaw v. Hunt*, and on July 9, 1996, the same three Tarboro residents joined the Plaintiffs in *Shaw* in filing an Amended Complaint in that case, similarly challenging District 1.

By Order dated September 12, 1997, the three-judge panel in *Shaw* approved a congressional redistricting plan enacted on March 31, 1997, by the General Assembly as a remedy for the constitutional violation found by the Supreme Court to exist in the Twelfth Congressional District (alternatively, "District 12"). The *Shaw* three-judge panel also dismissed without prejudice, as moot, the plaintiffs' claim that the First Congressional District in the 1992 Plan was unconstitutional. Although it was a final order, the September 12, 1997, decision of the *Shaw* three-judge panel was not preclusive of the instant cause of action, as the panel was not presented with a continuing challenge to the redistricting plan.

On October 17, 1997, ... two of the original three Plaintiffs [in this case], along with four residents of District 12, filed an amended Complaint challenging the 1997 remedial congressional redistricting plan (the "1997 Plan"), and seeking a declaration that the First and Twelfth Congressional Districts in the 1997 Plan are unconstitutional racial gerrymanders.

* * *

In compliance with the Supreme Court's decision, a three day bench trial was held in this matter, from November 29 to December 1, 1999. Plaintiffs called eight witnesses. Plaintiffs' first witness was Senator Hamilton Horton, a resident of Forsyth County and longtime member of the North Carolina General Assembly. Senator Horton testified as to his belief that Forsyth County and Winston-Salem were split along racial lines in the 1997 Plan and that District 12 was created with a predominantly racial motive.

Plaintiffs' second witness was Representative Steve Wood, a resident of High Point, North Carolina. Representative Wood testified that in 1997 he served in the North Carolina General Assembly in a leadership position. Representative Wood ran for Congress in the Twelfth District under the 1998 Plan and is convinced that the 1997 Plan divided High Point and Guilford County along racial lines for a predominantly racial motive.

As their third witness, Plaintiffs called Representative John Weatherly of King's Mountain, North Carolina, a member of the North Carolina General assembly during the consideration of the 1997 and

1998 redistricting plans who had previously served on a commission considering the State's legislative process. Representative Weatherly testified that he introduced legislation to facilitate the redistricting process through the use of a redistricting commission and that, on the basis of his political and legislative experience, he believed that both Districts 1 and 12 were drawn with a predominantly racial motive.

Plaintiffs' fourth witness was R.O. Everett, a longtime resident of Salisbury, North Carolina who has been active in politics and has run for the state legislature. Mr. Everett testified that he was familiar with the congressional districts in the Salisbury and Rowan County areas and is convinced that District 12 was drawn with a predominantly racial motive.

Plaintiffs' fifth witness was J.H. Froelich Jr., a lifetime resident of High Point, NC who testified that he has been active in state and local politics and believes that Guilford County was divided with a predominantly racial motive in both the 1992 and 1997 Plans and that the 1997 Plan's District 12 was drawn with a predominantly racial motive.

Plaintiffs' sixth witness was Neil Williams, a resident of Charlotte who served on its city council, is familiar with the Mecklenburg County precincts, and ran for Congress in the 1992 Plan's District 9. Mr. Williams testified that he is convinced that Mecklenburg County was divided along racial lines with a predominant racial motive and that the 1997 Plan's District 12 was drawn with a predominantly racial motive.

Plaintiffs' seventh witness was Don Frey of the North Carolina General Assembly's Information Systems Division, who presented statistical data from the General Assembly's database, including relative numbers of persons moved from the 1992 Plan to the 1997 Plan, and current precincts split by the 1997 Plan.

Plaintiffs' eighth and final witness, whose testimony carried over into the second day of trial, was Dr. Ronald Weber of the University of Wisconsin. Dr. Weber testified as an expert political scientist who has studied, consulted on, and testified in many redistricting cases. Referring to maps and other data, Dr. Weber testified that race predominated in the construction of Districts 1 and 12 under the 1997 Plan, and that cities, counties and precincts were divided along racial lines. Dr Weber concluded that no motivation other than race could adequately explain the legislature's decisions to include, exclude, or split certain precincts....

Defendants' first witness was Senator Roy Asberry Cooper, III, who testified as to the legislative history and enactment of the 1997 Plan in the North Carolina Senate, focusing on the creation of Districts 1 and 12. Senator Cooper testified that he was unsure whether he could get the

1997 Plan pre-cleared by the Justice Department without creating a majority-minority First District. Senator Cooper's testimony also brought to light a February 10, 1997 e-mail message (the "Cohen-Cooper Email") sent to him by Director of Bill Drafting Gerry Cohen, a state employee charged with the technical aspect of drawing the districts in 1991, 1992, and 1997 Plans. The Cohen-Cooper Email stated, in part, that "By shifting areas in Beaufort, Pitt, Craven and Jones Counties, I was able to boost the minority percentage in the first district from 48.1% to 49.25%. The district was only plurality white, as the white percentage was 49.67%." The email continues, "This was all the district could be improved by switching between the 1st and 3rd unless I went into Pasquotank, Perquimans, or Camden. I was able to make the district plurality black by switching precincts between the 1st and 4th ..." The Cohen-Cooper e-mail also states that "I [Cohen] have moved Greensboro Black community into the 12th, and now need to take bout [sic] 60,000 out of the 12th, I await your direction on this."

The Senator stated that he did not remember receiving the Cohen-Cooper e-mail and denied having given Cohen "specific instructions."

Additionally, Senator Cooper was questioned about a statement he made to the March 25, 1997 meeting of the House congressional redistricting committee, in which he argued that the 1997 Plan "provides for a fair geographical, racial and partisan balance throughout the state of North Carolina." The Senator claimed that the term "partisan balance" referred to maintaining the six-six Democrat-Republican split in the congressional delegation, but denied that the term "racial balance" would refer to maintaining the ten-two balance between whites and African Americans. Senator Cooper admitted that race was "one of the factors that was considered" in drafting the 1997 Plan, and but denied that it was the predominant factor.

Defendants began the third day of trial with their second witness, Representative W. Edwin McMahan, who testified as to the legislative history and enactment of the 1997 Plan in the North Carolina House of Representatives, especially the creation of Districts 1 and 12. Representative McMahan claimed that race was not the predominant factor in the creation of those districts.

Defendants' third witness was Dr. David Peterson of the University of North Carolina at Chapel Hill's Department of Geography and Sciences. Dr. Peterson presented a statistical analysis of data regarding the question whether race predominated over party affiliation in the construction of the 1997 Plan's District 12. Dr. Peterson also discussed the variance between Democratic registration and voting behavior, and analyzed Dr. Weber's reasoning on the predominance of race as a factor in the creation of District 12. In contrast to Dr. Weber, Dr. Peterson's conclusion was that political considerations, rather than race, might possibly account for the legislature's decisions to include, exclude, or split certain precincts.

Defendants' final witness was Gerry Cohen, Director of Bill Drafting for the North Carolina General Assembly. Mr. Cohen testified as to the legislative history and enactment of the 1997 Plan, especially with regard to Districts 1 and 12, as well as the technical aspects of redistricting, including the computer systems used.

FACTS

* * *

I. The Twelfth Congressional District

District 12 is one of the six predominantly Democratic districts established by the 1997 Plan to maintain the 6-6 partisan division in North Carolina's congressional delegation. District 12 is not a majority-minority district, but 46.67 percent of its total population is African-American. District 12 is composed of six counties, all of them split in the 1997 Plan. The racial composition of the parts of the six subdivided counties assigned to District 12 include three with parts over 50 percent African-American, and three in which the African-American percentage is under 50 percent. However, almost 75 percent of the total population in District 12 comes from the three county parts which are majority African-American in population: Mecklenburg, Forsyth, and Guilford counties. The other three county parts (Davidson, Iredell, and Rowan) have narrow corridors which pick up as many African Americans as are needed for the district to reach its ideal size.

Where Forsyth County was split, 72.9 percent of the total population of Forsyth County allocated to District 12 is African-American, while only 11.1 percent of its total population assigned to neighboring District 5 is African-American. Similarly, Mecklenburg County is split so 51.9 percent of its total population allocated to District 12 is African-American, while only 7.2 percent of the total population assigned to adjoining District 9 is African-American.

A similar pattern emerges when analyzing the cities and towns split between District 12 and its surrounding districts ....

An analysis of the voting precincts immediately surrounding District 12 reveals that the legislature did not simply create a majority Democratic district amidst surrounding Republican precincts. For example, around the Southwest edge of District 12 (in Mecklenburg County), the legislature included within the district's borders several precincts with racial compositions of 40 to 100 percent African-American, while excluding from the district voting precincts with less than 35 percent African-American population, but heavily Democratic voting registrations....

On the North Carolina map, District 12 has an irregular shape and is barely contiguous in parts....

Objective, numerical studies of the compactness of congressional districts are also available. In his report, "An Evaluation of North Carolina's 1998 Congressional Districts," Professor Gerald R. Webster, one of the Defendants' expert witnesses, presents statistical analyses of "comparator compactness indicators" for North Carolina's congressional districts under the 1997 Plan. In measuring the districts' dispersion compactness[7] and perimeter compactness,[8] Professor Webster offers two of the "most commonly recognized and applied" compactness indicators. (citing Pildes & Niemi, Expressive Harms, "Bizarre Districts," and Voting Rights: Evaluating Election-District Appearances After Shaw v. Reno, 92 MICH. L. REV. 483, 571-573, 6 (1993) (hereinafter, "Pildes & Niemi").

In discussing the relative normalcy of various compactness measures, Pildes and Niemi suggest that a "low" dispersion compactness measure would be equal to or less than 0.15. They suggest that a "low" perimeter compactness measure is equal to or less than 0.05. North Carolina's Twelfth Congressional District under the 1997 Plan has a dispersion compactness indicator of 0.109 and a perimeter compactness indicator of 0.041. These figures are much lower than the mean compactness indicators for North Carolina's twelve congressional districts under the 1997 Plan. The average dispersion compactness indicator for the State is 0.354, and the average perimeter compactness indicator is 0.192. The next lowest dispersion compactness indicator after District 12 is the 0.206 in the Fifth Congressional District, and the next lowest perimeter compactness indicator is the First Congressional District's 0.107.

Thus, it is clear that even after the changes detailed above, the primary characteristic of the Twelfth District is its "racial archipelago," stretching, bending and weaving to pick up predominantly African-American regions while avoiding many closer and more obvious regions of high Democratic registration, but low African-American population.

II.   *The First Congressional District*

District 1 is another predominantly Democratic district established by the 1997 Plan. Unlike District 12, it is a majority-

---

[7]

"Dispersion compactness" measures the geographic "dispersion" of a district. To calculate this a circle is circumscribed around a district. The reported coefficient is the proportion of the area of the circumscribed circle which is also included in the district. This measure ranges from 1.0 (most compact) to 0.0 (least compact).

[8]

"Perimeter compactness" is based upon the calculation of the district's perimeter. The reported coefficient is the proportion of the area in the district relative to a circle with the same perimeter. This measure ranges from 1.0 (most compact) to 0.0 (least compact)....

minority district, based on percentages of the total population of the District[6] as 50.27 percent of its total population is African-American. District 1 is composed of ten of the 22 counties split in drawing the statewide 12 district 1997 Plan. Half of the twenty counties represented in District 1 are split. Of the ten sub-divided counties assigned to District 1, four have parts with over 50 percent African-American population, four others have parts with over 40 percent African-American population, and two others have parts with over 30 percent African-American population.

In each of the ten counties that are split between District 1 and an adjacent district, the percent of the population that is African-American is higher inside the district than it is outside the district, but within the same county. The disparities are less significant than in the county splits involving District 12....

Similarly, nine of the 13 cities and towns split between District 1 and its neighboring districts are split along racial lines....

Viewed on the North Carolina map. District 1 is not as irregular as District 12.... It is shaped roughly like the state of Florida, although the protrusion to the South from its "panhandle" is only approximately 150 miles long (to Goldsboro, Wayne County, with two irregularities jutting into Jones, Craven, and Beaufort Counties. These irregularities surround the peninsular extension of the Third Congressional District from the East, allowing the incumbent from the previous Third Congressional District to retain his residence within the boundaries of the same district, and avoiding placing two incumbents in District 1.

The "comparator compactness indicators" from District 1 are much closer to the North Carolina mean compactness indicators than are those from District 12. For example, District I has a dispersion compactness indicator of 0.317 and a perimeter compactness indicator of 0.107. This dispersion compactness indicator is not significantly lower than the State's mean indicator of 0.354, and is higher than the dispersion compactness indicators of Districts 12 (0.109), 9 (0.292), and 5 (0.206). It may be noted that Districts 5 and 9 are next to, and necessarily shaped by, District 12. District 1 has a perimeter compactness indicator of 0.107, which is lower than North Carolina's mean perimeter compactness indicator (0.192), but much higher than Pildes and Niemi's suggested "low" perimeter compactness indicator (0.05). District 1's perimeter compactness indicator is also much higher than that of District 12 (0.041).

DISCUSSION

* * * * *

II.   The Twelfth Congressional District

* * * * *

In *Shaw I*, the Supreme Court described the 1992 Plan's District 12 as "unusually shaped ... approximately 160 miles long and, for much of its length, no wider than the [Interstate] 85 corridor. It winds in snake-like fashion through tobacco country, financial centers, and manufacturing areas until it gobbles in enough enclaves of black neighborhoods." The 1997 Plan's District 12 is similar: it is "unusually shaped," it is "snake-like," and it "gobbles in" African-American population centers. The evidence establishes that although its length has been shortened by approximately 65 miles, it still winds from Charlotte to Greensboro along the Interstate-85 corridor, detouring to envelop heavily African-American portions of cities such as Statesville, Salisbury, and Winston-Salem. It also connects communities not joined in a congressional district, other than in the unconstitutional 1992 Plan, since the whole of Western North Carolina was one district, nearly two hundred years ago.

As discussed above, where cities and counties are split between the Twelfth District and neighboring districts, the splits invariably occur along racial, rather than political, lines the parts of the divided cities and counties having a higher proportion of African-Americans are always included in the Twelfth. Defendants argue that the Twelfth was drawn not with race, but rather politics and partisanship in mind. They have described the District as a "Democratic island in a Republican sea," and presented expert evidence that political identification was the predominant factor determining the border of District 12. As the uncontroverted evidence demonstrates, however, the legislators excluded many heavily Democratic precincts from District 12, even when those precincts immediately border the Twelfth and would have established a far more compact district. The only clear thread woven throughout the districting process is that the border of the Twelfth district meanders to include nearly all of the precincts with African-American population proportions of over forty percent which lie between Charlotte and Greensboro, inclusive....

Additionally, Plaintiffs' expert, Dr. Weber, showed time and again how race trumped party affiliation in the construction of the 12th District and how political explanations utterly failed to explain the composition of the district. Of particular note is Dr. Weber's contention that a much more compact, solidly Democratic 12th District could have been created had race not predominated over traditional political considerations in the redistricting process. Additionally, Dr. Weber showed that, without fail, Democratic districts adjacent to District 12 yielded their minority areas to that district, retaining white Democratic precincts. This testimony served to undermine Defendants' contention that race was merely a factor in creating the 1997 Plan's 12th District, and that a desire to place high-performance Democratic areas (which happen to contain minority populations) within Democratic districts could explain the construction of the 12th.

The conclusion that race predominated was further bolstered by Senator Cooper's allusion to a need for "racial and partisan balance," cited above. The senator's contention that although he used the term "partisan balance" to refer to the maintenance of a six-six Democrat-Republican split in the congressional delegation, he did not mean the term "racial balance" to refer to the maintenance of a ten-two balance between whites and African-Americans is simply not credible.

Dr. Weber, who has testified as an expert in redistricting cases in Louisiana, Texas, Georgia, Virginia and Florida, also presented a convincing critique of the methodology used by Defendants' expert witness, Dr. Peterson. Dr. Weber characterized Dr. Peterson's boundary segment analysis as non-traditional, creating "erroneous" results by "ignoring the core" of each district in question. In summary, Dr. Weber found that Dr. Peterson's analysis and report "has not been appropriately done," and was therefore "unreliable" and not relevant.

Finally, the Cooper-Cohen-mail, discussed above, clearly demonstrates that the chief architects of the 1997 Plan had evolved a methodology for segregating voters by race, and that they had applied this method to the 12th District. The Cooper-Cohen e-mail refers specifically to the categorization of sections of Greensboro as "Black," and a scheme by which this section was added to the 12th District, creating a need to "take about 60,000" other citizens out. It is also relevant as evidence of the means by which the 1997 Plan's racial gerrymandering could be achieved with scientific precision, as the precise racial composition of another district (the First) is discussed at length, along with plans to "improve" that district by "boost[ing] the minority percentage."

.... Given that the Supreme Court struck down the 1992 Plan's 12th District, the clear inference here is that a motive existed to compose a new 12th District with just under a majority minority in order for it not to present a prima facie racial gerrymander. In fact, Senator Cooper argued before the legislature that the *Shaw* test for constitutionality would not be triggered because the 12th District was not a majority minority district. But using a computer to achieve a district that is just under 50% minority is no less a predominant use of race than using it to achieve a district that is just over 50% minority.

Based on the extensive direct and circumstantial evidence presented at trial, the Court finds as a matter of fact that the General Assembly, in redistricting, used criteria with respect to the Twelfth

District that are facially race driven. It is clear that the Twelfth District was drawn to collect precincts with high racial identification rather than political identification. Additionally, the evidence demonstrates that precincts with higher partisan representation (that is, more heavily Democratic precincts) were bypassed in the drawing of District 12 in favor of precincts with a higher African-American population. The legislature eschewed traditional distracting criteria such as contiguity, geographical integrity, community of interest, and compactness in redrawing the District as part of the 1997 Plan. Instead, the General Assembly utilized race as the predominant factor in drawing the District.

This Court finds that, in contrast to the state's claims regarding the 1st District, no evidence of a compelling state interest in utilizing race to create the new 12th District has been presented. Further, even if such an interest did exist, the 12th District is not narrowly tailored and therefore cannot survive the prescribed "strict scrutiny." The 1997 Plan's District 12 is an impermissible and unconstitutional racial gerrymander in violation of the Equal Protection Clause....

III.   First Congressional District

The three-judge panel in *Shaw* never ruled on the constitutionality of the 1992 Plan's First Congressional District. Standing problems on the part of the *Shaw* plaintiffs forced that court to narrow its focus to adjudicate only the issues raised regarding the Twelfth District. A comparison of the First and Twelfth Districts under the 1992 Plan reveals, however, that they are similarly egregious in their construction and that the First District would certainly have been subject to the same finding that it was not narrowly tailored. Both were majority-minority districts under the 1992 Plan, and neither evidenced even minimal geographical compactness.

The 1997 Plan's First District, once again presents this Court with a majority-minority district, this time containing a population that is 50.27 percent African-American, as opposed to the Twelfth District's 46.67 percent. The First District is, however, far more compact than the Twelfth and its shape is less irregular, as we have seen above.

This Court finds as a matter of fact that, under the 1992 Plan, the First District was not narrowly tailored and therefore that district was in violation of the Constitution. The evidence presented by the Defendants does not dispute this finding.

The statements of several key players in the 1997 redistricting process clearly show that, in an effort to gain preclearance under the Section 2 of the Voting Rights Act, 42 U.S.C. § 1973, they allowed race to predominate in the creation of the 1st District. The Cohen-Cooper e-mail is one such clear example, specifically referencing the desire to "boost the minority percentage in the first district" to create an "improved" district. The e-mail exposes a process in which voters were categorized by race, then shifted in and out of the 1st District by a computer program until a precise percentage of minority voters in the district was achieved. No other credible explanation has been offered.

The fact that race predominated in the construction of the 1st District is not surprising. The legislators faced the difficult task of remedying the unconstitutional aspects of the 1992 Plan's 1st District while complying with the mandates of the Voting Rights Act, discussed below. Indeed, Senator Cooper acknowledged that he felt he had to have over 50% minority representation in the First District. (Trial Transcript at 440) This admission reveals that the racial composition of the district was seen as a mandate, a necessity.

Thus, we further find that, in its 1997 Plan, the State continued to use race as the predominant factor in creating the majority-minority First District, and thus strict scrutiny must apply. This does not end our inquiry, however. Defendants may show that the district was narrowly tailored to achieve a compelling government interest.

Section 2 of the Voting Rights Act provides that "no voting qualification or prerequisite to voting or standard, practice, or procedure shall be imposed or applied by any State ... in a manner which results in a denial or abridgement of the right of any citizen of the United States to vote on account of race or color, ... " 42 U.S.C. § 1973(a) (1988). Congress instructed the courts, when determining whether a voting standard, practice, or procedure violates this prohibition, to examine "the totality of the circumstances" to ascertain whether "the political processes leading to nomination or election" are equally open to citizens of all races. § 1973(b)....

In *Thornburg v. Gingles*, the Supreme Court first examined the 1982 amendments to the Act. 478 U.S. 30 (1986).... The Court identified [three] "necessary preconditions" to a § 2 claim .... Once these preconditions are met, a court must consider the factors identified in the Senate Report accompanying the 1982 amendments.

Defendants presented evidence at trial to show that there was a strong basis for the General Assembly to have believed, at the time of the 1997 Plan's drafting, that the three *Gingles* preconditions and several of the factors set forth in the Senate Report existed in North Carolina. Specifically, the Defendants presented evidence that the African-American population in the area encompassed by District 1 was and is sufficiently large and geographically compact to constitute a majority in a congressional district. Additionally, Defendants contend, and Plaintiffs have stipulated for the purposes of this trial, that the African-American population is politically cohesive. Further, Defendants contend, and Plaintiffs have stipulated for the purposes of this trial, that the white majority votes sufficiently as a block to often enable it to defeat the minority's preferred candidate. Finally, all parties agree that, for many decades, African-Americans in North Carolina were victims of racial discrimination, and that a substantial majority of the State's African-American population is still at a disadvantage in comparison to white citizens with respect to income, housing, education and health.

This Court finds that Defendants have presented sufficient evidence to establish that the State Legislature of North Carolina did have a compelling reason to address race in the construction of the First District under the 1997 Plan. That compelling reason was the need to satisfy Section 2 of the Voting Rights Act in order to ensure that the State's African-American population have equal access to the political process.

Further, this Court finds that the specific composition of the First District's borders, while predominated by race, was narrowly tailored to meet the Section 2 requirements while also addressing other traditional, political considerations, including the desire to protect incumbency, both of a Democrat in the First District and a Republican in the Third District. The splitting of counties and lack of compactness display the interplay between these considerations: the borders were drawn to avoid putting two incumbents in a single district; the State Legislature intended to exclude as much of the First State Senatorial District from the 1997 Plan's 1st District as possible, resulting in modifications that forced the district's borders south and west. While race predominated, the legislature resisted the temptation to create a district reminiscent of the 1992 Plan's 1st District, which reflected little or no effort to achieve a narrow tailoring.

Thus, this Court finds that the 1997 Plan's 1st District meets the requisite standard of strict scrutiny. Race, while the predominant factor in its composition, was not impermissibly used in establishing its borders. There was a compelling state interest in obtaining pre-clearance under Section 2 [sic] of the Voting Rights Act, and the 1st District was narrowly tailored to meet this interest. Thus we find that the 1997 Plan's 1st District does not present an unconstitutional racial gerrymander....

THORNBURG, District Judge, sitting by designation as Circuit Judge, concurring in part and dissenting in part:

I join the majority in concluding that the First Congressional district is constitutionally drawn, but respectfully dissent from the reasoning of the majority in reaching that conclusion. I dissent from the majority opinion finding the Twelfth Congressional district to be an unconstitutional racial gerrymander....

* * * * *

IV. DISCUSSION

Initially, I note that the 1997 plan must be addressed based on its own merit, not on any resemblance to the 1992 Plan.... Nevertheless, the majority makes reference to the "unconstitutional" 1992 Plan in criticizing both the First and Twelfth Districts under the 1997 Plan. This criticism essentially mirrors the "footprint" argument advanced by Plaintiffs, and therefore is equally flawed.

Plaintiffs contend that any district which is based on the "footprint" of a prior unconstitutional district is inherently invalid. This suggests that the legislature *must* begin with a completely clean slate in order to wipe away the vestiges of prior unconstitutional districts. Thus, the North Carolina General Assembly could not use the unconstitutional 1992 Plan as the beginning point for creating the 1997 Plan. However, given that the task of the General Assembly in 1997 was to correct the defects of the 1992 plan, it should be permissible to use the 1992 Plan as the starting point for creating a constitutional plan. Further, it would be illogical to argue that the unconstitutional aspects of a decision made by legislators in 1992 somehow taints the actions of a completely different legislative body in 1997. Most importantly, requiring a legislature to start completely from scratch makes their task nearly impossible because congressional incumbents and state legislators will invariably demand the preservation of as much of the geographic core of districts as possible, a political reality explained in testimony at the trial. Indeed, the undersigned can think of no reason why a legislature may not simply address the offensive aspects of an unconstitutional district, cure those defects, and thereby create a constitutional district.

A.   The Twelfth Congressional District

To show that racial motives predominated in the drawing of the Twelfth District, Plaintiffs had the burden of proving by a preponderance of the evidence that the legislature substantially disregarded legitimate districting criteria and subordinated those criteria to the improper racial motivation. A thorough treatment of Plaintiffs' burden is noticeably absent from the majority opinion, but this burden must not be overlooked or disregarded. Plaintiffs quite simply have failed to carry their burden through either direct or circumstantial evidence. Defendants, on the other hand, have produced ample and convincing evidence which demonstrates that political concerns such as existing constituents, incumbency, voter performance, commonality of interests, and contiguity, not racial motivations, dominated the process surrounding the creation and adoption of the 1997 redistricting plan.

Finding that race was the predominant motivation and applying strict scrutiny to the Twelfth District fails to evalutate the redistricting process within the context of the legislative environment where such decisions occur.

Passing a redistricting plan in a limited time period, under a federal court order, and in a politically divided General Assembly seemed like an impossible task early in 1997. In order to succeed, the chairmen of the House and Senate Redistricting Committees recognized the necessity of creating a plan which would garner the support of both parties and both houses.

Consequently, they set out to design a plan which, in addition to addressing the constitutional deficiencies of past plans, would protect incumbents and thereby maintain the then existing 6-6 partisan split amongst North Carolina's congressional delegation. Because both the First and Twelfth Districts had Democrat incumbents, and maintaining the 6-6 split was viewed as imperative, preserving a strong Democratic Twelfth District which protected incumbent Mel Watts' political base was absolutely necessary. In creating such a district, common sense as well as political experience dictated ascertaining the strongest voter performing Democratic precincts in the urban Piedmont Crescent. That many of those strong Democratic performing precincts were majority African-American, and that the General Assembly leaders were aware of that fact, is not a constitutional violation.[9] Those precincts were included in the Twelfth District based primarily upon their Democratic performance, not their racial makeup.[10] North Carolina's legislative leaders have openly admitted to being aware of the race issue, to being conscious of the racial percentages of the districts they drew, and to recognizing that their reistricting plan could potentially be subjected to federal scrutiny yet again as a challenged racial gerrymander. Yet, these were merely some of the numerous political considerations which legislative leaders had to account for in designing a plan which would pass.

The expert testimony of Dr. David W. Peterson, the unbiased statistician whose opinions were referenced by the Supreme Court in *Hunt v. Cromartie*, supports Defendants' position. Dr. Peterson opined that, based purely on the Plaintiffs' circumstantial statistical evidence, politics was *at least* as plausible a motivating factor as race in the drawing of the Twelfth District. In other words, the statistical evidence before the Court does not support the proposition that race *predominated* as a motivation. Yet, it is this same equivocal statistical evidence which forms the backbone of the Plaintiffs' case.

---

[9]   All parties agree that African-American voters in North Carolina are extremely loyal Democratic voters, with over 95% of African-American voters in North Carolina registered and voting accordingly.

[10]   The fact that the majority of African-American legislators in the North Carolina House of Representatives voted *against* the enactment of the 1997 redistricting plan tends to undermine the conclusion that the legislature designed districts which impermissibly favored African-Americans.

In an attempt to rebut this argument, Plaintiffs relied primarily on the testimony of their expert witness, Dr. Ronald Weber.[11] Dr. Weber also plays a prominent role in the majority opinion. Dr. Weber argued that the North Carolina legislature failed to include numerous precincts in the Twelfth District which had high levels of Democratic support, but which were not majority African-American. Consequently, he contended the legislature must have been more focused on race than on creating a Democratic district. Dr. Weber also criticized Dr. Peterson's findings as "unreliable" and not relevant....

[H]is arguments still do little to advance Plaintiffs' position. First, there is no dispute that every one of the majority African-American precincts included in the Twelfth District are among the *highest*, if not the highest, Democratic performing districts in that geographic region. Thus, although Dr. Weber pointed to other precincts which he suggests are highly Democratic in performance, this does not explain why any of the highest performing Democratic precincts should be excluded from the Twelfth District. Furthermore, Dr. Weber's entire line of criticism ignored geographic realities and one-person, one-vote principles. Weber admitted that the precincts which he argued are strongly Democratic were chosen without considering where they were located.[12] Further, under one-person, one-vote principles, Weber's precincts could not all possibly be included in the Twelfth District without removing a corresponding number of voters from elsewhere in the district. Finally, Weber's analysis is flawed due to the incorrect assumptions under which he conducted his study. Weber admitted he considered no hypothesis other than race as the legislature's predominant motive, and he specifically failed to inquire about real world political or partisan factors which might have influenced the process. One reason for the focus on race was Dr. Weber's incorrect belief that the person drawing North Carolina's districts could only see racial data, when in fact North Carolina's computer screens displayed information on political breakdowns of both voter registration and voter performance. This error, his failure to account for other potential factors, [and] the flaws in his arguments ... combine to undermine his subsequent conclusions and criticisms. In the end, the undersigned sees no reason to give any weight to the opinions of Dr. Ronald Weber and fails to understand the majority reliance on such a thin reed.

---

[11]

Plaintiffs also provided the testimony of witnesses who were, at best, peripheral players in the General Assembly's decision-making process. Three of those witnesses were not members of the General Assembly when the plan in question was adopted and indicated no direct involvement with that process. Of the three witnesses who were members of the General Assembly during the relevant time period, none claimed to have had a significant involvement with or specific knowledge of the decision-making process. Nevertheless, each confidently expressed the opinion that racial motivations did predominate as to the Twelfth District.

[12]

On cross-examination, the Defendants presented maps which showed that few highly performing Democratic precincts actually abutted the Twelfth District. Consequently, few of the strong Democratic precincts to which Dr. Weber referred could have easily been included in the Twelfth District.

Another significant shortcoming of the majority's analysis is the failure to adequately credit the testimony of the two men who were the driving force behind the creation of the 1997 Redistricting Plan. Senator Roy Cooper, III, served as the Democrat chair of the Senate Redistricting Committee and Representative Edward McMahan acted as the Republican chair of the House Redistricting Committee. They were responsible for developing a redistricting plan that could pass both houses and for marshaling it through the legislative process. They indicated that the 1997 plan and the formulation of its boundaries came primarily from their personal negotiations with each other. Both testified that correcting the constitutional defects of the previous plan and passage of the bill by ensuring a 6-6 partisan split were the two central goals in developing the 1997 plan. Indeed, each testified under oath that politics, not race, was the predominant motivating factor in the Plan's development, with Senator Cooper going so far as to call partisan fairness an "overriding factor." This Court's finding that racial motives predominated in the legislative process directly contradicts their express testimony.

In contrast to Plaintiffs, the Defendants adequately supported their position with convincing evidence, even though they had no burden of proof in this trial. Senator Cooper and Representative McMahan detailed the motivations behind their actions, at times expressing regret for having to expose the naked political nature of their conduct. In addition to incumbency protection, other factors considered by the General Assembly included increasing geographic compactness and reducing the number of split counties and precincts. The 1997 Twelfth District as adopted reflected the legislators' focus on these legitimate districting criteria. The 1997 Twelfth District is more compact, splits fewer counties and precincts, and is much more pleasing to the eye than the previous District. The General Assembly shortened the District from 191 to 102 miles, moved 60 percent of the geographic area and 30 percent of the population out of the District," and eliminated the long narrow corridors and other objectionable characteristics which had previously been criticized. Most importantly, the Twelfth District is not a minority-majority district by any traditional measurement, numbering 46.67 percent African-American in total population and only 43.36 percent African-American in voting age population.

Furthermore, the General Assembly had before it abundant evidence of a clear community of interest in the Twelfth District.[13] The three urban areas located along the Interstate-85 industrial corridor, known as the Piedmont Crescent, share common characteristics and face similar problems. One statement submitted at a public hearing described the Twelfth District as "uniquely urban in its dominant

---

[13] Substantial evidence from both private citizens and politicians concerning the benefits of having a Piedmont Crescent district was submitted at the public hearings and therefore was before the legislature.

issues," some of which were described as affordable housing, alternative transportation, air and water quality, and various other complex issues found in an increasingly populated and urban area. As a consequence, the urban voters in the Twelfth District as presently configured have much more in common with each other than with rural voters living on the distant outskirts of those urban cities." Senator Cooper felt that maintaining this community of interest was one of the legislature's motivating factors, and indeed, the 1997 Twelfth District as drawn reflected and protected the clear community of interest in the Piedmont Crescent.[14]

The evidence presented by Defendants demonstrates that politics predominated in the drawing of the Twelfth District in 1997. Plaintiffs' evidence does nothing more than address the admitted fact that legislative leaders were aware of the race issue, or perhaps that the Twelfth District could have possibly been drawn in a different way to accomplish the legislature's stated political goals. Such evidence does not meet Plaintiffs' heavy burden of showing by a preponderance of the evidence that racial motives predominated in substantial disregard of legitimate districting criteria....

Therefore, I conclude that strict scrutiny should not be applied to the Twelfth District.

B. The First Congressional District

The First District in the 1997 Plan is 50.27 percent African-American in total population and 46.54 percent African-American in voting age population. Final Pre-Trial Order, at ¶27. Thus, the First District is the only majority-minority district in North Carolina in terms of total population, and no congressional district in this state is majority-minority in terms of voting age population. However, this fact does not change the applicable legal standard. A State's decision to intentionally create a majority-minority district is not necessarily subject to strict scrutiny. *Bush*, 517 U.S. at 958. Plaintiffs still have the burden of showing by a preponderance of the evidence that race was the predominant factor motivating the legislature's decision and that legitimate districting criteria were subordinated to race. *Miller*, 515 U.S. at 916.

Senator Cooper and Representative McMahan testified that they were motivated to create a majority-minority district in the Northeastern area of the state to avoid concerns under the Voting Rights Act. However, their motivation was predicated on the knowledge that

---

[14]
    The majority observes that Charlotte, Winston-Salem, and Greensboro have never before been joined in a congressional district prior to 1992. However, it is irrelevant that the impetus for first grouping these metropolitan areas together was a plan since declared unconstitutional. What currently is relevant is the clear community of interest in this Piedmont Crescent district which has been recognized by politicians and private citizens alike.

they could create a compact, contiguous district in Northeastern North Carolina which focused on an undeniable community of interests.

> [A]s we went through the process it became clear that we could draw a nice, compact district that made geographic sense, that put together communities of interest, that was a strongly leaning Democratic district, that was slightly majority-minority population.
>
> District 1 is a largely agrarian rural district. It has a lot of medium sized towns. I think uniquely [in] Eastern North Carolina you have the 30 to 50,000 population towns with largely rural areas. A lot of these counties are largely poorer counties, they are very high up on our economic tiers of depressed counties. So I think that there's a great community of interest in Northeastern North Carolina with those counties that are up there.

Likewise, Senator Cooper and Representative McMahan were concerned with creating a geographically compact district. McMahan in particular focused almost exclusively on geographical considerations and "making the district look good." And indeed, the 1997 redistricting process resulted in a fairly compact and normal looking congressional district in Northeastern North Carolina. The perimeter and dispersion compactness indicators of the First District are not much lower than the mean compactness indicators for North Carolina's twelve districts. Neither number is low enough to raise a "red flag" according to the criteria set out in the Pildes and Niemi study. Furthermore, as the majority correctly observes, where the borders of the First District have significant irregularities, those irregularities are attributable to political motivations, namely the desire to protect incumbents and avoid putting two congressional incumbents in a single district. Therefore, although it was the intent of Senator Cooper and Representative McMahan to create a minority-majority district in Northeastern North Carolina, this decision was based on legitimate districting principles. Quite simply, once they knew they *could* create a compact, contiguous district which addressed the community of interests in Northeastern North Carolina, they felt they *should* do so.

The majority reaches a different conclusion, however, and applies strict scrutiny to the First District. The majority characterizes the racial composition of the First District as "a mandate, a necessity," and therefore concludes that racial motives predominated. In support of this conclusion, the majority cites the Cooper-Cohen e-mail which refers to the desire to "boost the minority percentage in the first district" to create an "improved" district. Also, the majority points to Senator Cooper's acknowledgment at trial that he felt the need to have over 50 percent minority representation in the First District. Based upon these statements, the majority concludes that the General Assembly "continued to use race as the predominant factor in creating the majority-minority First District and thus strict scrutiny must apply."[15]

However, these statements merely highlight the admitted and permissible reality: the North Carolina General Assembly intentionally created a majority-minority district (in terms of population only) in Northeastern North Carolina. But despite the intent to create a majority-minority district, the evidence does not show that racial motives *predominated* in substantial disregard of legitimate criteria like compactness, contiguity, and communities of interest. On the contrary, the direct testimony shows that the legislature addressed traditional, legitimate districting criteria and determined that a majority-minority district in Northeastern North Carolina was appropriate. Indeed, the criteria of communities of interest and geographical compactness were uppermost in the legislators' minds. Considering the evidence before the Court in light of the deference due the state legislative decision, my understanding of the applicable legal standard forces me to conclude that race did not impermissibly predominate in the districting process and therefore strict scrutiny should not apply to the First Congressional District.

*   *   *   *   *

On page 612, add the following material at the end of note 16:

Despite the fact that *Miller* rejected the idea that geographic compactness is the linchpin of all *Shaw* claims, compactness continues to play a central role.   First, in deciding whether plaintiffs have shown the predominance of racial considerations, courts rely heavily on the irregularity of district shape: the fact that a district does not adhere to what the courts have viewed as 'traditional" standards of compactness raises suspicion. By contrast, if a black community is "geographically compact," then a reapportionment plan that concentrates members of the group in one district should not trigger strict scrutiny in the first place, since a compact majority-black district is fully consonant with traditional apportionment principles.

Second, at the justification stage, in deciding whether section 2 *could* provide a compelling interest for race-conscious districting, a court must again look at compactness. The question here is whether the black community is sufficiently numerous and geographically compact that it would have been able to establish a *prima facie* case under section 2 if no majority-black district had

---

[15]
    The majority purports to find that "under the 1992 plan, the First District was not narrowly tailored and therefore that district was in violation of the Constitution." However, this Court has no authority to find that the First District under the 1992 Plan was unconstitutional. Due to a standing issue, the Supreme Court in *Shaw II* did not make a ruling on that district. *Shaw v. Hunt*, 517 *U.S.* 899, 904 (1996). Neither this Court nor any court has made a legal ruling on the constitutionality of the 1992 First District. *Cromartie v. Hunt*, 4:96-CV104-BO(3), Order filed June 21, 1998, at 2. The 1992 Plan no longer exists, is not currently being challenged by Plaintiffs in this case, and simply is not an issue before this Court. To the extent the majority's application of the strict scrutiny is predicated on a comparison to the 1992 First District, such reliance is patently wrong.

been drawn. Only a reasonable fear of section 2 liability provides the requisite basis in evidence for subordinating other districting principles to racial concerns.

Third, compactness enters the picture again with regard to the question whether the district that was actually drawn is "narrowly tailored." If it would have been possible to comply with section 2 without doing substantial violence to the traditional principles of districting, including compactness, then a section 2 compliance district that is not compact fails the narrow tailoring test, since it was *unnecessary* to draw a bizarrely shaped district.

Is this triple counting coherent? If a district is narrowly tailored, in the sense that it complies with traditional districting principles and provides representation to a geographically compact black community, why is strict scrutiny triggered in the first place?

At least so far, courts have treated compliance with sections 2 and 5 of the Voting Rights Act as the sole "compelling state interests" that enable districts to survive strict scrutiny. As we point out in Chapter 7D of this supplement, however, the question of amended section 2's constitutionality has not been answered definitively. If you have not yet read the materials on the constitutionality of amended section 2, you should consider them here.

On page 615, at the end of Chapter 8, add the following new material:

D. RACE AND REPRESENTATION UNDER THE FIFTEENTH AMENDMENT

For the most part, contemporary controversies involving race and representation arise under the Fourteenth Amendment, rather than the Fifteenth Amendment. In part, this is a product of the voting rights revolution of the 1960's: outright race-based disenfranchisement is relatively rare (although consider the question whether, in light of the historical materials presented in Chapter 2 of the book, the exclusion of permanent residents and some felons from the franchise is the product of racial motivations). In part, this is also a product of the Supreme Court's constricted reading of the Fifteenth Amendment. In *City of Mobile v. Bolden*, 446 U.S. 55, 65 (1980), a plurality of the Court suggested that the Fifteenth Amendment is satisfied as long as minority citizens are able to "register and vote without hindrance," regardless of whether their votes are purposefully diluted, and a majority of the Court seemed to endorse the *Bolden* plurality's view in *Reno v. Bossier Parish School Board,* 528 U.S. 320, 120 S. Ct. 866, 875 n.3 (2000).

As the *Shaw* cases suggest, not every use of race in the reapportionment process violates the equal protection clause. First, some level of race-consciousness seems to be entirely permissible: as long as race is not a predominant factor in drawing district lines, the courts seem prepared to allow it to be part of the pluralist bargaining process. Second, the compelling governmental interest in complying with sections 2 and 5 of the Voting Rights Act also apparently justifies taking race into account.

But can race ever play a role in a case where the Fifteenth Amendment comes into play? Note the apparently categorical language of section 1 of the amendment: "The right of citizens of the United States to vote shall not be denied or abridged by the United States or by any State on account of race, color, or previous condition of servitude." Can restriction of the franchise on racial grounds ever be justified? And what does it mean to say that a restriction is "racial," rather than political? The Court confronted these questions in a case involving the election of a special governmental body in Hawaii.

RICE v. CAYETANO
528 U.S. 495 (2000)

JUSTICE KENNEDY delivered the opinion of the Court.

.... The Hawaiian Constitution limits the right to vote for nine trustees chosen in a statewide election. The trustees compose the governing authority of a state agency known as the Office of Hawaiian Affairs, or OHA. The agency administers programs designed for the benefit of two subclasses of the Hawaiian citizenry. The smaller class comprises those designated as "native Hawaiians," defined by statute ... as descendants of not less than one-half part of the races inhabiting the Hawaiian Islands prior to 1778. The second, larger class of persons benefited by OHA programs is "Hawaiians," defined to be ... those persons who are descendants of people inhabiting the Hawaiian Islands in 1778. The right to vote for trustees is limited to "Hawaiians," the second, larger class of persons, which of course includes the smaller class of "native Hawaiians."

Petitioner Rice, a citizen of Hawaii and thus himself a Hawaiian in a well-accepted sense of the term, does not have the requisite ancestry even for the larger class. He is not, then, a "Hawaiian" in terms of the statute; so he may not vote in the trustee election. The issue presented by this case is whether Rice may be so barred. Rejecting the State's arguments that the classification in question is not racial or that, if it is, it is nevertheless valid for other reasons, we hold Hawaii's denial of petitioner's right to vote to be a clear violation of the Fifteenth Amendment.

I

When Congress and the State of Hawaii enacted the laws we are about to discuss and review, they made their own assessments of the events which intertwine Hawaii's history with the history of America itself. We will begin with a very brief account of that historical background....

The origins of the first Hawaiian people and the date they reached the islands are not established with certainty, but the usual assumption is that they were Polynesians who voyaged from Tahiti and began to settle the islands around A.D. 750. When England's Captain Cook made landfall in Hawaii on his expedition in 1778, the Hawaiian people had developed, over the preceding 1,000 years or so, a cultural and political structure of their own. They had well-established traditions and customs and practiced a polytheistic religion. Agriculture and fishing sustained the people, and, though population estimates vary, some modern historians conclude that the population in 1778 was about 200,000-300,000....

In 1810, the islands were united as one kingdom under the leadership of an admired figure in Hawaiian history, Kamehameha I. It is difficult to say how many settlers from Europe and America were in Hawaii when the King consolidated his power. One historian estimates there were no more than 60 or so settlers at that time. An influx was soon to follow....

The 1800's are a story of increasing involvement of westerners in the economic and political affairs of the Kingdom. Rights to land became a principal concern, and there was unremitting pressure to allow non-Hawaiians to use and to own land and to be secure in their title....

The status of Hawaiian lands has presented issues of complexity and controversy from at least the rule of Kamehameha I to the present day. We do not attempt to interpret that history, lest our comments be thought to bear upon issues not before us. It suffices to refer to various of the historical conclusions that appear to have been persuasive to Congress and to the State when they enacted the laws soon to be discussed.

When Kamehameha I came to power, he reasserted suzerainty over all lands and provided for control of parts of them by a system described in our own cases as "feudal."....

In 1920, the Congress of the United States, in a Report on the bill establishing the Hawaiian Homes Commission, made an assessment of Hawaiian land policy in the following terms:

> Your committee thus finds that since the institution of private ownership of lands in Hawaii the native Hawaiians, outside of the King and the chiefs, were granted and have held but a very small portion of the lands of the Islands. Under the homestead laws somewhat more than a majority of the lands were homesteaded to Hawaiians, but a great many of these lands have been lost through improvidence and inability to finance farming operations. Most frequently, however, the native Hawaiian, with no thought of the future, has obtained the land for a nominal sum, only to turn about and sell it to wealthy interests for a sum more nearly approaching its real value. The Hawaiians are not business men and have shown themselves unable to meet competitive conditions unaided. In the end the speculators are the real beneficiaries of the homestead laws. Thus the tax returns for 1919 show that only 6.23 per centum of the property of

the Islands is held by native Hawaiians and this for the most part is lands in the possession of approximately a thousand wealthy Hawaiians, the descendents of the chiefs.

While these developments were unfolding, the United States and European powers made constant efforts to protect their interests and to influence Hawaiian political and economic affairs in general. The first "articles of arrangement" between the United States and the Kingdom of Hawaii were signed in 1826, and additional treaties and conventions between the two countries were signed in 1849, 1875, and 1887....

Tensions intensified between an anti-Western, pro-native bloc in the government on the one hand and Western business interests and property owners on the other. The conflicts came to the fore in 1887. Westerners forced the resignation of the Prime Minister of the Kingdom of Hawaii and the adoption of a new Constitution, which, among other things, reduced the power of the monarchy and extended the right to vote to non-Hawaiians.

Tensions continued through 1893, when they again peaked, this time in response to an attempt by the then Hawaiian monarch, Queen Liliuokalani, to promulgate a new constitution restoring monarchical control over the House of Nobles and limiting the franchise to Hawaiian subjects. A so-called Committee of Safety, a group of professionals and businessmen, with the active assistance of John Stevens, the United States Minister to Hawaii, acting with United States armed forces, replaced the monarchy with a provisional government. That government sought annexation by the United States. On December 18 of the same year, President Cleveland, unimpressed and indeed offended by the actions of the American Minister, denounced the role of the American forces and called for restoration of the Hawaiian monarchy. The Queen could not resume her former place, however, and, in 1894, the provisional government established the Republic of Hawaii. The Queen abdicated her throne a year later.

In 1898, President McKinley signed a Joint Resolution, sometimes called the Newlands Resolution, to annex the Hawaiian Islands as territory of the United States. According to the Joint Resolution, the Republic of Hawaii ceded all former Crown, government, and public lands to the United States. The resolution further provided that revenues from the public lands were to be "used solely for the benefit of the inhabitants of the Hawaiian Islands for educational and other public purposes." Two years later the Hawaiian Organic Act established the Territory of Hawaii, asserted United States control over the ceded lands, and put those lands "in the possession, use, and control of the government of the Territory of Hawaii . . . until otherwise provided for by Congress."

In 1993, a century after the intervention by the Committee of Safety, the Congress of the United States reviewed this history, and in particular the role of Minister Stevens. Congress passed a Joint Resolution recounting the events in some detail and offering an apology to the native Hawaiian people.

Before we turn to the relevant provisions two other important matters, which affected the demographics of Hawaii, must be recounted. The first is the tragedy inflicted on the early Hawaiian people by the introduction of western diseases and infectious agents. As early as the establishment of the rule of Kamehameha I, it was becoming apparent that the native population had serious vulnerability to diseases borne to the islands by settlers. High mortality figures were experienced in infancy and adulthood, even from common illnesses such as diarrhea, colds, and measles. More serious diseases took even greater tolls. In the smallpox epidemic of 1853, thousands of lives were lost. By 1878, 100 years after Cook's arrival, the native population had been reduced to about 47,500 people. These mortal illnesses no doubt were an initial cause of the despair, disenchantment, and despondency some commentators later noted in descendents of the early Hawaiian people.

The other important feature of Hawaiian demographics to be noted is the immigration to the islands by people of many different races and cultures. Mostly in response to the demand of the sugar industry for arduous labor in the cane fields, successive immigration waves brought Chinese, Portuguese, Japanese and Filipinos to Hawaii. Beginning with the immigration of 293 Chinese in 1852, the plantations alone drew to Hawaii, in one estimate, something over 400,000 men, women, and children over the next century. Each of these ethnic and national groups has had its own history in Hawaii, its own struggles with societal and official discrimination, its own successes, and its own role in creating the present society of the islands....

II

Not long after the creation of the new Territory, Congress became concerned with the condition of the native Hawaiian people. Reciting its purpose to rehabilitate the native Hawaiian population, Congress enacted the Hawaiian Homes Commission Act, which set aside about 200,000 acres of the ceded public lands and created a program of loans and long-term leases for the benefit of native Hawaiians. The Act defined "native Hawaiians" to include "any descendant of not less than one-half part of the blood of the races inhabiting the Hawaiian Islands previous to 1778."

Hawaii was admitted as the fiftieth State of the Union in 1959. With admission, the new State agreed to adopt the Hawaiian Homes Commission Act as part of its own Constitution. In addition, the United States granted Hawaii title to all public lands and public property within the boundaries of the State, save those which the Federal Government retained for its own use. This grant included the 200,000 acres set aside under the Hawaiian Homes Commission Act and almost 1.2 million additional acres of land.

The legislation authorizing the grant recited that these lands, and the proceeds and income they generated, were to be held "as a public trust" to be "managed and disposed of for one or more of" five purposes:

> [1] for the support of the public schools and other public educational institutions, [2] for the betterment of the conditions of native Hawaiians, as defined in the Hawaiian Homes Commission Act, 1920, as amended, [3] for the development of farm and home ownership on as widespread a basis as possible[,] [4] for the making of public improvements, and [5] for the provision of lands for public use.

In the first decades following admission, the State apparently continued to administer the lands that had been set aside under the Hawaiian Homes Commission Act for the benefit of native Hawaiians. The income from the balance of the public lands is said to have "by and large flowed to the department of education."

In 1978 Hawaii amended its Constitution to establish the Office of Hawaiian Affairs, which has as its mission "the betterment of conditions of native Hawaiians . . . [and] Hawaiians." Members of the 1978 constitutional convention, at which the new amendments were drafted and proposed, set forth the purpose of the proposed agency:

> Members [of the Committee of the Whole] were impressed by the concept of the Office of Hawaiian Affairs which establishes a public trust entity for the benefit of the people of Hawaiian ancestry. Members foresaw that it will provide Hawaiians the right to determine the priorities which will effectuate the betterment of their condition and welfare and promote the protection and preservation of the Hawaiian race, and that it will unite Hawaiians as a people.

Implementing statutes and their later amendments vested OHA with broad authority to administer two categories of funds: a 20 percent share of the revenue from the 1.2 million acres of lands granted to the State pursuant to ... the Admission Act, which OHA is to administer "for the betterment of the conditions of native Hawaiians," and any state or federal appropriations or private donations that may be made for the benefit of "native Hawaiians" and/or "Hawaiians." (The 200,000 acres set aside under the Hawaiian Homes Commission Act are administered by a separate agency.) The Hawaiian Legislature has charged OHA with the mission of "serving as the principal public agency . . . responsible for the performance, development, and coordination of programs and activities relating to native Hawaiians and Hawaiians" ....

OHA is overseen by a nine-member board of trustees, the members of which "shall be Hawaiians" and -- presenting the precise issue in this case -- shall be "elected by qualified voters who are Hawaiians, as provided by law." The term "Hawaiian" is defined by statute:

> "Hawaiian" means any descendant of the aboriginal peoples inhabiting the Hawaiian Islands which exercised sovereignty and subsisted in the Hawaiian Islands in 1778, and which peoples thereafter have continued to reside in Hawaii.

The statute defines "native Hawaiian" as follows:

> "Native Hawaiian" means any descendant of not less than one-half part of the races inhabiting the Hawaiian Islands previous to 1778, as defined by the Hawaiian Homes Commission Act, 1920, as amended; provided that the term identically refers to the descendants of such blood quantum of such aboriginal peoples which exercised sovereignty and subsisted in the Hawaiian Islands in 1778 and which peoples thereafter continued to reside in Hawaii.

Petitioner Harold Rice is a citizen of Hawaii and a descendant of pre-annexation residents of the islands. He is not, as we have noted, a descendant of pre-1778 natives, and so he is neither "native Hawaiian" nor "Hawaiian" as defined by the statute. Rice applied in March 1996 to vote in the elections for OHA trustees. To register to vote for the office of trustee he was required to attest: "I am also Hawaiian and desire to register to vote in OHA elections." Rice marked through the words "am also Hawaiian and," then checked the form "yes." The State denied his application.

Rice sued Benjamin Cayetano, the Governor of Hawaii, in the United States District Court for the District of Hawaii. (The Governor was sued in his official capacity, and the Attorney General of Hawaii defends the challenged enactments. We refer to the respondent as "the State.") Rice contested his exclusion from voting in elections for OHA trustees ....

III

The purpose and command of the Fifteenth Amendment are set forth in language both explicit and comprehensive. The National Government and the States may not violate a fundamental principle: They may not deny or abridge the right to vote on account of race. Color and previous condition of servitude, too, are forbidden criteria or classifications, though it is unnecessary to consider them in the present case.

Enacted in the wake of the Civil War, the immediate concern of the Amendment was to guarantee to the emancipated slaves the right to vote, lest they be denied the civil and political capacity to protect their new freedom. Vital as its objective remains, the Amendment goes beyond it. Consistent with the design of the Constitution, the Amendment is cast in fundamental terms, terms transcending the particular controversy which was the immediate impetus for its enactment. The Amendment grants protection to all persons, not just members of a particular race.

The design of the Amendment is to reaffirm the equality of races at the most basic level of the democratic process, the exercise of the voting franchise. A resolve so absolute required language as simple in command as it was comprehensive in reach. Fundamental in purpose and effect and self-executing in operation, the Amendment prohibits all provisions denying or abridging the voting franchise of any citizen or class of citizens on the basis of race. "By the inherent power of the Amendment the word white disappeared" from our voting laws, bringing those who had been excluded by reason of race within "the generic grant of suffrage made by the State." The Court has acknowledged the Amendment's mandate of neutrality in straightforward terms: "If citizens of one race having certain qualifications are permitted by law to vote, those of another having the same qualifications must be. Previous to this amendment, there was no constitutional guaranty against this discrimination: now there is." United States v. Reese, 92 U.S. 214, 218 (1876).

Though the commitment was clear, the reality remained far from the promise. Manipulative devices and practices were soon employed to deny the vote to blacks. We have cataloged before the "variety and persistence" of these techniques....

The Fifteenth Amendment was quite sufficient to invalidate a scheme which did not mention race but instead used ancestry in an attempt to confine and restrict the voting franchise. In 1910, the State of Oklahoma enacted a literacy requirement for voting eligibility, but exempted from that requirement the "'lineal descendants'" of persons who were "'on January 1, 1866, or at any time prior thereto, entitled to vote under any form of government, or who at that time resided in some foreign nation.'" Guinn [v. United States, 238 U.S. 347 (1915).] Those persons whose ancestors were entitled to vote under the State's previous, discriminatory voting laws were thus exempted from the eligibility test. Recognizing that the test served only to perpetuate those old laws and to effect a transparent racial exclusion, the Court invalidated it.

More subtle, perhaps, than the grandfather device in Guinn were the evasions attempted in the white primary cases; but the Fifteenth Amendment, again by its own terms, sufficed to strike down these voting systems, systems designed to exclude one racial class (at least) from voting....

Unlike the cited cases, the voting structure now before us is neither subtle nor indirect. It is specific in granting the vote to persons of defined ancestry and to no others. The State maintains this is not a racial category at all but instead a classification limited to those whose ancestors were in Hawaii at a particular time, regardless of their race. The State points to theories of certain scholars concluding that some inhabitants of Hawaii as of 1778 may have migrated from the Marquesas Islands and the Pacific Northwest, as well as from Tahiti. Furthermore, the State argues, the restriction in its operation excludes a person whose traceable ancestors were exclusively Polynesian if none of those ancestors resided in Hawaii in 1778; and, on the other hand, the vote would be granted to a person who could trace, say, one sixty-fourth of his or her ancestry to a Hawaiian inhabitant on the pivotal date. These factors, it is said, mean the restriction is not a racial classification. We reject this line of argument.

Ancestry can be a proxy for race. It is that proxy here. Even if the residents of Hawaii in 1778 had been of more diverse ethnic backgrounds and cultures, it is far from clear that a voting test favoring their descendants would not be a race-based qualification. But that is not this case. For centuries Hawaii was isolated from migration. The inhabitants shared common physical characteristics, and by 1778 they had a common culture. Indeed, the drafters of the statutory definition in question emphasized the "unique culture of the ancient Hawaiians" in explaining their work. The provisions before us reflect the State's effort to preserve that commonality of people to the present day. In the interpretation of the Reconstruction era civil rights laws we have observed that "racial discrimination" is that which singles out "identifiable classes of persons . . . solely because of their ancestry or ethnic characteristics." Saint Francis College v. Al-Khazraji, 481 U.S. 604 (1987). The very object of the statutory definition in question and of its earlier congressional counterpart in the Hawaiian Homes Commission Act is to treat the early Hawaiians as a distinct people, commanding their own recognition and respect. The State, in enacting the legislation before us, has used ancestry as a racial definition and for a racial purpose.

The history of the State's definition demonstrates the point....

A different definition of "Hawaiian" was first promulgated in 1978 as one of the proposed amendments to the State Constitution. As proposed, "Hawaiian" was defined as "any descendant of the races inhabiting the Hawaiian Islands, previous to 1778." Rejected as not ratified in a valid manner, the definition was modified and in the end promulgated in statutory form as quoted above. By the drafters' own admission, however, any changes to the language were at most cosmetic. Noting that "the definitions of 'native Hawaiian' and 'Hawaiian' are changed to substitute 'peoples' for 'races,'" the drafters of the revised definition "stressed that this change is non-substantive, and that 'peoples' does mean 'races.'"...

As for the further argument that the restriction differentiates even among Polynesian people and is based simply on the date of an ancestor's residence in Hawaii, this too is insufficient to prove the classification is nonracial in purpose and operation. Simply because a class defined by ancestry does not include all members of the race does not suffice to make the classification race neutral. Here, the State's argument is undermined by its express racial purpose and by its actual effects.

The ancestral inquiry mandated by the State implicates the same grave concerns as a classification specifying a particular race by name. One of the principal reasons race is treated as a forbidden classification is that it demeans the dignity and worth of a person to be judged by ancestry instead of by his or her own merit and essential qualities. An inquiry into ancestral lines is not consistent with respect based on the unique personality each of us possesses, a respect the Constitution itself secures in its concern for persons and citizens.

The ancestral inquiry mandated by the State is forbidden by the Fifteenth Amendment for the further reason that the use of racial classifications is corruptive of the whole legal order democratic elections seek to preserve. The law itself may not become the instrument for generating the prejudice and hostility all too often directed against persons whose particular ancestry is disclosed by their ethnic characteristics and cultural traditions.... Ancestral tracing of this sort achieves its purpose by creating a legal category which employs the same mechanisms, and causes the same injuries, as laws or statutes that use race by name. The State's electoral restriction enacts a race-based voting qualification.

IV

The State offers three principal defenses of its voting law, any of which, it contends, allows it to prevail even if the classification is a racial one under the Fifteenth Amendment. We examine, and reject, each of these arguments.

A

The most far reaching of the State's arguments is that exclusion of non-Hawaiians from voting is permitted under our cases allowing the differential treatment of certain members of Indian tribes. The decisions of this Court, interpreting the effect of treaties and congressional enactments on the subject, have held that various tribes retained some elements of quasi-sovereign authority, even after cession of their lands to the United States. The retained tribal authority relates to self-governance. In reliance on that theory the Court has sustained a federal provision giving employment preferences to persons of tribal ancestry. [*Morton v. Mancari*].

If Hawaii's restriction were to be sustained under *Mancari* we would be required to accept some beginning premises not yet established in our case law. Among other postulates, it would be necessary to conclude that Congress ... has determined that native Hawaiians have a status like that of Indians in organized tribes, and that it may, and has, delegated to the State a broad authority to preserve that status. These propositions would raise questions of considerable moment and difficulty. It is a matter of some dispute, for instance, whether Congress may treat the native Hawaiians as it does the Indian tribes. We can stay far off that difficult terrain, however.

The State's argument fails for a more basic reason. Even were we to take the substantial step of finding authority in Congress, delegated to the State, to treat Hawaiians or native Hawaiians as tribes, Congress may not authorize a State to create a voting scheme of this sort.

Of course, as we have established in a series of cases, Congress may fulfill its treaty obligations and its responsibilities to the Indian tribes by enacting legislation dedicated to their circumstances and needs. As we have observed, "every piece of legislation dealing with Indian tribes and reservations . . . singles out for special treatment a constituency of tribal Indians."

[Morton v. *Mancari*] presented the somewhat different issue of a preference in hiring and promoting at the federal Bureau of Indian Affairs (BIA), a preference which favored individuals who were "'one-fourth or more degree Indian blood and . . . members of a Federally-recognized tribe.'" Although the classification had a racial component, the Court found it important that the preference was "not directed towards a 'racial' group consisting of 'Indians,'" but rather "only to members of 'federally recognized' tribes." "In this sense," the Court held, "the preference [was] political rather than racial in nature." ....

Hawaii would extend the limited exception of *Mancari* to a new and larger dimension. The State contends that "one of the very purposes of OHA -- and the challenged voting provision -- is to afford Hawaiians a measure of self-governance," and so it fits the model of *Mancari*. It does not follow from *Mancari*, however, that Congress may authorize a State to establish a voting scheme that limits the electorate for its public officials to a class of tribal Indians, to the exclusion of all non-Indian citizens.

The tribal elections established by the federal statutes the State cites illuminate its error. If a non-Indian lacks a right to vote in tribal elections, it is for the reason that such elections are the internal affair of a quasi-sovereign. The OHA elections, by contrast, are the affair of the State of Hawaii. OHA is a state agency, established by the State Constitution, responsible for the administration of state laws and obligations. The Hawaiian Legislature has declared that OHA exists to serve "as the principal public agency in the State responsible for the performance, development, and coordination of programs and activities relating to native Hawaiians and Hawaiians." Foremost among the obligations entrusted to this agency is the administration of a share of the revenues and proceeds from public lands, granted to Hawaii to "be held by said State as a public trust."....

Although it is apparent that OHA has a unique position under state law, it is just as apparent that it remains an arm of the State.

The validity of the voting restriction is the only question before us. As the court of appeals did, we assume the validity of the underlying administrative structure and trusts, without intimating any opinion on that point. Nonetheless, the elections for OHA trustee are elections of the State, not of a separate quasi-sovereign, and they are elections to which the Fifteenth Amendment applies....

B

Hawaii further contends that the limited voting franchise is sustainable under a series of cases holding that the rule of one person, one vote does not pertain to certain special purpose districts such as water or irrigation districts. Just as the *Mancari* argument would have involved a significant extension or new application of that case, so too it is far from clear that [this] line of cases would be at all applicable to statewide elections for an agency with the powers and responsibilities of OHA.

We would not find those cases dispositive in any event, however. The question before us is not the one-person, one-vote requirement of the Fourteenth Amendment, but the race neutrality command of the Fifteenth Amendment. Our special purpose district cases have not suggested that compliance with the one-person, one-vote rule of the Fourteenth Amendment somehow excuses compliance with the Fifteenth Amendment. We reject that argument here.... The Fifteenth Amendment has independent meaning and force. A State may not deny or abridge the right to vote on account of race, and this law does so.

C

Hawaii's final argument is that the voting restriction does no more than ensure an alignment of interests between the fiduciaries and the beneficiaries of a trust. Thus, the contention goes, the restriction is based on beneficiary status rather than race.

As an initial matter, the contention founders on its own terms, for it is not clear that the voting classification is symmetric with the beneficiaries of the programs OHA administers. Although the bulk of the funds for which OHA is responsible appears to be earmarked for the benefit of "native Hawaiians," the State permits both "native Hawaiians" and "Hawaiians" to vote for the office of trustee. The classification thus appears to create, not eliminate, a differential alignment between the identity of OHA trustees and what the State calls beneficiaries.

Hawaii's argument fails on more essential grounds. The State's position rests, in the end, on the demeaning premise that citizens of a particular race are somehow more qualified than others to vote on certain matters. That reasoning attacks the central meaning of the Fifteenth Amendment. The Amendment applies to "any election in which public issues are decided or public officials selected." There is no room under the Amendment for the concept that the right to vote in a particular election can be allocated based on race. Race cannot qualify some and disqualify others from full participation in our democracy. All citizens, regardless of race, have an interest in selecting officials who make policies on their behalf, even if those policies will affect some groups more than others. Under the Fifteenth Amendment voters are treated not as members of a distinct race but as members of the whole citizenry. Hawaii may not assume, based on race, that petitioner or any other of its citizens will not cast a principled vote....

* * *

When the culture and way of life of a people are all but engulfed by a history beyond their control, their sense of loss may extend down through generations; and their dismay may be shared by many members of the larger community. As the State of Hawaii attempts to address these realities, it must, as always, seek the political consensus that begins with a sense of shared purpose. One of the necessary beginning points is this principle: The Constitution of the United States, too, has become the heritage of all the citizens of Hawaii.

In this case the Fifteenth Amendment invalidates the electoral qualification based on ancestry. The judgment of the Court of Appeals for the Ninth Circuit is reversed.

JUSTICE BREYER, with whom JUSTICE SOUTER joins, concurring in the result.

I agree with much of what the Court says and with its result, but I do not agree with the critical rationale that underlies that result. Hawaii seeks to justify its voting scheme by drawing an analogy between its Office of Hawaiian Affairs (OHA) and a trust for the benefit of an Indian Tribe....

[I]n my view, we should reject Hawaii's effort to justify its rules through analogy to a trust for an Indian tribe because the record makes clear that (1) there is no "trust" for native Hawaiians here, and (2) OHA's electorate, as defined in the statute, does not sufficiently resemble an Indian tribe....

[The lands ceded to by the federal government to Hawaii were given] to benefit all the people of Hawaii. The [relevant] Act specifies that the land is to be used for the education of, the developments of homes and farms for, the making of public improvements for, and public use by, all of Hawaii's citizens, as well as for the betterment of those who are "native."

Moreover, OHA funding comes from several different sources.... All of OHA's funding is authorized by ordinary state statutes.... OHA is simply a special purpose department of Hawaii's state government.

As importantly, the statute defines the electorate in a way that is not analogous to membership in an Indian tribe. Native Hawaiians, considered as a group, may be analogous to tribes of other Native Americans. But the statute does not limit the electorate to native Hawaiians. Rather it adds to approximately 80,000 native Hawaiians about 130,000 additional "Hawaiians," defined as including anyone with one ancestor who lived in Hawaii prior to 1778, thereby including individuals who are less than one five-hundredth original Hawaiian (assuming nine generations between 1778 and the present)....

I have been unable to find any Native American tribal definition that is so broad. The Alaska Native Claims Settlement Act, for example, defines a "Native" as "a person of one-fourth degree or more Alaska Indian" or one "who is regarded as an Alaska Native by the Native village or Native group of which he claims to be a member and whose father or mother is . . . regarded as Native by any village or group" (a classification perhaps more likely to reflect real group membership than any blood quantum requirement). Many tribal constitutions define membership in terms of having had an ancestor whose name appeared on a tribal roll -- but in the far less distant past. See, e.g., Constitution of the Choctaw Nation of Oklahoma, Art. II (membership consists of persons on final rolls approved in 1906 and their lineal descendants); Constitution of the Sac and Fox Tribe of Indians of Oklahoma, Art. II (membership consists of persons on official roll of 1937, children since born to two members of the Tribe, and children born to one member and a nonmember if admitted by the council); Revised Constitution of the Jicarilla Apache Tribe, Art. III (membership consists of persons on official roll of 1968 and children of one member of the Tribe who are at least three-eighths Jicarilla Apache Indian blood); Revised Constitution Mescalero Apache Tribe, Art. IV (membership consists of persons on the official roll of 1936 and children born to at least one enrolled member who are at least one-fourth degree Mescalero Apache blood).

Of course, a Native American tribe has broad authority to define its membership. There must, however, be some limit on what is reasonable, at the least when a State (which is not itself a tribe) creates the definition. And to define that membership in terms of 1 possible ancestor out of 500, thereby creating a vast and unknowable body of potential members -- leaving some combination of luck and interest to determine which potential members become actual voters -- goes well beyond any reasonable limit. It was not a tribe, but rather the State of Hawaii, that created this definition; and, as I have pointed out, it is not like any actual membership classification created by any actual tribe.

These circumstances are sufficient, in my view, to destroy the analogy on which Hawaii's justification must depend.... [T]he analogies they here offer are too distant to save a race-based voting definition that in their absence would clearly violate the Fifteenth Amendment. For that reason I agree with the majority's ultimate conclusion.

JUSTICE STEVENS, with whom JUSTICE GINSBURG joins as to Part II, dissenting.

The Court's holding today rests largely on the repetition of glittering generalities that have little, if any, application to the compelling history of the State of Hawaii. When that history is held up against the manifest purpose of the Fourteenth and Fifteenth Amendments, and against two centuries of this Court's federal Indian law, it is clear to me that Hawaii's election scheme should be upheld.

I

.... OHA was intended to advance multiple goals: to carry out the duties of the trust relationship between the Islands' indigenous peoples and the Government of the United States; to compensate for past wrongs to the ancestors of these peoples; and to help preserve the distinct, indigenous culture that existed for centuries before Cook's arrival. As explained by the senior Senator from Hawaii, Senator Inouye, who is not himself a native Hawaiian but rather (like petitioner) is a member of the majority of Hawaiian voters who supported the 1978 amendments, the amendments reflect "an honest and sincere attempt on the part of the people of Hawai'i to rectify the wrongs of the past, and to put into being the mandate of our Federal government -- the betterment of the conditions of Native Hawaiians."

Today the Court concludes that Hawaii's method of electing the trustees of OHA violates the Fifteenth Amendment. In reaching that conclusion, the Court has assumed that the programs administered by OHA are valid. That assumption is surely correct. In my judgment, however, the reasons supporting the legitimacy of OHA and its programs in general undermine the basis for the Court's decision holding its trustee election provision invalid. The OHA election provision violates neither the Fourteenth Amendment nor the Fifteenth.

That conclusion is in keeping with three overlapping principles. First, the Federal Government must be, and has been, afforded wide latitude in carrying out its obligations arising from the special relationship it has with the aboriginal peoples, a category that includes the native Hawaiians, whose lands are now a part of the territory of the United States. In addition, there exists in this case the State's own fiduciary responsibility -- arising from its establishment of a public trust -- for administering assets granted it by the Federal Government in part for the benefit of native Hawaiians. Finally, even if one were to ignore the more than two centuries of Indian law precedent and practice on which this case follows, there is simply no invidious discrimination present in this effort to see that indigenous peoples are compensated for past wrongs, and to preserve a distinct and vibrant culture that is as much a part of this Nation's heritage as any.

II

Throughout our Nation's history, this Court has recognized both the plenary power of Congress over the affairs of native Americans and the fiduciary character of the special federal relationship with descendants of those once sovereign peoples. The source of the Federal Government's responsibility toward the Nation's native inhabitants, who were subject to European and then American military conquest, has been explained by this Court in the crudest terms, but they remain instructive nonetheless.

> These Indian tribes are the wards of the nation. They are communities dependent on the United States. Dependent largely for their daily food. Dependent for their political rights . . . . From their very weakness and helplessness, so largely due to the course of dealing of the Federal Government with them and the treaties in which it has been promised, there arises the duty of protection, and with it the power. This has always been recognized by the Executive, and by Congress, and by this court, whenever the question has arisen.

.... Critically, neither the extent of Congress' sweeping power nor the character of the trust relationship with indigenous peoples has depended on the ancient racial origins of the people, the allotment of tribal lands, the coherence or existence of tribal self-government, or the varying definitions of "Indian" Congress has chosen to adopt. Rather, when it comes to the exercise of Congress' plenary power in Indian affairs, this Court has ... concluded that as "long as the special treatment can be tied rationally to the fulfillment of Congress' unique obligation

towards the Indians, such legislative judgments will not be disturbed."
Morton v. *Mancari*, 417 U.S. 535 (1974).

As the history recited by the majority reveals, the grounds for
recognizing the existence of federal trust power here are overwhelming.
Shortly before its annexation in 1898, the Republic of Hawaii (installed
by United States merchants in a revolution facilitated by the United
States Government) expropriated some 1.8 million acres of land that it
then ceded to the United States. In the Organic Act establishing the
Territory of Hawaii, Congress provided that those lands should remain
under the control of the territorial government "until otherwise provided
for by Congress," By 1921, Congress recognized that the influx of foreign
infectious diseases, mass immigration coupled with poor housing and
sanitation, hunger, and malnutrition had taken their toll. Confronted
with the reality that the Hawaiian people had been "frozen out of their
lands and driven into the cities," Congress decided that 27 specific tracts
of the lands ceded in 1898, comprising about 203,500 acres, should be
used to provide farms and residences for native Hawaiians. Relying on
the precedent of previous federal laws granting Indians special rights in
public lands, Congress created the Hawaiian Homes Commission to
implement its goal of rehabilitating the native people and culture.[17]
Hawaii was required to adopt this Act as a condition of statehood in the
Hawaii Statehood Admissions Act (Admissions Act). And in an effort to
secure the Government's duty to the indigenous peoples, § 5 of the Act
conveyed 1.2 million acres of land to the State to be held in trust "for the
betterment of the conditions of native Hawaiians" and certain other
public purposes.

The nature of and motivation for the special relationship between
the indigenous peoples and the United States Government was
articulated in explicit detail in 1993, when Congress adopted a Joint
Resolution containing a formal "apology to Native Hawaiians on behalf
of the United States for the overthrow of the Kingdom of Hawaii."
Among other acknowledgments, the resolution stated that the 1.8
million acres of ceded lands had been obtained "without the consent of
or compensation to the Native Hawaiian people of Hawaii or their
sovereign government."

In the end, however, one need not even rely on this official
apology to discern a well-established federal trust relationship with the

---

[17]

    .... [One cannot] pretend that this law fits simply within our non-Indian
cases under the Fifteenth Amendment. As the preceding discussion of *Mancari* and
our other Indian law cases reveals, this Court has never understood laws relating to
indigenous peoples simply as legal classifications defined by race. Even where, unlike
here, blood quantum requirements are express, this Court has repeatedly
acknowledged that an overlapping political interest predominates. It is only by
refusing to face this Court's entire body of Indian law, that the majority is able to hold
that the OHA qualification denies non-"Hawaiians" the right to vote "on account of
race."

native Hawaiians. Among the many and varied laws passed by Congress in carrying out its duty to indigenous peoples, more than 150 today expressly include native Hawaiians as part of the class of Native Americans benefited. By classifying native Hawaiians as "Native Americans" for purposes of these statutes, Congress has made clear that native Hawaiians enjoy many of "the same rights and privileges accorded to American Indian, Alaska Native, Eskimo, and Aleut communities."

While splendidly acknowledging this history -- specifically including the series of agreements and enactments the history reveals -- the majority fails to recognize its import. The descendants of the native Hawaiians share with the descendants of the Native Americans on the mainland or in the Aleutian Islands not only a history of subjugation at the hands of colonial forces, but also a purposefully created and specialized "guardian-ward" relationship with the Government of the United States. It follows that legislation targeting the native Hawaiians must be evaluated according to the same understanding of equal protection that this Court has long applied to the Indians on the continental United States: that "special treatment . . . be tied rationally to the fulfillment of Congress' unique obligation" toward the native peoples.

Declining to confront the rather simple logic of the foregoing, the majority would seemingly reject the OHA voting scheme for a pair of different reasons. First, Congress' trust-based power is confined to dealings with tribes, not with individuals, and no tribe or indigenous sovereign entity is found among the native Hawaiians. Second, the elections are "the affair of the State," not of a tribe, and upholding this law would be "to permit a State, by racial classification, to fence out whole classes of citizens from decision making in critical state affairs." In my view, neither of these reasons overcomes the otherwise compelling similarity, fully supported by our precedent, between the once subjugated, indigenous peoples of the continental United States and the peoples of the Hawaiian Islands whose historical sufferings and status parallel those of the continental Native Americans.

Membership in a tribe, the majority suggests, rather than membership in a race or class of descendants, has been the sine qua non of governmental power in the realm of Indian law .... But as scholars have often pointed out, tribal membership cannot be seen as the decisive factor in this Court's opinion upholding the BIA preferences in *Mancari*; the hiring preference at issue in that case not only extended to non-tribal member Indians, it also required for eligibility that ethnic Native Americans possess a certain quantum of Indian blood. Indeed, the Federal Government simply has not been limited in its special dealings with the native peoples to laws affecting tribes or tribal Indians alone. In light of this precedent, it is a painful irony indeed to conclude that native Hawaiians are not entitled to special benefits designed to restore a measure of native self-governance because they currently lack any vestigial native government -- a possibility of which history and the actions of this Nation have deprived them....

Of greater concern to the majority is the fact that we are confronted here with a state constitution and legislative enactment -- passed by a majority of the entire population of Hawaii -- rather than a law passed by Congress or a tribe itself. But as our own precedent makes clear, this reality does not alter our analysis. As I have explained, OHA and its trustee elections can hardly be characterized simply as an "affair of the State" alone; they are the instruments for implementing the Federal Government's trust relationship with a once sovereign indigenous people. This Court has held more than once that the federal power to pass laws fulfilling its trust relationship with the Indians may be delegated to the States. Most significant is our opinion in *Washington v. Confederated Bands and Tribes of Yakima Nation*, 439 U.S. 463 (1979), in which we upheld against a Fourteenth Amendment challenge a state law assuming jurisdiction over Indian tribes within a State. While we recognized that States generally do not have the same special relationship with Indians that the Federal Government has, we concluded that because the state law was enacted "in response to a federal measure" intended to achieve the result accomplished by the challenged state law, the state law itself need only "'rationally further the purpose identified by the State.'"

The state statutory and constitutional scheme here was without question intended to implement the express desires of the Federal Government....

The sole remaining question under *Mancari* and Yakima is thus whether the State's scheme "rationally furthers the purpose identified by the State." Under this standard, as with the BIA preferences in *Mancari*, the OHA voting requirement is certainly reasonably designed to promote "self-government" by the descendants of the indigenous Hawaiians, and to make OHA "more responsive to the needs of its constituent groups." The OHA statute provides that the agency is to be held "separate" and "independent of the [State] executive branch"; OHA executes a trust, which, by its very character, must be administered for the benefit of Hawaiians and native Hawaiians; and OHA is to be governed by a board of trustees that will reflect the interests of the trust's native Hawaiian beneficiaries....

The foregoing reasons are to me more than sufficient to justify the OHA trust system and trustee election provision under the Fourteenth Amendment.

III

Although the Fifteenth Amendment tests the OHA scheme by a different measure, it is equally clear to me that the trustee election provision violates neither the letter nor the spirit of that Amendment.

Section 1 of the Fifteenth Amendment provides:

The right of citizens of the United States to vote shall not be denied or abridged by the United States or by any State on account of race, color, or previous condition of servitude.

As the majority itself must tacitly admit, the terms of the Amendment itself do not here apply. The OHA voter qualification speaks in terms of ancestry and current residence, not of race or color.... The ability to vote is a function of the lineal descent of a modern-day resident of Hawaii, not the blood-based characteristics of that resident, or of the blood-based proximity of that resident to the "peoples" from whom that descendant arises.

The distinction between ancestry and race is more than simply one of plain language. The ability to trace one's ancestry to a particular progenitor at a single distant point in time may convey no information about one's own apparent or acknowledged race today. Neither does it of necessity imply one's own identification with a particular race, or the exclusion of any others "on account of race." The terms manifestly carry distinct meanings, and ancestry was not included by the framers in the Amendment's prohibitions.

Presumably recognizing this distinction, the majority relies on the fact that "ancestry can be a proxy for race." That is, of course, true, but it by no means follows that ancestry is always a proxy for race. Cases in which ancestry served as such a proxy are dramatically different from this one. For example, the literacy requirement at issue in *Guinn v. United States*, 238 U.S. 347 (1915), relied on such a proxy. As part of a series of blatant efforts to exclude blacks from voting, Oklahoma exempted from its literacy requirement people whose ancestors were entitled to vote prior to the enactment of the Fifteenth Amendment. The *Guinn* scheme patently "served only to perpetuate . . . old [racially discriminatory voting] laws and to effect a transparent racial exclusion." As in *Guinn*, the voting laws held invalid under the Fifteenth Amendment in all of the cases cited by the majority were fairly and properly viewed through a specialized lens -- a lens honed in specific detail to reveal the realities of time, place, and history behind the voting restrictions being tested.

That lens not only fails to clarify, it fully obscures the realities of this case, virtually the polar opposite of the Fifteenth Amendment cases on which the Court relies. In *Terry v. Adams*, 345 U.S. 461 (1953), for example, the Court held that the Amendment proscribed the Texas "Jaybird primaries" that used neutral voting qualifications "with a single proviso -- Negroes are excluded." Similarly, in *Smith v. Allwright*, 321 U.S. 649 (1944), it was the blatant "discrimination against Negroes" practiced by a political party that was held to be state action within the meaning of the Amendment. Cases such as these that "strike down these voting systems . . . designed to exclude one racial class (at least) from voting," have no application to a system designed to empower politically the remaining members of a class of once sovereign, indigenous people.

Ancestry surely can be a proxy for race, or a pretext for invidious racial discrimination. But it is simply neither proxy nor pretext here. All of the persons who are eligible to vote for the trustees of OHA share two qualifications that no other person old enough to vote possesses: They are beneficiaries of the public trust created by the State and administered by OHA, and they have at least one ancestor who was a resident of Hawaii in 1778. A trust whose terms provide that the trustees shall be elected by a class including beneficiaries is hardly a novel concept. The Committee that drafted the voting qualification explained that the trustees here should be elected by the beneficiaries because "people to whom assets belong should have control over them . . . . The election of the board will enhance representative governance and decision-making accountability and, as a result, strengthen the fiduciary relationship between the board member, as trustee, and the native Hawaiian, as beneficiary." The described purpose of this aspect of the classification thus exists wholly apart from race. It is directly focused on promoting both the delegated federal mandate, and the terms of the State's own trustee responsibilities.

The majority makes much of the fact that the OHA trust -- which it assumes is legitimate -- should be read as principally intended to benefit the smaller class of "native Hawaiians," who are defined as at least one-half descended from a native islander circa 1778, not the larger class of "Hawaiians," which includes "any descendant" of those aboriginal people who lived in Hawaii in 1778 and "which peoples thereafter have continued to reside in Hawaii." It is, after all, the majority notes, the larger class of Hawaiians that enjoys the suffrage right in OHA elections. There is therefore a mismatch in interest alignment between the trust beneficiaries and the trustee electors, the majority contends, and it thus cannot be said that the class of qualified voters here is defined solely by beneficiary status.

While that may or may not be true depending upon the construction of the terms of the trust, there is surely nothing racially invidious about a decision to enlarge the class of eligible voters to include "any descendant" of a 1778 resident of the Islands. The broader category of eligible voters serves quite practically to ensure that, regardless how "dilute" the race of native Hawaiians becomes -- a phenomenon also described in the majority's lavish historical summary -- there will remain a voting interest whose ancestors were a part of a political, cultural community, and who have inherited through participation and memory the set of traditions the trust seeks to protect. The putative mismatch only underscores the reality that it cannot be purely a racial interest that either the trust or the election provision seeks to secure; the political and cultural interests served are -- unlike racial survival -- shared by both native Hawaiians and Hawaiians.

Beyond even this, the majority's own historical account makes clear that the inhabitants of the Hawaiian Islands whose descendants comprise the instant class are identified and remain significant as much because of culture as because of race. By the time of Cook's arrival, "the Hawaiian people had developed, over the preceding 1,000 years or so, a cultural and political structure, . . . well-established traditions and customs and . . . a polytheistic religion." Prior to 1778, although there "was no private ownership of land," the native Hawaiians "lived in a highly organized, self-sufficient, subsistent social system based on communal land tenure with a sophisticated language, culture and religion." According to Senator Akaka, their society "was steeped in science [and they] honored their 'aina (land) and environment, and therefore developed methods of irrigation, agriculture, aquaculture, navigation, medicine, fishing and other forms of subsistence whereby the land and sea were efficiently used without waste or damage. Respect for the environment and for others formed the basis of their culture and tradition." Legends and oral histories passed from one generation to another are reflected in artifacts such as carved images, colorful feathered capes, songs, and dances that survive today. For some, Pele, the God of Fire, still inhabits the crater of Kilauea, and the word of the Kahuna is still law. It is this culture, rather than the Polynesian race, that is uniquely Hawaiian and in need of protection.

Even if one refuses to recognize the beneficiary status of OHA trustee voters entirely,[18] it cannot be said that the ancestry-based voting qualification here simply stands in the shoes of a classification that would either privilege or penalize "on account of" race. The OHA voting qualification -- part of a statutory scheme put in place by democratic vote of a multiracial majority of all state citizens, including those non-"Hawaiians" who are not entitled to vote in OHA trustee elections --

---

[18]

    JUSTICE BREYER's even broader contention that "there is no 'trust' for native Hawaiians here," appears to make the greater mistake of conflating the public trust established by Hawaii's Constitution and laws, with the "trust" relationship between the Federal Government and the indigenous peoples....

    .... [N]either the particular terms of the State's public trust nor the particular source of OHA funding "destroys" the centrally relevant trust "analogy" on which Hawaii relies -- that of the relationship between the Federal Government and indigenous Indians on this continent, as compared with the relationship between the Federal Government and indigenous Hawaiians in the now United States-owned Hawaiian Islands. That trust relationship -- the only trust relevant to the Indian law analogy -- includes the power to delegate authority to the States....

appropriately includes every resident of Hawaii having at least one ancestor who lived in the Islands in 1778. That is, among other things, the audience to whom the congressional apology was addressed. Unlike a class including only full-blooded Polynesians -- as one would imagine were the class strictly defined in terms of race -- the OHA election provision excludes all full-blooded Polynesians currently residing in Hawaii who are not descended from a 1778 resident of Hawaii. Conversely, unlike many of the old southern voting schemes in which any potential voter with a 'taint' of non-Hawaiian blood would be excluded, the OHA scheme excludes no descendant of a 1778 resident because he or she is also part European, Asian, or African as a matter of race. The classification here is thus both too inclusive and not inclusive enough to fall strictly along racial lines.

.... [T]he majority next posits that "one of the principal reasons race is treated as a forbidden classification is that it demeans the dignity and worth of a person to be judged by ancestry instead of by his or her own merit and essential qualities." That is, of course, true when ancestry is the basis for denying or abridging one's right to vote or to share the blessings of freedom. But it is quite wrong to ignore the relevance of ancestry to claims of an interest in trust property, or to a shared interest in a proud heritage. There would be nothing demeaning in a law that established a trust to manage Monticello and provided that the descendants of Thomas Jefferson should elect the trustees. Such a law would be equally benign, regardless of whether those descendants happened to be members of the same race.[19]

In this light, it is easy to understand why the classification here is not "demeaning" at all, for it is simply not based on the "premise that citizens of a particular race are somehow more qualified than others to vote on certain matters." It is based on the permissible assumption in this context that families with "any" ancestor who lived in Hawaii in 1778, and whose ancestors thereafter continued to live in Hawaii, have a claim to compensation and self-determination that others do not. For the multiracial majority of the citizens of the State of Hawaii to recognize that deep reality is not to demean their own interests but to honor those of others.

It thus becomes clear why the majority is likewise wrong to conclude that the OHA voting scheme is likely to "become the

---

[19]

Indeed, "in one form or another, the right to pass on property -- to one's family in particular -- has been part of the Anglo-American legal system since feudal times." *Hodel v. Irving*, 481 U.S. 704 (1987). Even the most minute fractional interests that can be identified after allotted lands are passed through several generations can receive legal recognition and protection. Thus, we held [in *Hodel v. Irving*] ... that inherited shares of parcels allotted to the Sioux in 1889 could not be taken without compensation even though their value was nominal and it was necessary to use a common denominator of 3,394,923,840,000 to identify the size of the smallest interest. Whether it is wise to provide recompense for all of the descendants of an injured class after several generations have come and gone is a matter of policy, but the fact that their interests were acquired by inheritance rather than by assignment surely has no constitutional significance.

instrument for generating the prejudice and hostility all too often directed against persons whose particular ancestry is disclosed by their ethnic characteristics and cultural traditions." The political and cultural concerns that motivated the nonnative majority of Hawaiian voters to establish OHA reflected an interest in preserving through the self-determination of a particular people ancient traditions that they value. The fact that the voting qualification was established by the entire electorate in the State -- the vast majority of which is not native Hawaiian -- testifies to their judgment concerning the Court's fear of "prejudice and hostility" against the majority of state residents who are not "Hawaiian," such as petitioner. Our traditional understanding of democracy and voting preferences makes it difficult to conceive that the majority of the State's voting population would have enacted a measure that discriminates against, or in any way represents prejudice and hostility toward, that self-same majority. Indeed, the best insurance against that danger is that the electorate here retains the power to revise its laws....

JUSTICE GINSBURG, dissenting.

I dissent essentially for the reasons stated by JUSTICE STEVENS in Part II of his dissenting opinion. Congress' prerogative to enter into special trust relationships with indigenous peoples ... is not confined to tribal Indians. In particular, it encompasses native Hawaiians, whom Congress has in numerous statutes reasonably treated as qualifying for the special status long recognized for other once-sovereign indigenous peoples. That federal trust responsibility, both the Court and JUSTICE STEVENS recognize, has been delegated by Congress to the State of Hawaii. Both the Office of Hawaiian Affairs and the voting scheme here at issue are "tied rationally to the fulfillment" of that obligation. No more is needed to demonstrate the validity of the Office and the voting provision under the Fourteenth and Fifteenth Amendments.

NOTES AND QUESTIONS

1. For more extensive discussions of the special status of native Hawaiians, see Jon Van Dyke, *The Political Status of the Hawaiian People*, 17 YALE L. & POL'Y REV. 95 (1998); Stuart Benjamin, Note, *Equal Protection and the Special Relationship: The Case of Native Hawaiians*, 106 YALE L. J. 537 (1996).

2. Is *Rice* simply a modern-day version of *Guinn*, or does it – like the *Shaw* cases – suggest a distinction between racial distinctions and race discrimination?

3. Given the *Shaw* cases, why did the Court decide *Rice* solely as a Fifteenth Amendment case, rather than under both the Fourteenth and Fifteenth Amendments?

4. In *Office of Hawaiian Affairs v. Cayetano*, 94 Haw. 1 (2000), the Hawaii Supreme Court addressed the implications of *Rice* for the continued tenure in office of the OHA trustees. Following the U.S. Supreme Court's decision, Rice and the State entered into a stipulation that judgment be entered "declaring only that denying plaintiff Harold F. Rice the right to vote in elections of trustees for the Office of Hawaiian Affairs because he is not "Hawaiian" violated the Fifteenth Amendment" and that "[o]ther than to apply for costs and move for an award of reasonable attorney's fees, plaintiff seeks no further relief in this case ...." Thus, although Rice had originally sought a declaratory judgment that the present trustees were unconstitutionally and unlawfully elected and had no power to act, no court ever reached that issue.

Governor Cayetano, however, took the position that the elections of the eight OHA Trustees were invalid, that their positions were therefore vacant, and that he had the authority under state law to appoint replacement trustees.

On that limited question, the Hawaii Supreme Court disagreed:

> [The U.S.] Supreme Court, itself, did not specifically invalidate the election or find that the unconstitutional nature of the voting requirement mandates a new election.... Voiding an election and ordering a new one represents one of the more extreme remedies available to a court sitting in equity and is not a necessary response to all unconstitutional practices....

> Although Respondent believes federal law would support invalidation and removal of the eight trustees, he contends it is unnecessary to consider federal jurisprudence and submits that eight "vacancies" were created ... Respondent bases this conclusion on the following two-step process: (1) the Rice ruling means that eight trustees are only de facto trustees, and not lawful, i.e., "de jure" trustees; and (2) because the eight trustees are not lawful "de jure" trustees, there are eight "vacancies" within the meaning of the relevant statutes....

> A[n] officer becomes a de facto officer ... by exercising his or her duties ... under color of any election or an appointment by or pursuant to a public unconstitutional law, before the same is adjudged as such. Courts have consistently held that actions taken by de facto officeholders are valid and enforceable.

> Respondent is correct in his assertion that the OHA trustees are now de facto trustees. The eight OHA trustees, elected in the 1996 and 1998 elections, are officers who were elected under the color of an election pursuant to an unconstitutional public law, before the law was adjudged to be unconstitutional.

> Nonetheless, even if the eight OHA trustees are de facto trustees, Respondent offers no legal authority, and we have found none, to support the conclusion that there is an automatic vacancy when an officer holder becomes a de facto official due to the finding by a federal court that a portion of an election statute is unconstitutional. By contrast, there is legal authority that further removal action is required before the office is deemed vacant.

[A New York court] considered the status of councilmen elected before entry of a judgment finding that a method of apportionment was unconstitutional. The New York court acknowledged that the district plan under which the councilmen were elected was unconstitutional and that any election held under it was illegal. The court noted, however, that the judgment determined only the constitutionality of the districting plan and did not question the right of the councilmen to serve their full terms as elected officials. Thus, the court concluded that the councilmen were de facto councilmen and could not be removed except in a proper proceeding directed to that end.

.... [In this case, too,] the State must take further action apart from this proceeding before the positions presently held by the eight OHA trustees, elected in 1996 and 1998, are deemed vacant and ready to be filled [by the Governor]....

Although we agree with Respondent's contention that the Supreme Court opinion changed the status of the elected OHA trustees from de jure officeholders to de facto officeholders, the instant proceeding is not the appropriate proceeding to determine the present status of the trustees. If, in addition to the questions presented in the instant case, the State wishes to seek judicial determination of the propriety of the trustees to remain in their positions and believes the trustees should no longer hold office as a result of Rice v. Cayetano, the State should seek relief through a quo warranto petition ... Proceeding in that manner would allow the parties to present their reasons as to why the trustees should or should not be allowed to continue in office until the next election.

For a fuller treatment of this remedial question, see the Special Supplement Chapter, *When Elections Go Bad*.

CHAPTER NINE

Page 632 after note 4:

5. *Colorado Republican II* - The Supreme Court in *Colorado Republican* concluded that the advertisement in question was an independent expenditure protected by the First Amendment under *Buckley* but did not reach the issue of whether the First Amendment forbids limits on coordinated expenditures between political parties and their candidates, which are considered contributions under the FECA. However, on remand the federal district court held that the Party Expenditure Provision, which limits the amount of money a political party may spend in coordination with its candidates, violated the First Amendment, and the Tenth Circuit Court of Appeals affirmed. Despite the fact that the Supreme Court has typically upheld limitations on contributions, and has subject them to a lower standard of scrutiny, the Tenth Circuit held that the labels "contribution" and "expenditure" did not decide the case at hand. In holding the limitations on coordinated expenditures unconstitutional, the court concluded:

> [T]he Party Expenditure Provision constitutes a "significant interference" with the First Amendment rights of political parties. This interference effects more than a "marginal restriction upon the [parties'] ability to engage in free communication." The FEC has not demonstrated on remand that coordinated spending by political parties corrupts, or creates the appearance of corrupting, the electoral process. Therefore, [the Party Expenditure Provision's] limit on party spending is not "closely drawn" to the recognized governmental interest but instead constitutes an "unnecessary abridgment" of First Amendment freedoms.

Federal Election Commission v. Colorado Republican Fed. Campaign Comm'n, 213 F.3d 1221 (10th Cir. 2000). The Supreme Court recently granted a writ of certiorari to address this issue. Recall, however, that as the Supreme Court addresses Colorado Republican II, the facts of the case concern the 1986 Colorado senatorial election. What does 14 years of legal review of the FEC's determination say about the efficacy of this approach to regulating electoral conduct in the heat of an election battle?

6. After *Colorado Republican*, there were a clear majority of votes on the Supreme Court to overturn *Buckley*. These divided, however, between the group represented by Justice Thomas, who sought to overturn *Buckley's* restrictions on contributions, and the group represented by Justice Stevens, who would have overturned *Buckley's* restrictions on expenditures. Both of the

anti-*Buckley* wings are united by rejecting the core insight of *Buckley* that different first amendment regimes govern the contributions and expenditures side of electoral regulation. But they are divided by an inability to agree on the direction in which the *Buckley* edifice should fall. Thus, it may be said that not only is the FECA regime as modified by *Buckley* one that no legislature ever envisioned as a policy matter, as Professor Sorauf argues, but that even the *Buckley* modification of FECA is not one that could command the consensus of the Court. Yet *Buckley* remains oddly stable because the antagonism of the dissenting views prevents the emergence of any majority coalition for overturning *Buckley* – at least thus far.

7. Curiously, despite the dissatisfaction with *Buckley,* subsequent caselaw has only entrenched the contributions/expenditures analytic divide inherited from *Buckley.* Consider the realignment of Justices when the issue presented for review is not expenditures but contributions, as in the Court's most recent pronouncement on campaign finance.

NIXON v. SHRINK MISSOURI GOVERNMENT PAC
528 U.S. 377 (2000).

JUSTICE SOUTER delivered the opinion of the Court.

The principal issues in this case are whether *Buckley v. Valeo,* is authority for state limits on contributions to state political candidates and whether the federal limits approved in *Buckley*, with or without adjustment for inflation, define the scope of permissible state limitations today. We hold *Buckley* to be authority for comparable state regulation, which need not be pegged to *Buckley*'s dollars.

I.

In 1994, the Legislature of Missouri enacted Senate Bill 650 (SB650) to restrict the permissible amounts of contributions to candidates for state office. Mo. Rev. Stat. § 130.032 (1994). Before the statute became effective, however, Missouri voters approved a ballot initiative with even stricter contribution limits, effective immediately. The United States Court of Appeals for the Eighth Circuit then held the initiative's contribution limits unconstitutional under the First Amendment, with the upshot that the previously dormant 1994 statute took effect

As amended in 1997, that statute imposes contribution limits ranging from $ 250 to a $ 1,000, depending on specified state office or size of constituency. The particular provision [Mo. Rev. Stat. § 130.032] challenged here reads that:

> to elect an individual to the office of governor, lieutenant governor, secretary of state, state treasurer, state auditor or attorney general, [the amount of contributions made by or accepted from any person other than the candidate in any one election shall not exceed] one thousand dollars.

***

Respondents Shrink Missouri Government PAC, a political action committee, and Zev David Fredman, a candidate for the 1998 Republican nomination for state auditor, sought to enjoin enforcement of the contribution statute as violating their First and Fourteenth Amendment rights (presumably those of free speech, association, and equal protection, although the complaint did not so state). Shrink Missouri gave $ 1,025 to Fredman's candidate committee in 1997, and another $ 50 in 1998. Shrink Missouri represented that, without the limitation, it would contribute more to the Fredman campaign. Fredman alleged he could campaign effectively only with more generous contributions than § 130.032.1 allowed. On cross-motions for summary judgment, the District Court sustained the statute. Applying *Buckley v. Valeo* the court found adequate support for the law in the proposition that large contributions raise suspicions of influence peddling tending to undermine citizens' confidence "in the integrity of . . . government." The District Court rejected respondents' contention that inflation since *Buckley*'s approval of a federal $1000 restriction meant that the state limit of !,075 for a statewide office could not be constitutional today.

The Court of Appeals for the Eighth Circuit nonetheless enjoined enforcement of the law pending appeal and ultimately reversed the District Court. Finding that *Buckley* had "'articulated and applied a strict scrutiny standard of review,'" the Court of Appeals held that Missouri was bound to demonstrate "that it has a compelling interest and that the contribution limits at issue are narrowly drawn to serve that interest." The appeals court treated Missouri's claim of a compelling interest "in avoiding the corruption or the perception of corruption brought about when candidates for elective office accept large campaign contributions" as insufficient by itself to satisfy strict scrutiny.

***

Given the large number of States that limit political contributions, we granted certiorari to review the congruence of the Eighth Circuit's decision with *Buckley*. We reverse.

II.

A.

***

B.

In defending its own statute, Missouri espouses those same interests [that were addressed in *Buckley*] of preventing corruption and the appearance of it that flows from munificent campaign contributions. Even without the authority of *Buckley*, there would be no serious question about the legitimacy of the interests claimed, which, after all,

underlie bribery and anti-gratuity statutes. While neither law nor morals equate all political contributions, without more, with bribes, we spoke in *Buckley* of the perception of corruption "inherent in a regime of large individual financial contributions" to candidates for public office as a source of concern "almost equal" to *quid pro quo* improbity. The public interest in countering that perception was, indeed, the entire answer to the overbreadth claim raised in the *Buckley* case. This made perfect sense. Leave the perception of impropriety unanswered, and the cynical assumption that large donors call the tune could jeopardize the willingness of voters to take part in democratic governance. Democracy works "only if the people have faith in those who govern, and that faith is bound to be shattered when high
officials and their appointees engage in activities which arouse suspicions of malfeasance and corruption." United States v. Mississippi Valley Generating Co., 364 U.S. 520 (1961).

Although respondents neither challenge the legitimacy of these objectives nor call for any reconsideration of *Buckley*, they take the State to task, as the Court of Appeals did, for failing to justify the invocation of those interests with empirical evidence of actually corrupt practices or of a perception among Missouri voters that unrestricted contributions must have been exerting a covertly corrosive influence. The state statute is not void, however, for want of evidence.

The quantum of empirical evidence needed to satisfy heightened judicial scrutiny of legislative judgments will vary up or down with the novelty and plausibility of the justification raised. *Buckley* demonstrates that the dangers of large, corrupt contributions and the suspicion that large contributions are corrupt are neither novel nor implausible. The opinion noted that "the deeply disturbing examples surfacing after the 1972 election demonstrate that the problem [of corruption] is not an illusory one." Although we did not ourselves marshal the evidence in support of the congressional concern, we referred to "a number of the abuses" detailed in the Court of Appeals's decision, which described how corporations, well-financed interest groups, and rich individuals had made large contributions, some of which were illegal under existing law, others of which reached at least the verge of bribery. The evidence before the Court of Appeals described public revelations by the parties in question more than sufficient to show why voters would tend to identify a big donation with a corrupt purpose.

While *Buckley*'s evidentiary showing exemplifies a sufficient justification for contribution limits, it does not speak to what may be necessary as a minimum. As to that, respondents are wrong in arguing that in the years since *Buckley* came down we have "supplemented" its holding with a new requirement that governments enacting contribution limits must "'demonstrate that the recited harms are real, not merely conjectural,'" a contention for which respondents rely principally on *Colorado Republican.*. We have never accepted mere conjecture as adequate to carry a First Amendment burden, and *Colorado Republican* did not deal with a government's burden to justify limits on contributions. Although the principal opinion in that case charged the Government with failure to show a real risk of corruption, the issue in question was limits on independent expenditures by political parties, which the principal opinion expressly distinguished from contribution limits: "limitations on independent expenditures are less directly related to preventing corruption" than contributions are. In that case, the "constitutionally significant fact" that there was no "coordination between the candidate and the source of the expenditure" kept the principal opinion "from assuming, absent convincing evidence to the contrary, that [a limitation on expenditures] is necessary to combat a substantial danger of corruption of the electoral system." *Colorado Republican* thus goes hand in hand with *Buckley*, not toe to toe.

     ***

In any event, this case does not present a close call requiring further definition of whatever the State's evidentiary obligation may be. *** Although Missouri does not preserve legislative history, the State presented an affidavit from State Senator Wayne Goode, the co-chair of the state legislature's Interim Joint Committee on Campaign Finance Reform at the time the State enacted the contribution limits, who stated that large contributions have "'the real potential to buy votes.'" The District Court cited newspaper accounts of large contributions supporting inferences of impropriety. One report questioned the state treasurer's decision to use a certain bank for most of Missouri's banking business after that institution contributed $20,000 to the treasurer's campaign. Another made much of the receipt by a candidate for state auditor of a $40,000 contribution from a brewery and one for $20,000 from a bank. *** And although majority votes do not, as such, defeat First Amendment protections, the statewide vote on Proposition A certainly attested to the perception relied upon here: "An overwhelming 74 percent of the voters of Missouri determined that contribution limits are necessary to combat corruption and the appearance thereof."

[T]he closest respondents come to challenging these conclusions is their invocation of academic studies said to indicate that large contributions to public officials or candidates do not actually result in changes in candidates' positions. Brief for Respondents Shrink Missouri Government PAC et al. 41; Smith, *Money Talks Speech, Corruption, Equality, and Campaign Finance*, 86 GEO. L. J. 45, 58 (1997); Smith, *Faulty Assumptions and Undemocratic Consequences of Campaign Finance Reform*, 105 YALE L. J. 1049, 1067-1068 (1995). Other studies, however, point the other way. Reply Brief for Respondent Bray 4-5; F. SORAUF, INSIDE CAMPAIGN FINANCE 169 (1992); Hall & Wayman, *Buying Time: Moneyed Interests and the Mobilization of Bias in Congressional Committees*, 84 AM. POL. SCI. REV. 797 (1990); D. Magleby & C. Nelson, THE MONEY CHASE 78 (1990). Given the conflict among these publications, and the absence of any reason to think that public perception has been influenced by the studies cited by respondents, there is little reason to doubt that sometimes large contributions will work actual corruption of our political system, and no reason to question the existence of a corresponding suspicion among voters.

C.

Nor do we see any support for respondents' various arguments that in spite of their striking resemblance to the limitations sustained in *Buckley*, those in Missouri are so different in kind as to raise essentially a new issue about the adequacy of the Missouri statute's tailoring to serve its purposes. Here, as in *Buckley*, "there is no indication . . . that the contribution limitations imposed by the [law] would have any dramatically adverse effect on the funding of campaigns and political associations," and thus no showing that "the limitations prevented the candidates and political committees from amassing the resources necessary for effective advocacy." The District Court found here that in the period since the Missouri limits became effective, "candidates for state elected office [have been] quite able to raise funds sufficient to run effective campaigns," and that "candidates for political office in the state are still able to amass impressive campaign war chests." The plausibility of these conclusions is buttressed by petitioners' evidence that in the 1994 Missouri elections (before any relevant state limitations went into effect), 97.62 percent of all contributors to candidates for state auditor made contributions of $ 2,000 or less. Even if we were to assume that the contribution limits affected respondent Fredman's ability to wage a competitive campaign (no small assumption given that Fredman only identified one contributor, Shrink Missouri, that would have given him more than $1,075 per election), a showing of one affected individual does not point up a system of suppressed political advocacy that would be unconstitutional under *Buckley*.

***

D.

The dissenters in this case think our reasoning evades the real issue. Justice Thomas chides us for "hiding behind" *Buckley*, and Justice Kennedy faults us for seeing this case as "a routine application of our analysis" in *Buckley* instead of facing up to what he describes as the consequences of *Buckley*. Each dissenter would overrule *Buckley* and thinks we should do the same.

The answer is that we are supposed to decide this case. Shrink and Fredman did not request that *Buckley* be overruled; the furthest reach of their arguments about the law was that subsequent decisions already on the books had enhanced the State's burden of justification beyond what *Buckley* required, a proposition we have rejected as mistaken.

III.

There is no reason in logic or evidence to doubt the sufficiency of *Buckley* to govern this case in support of the Missouri statute. The judgment of the Court of Appeals is, accordingly, reversed, and the case is remanded for proceedings consistent with this opinion.

It is so ordered.

JUSTICE STEVENS, concurring.

Justice Kennedy suggests that the misuse of soft money tolerated by this Court's misguided decision in *Colorado Republican* demonstrates the need for a fresh examination of the constitutional issues raised by Congress' enactment of the Federal Election Campaign Acts of 1971 and 1974 and this Court's resolution of those issues in *Buckley v. Valeo.* In response to his call for a new beginning, therefore, I make one simple point. Money is property; it is not speech.

Speech has the power to inspire volunteers to perform a multitude of tasks on a campaign trail, on a battleground, or even on a football field. Money, meanwhile, has the power to pay hired laborers to perform the same tasks. It does not follow, however, that the First Amendment provides the same measure of protection to the use of money to accomplish such goals as it provides to the use of ideas to achieve the same results.

***

JUSTICE BREYER, with whom JUSTICE GINSBURG joins, concurring.

The dissenters accuse the Court of weakening the First Amendment. They believe that failing to adopt a "strict scrutiny" standard "balances away First Amendment freedoms." But the principal dissent oversimplifies the problem faced in the campaign finance context. It takes a difficult constitutional problem and turns it into a lopsided dispute between political expression and government censorship. Under the cover of this fiction and its accompanying formula, the dissent would make the Court absolute arbiter of a difficult question best left, in the main, to the political branches. I write separately to address the critical question of how the Court ought to review this kind of problem, and to explain why I believe the Court's choice here is correct.

If the dissent believes that the Court diminishes the importance of the First Amendment interests before us, it is wrong. The Court's opinion does not question the constitutional importance of political speech or that its protection lies at the heart of the First Amendment. Nor does it question the need for particularly careful, precise, and independent judicial review where, as here, that protection is at issue. But this is a case where constitutionally protected interests lie on both sides of the legal equation. For that reason there is no place for a strong presumption against constitutionality, of the sort often thought to accompany the words "strict scrutiny." Nor can we expect that mechanical application of the tests associated with "strict scrutiny" -- the tests of "compelling interests" and "least restrictive means" -- will properly resolve the difficult constitutional problem that campaign finance statutes pose.

On the one hand, a decision to contribute money to a campaign is a matter of First Amendment concern -- not because money is speech (it is not); but because it enables speech. Through contributions the contributor associates himself with the candidate's cause, helps the candidate communicate a political message with which the contributor agrees, and helps the candidate win by attracting the votes of similarly minded voters. Both political association and political communication are at stake.

On the other hand, restrictions upon the amount any one individual can contribute to a particular candidate seek to protect the integrity of the electoral process -- the means through which a free society democratically translates political speech into concrete governmental action. Moreover, by limiting the size of the largest contributions, such restrictions aim to democratize the influence that money itself may bring to bear upon the electoral process. In doing so, they seek to build public confidence in that process and broaden the base of a candidate's meaningful financial support, encouraging the public participation and open discussion that the First Amendment itself presupposes.

In service of these objectives, the statute imposes restrictions of degree. It does not deny the contributor the opportunity to associate with the candidate through a contribution, though it limits a contribution's size. Nor does it prevent the contributor from using money (alone or with others) to pay for the expression of the same views in other ways. Instead, it permits all supporters to contribute the same amount of money, in an attempt to make the process fairer and more democratic.

Under these circumstances, a presumption against constitutionality is out of place.... In such circumstances -- where a law significantly implicates competing constitutionally protected interests in complex ways -- the Court has closely scrutinized the statute's impact on those interests, but refrained from employing a simple test that effectively presumes unconstitutionality. Rather, it has balanced interests. And in practice that has meant asking whether the statute burdens any one such interest in a manner out of proportion to the statute's salutary effects upon the others (perhaps, but not necessarily, because of the existence of a clearly superior, less restrictive alternative). Where a legislature has significantly greater institutional expertise, as, for example, in the field of election regulation, the Court in practice defers to empirical legislative judgments -- at least where that deference does not risk such constitutional evils as, say, permitting incumbents to insulate themselves from effective electoral challenge. This approach is that taken in fact by *Buckley* for contributions, and is found generally where competing constitutional interests are implicated, such as privacy, First Amendment interests of listeners or viewers, and the integrity of the electoral process.... For the dissenters to call the approach "sui generis" overstates their case.

***

But what if I am wrong about *Buckley*? Suppose *Buckley* denies the political branches sufficient leeway to enact comprehensive solutions to the problems posed [*914] by campaign finance. If so, like Justice Kennedy, I believe the Constitution would require us to reconsider *Buckley*. With that understanding I join the Court's opinion.

JUSTICE KENNEDY, dissenting.

***

I.

Zev David Fredman asks us to evaluate his speech claim in the context of a system which favors candidates and officeholders whose campaigns are supported by soft money, usually funneled through political parties. The Court pays him no heed. The plain fact is that the compromise the Court invented in *Buckley* set the stage for a new kind of speech to enter the political system. It is covert speech. The Court has forced a substantial amount of political speech underground, as contributors and candidates devise ever more elaborate methods of avoiding contribution limits, limits which take no account of rising campaign costs. The preferred method has been to conceal the real purpose of the speech. Soft money may be contributed to political parties in unlimited amounts, and is used often to fund so-called issue advocacy, advertisements that promote or attack a candidate's positions without specifically urging his or her election or defeat. Issue advocacy, like soft money, is unrestricted, while straightforward speech in the form of financial contributions paid to a candidate, speech subject to full disclosure and prompt evaluation by the public, is not. Thus has the Court's decision given us covert speech. This mocks the First Amendment. The current system would be unfortunate, and suspect under the First Amendment, had it evolved from a deliberate legislative choice; but its unhappy origins are in our earlier decree in *Buckley*, which by accepting half of what Congress did (limiting contributions) but rejecting the other (limiting expenditures) created a misshapen system, one which distorts the meaning of speech.

The irony that we would impose this regime in the name of free speech ought to be sufficient ground to reject *Buckley's* wooden formula in the present case. The wrong goes deeper, however. By operation of the *Buckley* rule, a candidate cannot oppose this system in an effective way without selling out to it first. Soft money must be raised to attack the problem of soft money. In effect, the Court immunizes its own erroneous ruling from change. Rulings of this Court must never be viewed with more caution than when they provide immunity from their own correction in the political process and in the forum of unrestrained speech. The melancholy history of campaign finance in *Buckley's* wake shows what can happen when we intervene in the dynamics of speech and expression by inventing an artificial scheme of our own.

*** I would overrule *Buckley* and then free Congress or state legislatures to attempt some new reform, if, based upon their own considered view of the First Amendment, it is possible to do so. Until any reexamination takes place, however, the existing distortion of speech caused by the half-way house we created in *Buckley* ought to be eliminated. The First Amendment ought to be allowed to take its own course without further obstruction from the artificial system we have imposed. It suffices here to say that the law in question does not come even close to passing any serious scrutiny.

For these reasons, though I am in substantial agreement with what Justice Thomas says in his opinion, I have thought it necessary to file a separate dissent.

JUSTICE THOMAS, with whom JUSTICE SCALIA joins, dissenting.

...[O]ur decision in *Buckley* was in error, and I would overrule it. I would subject campaign contribution limitations to strict scrutiny, under which Missouri's contribution limits are patently unconstitutional.

I.

I begin with a proposition that ought to be unassailable: Political speech is the primary object of First Amendment protection. The Founders sought to protect the rights of individuals to engage in political speech because a self-governing people depends upon the free exchange of political information. And that free exchange should receive the most protection when it matters the most -- during campaigns for elective office....

I do not start with these foundational principles because the Court openly disagrees with them -- it could not, for they are solidly embedded in our precedents. Instead, I start with them because the Court today abandons them. For nearly half a century, this Court has extended First Amendment protection to a multitude of forms of "speech," such as making false defamatory statements, filing lawsuits, dancing nude, exhibiting drive-in movies with nudity, burning flags, and wearing military uniforms. Not surprisingly, the Courts of Appeals have followed our lead and concluded that the First Amendment protects, for example, begging, shouting obscenities, erecting tables on a sidewalk, and refusing to wear a necktie. In light of the many cases of this sort, today's decision is a most curious anomaly. Whatever the proper status of such activities under the First Amendment, I am confident that they are less integral to the functioning of our Republic than campaign contributions. Yet the majority today, rather than going out of its way to protect political speech, goes out of its way to avoid protecting it. As I explain below, contributions to political campaigns generate essential political speech. And contribution caps, which place a direct and substantial limit on core speech, should be met with the utmost skepticism and should receive the strictest scrutiny.

II.

At bottom, the majority's refusal to apply strict scrutiny to contribution limits rests upon *Buckley's* discounting of the First Amendment interests at stake. The analytic foundation of *Buckley*, however, was tenuous from the very beginning and has only continued to erode in the intervening years. What remains of *Buckley* fails to provide an adequate justification for limiting individual contributions to political candidates.

A.

To justify its decision upholding contribution limitations while striking down expenditure limitations, the Court in *Buckley* explained that expenditure limits "represent substantial rather than merely theoretical restraints on the quantity and diversity of political speech," while contribution limits "entail only a marginal restriction upon the contributor's ability to engage in free communication." In drawing this distinction, the Court in *Buckley* relied on the premise that contributing to a candidate differs qualitatively from directly spending money. It noted that "while contributions may result in political expression if spent by a candidate or an association to present views to the voters, the transformation of contributions into political debate involves speech by someone other than the contributor." . . .

The decision of individuals to speak through contributions rather than through independent expenditures is entirely reasonable. Political campaigns are largely candidate focused and candidate driven. Citizens recognize that the best advocate for a candidate (and the policy positions he supports) tends to be the candidate himself. And candidate organizations also offer other advantages to citizens wishing to partake in political expression. Campaign organizations offer a ready-built, convenient means of communicating for donors wishing to support and amplify political messages. Furthermore, the leader of the organization -- the candidate -- has a strong self-interest in efficiently expending funds in a manner that maximizes the power of the messages the contributor seeks to disseminate. Individual citizens understandably realize that they "may add more to political discourse by giving rather than spending, if the donee is able to put the funds to more productive use than can the individual." *Colorado Republican.*

In the end, *Buckley's* claim that contribution limits "do not in any way infringe the contributor's freedom to discuss candidates and issues," ignores the distinct role of candidate organizations as a means of individual participation in the Nation's civic dialogue. The result is simply the suppression of political speech. By depriving donors of their right to speak through the candidate, contribution limits relegate donors' points of view to less effective modes of communication. Additionally, limiting contributions curtails individual participation.... *Buckley* completely failed in its attempt to provide a basis for permitting government to second-guess the individual choices of citizens partaking in quintessentially democratic activities....

B.

The Court in Buckley denigrated the speech interests not only of contributors, but also of candidates. Although the Court purported to be concerned about the plight of candidates, it nevertheless proceeded to disregard their interests without justification. The Court did not even attempt to claim that contribution limits do not suppress the speech of political candidates. It could not have, given the reality that donations "make a significant contribution to freedom of expression by enhancing the ability of candidates to present, and the public to receive, information necessary for the effective operation of the democratic process." *CBS, Inc. v. FCC*, 453 U.S. 367 (1981). Instead, the Court abstracted from a candidate's individual right to speak and focused exclusively on aggregate campaign funding.

The Court's flawed and unsupported aggregate approach [also]ignores both the rights and value of individual candidates. The First Amendment "is designed and intended to remove governmental restraints from the arena of public discussion, putting the decision as to what views shall be voiced largely into the hands of *each of us*, in the hope that use of such freedom will ultimately produce a more capable citizenry and more perfect polity and in the belief that no other approach would comport with the premise of *individual* dignity and choice upon which our political system rests." *Cohen v. California*, 403 U.S. 15 (1971). In short, the right to free speech is a right held by each American, not by Americans en masse. The Court in Buckley provided no basis for suppressing the speech of an individual candidate simply because other candidates (or candidates in the aggregate) may succeed in reaching the voting public. And any such reasoning would fly in the face of the premise of our political system -- liberty vested in individual hands safeguards the functioning of our democracy. In the case at hand, the Missouri scheme has a clear and detrimental effect on a candidate such as petitioner Fredman, who lacks the advantages of incumbency, name recognition, or substantial personal wealth, but who has managed to attract the support of a relatively small number of dedicated supporters: It forbids his message from reaching the voters. And the silencing of a candidate has consequences for political debate and competition overall.

In my view, the Constitution leaves it entirely up to citizens and candidates to determine who shall speak, the means they will use, and the amount of speech sufficient to inform and persuade. Buckley's ratification of the government's attempt to wrest this fundamental right from citizens was error.

***

IV.

In light of the importance of political speech to republican government, Missouri's substantial restriction of speech warrants strict scrutiny, which requires that contribution limits be narrowly tailored to a compelling governmental interest.

Missouri does assert that its contribution caps are aimed at preventing actual and apparent corruption. As we have noted, "preventing corruption or the appearance of corruption are the only legitimate and compelling government interests thus far identified for restricting campaign finances." National Conservative Political Action Comm., 470 U.S. at 496-497. But the State's contribution limits are not narrowly tailored to that harm. The limits directly suppress the political speech of both contributors and candidates, and only clumsily further the governmental interests that they allegedly serve. They are crudely tailored because they are massively overinclusive, prohibiting all donors who wish to contribute in excess of the cap from doing so and restricting donations without regard to whether the donors pose any real corruption risk. Moreover, the government has less restrictive means of addressing its interest in curtailing corruption. Bribery laws bar precisely the *quid pro quo* arrangements that are targeted here. And disclosure laws "deter actual corruption and avoid the appearance of corruption by exposing large contributions and expenditures to the light of publicity." *Buckley v. Valeo.* In fact, Missouri has enacted strict disclosure laws.

***

V.

Because the Court unjustifiably discounts the First Amendment interests of citizens and candidates, and consequently fails to strictly scrutinize the inhibition of political speech and competition, I respectfully dissent.

NOTES AND QUESTIONS

1. How would one explain the apparent shift in Chief Justice Rehnquist's views from *Colorado Republican I* to *Shrink Missouri*? How would one explain Justice Ginsburg's shift from joining the complete repudiation of *Buckley* by Justice Stevens in *Colorado Republican I* to joining the more

nuanced position of Justice Breyer in *Shrink Missouri,* who in turn seems less convinced by the *Buckley* edifice than he did in *Colorado Republican?*

2. Both Justice Breyer in concurrence and Justice Kennedy in dissent introduce a new element to the Court's debates over *Buckley*: is it working? Each appears willing to evaluate the constitutionality of various state regulations in terms of their efficacy in promoting healthy electoral practices and according to the incentives they give for vigorous electoral debate? Is this the proper framework for constitutional adjudication? Is the Court particularly adept at making such evaluations of the functioning of electoral regulations?

3. How much of the constitutional debate regarding campaign-finance regulation is an empirical dispute over the measurable effects of such regulation? Note the kind of evidence the Court is prepared to find sufficient in *Shrink.* In particular, how much should it matter to constitutional analysis that campaign-finance regulation emerges from a voter initiative process, as opposed to legislation? In *Shrink,* the fact that the measure was voter-initiated *itself* seemed to provide, in part, the empirical evidence the First Amendment requires. Is that appropriate? Compare the way the Court treats the empirical requirements here with the kind of evidence the Court found insufficient in *First National Bank of Boston v. Bellotti,* casebook at 633, to justify state bans on corporate spending for ballot measures.

In general, keep in mind the relationship between normative judgments and demands for empirical justification in constitutional cases involving democracy, particularly in the campaign-finance area. How much do disputes over purportedly empirical facts masquerade for what are really disputes about normative judgments?

Page 664 after last materials:

G. THE NEW FRONTIER: ISSUE ADVOCACY

I. The Conceptual Problem: The Boundary Between Electoral Speech and Public Discourse

Any regulation of campaign-related spending must confront the need to define a boundary between campaigns (the "electoral domain") and more general public debate over issues, ideas, and policies (the "domain of public discourse"). For general discussion of this important point, see C. Edwin Baker, *Campaign Expenditures and Free Speech,* 33 HARV. C.R.-C.L. L. REV. 1 (1998). Even in the absence of *Buckley v. Valeo,* this task would be required as a matter of core First Amendment principles more deeply embedded, and less controversial, than *Buckley* itself. For the central concern of the First Amendment has long been understood to be a "profound national commitment to the principle that debate on public issues should be uninhibited, robust, and wide-open, and that it may well include vehement, caustic, and sometimes unpleasantly sharp attacks on government and public officials." *New York Times v. Sullivan,* 376 U.S. 254, 270 (1964). This principle is currently contested in discrete areas, like the regulation of hate speech or pornography, but it is not significantly disputed with respect to the ordinary issues of political debate and public discourse.

Long before *Buckley*, therefore, it was established that government could not regulate the domain of public discourse -- most especially, political speech -- for the purpose of establishing a greater "equality of voice" or "influence" among participants engaged in public debate. When large government and small government proponents are competing to control public opinion, for example, the First Amendment commitment to robust, wide-open debate does not permit government itself to favor either side -- whether in the name of fairness, equality, or virtually any other justification. "As a general matter, the American First Amendment tradition requires that the financial, political, or rhetorical imbalance between the proponents of competing arguments is insufficient to justify government intervention to correct that imbalance." Frederick Schauer and Richard H. Pildes, *Electoral Exceptionalism and the First Amendment*, 77 TEX. L. REV. 1803, 1825 (1999).

As a result, any form of campaign-finance regulation must meet at least two requirements: (1) in principle, there must be a theoretical distinction that can be justified between an arena that can be demarcated as "the electoral domain" and that which can be considered "the domain of public discourse;" and (2) in terms of practicable and administrative regulatory and constitutional doctrine, there must be a way of giving operational content to whatever boundary, in theory, can be offered to distinguish these two domains. Another way of putting this point is that when it comes to political participation, the governing principle is that of political equality among all citizens; the one-vote, one-person principle of Chapter 3 in the casebook reflects this principle. Yet when it comes to public discourse, the central governing principle is that of political liberty; each citizen should be able to express his or her opinions fully and without constraint. The First Amendment reflects *that* principle.

How does this relate to *Buckley v. Valeo*? At the time of *Buckley*, the landscape was essentially thought to include only campaign contributions and expenditures. By assumption, both these funding modes involve *campaigns* and hence the electoral domain. But by the 1996 elections, a major new form of influencing policy and elections came to the fore: this mode is known as issue advocacy. Issue advocacy is best understood by what it does *not* do -- it is a communication that does not seek to advance the election of a clearly identified candidate (or perhaps group of candidates -- such as Democrats). In its pure form, issue advocacy would involve advertising that sought to influence public opinion regarding political issues. An example would be the famous "Harry and Louise" advertisements, financed by the insurance industry, that successfully sought to build public opposition to President Clinton's health-care reform proposals. No national elections were pending; these advertisements were designed to change public opinion. As such, they were clearly in the "domain of public discourse" and subject to the First Amendment protections that govern that domain.

But issue advertisements can easily merge into forms of electoral influence -- and can be intentionally designed to do so. Imagine advertisements run two weeks before the 2000 Presidential election, financed by pharmaceutical companies, that urged voters not to support extending Medicare coverage to prescription drugs -- when one of the major-party candidates had made support for such extension a central issue in his campaign and the other had strongly opposed it. Would/should this be an "issue ad?" Or an "electoral ad?" Should the law treat such an ad as part of the domain of public discourse -- and hence unregulable? Or as part of the electoral domain -- and hence subject to regulation as a form of campaign financing?

Buckley avoided coming to terms in any final way with the tension between equality and liberty, and the tension between the electoral domain and the domain of public discourse. As Professor Kathleen Sullivan has put it, *Buckley* tried to "split the difference." It treated campaign expenditures as essentially unregulable speech, but campaign contributions as regulable electoral funding. As Professor Sullivan nicely elaborates:

> *Buckley* involved nothing less than a choice between two of our most powerful traditions: equality in the realm of democratic polity, and liberty in the realm of political speech. The Court had to decide whether outlays of political money more resemble voting, on the one hand, or political debate, on the other. The norm in voting is equality: one person, one vote. The norm in political speech is negative liberty: freedom of exchange, against a backdrop of unequal distribution of resources (it has been said that freedom of the press belongs to those who own one). Faced with the question of which regime ought to govern regulation of political money, the Court in effect chose a little of both. It treated campaign contributions as more like voting, where individual efforts may be equalized, and campaign expenditures as more like speech, where they may not.

Kathleen Sullivan, *Political Money and Freedom of Speech*, 30 U. C. DAVIS L. REV. 633, 667 (1997).

In a similar fashion, the problem of issue advocacy will require constitutional law to define the boundary between genuine issue-oriented debate and election-oriented campaign advocacy. *Buckley's* effort to split the difference between equality and liberty is widely regarded as having failed. Will the law be able to do any better when it comes to determining the line between issue ads -- where political liberty should presumably govern -- and electoral ads -- where reformers advocate political equality should govern?

II. Judicial Administration of the Boundary: The Law of Issue Advocacy

1. The Supreme Court. The Supreme Court has addressed issue advocacy in only two cases. In neither was the question central, nor has the Court yet devoted elaborate attention to the issue. In *Buckley* itself, 424 U.S. at 42, the Court articulated the general nature of the problem:

> The distinction between discussion of issues and candidates and advocacy of election or defeat of candidates may often dissolve in practical application. Candidates, especially incumbents, are intimately tied to public issues involving legislative proposals and governmental actions. Not only do candidates campaign on the basis of their positions on various public issues, but campaigns themselves generate issues of public interest.

Despite the inevitable mix of candidates and issues, though, any system of campaign-finance regulation requires some method of distinguishing the two.

Among other features, the 1974 FECA legislation included broad regulation of what was arguably both issue and election advocacy. Congress regulated all spending "in connection with" or "for the purpose of influencing" a federal election, or "relative to" a federal candidate. Violation of the resulting regulations resulted in criminal penalties.

Based on First Amendment concerns, the Court in *Buckley* held these provisions unconstitutional. The Court held that the statutory definitions were so vague and overbroad that they failed to provide constitutionally adequate notice to persons the statute potentially regulated. According to the Court, "[t]he test is whether the language . . . affords the '[p]recision of regulation [that] must be the touchstone in an area so closely touching our most precious freedoms[20]." Only what came to be known as express advocacy could constitutionally be regulated: that includes only "expenditures for communications that in express terms advocate the election or defeat of a clearly identified candidate." In an important footnote, the Court offered as a non-exclusive list of "express words of advocacy" the following examples: "'vote for,' 'elect,' 'support,' 'cast your ballot for[1], 'Smith for Congress,' 'vote against,' 'defeat,' [and] 'reject.'"

Notice that this definition enables speech to be treated as express advocacy only if it can essentially pass through the eye of a needle. In the Court's second encounter with the problem, it suggested a slightly broader definition. *Federal Election Commission v. Massachusetts Citizens for Life, Inc.*, 479 U.S. 238 (1986), involved an anti-abortion group's "special edition" newsletter. This publication listed state and federal candidates in an upcoming primary; identified their positions on three key issues of concern to the group; provided photographs of those with one hundred percent favorable voting records, but not of others; and urged readers to vote for anti-abortion candidates. The Court concluded that the newsletter constituted express advocacy, even though it never explicitly called for votes for a particular candidate. Yet the newsletter could not "be regarded as a mere discussion of public issues that by their nature raise the names of certain politicians. Rather, it provides in effect an explicit directive: vote for these (named) candidates." 479 U.S. at 248-50.

The result of these doctrines is that ads that are rather clearly aimed at influencing elections, at least in part, are treated to First Amendment protection and hence not reachable by campaign-finance regulation. Rather than contributing to a campaign, then, or engaging in "electoral" expenditures, those seeking to affect outcomes can simply finance the broadcasting of "issue" ads. The following example, taken from Richard Briffault, *Issue Advocacy: Redrawing the Elections/Politics Line*, 77 TEX. L. REV. 1751 (1999), is of a television ad that was repeatedly run in the closing weeks of the 1996 state elections in Montana:

> **Who is Bill Yellowtail? He preaches family values, but he took a swing at his wife. Yellowtail's explanation? He "only slapped her," but her nose was broken. He talks law and order, but is himself a convicted criminal. And though he talks about protecting children, Yellowtail failed to make his own child support payments, then voted against child support enforcement. Call Bill Yellowtail and tell him we don't approve of his wrongful behavior. Call (406) 443-3620.**

---

[20]Id. at 41.

As Briffault describes the current state of the law:

> The anti-Yellowtail ad, financed by an organization crypti-
> cally named Citizens for Reform, was a classic instance of
> contemporary "issue advocacy." It was an issue ad not
> because it discussed any issues, but because it avoided
> "express advocacy" of either Democrat Yellowtail's defeat or
> the election of Rick Hill, Yellowtail's Republican opponent, in
> the race for Montana's seat in the House of Representatives.
> The ad featured harsh criticism of Yellowtail by name, was
> broadcast on the eve of the election, and was paid for by an
> organization that spent $ 2 million supporting Republican
> candidates in elections across the country. The ad contained
> an electioneering message but, because it carefully refrained
> from any call to vote against Yellowtail or for Hill, the ad fell
> short of express advocacy and was, instead, an issue ad. As a
> result, it was exempt from regulation under the Federal
> Election Campaign Act -- even the provisions requiring the
> sponsor to disclose who paid for the ad.

Is this result correct? Should it be constitutionally required, as might
well be the case under current law? What is the effect on a system of
regulating campaign contributions if such ads are constitutionally
protected?

   *2. The Magnitude of Issue Advocacy and the Stakes for Campaign
Finance Regulation.*

   Issue advocacy is completely beyond the scope of current federal
election regulations. Recall that campaign contributions and expenditures
are subject to reporting and disclosure requirements; contributions and
expenditures by corporations and unions are prohibited. Contributions to
candidates and parties are capped. In contrast, reporting and disclosure
laws do not apply to issue advocacy. There are no restrictions on corporate
or union issue advocacy. Contributions for issue advocacy are not subject
to any caps Thus, whether material is considered issue advocacy (hence in
the "domain of public discourse") or express advocacy (and hence in the
"electoral domain") determines whether it is reachable by campaign-finance
regulation or wholly outside such regulation -- and constitutionally
protected.

   In the 1996 election cycle, campaigns and organizations learned to
exploit the concept of issue advocacy. Recall that the Supreme Court has
offered an extremely narrow conception of express advocacy, which means
that much of the terrain of election-related advertising falls under the
category of issue advocacy. Moreover, because the Court has tried to create
a bright-line rule for what constitutes "express advocacy," it has become
easy to manipulate the presentation of ads to avoid having them considered
express advocacy. Before 1996, reformers worried about the "soft money"
problem. But by 1996, campaigns and organizations had learned that it
was perhaps even easier to exploit the issue advocacy opening, and the 1996
elections saw a massive rise in "issue ads" -- a trend sure to continue and
expand in the 2000 elections. Indeed, soft money can now be combined with
so-called "issue ads" that are for all practical purposes forms of electoral

advocacy; the result is a near perfect circumvention of the 1974 FECA. As the leading article on issue advocacy puts it:

> Pragmatically, the current test is an open invitation for evasion. It is child's play for political advertisers and campaign professionals to develop ads that effectively advocate or oppose the cause of a candidate but stop short of the formal express advocacy that the courts permit to be regulated. The most common tactic for political advertisers is to include some language calling for the reader, viewer, or listener to respond to the message by doing something other than voting. In [one case], for example, the ad called on viewers to telephone the sponsor "for more information on traditional family values." Other ads urged voters to telephone the candidate targeted by the sponsor and ask him why he opposes tax cuts or term limits. A survey by the Annenberg Public Policy Center of 107 issue advocacy advertisements that aired on television or radio during the 1996 election cycle found that 70.1% urged audience members to either contact a public official or the organization sponsoring the ad to express their views concerning a particular policy position. A similar study by the Annenberg Center of 423 issue ads aired in 1997-98 found that 77.5% urged audience members to "call" or to "tell" an elected official something or call the sponsoring organization. By combining sharp criticism of a candidate with an exhortation to call the sponsor or the candidate criticized, these ads can inoculate themselves from the charge that they constitute express advocacy.

Richard Briffault, *Issue Advocacy: Redrawing the Elections/Politics Line*, 77 TEX. L. REV. 1751, 1759 (1999).

3. The structure of the Regulatory Problem.

As a practical problem in legal regulation, two aspects of the issue advocacy problem that are in tension with each other reveal precisely why an administrable regulatory regime will be difficult to achieve. On the one hand, any realistic understanding of what makes for an "electoral" ad will require highly-context specific judgments. The law could make those judgments turn on assessments of the subjective intent of the actor: was the ad intended to be an electoral ad or an issue ad. Alternatively, the context-specific assessment could turn on specific external features of the context in which the ad appeared: what was the exact content of the ad, how long before the election did it appear, who financed it, and the like. That the meaning and interpretation of communication is, realistically, context specific, is recognized not just in the philosophy of language, but in judicial decisions. Thus, in *Christian Action Network*, to be discussed *infra*, the Fourth Circuit acknowledged, as the FEC argued, that it might well be the case that "metaphorical and figurative speech can be more pointed and compelling, and can thus more successfully express advocacy, than a plain, literal recommendation to 'vote' for a particular person." 110 F.3d, at 1064. *FEC v. Christian Action Network, Inc.*, 110 F. 3d 1049, 1064 (4th Cir. 1997). Similarly, in an important issue-advocacy case, a federal district judge noted that "[l]anguage . . . is an elusive thing" and that communication depends "heavily on context." *Maine Right to Life Committee, Inc., v. Federal Election Commission*, 98 F.3d 1, 11 (1996), *cert. denied*, 522 U.S.

810 (1997). These considerations argue in favor of a case-by-case explora-
tion of the meaning (or perhaps the intent) of specific ads.

Yet both the decisions just quoted went on to reject such context-
specific approaches to defining issue advocacy.   In striking down the
Congressional definition of electoral advertising at issue in *Buckley*, the
Court offered some of the considerations against context-specific approaches. First, intent-based inquiries would lead to administrative and
judicial probing of whether speakers "intended" to influence elections -- and
this inquiry itself was deeply troubling to First Amendment values. Thus,
the Court required that regulation focus on the content of the communication itself. Second, the First Amendment generally requires exceptionally
clear dividing lines between protected and regulated speech so that
speakers who want to engage in protected speech are not "chilled" by legal
uncertainty. Context-specific legal standards tolerable in other regulatory
areas are not, for this reason, acceptable in First Amendment sensitive
domains. In addition to these considerations the Court expressed, there are
others as well. Keep in mind that these standards are going to be enforced,
in the first instance, by a federal regulatory agency, the FEC. The agency
will have to enforce these rules in hotly contested elections with enormous
partisan and political stakes. To the extent the rules are not clear in
advance, any enforcement action raises the specter of politically motivated
enforcement -- either in reality or in appearance. Moreover, for the FEC to
be effective, it will have to enforce the rules in the midst of elections; *ex post*
monetary sanctions are never as effective because they are hard to make
commensurate with the stakes in winning or losing elections. Clear, bright-
line rules will not only make for more self-enforcement by the regulated
actors, but will make for more effective, immediate FEC enforcement. For
all these reasons, the issue advocacy problem argues in favor of minimizing
case-by-case explorations of meaning and intent; instead, the problem
seems to require clear, easily administered, First Amendment-sensitive
rules.

Thus, the administrability problem reduces to this: there are
powerful considerations, grounded in First Amendment principle and
practical imperatives, that argue in favor of clear, bright-line legal rules to
separate issue and election advocacy. Yet any bright-line rule that defines
"electoral" ads narrowly will be easy to evade; clear but narrow rules will
make regulation futile. On the other hand, any bright-line that defines
"electoral" ads broadly -- by including all communication, for example, one
or two months before an election -- will inevitably sweep in much genuine
"issue" advocacy. Clear but broad rules trample significantly on political
discourse, the most protected of all forms of free speech. And yet, any
intermediate approach that seeks to avoid the use of bright-line rules by
trying to separate electoral from issue ads on a more indeterminate,
context-specific basis, inevitably runs the risk of subjective administration,
vagueness, chilling effects on protected speech, and the like. How should
the tradeoff between the need for clarity and the need for accurate
interpretive judgments be made? While this is a variation of more familiar
debates about the role for clear legal rules versus more standard-oriented
legal norms – the latter of which leave more discretion to those who apply
the norms – note that the problem here arises where the political stakes are
extremely high and the First Amendment values exceptionally powerful.

4. Lower court approaches. For two contrasting, important
approaches, compare *Federal Election commission v. Furgatch*, 807 F.2d 857

(9th Cir. 1987) and *Federal Election Commission v. Christian Action Network*, 894 F. Supp. 946 (W.D. Va. 1995), *aff'd mem*. 92 F.3d 1178 (4th Cir. 1996). *Furgatch* involved a full page advertisement in the New York Times one week before the 1980 Presidential election between Jimmy Carter and Ronald Reagan. The ad was captioned "Don't let him do it." It was placed and paid for by Harvey Furgatch. The advertisement read:

> **DON'T LET HIM DO IT.**
>
> **The President of the United States continues degrading the electoral process and lessening the prestige of the office.**
>
> **It was evident months ago when his running mate outrageously suggested Ted Kennedy was unpatriotic. The President remained silent.**
>
> **And we let him.**
>
> **It continued when the President himself accused Ronald Reagan of being unpatriotic.**
>
> **And we let him do it again.**
>
> **In recent weeks, Carter has tried to buy entire cities, the steel industry, the auto industry, and others with public funds.**
>
> **We are letting him do it.**
>
> **He continues to cultivate the fears, not the hopes, of the voting public by suggesting the choice is between "peace and war," "black or white," "north or south," and "Jew vs. Christian." His meanness of spirit is divisive and reckless McCarthyism at its worst. And from a man who once asked, "Why Not the Best?"**
>
> **It is an attempt to hide his own record, or lack of it. If he succeeds the country will be burdened with four more years of incoherencies, ineptness and illusion, as he leaves a legacy of low-level campaigning.**
>
> **DON'T LET HIM DO IT.**

Despite the ad not advocating a vote against Carter in express terms, the Ninth Circuit found it to constitute express advocacy. That court held that an ad need not use any of the "magic words" listed in *Buckley* to constitute express electoral advocacy. Instead, courts should examine any communication "as a whole, . . . with limited reference to external events" such as the timing of the ad. The court emphasized the narrowness of its extension of *Buckley*. Only if a message could be "susceptible of no other reasonable interpretation but as an exhortation to vote" could it be treated as express advocacy. The message must be "unmistakable and unambiguous, suggestive of only one plausible meaning." In this case, voting against Carter "was the only action open to those who would not 'let him do it.'" As a result, Furgatch was liable for civil sanctions, pursuant to the FECA, for having failed to report his expenditure to the FEC and failing to have included a disclaimer in the ad stating that he had paid for it and it "was not authorized by any candidate."

Does a test that focuses on "communication as a whole" and that makes reference to "external events" provide fair notice to those who want to speak about public issues without running into the FECA regulatory domain? Does it provide sufficiently clear guidance and breathing room for First Amendment concerns?

Most courts have rejected the *Furgatch* approach. At the other pole stands the Fourth Circuit's decision in *Christian Action Network*. As found in the lower court, that case involved a 1992 television advertisement that referred to Bill Clinton's support for "radical homosexual causes," presented "a series of pictures depicting advocates of homosexual rights, apparently gay men and lesbians, demonstrating at a political march," and combined "the visual degrading of candidate Clinton's picture into a black and white negative," "ominous music," and "unfavorable coloring" in a manner that "raised strong emotions [among] viewers." Yet both the district court and the court of appeals concluded that the message did not constitute express advocacy of Clinton's defeat. Although the advertising named Clinton and used his picture, was broadcast in the weeks immediately preceding the November 1992 general election, and was "openly hostile" to the gay rights positions it attributed to Clinton, the ad was "devoid of any language that directly exhorted the public to vote." The Fourth Circuit concluded that a viewer could just as readily interpret the ad as election advocacy for the defeat of President Clinton or as issue advocacy on the question of homosexual rights. Indeed, so sure was the Fourth Circuit that this ad was protected issue advocacy that in a follow-up case it sanctioned the FEC (by requiring that it pay fees and costs of the Christian Action Network) for even bringing the action. 110 F.3d 1049 (4th Cir. 1997) (per Luttig, J.).

Does the *Christian Action* approach allow campaigns and ad consultants simply to game the system by transparently masking ads obviously designed to defeat or elect candidates as "issue ads?" First Amendment law requires that otherwise pornographic material be treated as protected speech if it contains any other "redeeming social value;" this has led to a whole industry in which pornography is surrounded with enough indicators of "other value" to enter this safe harbor. Under the approach of *Christian Action*, are "issue ads" becoming the pornography of the electoral arena? Or does *Christian Action* reflect important and genuine First Amendment values that ought to be respected and hence treated as part of the "domain of public discourse"-- and therefore beyond the reach of federal election laws?

For other important lower-court treatments of issue advocacy, see *Clifton v. Federal Election Comm'n*, 114 F.3d 1309, 1320 (1st Cir. 1997), cert. denied, 522 U.S. 1108 (1998); *Federal Election Comm'n v. Survival Educ. Fund, Inc.*, 65 F.3d 285, 299 (2d Cir. 1995); *Faucher v. Federal Election Comm'n*, 928 F.2d 468, 470 (1st Cir. 1991); *Federal Election Comm'n v. Central Long Island Tax Reform Immediately Comm.*, 616 F.2d 45, 53 (2d Cir. 1980); *North Carolina Right to Life, Inc. v. Bartlett*, 3 F. Supp. 2d 675, 678-79 (E.D.N.C. 1998); *West Virginians for Life, Inc. v. Smith*, 960 F. Supp. 1036, 1038-39 (S.D.W. Va. 1996); *Federal Election Comm'n v. National Org. for Women*, 713 F. Supp.428, 433 (D.D.C. 1989).

5. *The FEC Approach.* Current FEC regulations draw on the *Furgatch* approach to adopt a context-specific assessment. These regulations define express advocacy to include communications which:

[w]hen taken as a whole and with limited reference to external events, such as the proximity to the election, could only be

interpreted by a reasonable person as containing advocacy of the election or defeat of one or more clearly identified candidate(s) because --

(1) The electoral portion of the communication is unmistakable, unambiguous, and suggestive of only one meaning; and

(2) Reasonable minds could not differ as to whether it encourages actions to elect or defeat one or more clearly identified candidate(s) or encourage some other kind of action. 11 C.F.R. Sec. 100.22(b) (2000).

Can this standard be applied with the ease required in the midst of a hotly contested election? Is it likely to be applied consistently? How easy would it be to evade? The First Circuit has found this regulation unconstitutional. *Maine Right to Life Committee, Inc., v. Federal Election Commission*, 98 F.3d 1 (1996), *cert. denied*, 522 U.S. 810 (1997); *see also Right to Life of Dutchess County, Inc. v. Federal Election Commission*, 6 F. Supp. 2d 248, 253 (S.D. N.Y. 1998) (also holding this regulation unconstitutional); *Vermont Right to Life Committee v. Sorrell*, 19 F. Supp. 2d 204 (D. Vt. 1998) (construing state law that treated as electoral advocacy any communication that "expressly or implicitly" advocated the success or defeat of a candidate as constitutional only as applied to communications that "in express terms" advocate the election or defeat of a "clearly identified candidate").

6. *Other Proposals.*

Professor Briffault, in the important article noted above, offers the following proposed approach, which he argues should be constitutional. Express advocacy should be defined as any communication that (1) refers to a clearly identified candidate; (2) is made within a defined period before an election (probably four weeks before a general election and two weeks before a primary); and (3) involves a sufficiently large expenditure -- at least one percent, and possibly at least five percent -- of the average expenditure of the winning candidate for the office in question in the two preceding elections. Briffault argues that (1) is required to distinguish election-related speech from other forms of political speech. He suggests that (2) seems roughly consistent with data that show a sharp shift in the content of issue ads in the period leading up to an election, though he notes it is both important for First Amendment purposes to establish a bright-line test and that any such line will inherently be somewhat too broad and too narrow in getting at genuine electoral advocacy. He justifies (3) on the grounds that regulation should focus on communications that have a reasonable likelihood of actually affecting electoral outcomes, in part to reduce the risk of regulating political speech. Does this proposal draw the boundary at the right place between the electoral domain and the domain of public discourse? Would the courts be likely to accept this proposal as constitutional? Should the courts do so? Consider the following view prompted by concern that it is only when elections appear imminent that political speech has any real salience: "It is only with some horror that readers steeped in anything resembling the First Amendment tradition can view proposals to limit advocacy within thirty or sixty or ninety days of an election . . . ." Samuel Issacharoff and Pamela S. Karlan, *The Hydraulics of Campaign Finance Reform*, 77 TEX. L. REV. 1705 (1999).

Congressional reform proposals have not yet come to terms with the issue advocacy question. In one version of proposed legislation, which passed The House of Representatives in the summer of 1998 as the Shays-

Meehan Bipartisan Campaign Reform Act of 1998, the House defined an election-related communication is one that advocates the election or defeat of a candidate by "expressing unmistakable and unambiguous support for or opposition to one or more clearly identified candidates when taken as a whole and with limited reference to external events, such as proximity to an election." This definition appears to draw on *Furgatch* and the FEC regulations. Is it a more or less appropriate proposal than the Briffault proposal?

III. Conclusion: Can Campaign Finance Regulation Overcome the Problem of Issue Advocacy?

Recall that under the First Amendment, any system of campaign-finance regulation must be able to draw a boundary between the electoral domain and the domain of public discourse. At the outset, we suggested that this was a two-fold problem: (1) as a matter of principle or normative analysis, there is a question as to whether it is justifiable to attempt to distinguish ideas, debates, and issues from candidates, elections, and campaigns. What is the nature of the distinction, and the justifications for it, that the law would seek to draw? (2) once we are clear on the theoretical aim, can regulatory policy generate an administrable line that is both effective at achieving the aims of regulation but consistent with First Amendment concerns for vagueness, fair notice, and adequate protection of political debate?

Keep in mind that the problem of issue advocacy transcends the more familiar debates over regulating campaign contributions, expenditures, or both. Even if both expenditures and contributions could, constitutionally, be regulated, the problem of issue advocacy would remain. Issue advocacy also transcends the debate about whether *Buckley* was "rightly" decided. Even if *Buckley* were overruled, the problem would remain, whatever the direction in which *Buckley* might be overruled. If the Constitution were reinterpreted or amended to permit greater regulation of election-related speech, in the name of political equality, for example, the necessity to determine what constitutes an election-related expenditure versus a public-discourse expenditure would still remain. On the other hand, were the Constitution reinterpreted to give First Amendment protection to campaign contributions in the same way that expenditures are protected, the necessity to determine what constitutes election-related activity -- for purposes of disclosure laws, if not for regulatory proscriptions -- would still remain.

The question is therefore stark: Can the problem of campaign-finance regulation be solved without solving the problem of issue advocacy? If not, can the problem of issue advocacy be solved?

CHAPTER TEN

On page 712, after the existing materials add the following:

DIRECT DEMOCRACY IN THE AGE OF THE INTERNET?

As voting over the internet becomes an imaginable possibility, questions of direct democracy have assumed an additional importance. So-called "cyberpopulists" see the Internet as increasing citizen participation, not merely by making it easier to vote but, more importantly, by increasing the array of voting opportunities. *See generally* Neil Netanel, *Cyberspace Self-Governance: A Skeptical View from Liberal Democratic Theory* 88 CAL. L. REV. 395 (1999). The standard Internet-based pitch for direct democracy goes something like this. The Internet will enable citizens to become far better informed about public issues. First, they have access to more sources of information overall (and perhaps they can process that information in more useful ways). Second, the decreased (essentially trivial) cost of communication makes it possible to disseminate good ideas even if those ideas are not initially backed by large amount of money. Finally, voters can vote costlessly, without having to go to the polls at inconvenient times. According to the Direct Democracy Online Project, one website promoting the idea, "[r]epresentative democracy, such as we have in the United States" was "originally devised to get around the practical problem of transportation in a large democracy; specifically, that all of the people in a nation could not economically vote on a great number of issues, simply because they could not all be physically present to debate and cast a ballot in one location."

Is this view correct as either a descriptive or normative matter? In this light, consider the following argument:

> Even on its own terms, of course, this account has problems. What does it mean to say that it's easier to become well informed? It's rather expensive, actually, not so much in financial terms -- on this, the net partisans are right, since it costs very little to gain access to literally millions of information providers -- but rather in terms of time and comprehension. Anyone who wants to increase the opportunities for direct democracy should be forced to read through the current official voter information pamphlets in California: more than a hundred pages of densely written statutory text for the two dozen or so propositions already on the ballot. Surely, the minimum that can be expected is knowing the text of a proposition on which one is voting, but even that task

seems beyond the competence or interest of most of the eligible electorate....

So what will voters do? Three responses seem particularly likely. The first is not voting on an issue at all unless one feels sufficiently well informed, a response that may leave the field to the less conscientious elements of the electorate or may result in disproportionate influence for single-issue voters who care about that issue. Second, one could vote essentially at random or according to some rule largely unrelated to the merits of specific measures. Consider, for example, the well-documented phenomenon that people tend to vote "no" when they don't understand a ballot proposition -- a consideration that might be thought of as essentially conservative or risk-averse until one realizes that framers of ballot language are aware of this point and draft propositions to take advantage of this tendency. Third, voters may spend their scarce comprehension effort looking for short-hand clues that tell them how to vote -- for example, looking to see which groups support or oppose a particular measure. This last response seems the most reasonable, ... but note that it reintroduces the idea of relying on mediating institutions. Those institutions may be different in the Internet world, but they're no less useful. Indeed, they may be more so precisely because the costs of sending communication are so reduced.... In deciding how to vote, then, citizens should rely on information generated over the Internet only to the extent that the information is reliable, and that may be a function of its being provided by "brand-name" intermediaries: the political parties, large media outlets, long-established interest groups, and the like.

Eben Moglen and Pamela S. Karlan, *The Soul of a New Political Machine: The Online, the Color Line, and Electronic Democracy*, ___ 34 LOY. L.A.L. REV. ___ (2001). After surveying the relatively standard arguments about the differences between direct and representative democracy, particularly with respect to the interests of minority groups, the authors conclude:

Internet voting, then, may often produce outcomes that are quick, certain, and wrong. Ironically, representative government may be even *more* desirable in the age of the Internet precisely because it's sometimes slow and creaky. It may perform its traditional braking function with respect to a new source of what Madison described as factional passion: immediate access and expression, without an opportunity for reflection.

CHAPTER ELEVEN

Page 720 after note 1:

1. Proportional Representation in the Home of First Past the Post? First past the post elections (FPTP) originated in the United Kingdom and were inherited in countries, like the United States, that adopted their electoral systems under strong British influence, such as former British colonies. What does it say about the continuing appeal of FPTP elections that even in the United Kingdom, there is now serious political effort underway to shift that country's elections to a more proportional form of representation? How might it affect debates in the United States were the United Kingdom actually to make this shift -- which would leave the United States as the only major Western democracy to use FPTP to elect all its lower house members?

In December, 1997, the Labour Government of the United Kingdom convened an Independent Commission on the British voting system. In October, 1998, the Commission, headed by Lord Jenkins of Hillhead, submitted a report in which it recommended a referendum to consider switching from first past the post single member constituencies to a more proportional system that eliminates some of the problems of multiparty votes. *See* Report of the Independent Commission on the Voting System, <http://lightning.prohosting.com/~mvc-uk/volI.pdf>. The Commission recommended that between 80 and 85 percent of the House of Commons continue to be elected by single member constituencies because of the important constituency service role that Members of Parliament play for all of the residents of their constituency. However, the Commission also recommended switching to Alternative Voting (AV) -- also sometimes known as Instant Runoff Voting -- to select the MPs from the single member districts. AV is essentially Single Transferrable Vote with a single member district; if no candidate has a majority, the candidate with the lowest number of votes is eliminated and the ballots are transferred to the second choices of that candidate's supporters. The process repeats until some candidate has a majority. AV consequently produces at least majority acquiescence to the victor (except in cases where the polity is extremely polarized in more than two directions).

The principal effect of AV is to allow voters to select their preferred candidate out of a three or more party race without having to weigh tactical concerns; the ability to designate a candidate who has a stronger chance as a second choice prevents the vote from being "lost." In addition to implementing AV, the Commission proposed that the remaining 15 to 20 percent of the seats be filled with a regionally based proportional representation system. Each voter would vote for both a candidate and a party; for each of 80 areas within the United Kingdom, the extra seat or seats to be assigned through proportional means would be assigned to the party that is most underrepresented by the single member seats within that area. The system would allow some representation for parties that consistently lose elections in certain areas (such as the Conservative Party invariably losing in major cities and Labour invariably losing in rural areas) while receiving consistent, substantial minority support. The Commission considered extensive reports of alternative voting system employed in other countries and also highlighted some of the "perverse" results that FPTP can produce, including several elections where minority parties won majorities and where parties with small pluralities won landslide majorities in Parliament. The Commission also extensively considered STV, but concluded that this would require either extremely large districts or enlarging the House of Commons (currently a 659 member body) and that either of those changes was undesirable. The Commission concluded that its proposal would ameliorate these effects, although it warned that AV without a "top-up" provision could accentuate some of the disproportional landslide results based on antipathy towards the ruling party. The Labour Government has not decided whether to submit a referendum to the people on changing the voting system and whether to propose the Commission's proposal or AV without a "top-up" provision.

2. *Instant Runoff Voting*. What the British "Jenkins Report" calls Alternative Voting is often, in the United States, called Instant Runoff Voting (IRV). IRV works much as the same as Single Transferrable Voting, but is of potential use within single-member districts. Voters rank candidates in the order they prefer. If no candidate receives a majority, the bottom candidate is eliminated and the ballots for that candidate are transferred to their second choice candidate. The process is repeated until one candidate has a majority. IRV thus produces an actual majority winner without requiring multiple rounds of voting.

IRV is another alternative voting system gaining increasing political support various places. It is particularly attractive in areas with significant third-party politics, because it enables voters to express a preference for such a party without "wasting" the vote in the way that occurs in the conventional First Past the Post (FPTP) voting system. Vermont is now in the midst of serious consideration of a shift to IRV. After substantial discussion of a bill to establish IRV for Vermont elections, Vermont established the Vermont Commission to Study Preference Voting in April, 1998. In January, 1999 the Commission presented its report, "As Easy as 1-2-3." The report strongly endorsed IRV. Under current Vermont election law, FPTP is used for legislative elections. In statewide elections for Governor, Lieutenant Governor, and Treasurer, if no candidate receives a majority, the General Assembly selects the winner in January.

This rule has resulted in 69 elections being decided in the state legislature, with 35% of all elections including at least one statewide race with no majority winner. *See* Vermont Commission to Study Preference Voting, "As Easy as 1-2-3," January, 1999, p. 3. Because Vermont is instituting public financing in 2000, the number of elections with no majority winner is expected to increase. *Id.* Vermont is one of several states that, because of strong third parties and independent candidates, are particularly likely to elect plurality candidates. Vermont currently has a third party representative in Congress and regularly elects several Progressives to the state legislature. New Mexico is also studying IRV because the strong Green Party support in New Mexico has been believed to swing elections from the Democrats to the Republicans. Similarly, in Alaska, Governor Knowles was elected as a Democratic candidate despite a solid Republican majority in the legislature following a strong independent candidacy. *Id.* at 6. A ballot initiative to consider adopting IRV will be on the November 2002 ballot in Alaska. In addition to recommending the adoption of IRV for executive elections and for Congressional elections, the Commission recommended further study of proportional representation for legislative elections. *Id.* at 5.

FURTHER LITIGATION ON CUMULATIVE VOTING

Page 745 after *Cane v. Worcester County*:

The most important federal court discussion of cumulative voting in recent years arose out of protracted voting-rights litigation in Chicago Heights, Illinois, a Chicago suburb with a longstanding history of racial conflict. The structure of the problem posed reflects a set of factors increasingly likely to arise in voting rights litigation after the 2000 Census: a multi-racial and ethnic contest for political power; polarized voting patterns; the constraints of the *Shaw v. Reno* line of cases; and the effort to find alternative remedies to the conventional approach of the preceding decade, in which single-member districts were nearly always the remedy of choice when at-large local government structures were found to violate the Voting Rights Act. The District Court's opinion appears first, followed by the Seventh Circuit's response to the District Court's efforts.

McCoy v. Chicago Heights
6 F. Supp. 2d 973 (N.D. Ill. 1998)

District Judge David H. Coar:

The instant case originated in 1987 and 1988 when the plaintiff class ... alleged that the non-partisan, at-large elections in Chicago Heights City Council . . . violated Section 2 of the Voting Rights Act of 1965 . . .

[Pursuant to a federal-court approved consent decree in 1994, the City abandoned its at-large election system and substituted a six single-member district plan with a mayor elected at-large. Under this plan, two districts would be majority African-American and a third would have a substantial Hispanic population. In addition, the mayor had the ability to break ties and a veto, as well as substantial appointive powers.

Eventually, voters of Chicago Heights approved this plan in a referendum. But some members of the plaintiff class believed the plan was inadequate. The plaintiff class therefore split. Dissident plaintiffs Perkins and McCoy argued for an aldermanic system, with a seven member council and a weak mayor elected at large].

II. DISCUSSION

The district court need not defer to a state-proposed remedial plan if the plan does not completely remedy the violation or if the plan itself violates Section 2 of the Act. This court finds that the modified strong mayor government is not a complete remedy to the Section 2 violation.... Notably, by granting significant power to the mayor ... who [is] elected at-large, the proposed systems perpetuate the race-based violation of the Voting Rights Act that occurred in the previous at-large voting system...

The City ... and class plaintiffs do not propose any alternate remedy for the voting rights violations. Therefore, this court turns to the remedy proposed by the individual plaintiffs Perkins and McCoy. In terms of the City government, this court is in agreement with the individual plaintiffs that a traditional aldermanic form of government would reduce the power of the mayor, who is necessarily elected at-large. One significant difference between these forms of government is that in the aldermanic form a mayor's veto may be overridden by a two-thirds vote of the aldermen, whereas in the strong mayor format a three-fifths majority is required. While it is true that both the aldermanic government and the strong mayor government allow the mayor to cast tie-breaking votes, the Perkins/McCoy proposal provides for seven aldermen, thus ensuring that tie votes will not result. . . . Another significant difference is that the modified strong mayor government proposed by the City and the class plaintiffs allows the mayor to appoint the city clerk and city treasurer; however, in the aldermanic form of government these officers would be elected at-large. . . .

In conclusion, this court finds that the remedies proposed by the City ... and class plaintiffs do not adequately address the Section 2 violation. . . . In contrast, the Perkins/McCoy remedy for governmental structure offers a more complete remedy, yet is not without its own problems. In particular, this court is troubled by the potential of the seven-district structure to be challenged on Equal Protection grounds.

b. Drawing District Lines

Although the Perkins/McCoy proposal is a satisfactory remedy with regards to the governmental structures for the City and the Park District, this court is hesitant to divide Chicago Heights into seven districts. The Supreme Court has held that race must not be a predominant factor in drawing district lines. Voter classifications based upon race are considered suspect and therefore subject to strict scrutiny if they subordinate traditional districting criteria to race.

See, e.g., Bush v. Vera, 517 U.S. 952 (1996); *Shaw v. Hunt,* 517 U.S. 899 (1996); *Miller v. Johnson,* 515 U.S. 900 (1995); *Shaw v. Reno,* 509 U.S. 630 (1993).

Thus, fashioning a remedy that will draw district lines so as to remedy a voting rights violation, but without making race a predominant factor, is a complicated undertaking. The opponents of the Perkins/McCoy plan have justifiably argued that the creation of seven wards with the predominant intent of racial gerrymandering runs the risk of being challenged on an Equal Protection basis. Creating majority-minority districts as a remedy to voting rights violations inevitably relies on "a quintessentially race-conscious calculus aptly described as the 'politics of second best.'" *Johnson v. De Grandy*, 512 U.S. 997, 1020 (1994) (Souter, concurring) (*citing* B. GROFMAN, L. HANDLEY & R. NEIMI, MINORITY REPRESENTATION AND THE QUEST FOR VOTING EQUALITY, 136 (1992)). Thus emerges the paradox of fashioning a voting rights remedy based on districts in voting remedy cases. As one district court has aptly noted, any remedial plan "(even one fashioned solely with race-neutral principles) must be ultimately tested by whether it cures the § 2 violation, ... race will always be a factor, for the ultimate question is whether the proposed plan provides the complaining racial group (in this case, African-Americans) equal access to the political process within the context of § 2." *Dillard v. City of Greensboro*, 946 F. Supp. 946, 955 (M.D. Ala. 1996) (Thompson, C.J.). Finally, any redistricting plan that this court may approve would be subject to continued constitutional challenges and would require being redrawn after the 2000 census.

5. Cumulative Voting

a. Cumulative Voting Defined

Thus, while this court favors a seven-member structure for the ... City, seven, single-membered districts would not be an effective remedy for the Section 2 violation in Chicago Heights. However, a drawing of district lines is not required in order to remedy the voting rights violation in Chicago Heights. Rather than dividing the city into seven districts, this court finds that a system of at-large voting that utilizes cumulative voting, in combination with the Perkins/McCoy plan, would successfully remedy the voting rights violation.

Cumulative voting as a remedy functions in the following manner:

> Voters receive as many votes to cast as there are seats to fill; voters then may distribute these multiple votes among minority candidates in any way they prefer. Thus, voters may "plump" all their votes on one candidate -- the

strategy of choice for minority groups with intense preferences for a particular candidate -- or give one vote each to several candidates. If five seats on a city council are to be filled, voters would have five votes each to distribute as they saw fit.

Richard Pildes & Kristen Donoghue, *Cumulative Voting in the United States*, 1995 U. CHI. LEGAL F. 241, 254 (1995). See generally Richard L. Engstrom, *Modified Multi-Seat Election Systems as Remedies for Minority Vote Dilution*, 21 STETSON L. REV. 743 (1992); Edward Still, *Alternatives to Single Member Districts, in Chandler Davidson*, ed., MINORITY VOTE DILUTION 249 (1989). Cumulative voting is frequently used to elect directors of corporations as a strategy for ensuring representation of minority shareholders in the board. *See* HARRY HENN & JOHN ALEXANDER, LAWS OF CORPORA- TIONS, (3d Ed. 1983) at 495-97. In fact, most states permit cumula- tive voting for corporations, allowing the individual corporation to elect whether to utilize the voting scheme. *See* ROBERT CLARK, CORPORATE LAW § 9.1 at 362 (1986).

If a cumulative voting system were applied to the Perkins/McCoy plan, the seven aldermen ... would be elected at-large using cumula- tive voting, rather than electing one alderman ... from each district as proposed by Perkins and McCoy. Each voter would be allocated seven votes to use as he or she chooses. Thus, the voter could use all seven votes to elect on candidate, or distribute the votes among several candidates. The seven candidates with the highest number of votes would be elected to office.

There are several distinct advantages to a system of regionwide cumulative voting for local office. In particular, rather than using race as a proxy for voting preference, such a system allows voters to "draw their own jurisdictional boundaries, decide which local governments were most important to them, and allocate their votes accordingly." Richard Briffault, *The Local Government Boundary Problem in Metropolitan Areas,* 48 STAN. L. REV. 1115, 1156 (1996). All minority groups may potentially benefit from such a system -- not just racial minorities. For example, in a region where Republicans are in a minority, cumulative voting could allow them to elect a candidate of choice. . . . Relevant to the instant case is the fact that cumulative voting would allow minority voters in Chicago Heights, including the African-Americans and Latinos, to elect candidates of choice without creating race-conscious district lines that would be subject to constitutional challenge. Indeed, cumulative voting does not compartmentalize voters according to their race: "the state does not directly single out any particular minorities for special protection through concentration into 'safe' districts." Pildes & Donoghue, *supra,* at 255.

b. Federal Court Precedent

The Supreme Court has held that . . . although single-member districts may be preferred, they are not by any means an exclusive remedy to voting rights violations.

Indeed, in a recent Voting Rights Act case, Justices Thomas and Scalia suggested that cumulative voting is a "more efficient and straightforward mechanism[] for achieving what has already become our tacit objective: roughly proportional allocation of power according to race." *Holder v. Hall,* 512 U.S. 874, 912 (1994) (Thomas, J. concurring, joined by Scalia, J.). Although it is by far the most common remedy for a Voting Rights Act violation, geographic districting is not a requirement of our political system:

> The decision to rely on single-member geographic districts as a mechanism for conducting elections is merely a political choice -- and one that we might reconsider in the future. Indeed, it is a choice that has undoubtedly been influenced by the adversary process: In the cases that have come before us, plaintiffs have focused largely upon attacking multimember districts and have offered single-member schemes as the benchmark of an "undiluted" alternative. But as the destructive effects of our current penchant for majority-minority districts become more apparent, courts will undoubtedly be called upon to reconsider adherence to geographic districting as a method for ensuring minority voting power. Already, some advocates have criticized the current strategy of creating majority-minority districts and have urged the adoption of other voting mechanisms - for example, cumulative voting or a system using transferable votes - that can produce proportional results without requiring division of the electorate into racially segregated districts.

> ... Such changes may seem radical departures from the electoral systems with which we are most familiar. Indeed, they may be unwanted by the people in the several States who purposely have adopted districting systems in their electoral laws. But nothing in our present understanding of the Voting Rights Act places a principled limit on the authority of federal courts that would prevent them from instituting a system of cumulative voting as a remedy under § 2, or even from establishing a more elaborate mechanism for securing proportional representation based on transferable votes. As some Members of the Court have already recognized, geographic districting is not a requirement inherent in our political system.

c. One-Person, One-Vote

This court finds that a system of cumulative voting complies with the requirements that the court be mindful of the "one-person, one-vote" requirement of the Equal Protection Clause. . . .

d. Illinois Voting Principles

Cumulative voting also conforms with Illinois' traditional voting principles. The fact that cumulative voting as a remedy has strong roots in Illinois is important given that the Supreme Court has held that district courts should not "intrude upon state policy any more than necessary" in fashioning remedies for voting rights violations.

Illinois was the first state to introduce a cumulative voting system. *See* Henn & Alexander, *supra*, at 495 n.12. Cumulative voting for directors of corporations was introduced in Illinois in 1870. See id. In addition, cumulative voting was adopted by the Illinois Constitutional Convention of 1869-70 as a device to assure minority representation in the legislature. *See* Charles Hynerman & Julian Morgan, *Cumulative Voting in Illinois*, 32 ILL. L. REV. 12, 13 (1937). The main reason for the adoption of the cumulative voting system "was a desire to correct the situation wherein southern Republicans and northern Democrats were going unrepresented in the legisla-ture." *Id.* Under this system, three representatives were elected for two-year terms from 51 different districts. Voters could cast one vote for three candidates, one and one-half votes for two candidates, or one vote for one candidate and two votes for a second candidate. *See id. See also* Ill. Const. of 1870, art. IV, § § 6, 7, 8. The cumulative voting system in Illinois corporations is still prescribed in some situations; however, cumulative voting for the legislature was repealed in 1980.

Cumulative voting nonetheless remains firmly established as a statutory form of city government in Illinois. As previously noted, the Illinois Municipal Code provides for a form of cumulative voting in a variant of the aldermanic form of government. [Under this State Code, cities are divided into several three-member districts for aldermanic elections].

III. CONCLUSION

In accordance with the Perkins/McCoy plan, the City must adopt an aldermanic form of government, as provided in Article 3.1 of the Illinois Municipal Code. The City will have a total of seven aldermen, who will be elected at-large by cumulative voting for four-year terms. The voting procedure will be as outlined in this opinion - a modified form of the "minority representation plan" provided for by Illinois law in the aldermanic form of government. Each voter will be allocated seven votes to use as he or she chooses, and the seven candidates with the most votes will be elected to office. The mayor, city treasurer, and city clerk will be elected at-large.

Harper v. City of Chicago Heights
223 F.3d 593 (7th Cir. July 27, 2000)

Diane P. Wood, Circuit Judge:

...The district court . . . ordered the implementation of a new election method that relies on cumulative voting....

* * *

II

A.

Standing behind the district court's judgment is the earlier finding -- unchallenged, as we said -- that the at-large system violated Section 2 of the Voting Rights Act. We think it was correct for the court to ask whether the replacement system eventually approved through referendum would remedy the violation; there was no need for the court to view it as if it had emerged from thin air. When a Section 2 violation has been found, the district court "must, wherever practicable, afford the jurisdiction an opportunity to remedy the violation first, . . . with deference afforded the jurisdiction's plan if it provides a full, legally acceptable remedy. . . . But if the jurisdiction fails to remedy completely the violation or if a proposed remedial plan itself constitutes a § 2 violation, the court must itself take measures to remedy the violation." *Dickinson v. Indiana State Election Bd.*, 933 F.2d 497, 501 n.5 (7th Cir. 1991) (citation and quotations omitted).

* * *

The evidence of the mayor's pattern of voting in tie-breaking situations, taken with the likelihood of ties on an even-numbered council, is enough to support the district court's conclusion that the referendum system did not adequately address the acknowledged problem in the City elections. . . .

B.

[But] we are compelled to find here that the remedy for the City crafted by the court cannot stand at this time. . . .

The district court's plan suffers from the same procedural flaw as did the consent decree when it was first presented to this court:

the court's plan modifies the election methods set forth in the Illinois Municipal Code without either going through the statutorily required procedures for making such changes to electoral methods or making a judicial finding that it was necessary to make these changes in order to comply with federal law. As this court explained in *Perkins*, [any consent-decree modification of state electoral structures are permissible only if necessary to remedy a federal-law violation].

The procedural holding in *Perkins*, while addressed to a slightly different problem, is equally applicable here, though we note that nothing in our earlier opinion disapproved of cumulative voting in the abstract. The Illinois Municipal Code makes available to cities a variety of election methods. The district court should either have selected one of these methods or found that the Illinois options violate federal law. Instead, as it had done before, it opted for a hybrid system without submitting that plan to the voters, as Illinois law would require, and without explaining why one of the State's authorized systems would not do the job. Although the Municipal Code allows for cumulative voting, it specifies that a city is to be divided into districts (not less than two and not more than six) and that each district is entitled to three aldermen. Without a finding that the Code's cumulative voting method violates federal law, the district court modified the plan to call for the city-wide election of seven council members.

The district court's plan also suffers from a failure to respect the City's preference for single-member districts. The Supreme Court has held that in fashioning an electoral system to remedy a voting rights violation, courts "should follow the policies and preferences of the State, as expressed in statutory and constitutional provisions or in the . . . plans proposed by the state legislature, whenever adherence to state policy does not detract from the Federal Constitution." *White v. Weiser*, 412 U.S. 783, 795 (1973). Accordingly, when a legislative body fails to offer an acceptable remedy, "the court, in exercising its discretion to fashion a remedy that complies with § 2, must to the greatest extent possible give effect to the legislative policy judgments underlying the current electoral scheme or the legally unacceptable remedy offered by the legislative body." *Cane v. Worcester County, Md.*, 35 F.3d 921, 928 (4th Cir. 1994).

Here, the City has demonstrated a clear preference for single-member districts. It proposed a remedial plan that relies on single-member districts and, in doing so, made a policy judgment about which electoral schemes are best suited for the locality. We should defer to the City's plan to the extent possible as long as it does not violate federal law. Although the district court found that the referendum system was inadequate, it did not find that any use of single-member districts violates federal law.

The United States, appearing as amicus curiae, defends the district court's plan on the ground that, under Illinois law, cumulative voting is an accepted electoral practice. Thus, the United States argues, while the district court's plan may have violated the City's preference for single-member districts, the State has no such preference. We find this distinction unconvincing. First, the United States overstates the popularity of cumulative voting in Illinois: although cumulative voting is lawful under the Municipal Code, the use of single-member districts is an equally acceptable electoral practice. . . . The City proposed and must function under the remedial plan and accordingly its judgments are entitled to deference.

It is somewhat troubling that the City has not articulated why it prefers single-member districts over cumulative voting, but this is not an ironclad requirement for public bodies as long as the entity's actual preference can legitimately be inferred from facts on the record. It is obviously true that deference to legislative policy judgments is predicated on the legislature actually having made a policy judgment rather than an arbitrary choice. But we are satisfied that the City did so. Prior to the district court's order, the parties had never thought of cumulative voting. In the absence of a finding that cumulative voting is the only legally viable remedy, the City should have an opportunity to consider the merits and deficiencies of cumulative voting before that system is imposed upon it. We emphasize that our decision should not be understood as a condemnation of cumulative voting. Cumulative voting is, as the Illinois Municipal Code makes clear, a lawful election method that may be implemented under circumstances demonstrating suitable deference to the legislative body. It also has the virtues the district court identified:

> Rather than using race as a proxy for voting preference, such a system allows voters to draw their own jurisdictional boundaries, decide which local governments were most important to them, and allocate their votes accordingly. . . . All minority groups may potentially benefit from such a system--not just racial minorities. . . . Indeed, cumulative voting does not compartmentalize voters according to their race. (citation omitted).

For the reasons discussed above, we AFFIRM the district court's holding that the current election method violates Section 2 of the Voting Rights Act as applied to the City; however, we REVERSE the district court's remedy and REMAND to the court to craft a suitable remedy.

NOTES AND QUESTIONS

1. Does the Seventh Circuit's opinion reflect an attitude of greater acceptance of cumulative voting, at least potentially, than earlier Courts of Appeals encounters with the issue? Compare this decision with *Worcester County*, at casebook p.741, which is also cited in the Seventh Circuit's decision. Note the strongly positive comments both courts appear to make about the virtues of cumulative-voting remedies.

2. Do *Shaw v. Reno* and its progeny put tremendous pressure on District Courts that have found Voting Rights Act violations to move toward cumulative voting, as the District Court did here? Under what circumstances would a District Court be permitted to impose a cumulative-voting remedy over the objections of a recalcitrant jurisdiction? For discussions of this issue, see, e.g., Pamela S. Karlan, *Our Separatism? The Voting Rights Act as an American Nationalities Policy*, 1995 U. CHI. LEGAL F. 83; Eben Moglen and Pamela S. Karlan, *The Soul of a New Political Machine: The Online, the Color Line, and Electronic Democracy*, 34 LOY. L.A.L. REV. ___ (2001); Steven J. Mulroy, *Alternative Ways Out: A Remedial Road Map for the Use of Alternative Electoral Systems as Voting Rights Act Remedies*, 77 N.C.L. REV. 1867 (1999).

Page 746 after note 1:

Illinois has recently begun considering a return to cumulative voting (CV) for its state legislature. With the elimination of CV in 1980, and perhaps other changes, the state legislature is now radically polarized along regional lines, in just the way CV sought to avoid when it was instituted after the Civil War in 1870 and seemed to succeed in doing until 1980. All the Democrats come from Chicago and southern Illinois; all the Republicans come from the suburbs and farm counties. According to current sponsors, the end of CV "eliminated the independent voice from the legislature." It gave both parties some representation in regions in which they were the minority, which facilitated the locating of common interests across party lines and made for less unified party domination of the state legislature. The effort to restore CV in Illinois is supported by the current Governor, George Ryan, who was Speaker of the House the last time Illinois used CV. The proposal would divide the state into 39 districts, each of which would elect three representatives through CV. *See* Ted Kleine, *Triple Threat,* (last modified Aug. 23, 2000) <http://www.fairvote.org/e_news/991015.htm>.

The 1980 constitutional amendment to eliminate CV was presented as a cost-saving measure. At that time the state house had 177 members and had just voted itself a large pay raise. The sponsor of the ballot measure that eliminated CV, the "Cutback Amendment," presented it as a way of establishing a system with 118 house members elected from single-member districts -- thus firing in one stroke 59 legislators who had just given themselves a large pay raise. *See id.*

Page 747 after note 1(c):

Recently, Amarillo, Texas, became the largest jurisdiction to switch to cumulative voting. Starting on May 6, 2000, elections for the four-seat school board have been filled through cumulative voting. Thus, far, the system has been credited with the first African-American elected to the board and the first election of a Latino candidate since the 1970s. The population of Amarillo is around 10% African American and 20% Latino. *See* Center for Voting and Democracy, *Cumulative Voting Has Major Impact in Amarillo* (last modified Sept. 19, 2000) <http://www.fairvote.org/frames/vra/impact.htm>. The increasing experimentation and apparent success of cumulative voting in Texas and elsewhere has led more newspapers to endorse this voting system. *See, e.g.,* Birmingham News, *Disfranchised Voters*, Aug. 31, 2000. (The Birmingham News, Alabama's largest paper, advocated using cumulative voting to resolve a Voting Rights Act dispute over council elections in Alabaster).

Page 763 after note 3:

In Congressional hearings on the proposed Voter's Choice Act for congressional elections, discussed in the casebook at p.763, Rep. Tom Campbell, a moderate Republican from California, offered the following noteworthy testimony in favor of the Act and of cumulative voting in particular:

STATEMENT OF THE HON. TOM CAMPBELL, A REPRE-
SENTATIVE IN CONGRESS FROM THE STATE OF CALI-
FORNIA

Mr. CAMPBELL.

Cumulative voting allows a self-defined minority to achieve representation. . . .

Now, I emphasize the word self-defined minority because that, to me, is essential. I think it is wrong for government to divide us according to race. I believe a color-blind government is the correct constitutional maxim as well as good public policy. And thus whereas the Supreme District Court has struck down race conscious drawing of lines in order to create majority-minority- districts, cumulative voting with multi-member districts allows a self-defined minority, whether it be racial or not.

Whether it be economic or political or social or of any particular variety, it is not defined by government. It is, rather, defined by the individuals; and thus it seems to me to escape any condemnation under the fifth or fourteenth amendments and yet account for something very valuable.

I will hopefully humorously and not for any offense purposes explain the plight of a modern Republican in a conservative Republican caucus.

I am routinely outvoted. It would be nice if, for example, of the nine elected leadership positions three of them were moderates. It cannot be so, however, where as each one of them is put up to a majority vote it will always go to a conservative. If, however, we were to elect those nine as we elect a board of directors, cumulative voting, I would have nine votes. So would every other member of my Republican conference, and I would cast all of my nine for three individuals, as opposed to one for each of nine individuals. I would cast three for each, and the three moderates would make it to what I call the board of directors of the Republican Congress of the House of Representatives.

. . . I define the minority within the majority. And this particular example I used was moderate Republican. It is not done by government, and it is not necessarily done by race. It does strike me as a very farsighted solution . . . .

Page 765 after note D:

For reliable information about alternative voting systems in the United States, including up-to-date reports on new uses of these systems, the most comprehensive source is an entity named The Center for Voting and Democracy. The Center, a nonpartisan, non-profit organization, studies voting systems and provides support to organizations that advocate changes in voting structures. The Center has been active in promoting redistricting alternatives, proportional and semi-proportional representation systems, and instant runoff voting. *See* Center for Voting and Democracy, *About Us*, (last modified Nov. 5, 2000) <http://www.fairvote.org/about_us/index.html>. In addition to the direct support to organizers and government officials interested in alternative voting systems, representatives of the Center have published op-ed pieces in major newspapers advocating changes in the electoral system. *See, e.g.*, John B. Anderson, *Electoral College Outlives Usefulness*, USA Today, Nov. 2, 2000, at 17A (advocating replacing the Electoral College with direct elections with instant runoff voting). The Center is a welcoming resource for student work on alternative voting systems, and also seeks interns to assist in the Center's educational and information-gathering work.

4.   As the materials on the history of territorial districting (pages 769-73 of the casebook) suggest, the decision to use geographic districts was a product of a particular set of political, economic, technological, and logistical conditions. Will changes in those dimensions change popular receptivity to alternative voting systems? For a recent suggestion along these lines, see Eben Moglen and Pamela S. Karlan, *The Soul of a New Political Machine: The Online, the Color Line, and Electronic Democracy,* 34 LOY. L.A.L. REV. ___ (2001):

But despite the traditionalism, stickiness and convenient manipulability of geographic districting, life in the Internet society accustoms us to a much reduced respect for its factual predicates. As we spend greater and more meaningful portions of our lives in computer-mediated communications with other people, three pervasive changes occur: location doesn't matter, our interests determine our communities, and we don't have to use our feet to vote with them.

In the first place, in the Internet society, everyone is adjacent to everyone else....During any given day we are at least as likely to communicate with people on other continents as in other parts of our county, or to shop with merchants in other time zones as in other neighborhoods of our town. Locality ceases to have a normative significance: our neighborhood pub is less likely to contain our friends than a chat room, the local merchant who charges more than the seller we can find on the net is more likely to gain our resentment than our business, and the sagacity of our local doctor is under constant challenge from the flood of medical information we can find for ourselves online. Being close by is nothing special because everyone's close by. An accessible Congressman is one who gives us a quick substantive answer to our email, not someone who comes home for the weekend and hangs around the mall we don't shop at anymore.

Replacing the normative value of the local is the power of affinity. The network's media allow us to locate others who share our interests and concerns with ease, and thus we increasingly occupy the locality of the like-minded. Nor is our locality in these terms singular: we are simultaneously part of the communities of sea kayakers, gamelon musicians, ex-Bahai atheists, melanoma survivors, lukewarm libertarians (not yet ready to eliminate public libraries and slightly queasy about do-it-yourself howitzer construction) and shiatsu fanciers. A conclave of the people who share all our affinities would be more depopulated than a New Hampshire village meeting on a blizzard evening–in fact it is almost guaranteed to be a solo. But each of the communities comprising our social context will be vibrant, noisy and disputatious....

As geographic proximity assumes less importance in individuals' sense of community, and as people become more connected with one another along dimensions other than physical proximity, they may become more skeptical of the idea that political representation ought to be organized invariably along geographical lines....

Page 778, at the end of note 4:

With respect to the relationship between voting systems and the election of female legislators in the United States, Robert Darcy, Susan Welch, and Janet Clark examined election results from fourteen states and found that women were more likely to run and to be elected from multi-member districts than from single-member ones. Robert Darcy, Susan Welch & Janet Clark, *Women Candidates in Single-and Multi-Member Districts: American State Legislative Races,* 66 SOC. SCI. Q. 945 (1985). This relationship was confirmed by a recent study of Montana, which changed its electoral system to an exclusively single-member district one following one-person, one-vote litigation arising out of the post-1990 reapportionment. *See* Michael J. Horan and James D. King, *The Demise of the Multi-Member District System and Its Effect Upon the Representation of Women,* 34 LAND & WATER L. REV. 407 (1999). Horan and King offer several explanations for women's greater success in multi-member systems:

First, party elites may exercise a kind of affirmative action, slating women or providing more campaign resources to women in multi-member districts. Pressure to support women candidates is more easily accommodated in multi-member districts than in single-member districts. Also, voters may similarly practice a form of affirmative action. Those with reservations concerning the qualifications of women for public office can cast one ballot for a woman in a multimember district knowing that they will also be represented by a man. Finally, the characteristics and accomplishments of individual candidates are often highlighted more than partisanship in multimember districts. The typical head-to-head battle between a Republican and Democrat is replaced by something of a free-for-all where each candidate emphasizes his/her own strengths rather than his/her opponent's weaknesses. In this environment, gender gives women a distinctive characteristic, especially in districts where women candidates are novelties.

Id. at 413. Does Horan and King's analysis suggest that there has been a tradeoff between greater representation of minorities through the switch to single-member districts and less representation of women?

DOCUMENTARY APPENDIX

THE UNITED STATES CONSTITUTION

We the People of the United States, in order to form a more perfect Union, establish Justice, insure domestic tranquility, provide for common defense, promote the general Welfare, and secure the Blessings of Liberty to ourselves and our Posterity, do ordain and establish this Constitution for the United States of America.

Article. I.

Section 1.
All legislative Powers herein granted shall be vested in a Congress of the United States, which shall consist of a Senate and House of Representatives.

Section. 2.
The House of Representatives shall be composed of Members chosen every second Year by the People of the several States, and the Electors in each State shall have the Qualifications requisite for Electors of the most numerous Branch of the State Legislature.

No Person shall be a Representative who shall not have attained to the Age of twenty five Years, and been seven Years a Citizen of the United States, and who shall not, when elected, be an Inhabitant of that State in which he shall be chosen.

Representatives and direct Taxes shall be apportioned among the several States which may be included within this Union, according to their respective numbers, which shall be determined by adding to the whole Number of free Persons, including those bound to Service for a Term of Years, and excluding Indians not taxed, three fifths of all other Persons. The actual Enumeration shall be made within three Years after the first Meeting of the Congress of the United States, and within every subsequent Term of ten Years, in such Manner as they shall by Law direct. The Number of Representatives shall not exceed one for every thirty Thousand, but each State shall have at Least one

Representative; and until such enumeration shall be made, the State of New Hampshire shall be entitled to choose three, Massachusetts eight, Rhode-Island and Providence Plantations one, Connecticut five, New-York six, New Jersey four, Pennsylvania eight, Delaware one, Maryland six, Virginia ten, North Carolina five, South Carolina five, and Georgia three.

When vacancies happen in the Representation from any State, the Executive Authority thereof shall issue Writs of Election to fill such Vacancies.

The House of Representatives shall chuse their Speaker and other Officers and shall have the sole Power of Impeachment.

Section. 3.
The Senate of the United States shall be composed of two Senators from each State, chosen by the Legislature thereof, for six Years; and each Senator shall have one Vote.

Immediately after they shall be assembled in Consequence of the first Election, they shall be divided as equally as may be into three Classes. The Seats of the Senators of the first Class shall be vacated at the Expiration of the second Year, of the second Class at the Expiration of the fourth Year, and of the third Class at the Expiration of the sixth Year, so that one third may be chosen every second Year; and if Vacancies happen by Resignation, or otherwise, during the Recess of the Legislature of any State, the Executive thereof may make temporary Appointments until the next Meeting of the Legislature, which shall then fill such Vacancies.

No Person shall be a Senator who shall not have attained to the Age of thirty Years, and been nine Years a Citizen of the United States, and who shall not, when elected, be an Inhabitant of that State for which he shall be chosen.

The Vice President of the United States shall be President of the Senate, but shall have no Vote, unless they be equally divided.

The Senate shall choose their other Officers, and also a President pro tempore, in the Absence of the Vice President, or when he shall exercise the Office of President of the United States.

The Senate shall have the sole Power to try all Impeachment's. When sitting for that Purpose, they shall be on Oath or Affirmation. When the President of the United States is tried, the Chief Justice shall preside: And no Person shall be convicted without the Concurrence of two thirds of the Members present.

Judgment in Cases of Impeachment shall not extend further than to removal from Office, and disqualification to hold and enjoy any Office of honor, Trust or Profit under the United States: but the Party convicted shall nevertheless be liable and subject to Indictment, Trial, Judgment and Punishment, according to Law.

Section. 4.
The Times, Places and Manner of holding Elections for Senators and Representatives, shall be prescribed in each State by the Legislature thereof; but the Congress may at any time by Law make or alter such Regulations, except as to the Places of choosing Senators.

The Congress shall assemble at least once in every Year, and such Meeting shall be on the first Monday in December, unless they shall by Law appoint a different Day.

Section. 5.
Each House shall be the Judge of the Elections, Returns and Qualifications of its own Members, and a Majority of each shall constitute a Quorum to do Business; but a smaller Number may adjourn from day to day, and may be authorized to compel the Attendance of absent Members, in such Manner, and under such Penalties as each House may provide.

Each House may determine the Rules of its Proceedings, punish its Members for disorderly Behaviour, and, with the Concurrence of two thirds, expel a Member.

Each House shall keep a Journal of its Proceedings, and from time to time publish the same, excepting such Parts as may in their Judgment require Secrecy; and the Yeas and Nays of the Members of either House on any question shall, at the Desire of one fifth of those Present, be entered on the Journal.

Neither House, during the Session of Congress, shall, without the Consent of the other, adjourn for more than three days, nor to any other Place than that in which the two Houses shall be sitting.

Section. 6.
The Senators and Representatives shall receive a Compensation for their Services, to be ascertained by Law, and paid out of the Treasury of the United States. They shall in all Cases, except Treason, Felony and Breach of the Peace, be privileged from Arrest during their Attendance at the Session of their respective Houses, and in going to and returning

from the same; and for any Speech or Debate in either House, they shall not be questioned in any other Place.

No Senator or Representative shall, during the Time for which he was elected, be appointed to any civil Office under the Authority of the United States, which shall have been created, or the Emoluments whereof shall have been encreased during such time; and no Person holding any Office under the United States, shall be a Member of either House during his Continuance in Office.

Section. 7.
All Bills for raising Revenue shall originate in the House of Representatives; but the Senate may propose or concur with Amendments as on other Bills.

Every Bill which shall have passed the House of Representatives and the Senate, shall, before it become a Law, be presented to the President of the United States; If he approve he shall sign it, but if not he shall return it, with his Objections to that House in which it shall have originated, who shall enter the Objections at large on their Journal, and proceed to reconsider it. If after such Reconsideration two thirds of that House shall agree to pass the Bill, it shall be sent, together with the Objections, to the other House, by which it shall likewise be reconsidered, and if approved by two thirds of that House, it shall become a Law. But in all such Cases the Votes of both Houses shall be determined by yeas and Nays, and the Names of the Persons voting for and against the Bill shall be entered on the Journal of each House respectively. If any Bill shall not be returned by the President within ten Days (Sundays excepted) after it shall have been presented to him, the Same shall be a Law, in like Manner as if he had signed it, unless the Congress by their Adjournment prevent its Return, in which Case it shall not be a Law.

Every Order, Resolution, or Vote to which the Concurrence of the Senate and House of Representatives may be necessary (except on a question of adjournment) shall be presented to the President of the United States; and before the Same shall take Effect, shall be approved by him, or being disapproved by him, shall be repassed by two thirds of the Senate and House of Representatives, according to the Rules and Limitations prescribed in the Case of a Bill.

Section. 8.
The Congress shall have Power To lay and collect Taxes, Duties, Imposts and Excises, to pay the Debts and provide for the common Defense and general Welfare of the United States; but all Duties, Imposts and Excises shall be uniform throughout the United States;

To borrow Money on the credit of the United States;

To regulate Commerce with foreign Nations, and among the several States, and with the Indian Tribes;

To establish an uniform Rule of Naturalization, and uniform Laws on the subject of Bankruptcies throughout the United States;

To coin Money, regulate the Value thereof, and of foreign Coin, and fix the Standard of Weights and Measures;

To provide for the Punishment of counterfeiting the Securities and current Coin of the United States;

To establish Post Offices and post Roads;

To promote the Progress of Science and useful Arts, by securing for limited Times to Authors and Inventors the exclusive Right to their respective Writings and Discoveries;

To constitute Tribunals inferior to the supreme Court;

To define and punish Piracies and Felonies committed on the high Seas, and Offences against the Law of Nations;

To declare War, grant Letters of Marque and Reprisal, and make Rules concerning Captures on Land and Water;

To raise and support Armies, but no Appropriation of Money to that Use shall be for a longer Term than two Years;

To provide and maintain a Navy;

To make Rules for the Government and Regulation of the land and naval Forces;

To provide for calling forth the Militia to execute the Laws of the Union, suppress Insurrections and repel Invasions;

To provide for organizing, arming, and disciplining, the Militia, and for governing such Part of them as may be employed in the Service of the United States, reserving to the States respectively, the Appointment of the Officers, and the Authority of training the Militia according to the discipline prescribed by Congress;

To exercise exclusive Legislation in all Cases whatsoever, over such District (not exceeding ten Miles square) as may, by Cession of particular States, and the Acceptance of Congress, become the Seat of the Government of the United States, and to exercise like Authority over all Places purchased by the Consent of the Legislature of the State in which the Same shall be, for the Erection of Forts, Magazines, Arsenals, dock-Yards, and other needful Buildings;--And

To make all Laws which shall be necessary and proper for carrying into Execution the foregoing Powers, and all other Powers vested by this Constitution in the Government of the United States, or in any Department or Officer thereof.

Section. 9.
The Migration or Importation of such Persons as any of the States now existing shall think proper to admit, shall not be prohibited by the Congress prior to the Year one thousand eight hundred and eight, but a Tax or duty may be imposed on such Importation, not exceeding ten dollars for each Person.

The Privilege of the Writ of Habeas Corpus shall not be suspended, unless when in Cases of Rebellion or Invasion the public Safety may require it.

No Bill of Attainder or ex post facto Law shall be passed.

No Capitation, or other direct, Tax shall be laid, unless in Proportion to the Census or Enumeration herein before directed to be taken.

No Tax or Duty shall be laid on Articles exported from any State.

No Preference shall be given by any Regulation of Commerce or Revenue to the Ports of one State over those of another: nor shall Vessels bound to, or from, one State, be obliged to enter, clear, or pay Duties in another.

No Money shall be drawn from the Treasury, but in Consequence of Appropriations made by Law; and a regular Statement and Account of the Receipts and Expenditures of all public Money shall be published from time to time.

No Title of Nobility shall be granted by the United States: And no Person holding any Office of Profit or Trust under them, shall, without the Consent of the Congress, accept of any present, Emolument, Office, or Title, of any kind whatever, from any King, Prince, or foreign State.

Section. 10.
No State shall enter into any Treaty, Alliance, or Confederation; grant Letters of Marque and Reprisal; coin Money; emit Bills of Credit; make any Thing but gold and silver Coin a Tender in Payment of Debts; pass any Bill of Attainder, ex post facto Law, or Law impairing the Obligation of Contracts, or grant any Title of Nobility.

No State shall, without the Consent of the Congress, lay any Imposts or Duties on Imports or Exports, except what may be absolutely necessary for executing it's inspection Laws: and the net Produce of all Duties and Imposts, laid by any State on Imports or Exports, shall be for the Use of the Treasury of the United States; and all such Laws shall be subject to the Revision and Control of the Congress.

No State shall, without the Consent of Congress, lay any Duty of Tonnage, keep Troops, or Ships of War in time of Peace, enter into any Agreement or Compact with another State, or with a foreign Power, or engage in War, unless actually invaded, or in such imminent Danger as will not admit of delay.

Article. II.

Section. 1.
The executive Power shall be vested in a President of the United States of America. He shall hold his Office during the Term of four Years, and, together with the Vice President, chosen for the same Term, be elected, as follows

Each State shall appoint, in such Manner as the Legislature thereof may direct, a Number of Electors, equal to the whole Number of Senators and representatives to which the State may be entitled in the Congress: but no Senator or Representative, or Person holding an Office of Trust or Profit under the United States, shall be appointed an Elector.

The Electors shall meet in their respective States, and vote by Ballot for two Persons, of whom one at least shall not be an Inhabitant of the same State with themselves. And they shall make a List of all the Persons voted for, and of the Number of Votes for each; which List they shall sign and certify, and transmit sealed to the Seat of the Government of the United States, directed to the President of the Senate. The President of the Senate shall, in the Presence of the Senate and House of Representatives, open all the Certificates, and the Votes shall then be counted. The Person having the greatest Number of Votes shall be the President, if such Number be a Majority of the whole Number of Electors appointed; and if there be more than one who have such

Majority, and have an equal Number of Votes, then the House of Representatives shall immediately chuse by Ballot one of them for President; and if no Person have a Majority, then from the five highest on the List the said House shall in like Manner chuse the President. But in chusing the President, the Votes shall be taken by States, the Representation from each State having one Vote; A quorum for this Purpose shall consist of a Member or Members from two thirds of the States, and a Majority of all the States shall be necessary to a Choice. In every Case, after the Choice of the President, the Person having the greatest Number of Votes of the Electors shall be the Vice President. But if there should remain two or more who have equal Votes, the Senate shall chuse from them by Ballot the Vice President.

The Congress may determine the Time of chusing the Electors, and the Day on which they shall give their Votes; which Day shall be the same throughout the United States.

No Person except a natural born Citizen, or a Citizen of the United States, at the time of the Adoption of this Constitution, shall be eligible to the Office of President; neither shall any Person be eligible to that Office who shall not have attained to the Age of thirty five Years, and been fourteen Years a Resident within the United States.

In Case of the Removal of the President from Office, or of his Death, Resignation, or Inability to discharge the Powers and Duties of the said Office, the Same shall devolve on the Vice President, and the Congress may by Law provide for the Case of Removal, Death, Resignation or Inability, both of the President and Vice President, declaring what Officer shall then act as President, and such Officer shall act accordingly, until the Disability be removed, or a President shall be elected.

The President shall, at stated Times, receive for his Services, a Compensation, which shall neither be encreased nor diminished during the Period for which he shall have been elected, and he shall not receive within that Period any other Emolument from the United States, or any of them.

Before he enter on the Execution of his Office, he shall take the following Oath or Affirmation:--"I do solemnly swear (or affirm) that I will faithfully execute the Office of President of the United States, and will to the best of my Ability, preserve, protect and defend the Constitution of the United States."

Section. 2.
The President shall be Commander in Chief of the Army and Navy of

the United States, and of the Militia of the several States, when called into the actual Service of the United States; he may require the Opinion, in writing, of the principal Officer in each of the executive Departments, upon any Subject relating to the Duties of their respective Offices, and he shall have Power to grant Reprieves and Pardons for Offences against the United States, except in Cases of Impeachment.

He shall have Power, by and with the Advice and Consent of the Senate, to make Treaties, provided two thirds of the Senators present concur; and he shall nominate, and by and with the Advice and Consent of the Senate, shall appoint Ambassadors, other public Ministers and Consuls, Judges of the supreme Court, and all other Officers of the United States, whose Appointments are not herein otherwise provided for, and which shall be established by Law: but the Congress may by Law vest the Appointment of such inferior Officers, as they think proper, in the President alone, in the Courts of Law, or in the Heads of Departments.

The President shall have Power to fill up all Vacancies that may happen during the Recess of the Senate, by granting Commissions which shall expire at the End of their next Session.

Section. 3.
He shall from time to time give to the Congress Information of the State of the Union, and recommend to their Consideration such Measures as he shall judge necessary and expedient; he may, on extraordinary Occasions, convene both Houses, or either of them, and in Case of Disagreement between them, with Respect to the Time of Adjournment, he may adjourn them to such Time as he shall think proper; he shall receive Ambassadors and other public Ministers; he shall take Care that the Laws be faithfully executed, and shall Commission all the Officers of the United States.

Section. 4.
The President, Vice President and all civil Officers of the United States, shall be removed from Office on Impeachment for, and Conviction of, Treason, Bribery, or other high Crimes and Misdemeanors.

Article. III.

Section. 1.
The judicial Power of the United States, shall be vested in one supreme Court, and in such inferior Courts as the Congress may from time to time ordain and establish. The Judges, both of the supreme and inferior Courts, shall hold their Offices during good Behaviour, and shall, at stated Times, receive for their Services, a Compensation, which shall not be diminished during their Continuance in Office.

Section. 2.

The judicial Power shall extend to all Cases, in Law and Equity, arising under this Constitution, the Laws of the United States, and Treaties made, or which shall be made, under their Authority;--to all Cases affecting Ambassadors, other public Ministers and Consuls;--to all Cases of admiralty and maritime Jurisdiction;--to Controversies to which the United States shall be a Party;--to Controversies between two or more States;--between a State and Citizens of another State; between Citizens of different States, --between Citizens of the same State claiming Lands under Grants of different States, and between a State, or the Citizens thereof, and foreign States, Citizens or Subjects.

In all Cases affecting Ambassadors, other public Ministers and Consuls, and those in which a State shall be Party, the supreme Court shall have original Jurisdiction. In all the other Cases before mentioned, the supreme Court shall have appellate Jurisdiction, both as to Law and Fact, with such Exceptions, and under such Regulations as the Congress shall make.

The Trial of all Crimes, except in Cases of Impeachment, shall be by Jury; and such Trial shall be held in the State where the said Crimes shall have been committed; but when not committed within any State, the Trial shall be at such Place or Places as the Congress may by Law have directed.

Section. 3

Treason against the United States, shall consist only in levying War against them, or in adhering to their Enemies, giving them Aid and Comfort. No Person shall be convicted of Treason unless on the Testimony of two Witnesses to the same overt Act, or on Confession in open Court.

The Congress shall have Power to declare the Punishment of Treason, but no Attainder of Treason shall work Corruption of Blood, or Forfeiture except during the Life of the Person attainted.

Article. IV.

Section. 1.

Full Faith and Credit shall be given in each State to the public Acts, Records, and judicial Proceedings of every other State. And the Congress may by general laws prescribe the Manner in which such Acts, Records and Proceedings shall be proved, and the Effect thereof.

Section. 2.

The Citizens of each State shall be entitled to all Privileges and Immunities of Citizens in the several States.

A Person charged in any State with Treason, Felony, or other Crime, who shall flee from Justice, and be found in another State, shall on Demand of the executive Authority of the State from which he fled, be delivered up, to be removed to the State having Jurisdiction of the Crime.

No Person held to Service or Labour in one State, under the Laws thereof, escaping into another, shall, in Consequence of any Law or Regulation therein, be discharged from such Service or Labour, but shall be delivered up on Claim of the Party to whom such Service or Labour may be due.

Section. 3.

New States may be admitted by the Congress into this Union; but no new State shall be formed or erected within the Jurisdiction of any other State; nor any State be formed by the Junction of two or more States, or Parts of States, without the Consent of the Legislatures of the States concerned as well as of the Congress.

The Congress shall have Power to dispose of and make all needful Rules and Regulations respecting the Territory or other Property belonging to the United States; and nothing in this Constitution shall be so construed as to Prejudice any Claims of the United States, or of any particular State.

Section. 4.

The United States shall guarantee to every State in this Union a Republican Form of Government, and shall protect each of them against Invasion; and on Application of the Legislature, or of the Executive (when the Legislature cannot be convened) against domestic Violence.

Article. V.

The Congress, whenever two thirds of both Houses shall deem it necessary, shall propose Amendments to this Constitution, or, on the Application of the Legislatures of two thirds of the several States, shall call a Convention for proposing Amendments, which, in either Case, shall be valid to all Intents and Purposes, as Part of this Constitution, when ratified by the Legislatures of three fourths of the several States, or by Conventions in three fourths thereof, as the one or the other Mode of Ratification may be proposed by the Congress; Provided that no Amendment which may be made prior to the Year One thousand eight hundred and eight shall in any Manner affect the first and fourth Clauses in the Ninth Section of the first Article; and that no State, without its Consent, shall be deprived of its equal Suffrage in the Senate.

Article. VI.

All Debts contracted and Engagements entered into, before the Adoption of this Constitution, shall be as valid against the United States under this Constitution, as under the Confederation.

This Constitution, and the Laws of the United States which shall be made in Pursuance thereof; and all Treaties made, or which shall be made, under the Authority of the United States, shall be the supreme Law of the Land; and the Judges in every State shall be bound thereby, any Thing in the Constitution or Laws of any State to the Contrary notwithstanding.

The Senators and Representatives before mentioned, and the Members of the several State Legislatures, and all executive and judicial Officers, both of the United States and of the several States, shall be bound by Oath or Affirmation, to support this Constitution; but no religious Test shall ever be required as a Qualification to any Office or public Trust under the United States.

Article. VII.

The Ratification of the Conventions of nine States, shall be sufficient for the Establishment of this Constitution between the States so ratifying the Same. done in Convention by the Unanimous Consent of the States present the Seventeenth Day of September in the Year of our Lord one thousand seven hundred and Eighty seven and of the Independence of the United States of America the Twelfth In witness whereof We have hereunto subscribed our Names,

AMENDMENTS

AMENDMENT I
(Ratified in 1791.)
Congress shall make no law respecting an establishment of religion, or prohibiting the free exercise thereof; or abridging the freedom of speech, or of the press; or the right of the people peaceably to assemble, and to petition the Government for a redress of grievances.

AMENDMENT II
(Ratified in 1791.)
A well regulated Militia, being necessary to the security of a free State, the right of the people to keep and bear Arms, shall not be infringed.

AMENDMENT III
(Ratified in 1791.)
No Soldier shall, in time of peace be quartered in any house, without the consent of the Owner, nor in time of war, but in a manner to be prescribed by law.

AMENDMENT IV
(Ratified in 1791.)
The right of the People to be secure in their persons, houses, papers, and effects, against unreasonable searches and seizures, shall not be violated, and no Warrants shall issue, but upon probable cause, supported by Oath or affirmation, and particularity describing the place to be searched, and the persons or things to be seized.

AMENDMENT V
(Ratified in 1791.)
No person shall be held to answer for a capital, or otherwise infamous crime, unless on a presentment or indictment of a Grand Jury, except in cases arising in the land or naval forces, or in the Militia, when in actual service in time of War or public danger; nor shall any person be subject for the same offence to be twice put in jeopardy of life or limb; nor shall be compelled in any criminal case to be a witness against himself, nor be deprived of life, liberty, or property, without due process of law; nor shall private property be taken for public use, without just compensation.

AMENDMENT VI
(Ratified in 1791.)
In all criminal prosecutions, the accused shall enjoy the right to a speedy and public trial, by an impartial jury of the State and district wherein the crime shall have been committed, which district shall have been previously ascertained by law, and to be informed of the nature

and cause of the accusation; to be confronted with the witnesses against him; to have compulsory process for obtaining witnesses in his favor, and to have Assistance of Counsel for his defense.

AMENDMENT VII
(Ratified in 1791.)
In Suits at common law, where the value in controversy shall exceed twenty dollars, the right of trial by jury shall be preserved, and no fact tried by a jury, shall be otherwise re-examined in any Court of the United States, than according to the rules of the common law.

AMENDMENT VIII
(Ratified in 1791.)
Excessive bail shall not be required, nor excessive fines imposed, nor cruel and unusual punishments inflicted.

AMENDMENT IX
(Ratified in 1791.)
The enumeration in the Constitution, of certain rights, shall not be construed to deny or disparage others retained by the people.

AMENDMENT X
(Ratified in 1791.)
The powers not delegated to the United States by the Constitution, nor prohibited by it to the States, are reserved to the States respectively, or to the people.

AMENDMENT XI
(Ratified in 1795.)
The Judicial power of the United States shall not be construed to extend to any suit in law or equity, commenced or prosecuted against one of the United States by Citizens of another State, or by Citizens or Subjects of any Foreign State.

AMENDMENT XII
(Ratified in 1804.)
The Electors shall meet in their respective states and vote by ballot for President and Vice-President, one of whom, at least, shall not be an inhabitant of the same state with themselves; they shall name in their ballots the person voted for as President, and in distinct ballots the person voted for as Vice-President, and they shall make distinct lists of all persons voted for as President, and of all persons voted for as Vice-President, and of the number of votes for each, which lists they shall sign and certify, and transmit sealed to the seat of the government of the United States, directed to the President of the Senate; -- The President of the Senate shall, in the presence of the Senate and House

of Representatives, open all the certificates and the votes shall then be counted; -- The person having the greatest number of votes for President, shall be the President, if such number be a majority of the whole number of Electors appointed; and if no person have such majority, then from the persons having the highest numbers not exceeding three on the list of those voted for as President, the House of Representatives shall choose immediately, by ballot, the President. But in choosing the President, the votes shall be taken by states, the representation from each state having one vote; a quorum for this purpose shall consist of a member or members from two-thirds of the states, and a majority of all the states shall be necessary to a choice. And if the House of Representatives shall not choose a President whenever the right of choice shall devolve upon then, before the fourth day of March next following, then the Vice-President shall act as President, as in the case of the death or other constitutional disability of the President. -- The person having the greatest number of votes as Vice-President, shall be the Vice-President, if such number be a majority of the whole number of Electors appointed, and if no person have a majority, then from the two highest numbers on the list, the Senate shall choose the Vice-President; a quorum for the purpose shall consist of two-thirds of the whole number of Senators, and a majority of the whole number shall be necessary to a choice. But no person constitutionally ineligible to the office of President shall be eligible to that of Vice-President of the United States.

AMENDMENT XIII
(Ratified in 1865.)
Section 1.
Neither slavery nor involuntary servitude, except as a punishment for crime whereof the party shall have been duly convicted, shall exist within the United States, or any place subject to their jurisdiction.

Section 2.
Congress shall have power to enforce this article by appropriate legislation.

AMENDMENT XIV
(Ratified in 1868.)
Section 1.
All persons born or naturalized in the United States, and subject to the jurisdiction thereof, are citizens of the United States and of the State wherein they reside. No State shall make or enforce any law which shall abridge the privileges or immunities of citizens of the United States; nor shall any State deprive any person of life, liberty, or property, without due process of law; nor deny to any person within its jurisdiction the equal protection of the laws.

Section 2.

Representatives shall be apportioned among the several States according to their respective numbers, counting the whole number of persons in each State, excluding Indians not taxed. But when the right to vote at any election for the choice of electors for President and Vice President of the United States, Representatives in Congress, the Executive and Judicial officers of a State, or the members of the Legislature thereof, is denied to any of the male inhabitants of such State, being twenty-one years of age, and citizens of the United States, or in any way abridged, except for participation in rebellion, or other crime, the basis of representation therein shall be reduced in the proportion which the number of such male citizens shall bear to the whole number of male citizens twenty-one years of age in such State.

Section 3.

No person shall be a Senator or Representative in Congress, or elector of President and Vice President, or hold any office, civil or military, under the United States, or under any State, who, having previously taken an oath, as a member of Congress, or as an officer of the United States, or as a member of any State legislature, or as an executive or judicial officer of any State, to support the Constitution of the United States, shall have engaged in insurrection or rebellion against the same, or given aid or comfort to the enemies thereof. But Congress may by a vote of two-thirds of each House, remove such disability.

Section 4.

The validity of the public debt of the United States, authorized by law, including debts incurred for payment of pensions and bounties for services in suppressing insurrection or rebellion, shall not be questioned. But neither the United States nor any State shall assume or pay any debt or obligation incurred in aid of insurrection or rebellion against the United States, or any claim for the loss or emancipation of any slave; but all such debts, obligations and claims shall be held illegal and void.

Section 5.

The Congress shall have power to enforce, by appropriate legislation, the provisions of this article.

AMENDMENT XV
(Ratified in 1870.)
Section 1.

The right of citizens of the United States to vote shall not be denied or abridged by the United States or by any State on account of race, color, or previous condition of servitude.

Section 2.

The Congress shall have power to enforce this article by appropriate legislation.

AMENDMENT XVI

(Ratified in 1913.)

The Congress shall have power to lay and collect taxes on incomes, from whatever source derived, without apportionment among the several States, and without regard to any census or enumeration.

AMENDMENT XVII

(Ratified in 1913.)

The Senate of the United States shall be composed of two Senators from each State, elected by the people thereof for six years; and each Senator shall have one vote. The electors in each State shall have the qualifications requisite for electors of the most numerous branch of the State legislatures. When vacancies happen in the representation of any State in the Senate, the executive authority of such State shall issue writs of election to fill such vacancies: Provided, That the legislature of any State may empower the executive thereof to make temporary appointments until the people fill the vacancies by election as the legislature may direct. This amendment shall not be so construed as to affect the election or term of any Senator chosen before it becomes valid as part of the Constitution.

AMENDMENT XVIII

(Ratified in 1919.)

Section 1.

After one year from the ratification of this article the manufacture, sale, or transportation of intoxicating liquors within, the importation thereof into, or the exportation thereof from the United States and all territory subject to the jurisdiction thereof for beverage purposes is hereby prohibited.

Section 2.

The Congress and the several States shall have concurrent power to enforce this article by appropriate legislation.

Section 3. This article shall be inoperative unless it shall have been ratified as an amendment to the Constitution by the legislatures of the several States as provided in the Constitution, within seven years from the date of the submission hereof to the States by the Congress.

AMENDMENT XIX

(Ratified in 1920.)

The right of citizens of the United States to vote shall not be denied or abridged by the United States or by any State on account of sex. Congress shall have power to enforce this article by appropriate legislation.

AMENDMENT XX
(Ratified in 1933.)
Section 1.
The terms of the President and Vice President shall end at noon on the 20th day of January, and the terms of Senators and Representatives at noon on the 3d day of January, of the years in which such terms would have ended if this article had not been ratified; and the terms of their successors shall then begin.

Section 2.
The Congress shall assemble at least once in every year, and such meeting shall begin at noon on the 3d day of January, unless they shall by law appoint a different day.

Section 3.
If, at the time fixed for the beginning of the term of the President, the President elect shall have died, the Vice President elect shall become President. If a President shall not have been chosen before the time fixed for the beginning of his term, or if the President elect shall have failed to qualify, then the Vice President elect shall act as President until a President shall have qualified; and the Congress may by law provide for the case wherein neither a President elect nor a Vice President elect shall have qualified, declaring who shall then act as President, or the manner in which one who is to act shall be selected, and such person shall act accordingly until a President or Vice President shall have qualified.

Section 4.
The Congress may by law provide for the case of the death of any of the persons from whom the House of Representatives may choose a President whenever the right of choice shall have devolved upon them, and for the case of the death of any of the persons from whom the Senate may choose a Vice President whenever the right of choice shall have devolved upon them.

Section 5.
Sections 1 and 2 shall take effect on the 15th day of October following the ratification of this article.

Section 6. This article shall be inoperative unless it shall have been ratified as an amendment to the Constitution by the legislatures of three-fourths of the several States within seven years from the date of its submission.

AMENDMENT XXI
(Ratified in 1933.)
Section 1.
The eighteenth article of amendment to the Constitution of the United States is hereby repealed.

Section 2.
The transportation or importation into any State, Territory, or possession of the United States for delivery or use therein of intoxicating liquors, in violation of the laws thereof, is hereby prohibited.

Section 3. This article shall be inoperative unless it shall have been ratified as an amendment to the Constitution by conventions in the several States, as provided in the Constitution, within seven years from the date of the submission hereof to the States by the Congress.

AMENDMENT XXII
(Ratified in 1951.)
Section 1.
No person shall be elected to the office of the President more than twice, and no person who has held the office of President, or acted as President, for more than two years of a term to which some other person was elected President shall be elected to the office of the President more than once. But this Article shall not apply to any person holding the office of President when this Article was proposed by the Congress, and shall not prevent any person who may be holding the office of President, or acting as President, during the term within which this Article becomes operative from holding the office of President or acting as President during the remainder of such term.

Section 2.
This Article shall be inoperative unless it shall have been ratified as an amendment to the Constitution by the legislatures of three-fourths of the several States within seven years from the date of its submission to the States by the Congress.

AMENDMENT XXIII
(Ratified in 1961.)
Section 1.
The District constituting the seat of Government of the United States shall appoint in such manner as the Congress may direct: A number of electors of President and Vice President equal to the whole number of Senators and Representatives in Congress to which the District would be entitled if it were a State, but in no event more than the least

populous State; they shall be in addition to those appointed by the States, but they shall be considered, for the purposes of the election of President and Vice President, to be electors appointed by a State; and they shall meet in the District and perform such duties as provided by the twelfth article of amendment.

Section 2. The Congress shall have power to enforce this article by appropriate legislation.

AMENDMENT XXIV
(Ratified in 1964.)
Section 1.
The right of citizens of the United States to vote in any primary or other election for President or Vice President, for electors for President or Vice President, or for Senator or Representative in Congress, shall not be denied or abridged by the United States or any State by reason of failure to pay any poll tax or other tax.

Section 2.
The Congress shall have power to enforce this article by appropriate legislation.

AMENDMENT XXV
(Ratified in 1967.)
Section 1.
In case of the removal of the President from office or of his death or resignation, the Vice President shall become President.

Section 2.
Whenever there is a vacancy in the office of the Vice President, the President shall nominate a Vice President who shall take office upon confirmation by a majority vote of both Houses of Congress.

Section 3.
Whenever the President transmits to the President pro tempore of the Senate and the Speaker of the House of Representatives his written declaration that he is unable to discharge the powers and duties of his office, and until he transmits to them a written declaration to the contrary, such powers and duties shall be discharged by the Vice President as Acting President.

Section 4.
Whenever the Vice president and a majority of either the principal officers of the executive departments or of such other body as Congress may by law provide, transmit to the President pro tempore of the Senate and the Speaker of the House of Representatives their written

declaration that the President is unable to discharge the powers and duties of his office, the Vice President shall immediately assume the powers and duties of the office as Acting President. Thereafter, when the President transmits to the President pro tempore of the Senate and the Speaker of the House of Representatives his written declaration that no inability exists, he shall resume the powers and duties of his office unless the Vice President and a majority of either the principal officers of the executive department or of such other body as Congress may by law provide, transmit within four days to the President pro tempore of the Senate and the Speaker of the House of Representatives their written declaration that the President is unable to discharge the powers and duties of his office. Thereupon Congress shall decide the issue, assembling within forty-eight hours for that purpose if not in session. If the Congress, within twenty-one days after receipt of the latter written declaration, or, if Congress is not in session, within twenty-one days after Congress is required to assemble, determines by two-thirds vote of both Houses that the President is unable to discharge the powers and duties of his office, the Vice President shall continue to discharge the same as Acting President; otherwise, the President shall resume the powers and duties of his office.

AMENDMENT XXVI
(Ratified in 1971.)
Section 1.
The right of citizens of the United States, who are eighteen years of age or older, to vote shall not be denied or abridged by the United States or by any State on account of age.

Section 2.
The Congress shall have power to enforce this article by appropriate legislation.

AMENDMENT XXVII
(Ratified in 1992.)
No law, varying the compensation for the services of the Senators and Representatives, shall take effect, until an election of Representatives shall have intervened.

THE ELECTORAL COUNT ACT

UNITED STATES CODE ANNOTATED
TITLE 3. THE PRESIDENT
CHAPTER 1–PRESIDENTIAL ELECTIONS AND VACANCIES

§ 1. Time of appointing electors

The electors of President and Vice President shall be appointed, in each State, on the Tuesday next after the first Monday in November, in every fourth year succeeding every election of a President and Vice President.

§ 2. Failure to make choice on prescribed day

Whenever any State has held an election for the purpose of choosing electors, and has failed to make a choice on the day prescribed by law, the electors may be appointed on a subsequent day in such a manner as the legislature of such State may direct.

§ 3. Number of electors

The number of electors shall be equal to the number of Senators and Representatives to which the several States are by law entitled at the time when the President and Vice President to be chosen come into office; except, that where no apportionment of Representatives has been made after any enumeration, at the time of choosing electors, the number of electors shall be according to the then existing apportionment of Senators and Representatives.

§ 4. Vacancies in electoral college

Each State may, by law, provide for the filling of any vacancies which may occur in its college of electors when such college meets to give its electoral vote.

§ 5. Determination of controversy as to appointment of electors

If any State shall have provided, by laws enacted prior to the day fixed for the appointment of the electors, for its final determination of any controversy or contest concerning the appointment of all or any of the electors of such State, by judicial or other methods or procedures, and such determination shall have been made at least six days before the time fixed for the meeting of the electors, such determination made pursuant to such law so existing on said day, and made at least six

days prior to said time of meeting of the electors, shall be conclusive, and shall govern in the counting of the electoral votes as provided in the Constitution, and as hereinafter regulated, so far as the ascertainment
of the electors appointed by such State is concerned.

§ 6. Credentials of electors; transmission to Archivist of the United States and to Congress; public inspection

It shall be the duty of the executive of each State, as soon as practicable after the conclusion of the appointment of the electors in such State by the final ascertainment, under and in pursuance of the laws of such State providing for such ascertainment, to communicate by registered mail under the seal of the State to the Archivist of the
United States a certificate of such ascertainment of the electors appointed, setting forth the names of such electors and the canvass or other ascertainment under the laws of such State of the number of votes given or cast for each person for whose appointment any and all votes have been given or cast; and it shall also thereupon be the duty of the executive of each State to deliver to the electors of such State, on or before the day on which they are required by section 7 of this title to meet, six duplicate-originals of the same certificate under the seal of the State; and if there shall have been any final determination in a State in the manner provided for by law of a controversy or contest concerning the appointment of all or any of the electors of such State, it shall be the duty of the executive of such State, as soon as practicable after such determination, to communicate under the seal of the State to the Archivist of the United States a certificate of such determination
in form and manner as the same shall have been made; and the certificate or certificates so received by the Archivist of the United States shall be preserved by him for one year and shall be a part of the public records of his office and shall be open to public inspection; and the Archivist of the United States at the first meeting of Congress thereafter shall transmit to the two Houses of Congress copies in full of each and every such certificate so received at the National Archives and Records Administration.

§ 7. Meeting and vote of electors

The electors of President and Vice President of each State shall meet and give their votes on the first Monday after the second Wednesday in December next following their appointment at such place in each State as the legislature of such State shall direct.

§ 8. Manner of voting

The electors shall vote for President and Vice President, respectively, in the manner directed by the Constitution.

§ 9. Certificates of votes for President and Vice President

The electors shall make and sign six certificates of all the votes given by them, each of which certificates shall contain two distinct lists, one of the votes for President and the other of the votes for Vice President, and shall annex to each of the certificates one of the lists of the electors which shall have been furnished to them by direction of the executive of the State.

§ 10. Sealing and endorsing certificates

The electors shall seal up the certificates so made by them, and certify upon each that the lists of all the votes of such State given for President, and of all the votes given for Vice President, are contained therein.

§ 11. Disposition of certificates

The electors shall dispose of the certificates so made by them and the lists attached thereto in the following manner:

First. They shall forthwith forward by registered mail one of the same to the President of the Senate at the seat of government.

Second. Two of the same shall be delivered to the secretary of state of the State, one of which shall be held subject to the order of the President of the Senate, the other to be preserved by him for one year and shall be a part of the public records of his office and shall be open to public inspection.

Third. On the day thereafter they shall forward by registered mail two of such certificates and lists to the Archivist of the United States at the seat of government, one of which shall be held subject to the order of the President of the Senate. The other shall be preserved by the Archivist of the United States for one year and shall be a part of the public records of his office and shall be open to public inspection.

Fourth. They shall forthwith cause the other of the certificates and lists to be delivered to the judge of the district in which the electors shall have assembled.

§ 12. Failure of certificates of electors to reach President of the Senate or Archivist of the United States; demand on State for certificate

When no certificate of vote and list mentioned in sections 9 and 11 of this title from any State shall have been received by the President of the Senate or by the Archivist of the United States by the fourth Wednesday in December, after the meeting of the electors shall have been held, the President of the Senate or, if he be absent from the seat of government, the Archivist of the United States shall request, by the most expeditious method available, the secretary of state of the State to send up the certificate and list lodged with him by the electors of such State; and it shall be his duty upon receipt of such request immediately to transmit same by registered mail to the President of the Senate at the seat of government.

§ 13. Same; demand on district judge for certificate

When no certificates of votes from any State shall have been received at the seat of government on the fourth Wednesday in December, after the meeting of the electors shall have been held, the President of the Senate or, if he be absent from the seat of government, the Archivist of the United States shall send a special messenger to the district judge in whose custody one certificate of votes from that State has been lodged, and such judge shall forthwith transmit that list by the hand of such messenger to the seat of government.

§ 14. Forfeiture for messenger's neglect of duty

Every person who, having been appointed, pursuant to section 13 of this title, to deliver the certificates of the votes of the electors to the President of the Senate, and having accepted such appointment, shall neglect to perform the services required from him, shall forfeit the sum of $1,000.

§ 15. Counting electoral votes in Congress

Congress shall be in session on the sixth day of January succeeding every meeting   of   the electors. The Senate and House of Representatives shall meet in the Hall of   the   House of Representatives at the hour of 1 o'clock in the afternoon on that day, and the President of the Senate shall be their presiding officer. Two tellers shall be previously appointed on the part of the Senate and two on the part of the House of Representatives, to whom shall be handed, as they are opened by the President of the Senate, all the certificates and papers purporting to be certificates of the electoral votes, which certificates and papers shall be opened, presented, and acted upon in the alphabetical order of the States, beginning with the letter A; and said tellers, having then read the same in the presence and hearing of the two Houses, shall make a list of the votes as they shall appear from the said certificates; and the votes having been ascertained and counted according to the rules in this subchapter provided, the result of the same shall be delivered to the President of the Senate, who shall thereupon announce the state of the vote, which announcement shall be deemed a sufficient declaration of the persons, if any, elected President and Vice President of the United States, and, together with a list of the votes, be entered on the Journals of the two Houses. Upon such reading of any such certificate or paper, the President of the Senate shall call for objections, if any. Every objection shall be made in writing, and shall state clearly and concisely, and without argument, the ground thereof, and shall be signed by at least one Senator and one Member of the House of Representatives before the same shall be received. When all objections so made to any vote or paper from a State shall have been received and read, the Senate shall thereupon withdraw, and such objections shall be submitted to the Senate for its decision; and the Speaker of the House of Representatives shall, in like manner, submit such objections to the House of Representatives for its decision; and no electoral vote or votes from any State which shall have been regularly given by electors whose appointment has been lawfully certified to according to section 6 of this title from which but one return has been received shall be rejected, but the two Houses concurrently may reject the vote or votes when they agree that such vote or votes have not been so regularly given by electors whose appointment has been so certified. If more than one return or paper purporting to be a return from a State shall have been received by the President of the Senate, those votes, and those only, shall be counted which shall have been regularly given by the electors who are shown by the determination mentioned in section 5 of this title to have been appointed, if the determination in said section provided for shall have been made, or by such successors or substitutes, in case of a vacancy in the board of electors so ascertained, as have been appointed to fill such vacancy in the mode provided by the laws of the State; but in case there shall arise the question which of two or more of such State authorities determining what electors have been appointed, as mentioned in section 5 of this title, is the lawful tribunal of such state, the votes regularly given of those electors, and those only, of such State shall be counted whose title as electors the two Houses, acting separately, shall concurrently decide is supported by the decision of such State so authorized by its law; and in such case of more than one return or paper purporting to be a return from a State, if there shall have been no such determination of the question in the State aforesaid, then those votes, and those only, shall be counted which the two Houses shall concurrently decide were cast by lawful electors appointed in accordance with the laws of the State, unless the two Houses, acting separately, shall concurrently decide such votes not to be the lawful votes of the legally appointed electors of such State. But if the two Houses shall disagree in respect of the counting of such votes, then, and in that case, the votes of the electors whose appointment shall have been certified by the executive of the State, under the seal thereof, shall be counted. When the two Houses have voted, they shall immediately again meet, and the presiding officer shall then announce the decision of the questions submitted. No votes or papers from any other State shall be acted upon until the objections previously made to the votes or papers from any State shall have been finally disposed of.

§ 16. Same; seats for officers and Members of two Houses in joint meeting

At such joint meeting of the two Houses seats shall be provided as follows: For the President of the Senate, the Speaker's chair; for the Speaker, immediately upon his left; the Senators, in the body of the Hall upon the right of the presiding officer; for the Representatives, in the body of the Hall not provided for the Senators; for the tellers, Secretary of the Senate, and Clerk of the House of Representatives, at the Clerk's desk; for the other officers of the two Houses, in front of the Clerk's desk and upon each side of the Speaker's platform. Such joint meeting shall not be dissolved until the count of electoral votes shall be completed and the result declared; and no recess shall be taken unless a question shall have arisen in regard to counting any such votes, or otherwise under this subchapter, in which case it shall be competent for either House, acting separately, in the manner hereinbefore provided, to direct a recess of such House not beyond the next calendar day, Sunday excepted, at the hour of 10 o'clock in the forenoon. But if the counting of the electoral votes and the declaration of the result shall not have been completed before the fifth calendar day next after such first meeting of the two Houses, no further or other recess shall be taken by either House.

§ 17. Same; limit of debate in each House

When the two Houses separate to decide upon an objection that may have been made to the counting of any electoral vote or votes from any State, or other question arising in the matter, each Senator and Representative may speak to such objection or question five minutes, and not more than once; but after such debate shall have lasted two hours it shall be the duty of the presiding officer of each House to put the main question without further debate.

§ 18. Same; parliamentary procedure at joint meeting

While the two Houses shall be in meeting as provided in this chapter, the President of the Senate shall have power to preserve order; and no debate shall be allowed and no question shall be put by the presiding officer except to either House on a motion to withdraw.

VOTING RIGHTS ACT

As codified at 42 U.S.C. § 1973 et seq. (2000) [Selected Sections: 2, 4, 5 and 14 (c) (3) of the Act]:

§ 2. Denial or abridgement of right to vote on account of race or color through voting qualifications or prerequisites; establishment of violation

(a) No voting qualification or prerequisite to voting or standard, practice, or procedure shall be imposed or applied by any State or political subdivision in a manner which results in a denial or abridgement of the right of any citizen of the United States to vote on account of race or color, or in contravention of the guarantees set forth in section 4(f)(2) [*42 USCS § 1973b*(f)(2)], as provided in subsection (b).

(b) A violation of subsection (a) is established if, based on the totality of circumstances, it is shown that the political processes leading to nomination or election in the State or political subdivision are not equally open to participation by members of a class of citizens protected by subsection (a) in that its members have less opportunity than other members of the electorate to participate in the political process and to elect representatives of their choice. The extent to which members of a protected class have been elected to office in the State or political subdivision is one circumstance which may be considered: Provided, That nothing in this section establishes a right to have members of a protected class elected in numbers equal to their proportion in the population.

§ 4. Suspension of the use of tests or devices in determining eligibility to vote

(a) Action by state or political subdivision for declaratory judgment of no denial or abridgement; three-judge district court; appeal to Supreme Court; retention of jurisdiction by three-judge court.

(1) To assure that the right of citizens of the United States to vote is not denied or abridged on account of race or color, no citizen shall be denied the right to vote in any Federal, State, or local election because of his failure to comply with any test or device in any State with respect to which the determinations have been made under the first two sentences of subsection (b) or in any political subdivision of such State (as such subdivision existed on the date such determinations were made with respect to such State), though such determinations were not made with respect to such subdivision as a separate unit, or in any political subdivision with respect to which such determinations have

been made as a separate unit, unless the United States District Court for the District of Columbia issues a declaratory judgment under this section. No citizen shall be denied the right to vote in any Federal, State, or local election because of his failure to comply with any test or device in any State with respect to which the determinations have been made under the third sentence of subsection (b) of this section or in any political subdivision of such State (as such subdivision existed on the date such determinations were made with respect to such State), though such determinations were not made with respect to such subdivision as a separate unit, or in any political subdivision with respect to which such determinations have been made as a separate unit, unless the United States District Court for the District of Columbia issues a declaratory judgment under this section. A declaratory judgment under this section shall issue only if such court determines that during the ten years preceding the filing of the action, and during the pendency of such action–

(A) no such test or device has been used within such State or political subdivision for the purpose or with the effect of denying or abridging the right to vote on account of race or color or (in the case of a State or subdivision seeking a declaratory judgment under the second sentence of this subsection) in contravention of the guarantees of subsection (f)(2);

(B) no final judgment of any court of the United States, other than the denial of declaratory judgment under this section, has determined that denials or abridgements of the rights to vote on account of race or color have occurred anywhere in the territory of such State or political subdivision or (in the case of a State or subdivision seeking a declaratory judgment under the second sentence of this subsection) that denials or abridgements of the right to vote in contravention of the guarantees of subsection (f)(2) have occurred anywhere in the territory of such State or subdivision and no consent decree, settlement, or agreement has been entered into resulting in any abandonment of a voting practice challenged on such grounds; and no declaratory judgment under this section shall be entered during the pendency of an action commenced before the filing of an action under this section and alleging such denials or abridgments of the right to vote;

(C) no Federal examiners under this Act have been assigned to such State or political subdivision;

(D) such State or political subdivision and all governmental units within its territory have complied with section 5 of this Act [*42 USCS § 1973c*], including compliance with the requirement that no change covered by section 5 [*42 USCS § 1973c*] has been enforced without preclearance under section 5 [*42 USCS § 1973c*], and have repealed all changes covered by section 5 [*42 USCS § 1973c*] to which the Attorney General has successfully objected or as to which the United States

District Court for the District of Columbia has denied a declaratory judgment;

(E) the Attorney General has not interposed any objection (that has not been overturned by a final judgment of a court) and no declaratory judgment has been denied under section 5 [*42 USCS § 1973c*], with respect to any submission by or on behalf of the plaintiff or any governmental unit within its territory under section 5 [*42 USCS § 1973c*], and no such submissions or declaratory judgment actions are pending; and

(F) such State or political subdivision and all governmental units within its territory--

(i) have eliminated voting procedures and methods of election which inhibit or dilute equal access to the electoral process;

(ii) have engaged in constructive efforts to eliminate intimidation and harassment of persons exercising rights protected under this Act; and

(iii) have engaged in other constructive efforts, such as expanded opportunity for convenient registration and voting for every person of voting age and the appointment of minority persons as election officials throughout the jurisdiction and at all stages of the election and registration process.

(2) To assist the court in determining whether to issue a declaratory judgment under this subsection, the plaintiff shall present evidence of minority participation, including evidence of the levels of minority group registration and voting, changes in such levels over time, and disparities between minority-group and non-minority-group participation.

(3) No declaratory judgment shall issue under this subsection with respect to such State or political subdivision if such plaintiff and governmental units within its territory have, during the period beginning ten years before the date the judgment is issued, engaged in violations of any provision of the Constitution or laws of the United States or any State or political subdivision with respect to discrimination in voting on account of race or color or (in the case of a State or subdivision seeking a declaratory judgment under the second sentence of this subsection) in contravention of the guarantees of subsection (f)(2) unless the plaintiff establishes that any such violations were trivial, were promptly corrected, and were not repeated.

(4) The State or political subdivision bringing such action shall publicize the intended commencement and any proposed settlement of such action in the media serving such State or political subdivision and in appropriate United States post offices. Any aggrieved party may as of right intervene at any stage in such action.

(5) An action pursuant to this subsection shall be heard and determined by a court of three judges in accordance with the provisions of section 2284 of title 28 of the United States Code [*28 USCS § 2284*] and any appeal shall lie to the Supreme Court. The court shall retain jurisdiction of any action pursuant to this subsection for ten years after judgment and shall reopen the action upon motion of the Attorney General or any aggrieved person alleging that conduct has occurred which, had that conduct occurred during the ten-year periods referred to in this subsection, would have precluded the issuance of a declaratory judgment under this subsection. The court, upon such reopening, shall vacate the declaratory judgment issued under this section if, after the issuance of such declaratory judgment, a final judgment against the State or subdivision with respect to which such declaratory judgment was issued, or against any governmental unit within the State or subdivision, determines that denials or abridgements of the right to vote on account of race or color have occurred anywhere in the territory of such State or political subdivision or (in the case of a State or subdivision which sought a declaratory judgment under the second sentence of this subsection) that denials or abridgements of the right to vote in contravention of the guarantees of subsection (f)(2) have occurred anywhere in the territory of such State or subdivision, or if, after the issuance of such declaratory judgment, a consent decree, settlement, or agreement has been entered into resulting in any abandonment of a voting practice challenged on such grounds.

(6) If, after two years from the date of the filing of a declaratory judgment under this subsection, no date has been set for a hearing in such action, and that delay has not been the result of an avoidable delay on the part of counsel for any party, the chief judge of the United States District Court for the District of Columbia may request the Judicial Council for the Circuit of the District of Columbia to provide the necessary judicial resources to expedite any action filed under this section. If such resources are unavailable within the circuit, the chief judge shall file a certificate of necessity in accordance with section 292(d) of title 28 of the United States Code [*28 USCS § 292*(d)].

(7) The Congress shall reconsider the provisions of this section at the end of the fifteen-year period following the effective date of the amendments made by the Voting Rights Act Amendments of 1982.

(8) The provisions of this section shall expire at the end of the twenty-five year period following the effective date of the amendments made by the Voting Rights Act Amendments of 1982.

(9) Nothing in this section shall prohibit the Attorney General from consenting to an entry of judgment if based upon a showing of objective

and compelling evidence by the plaintiff, and upon investigation, he is satisfied that the State or political subdivision has complied with the requirements of section 4(a)(1) [subsec. (a)(1) of this section]. Any aggrieved party may as of right intervene at any stage in such action.

(b) Required factual determinations necessary to allow suspension of compliance with tests and devices; publication in Federal Register. The provisions of subsection (a) shall apply in any State or in any political subdivision of a state which (1) the Attorney General determines maintained on November 1, 1964, any test or device, and with respect to which (2) the Director of the Census determines that less than 50 per centum of the persons of voting age residing therein were registered on November 1, 1964, or that less than 50 per centum of such persons voted on the presidential election of November 1964. On and after August 6, 1970, in addition to any State or political subdivision of a State determined to be subject to subsection (a) pursuant to the previous sentence, the provisions of subsection (a) shall apply in any State or any political subdivision of a State which (i) the Attorney General determines maintained on November 1, 1968, any test or device, and with respect to which (ii) the Director of the Census determines that less than 50 per centum of the persons of voting age residing therein were registered on November 1, 1968, or that less than 50 per centum of such persons voted in the presidential election of November 1968. On and after August 6, 1975, in addition to any State or political subdivision of a State determined to be subject to subsection (a) pursuant to the previous two sentences, the provisions of a subsection (a) shall apply in any State or any political subdivision of a State which (i) the Attorney General determines maintained on November 1, 1972, any test or device, and with respect to which (ii) the Director of the Census determines that less than 50 per centum of the citizens of voting age were registered on November 1, 1972, or that less than 50 per centum of such persons voted in the Presidential election of November 1972.

A determination or certification of the Attorney General or of the Director of the Census under this section or under section 6 or section 13 [*42 USCS § 1973d* or 1973k] shall not be reviewable in any court and shall be effective upon publication in the Federal Register.

(c) "Test or device" defined. The phrase "test or device" shall mean any requirement that a person as a prerequisite for voting or registration for voting (1) demonstrate the ability to read, write, understand, or interpret any matter, (2) demonstrate any educational achievement or his knowledge of any particular subject, (3) possess good moral character, or (4) prove his qualifications by the voucher of registered voters or members of any other class.

(d) Required frequency, continuation and probable recurrence of incidents of denial or abridgement to constitute forbidden use of tests or devices. For purposes of this section no State or political subdivision shall be determined to have engaged in the use of tests or devices for the purpose or with the effect of denying or abridging the right to vote on account of race or color, or in contravention of the guarantees set forth in section 4(f)(2) [subsec. (f)(2) of this section] if (1) incidents of such use have been few in number and have been promptly and effectively corrected by State or local action, (2) the continuing effect of such incidents has been eliminated, and (3) there is no reasonable probability of their recurrence in the future.

(e) Completion of requisite grade level of education in American-flag schools in which the predominant classroom language was other than English.

(1) Congress hereby declares that to secure the rights under the fourteenth amendment [USCS Constitution, Amendment 14] of persons educated in American-flag schools in which the predominant classroom language was other than English, it is necessary to prohibit the States from conditioning the right to vote of such persons on ability to read, write, understand, or interpret any matter in the English language.

(2) No person who demonstrates that he has successfully completed the sixth primary grade in a public school in, or a private school accredited by, any State or territory, the District of Columbia, or the Commonwealth of Puerto Rico in which the predominant classroom language was other than English, shall be denied the right to vote in any Federal, State, or local election because of his inability to read, write, understand, or interpret any matter in the English language, except that in States in which State law provides that a different level of education is presumptive of literacy, he shall demonstrate that he has successfully completed an equivalent level of education in a public school in, or a private school accredited by, any State or territory, the District of Columbia, or the Commonwealth of Puerto Rico in which the predominant classroom language was other than English.

(f) Congressional findings of voting discrimination against language minorities; prohibition of English-only elections; other remedial measures.

(1) The Congress finds that voting discrimination against citizens of language minorities is pervasive and national in scope. Such minority citizens are from environments in which the dominant language is other than English. In addition they have been denied equal educational opportunities by State and local governments, resulting in severe disabilities and continuing illiteracy in the English language. The Congress further finds that, where State and local officials conduct elections only in English, language minority citizens are excluded from

participating in the electoral process. In many areas of the country, this exclusion is aggravated by acts of physical, economic, and political intimidation. The Congress declares that, in order to enforce the guarantees of the fourteenth and fifteenth amendments to the United States Constitution [USCS Constitution, Amendments 14, 15], it is necessary to eliminate such discrimination by prohibiting English-only elections, and by prescribing other remedial devices.

(2) No voting qualification or prerequisite to voting, or standard, practice, or procedure shall be imposed or applied by any State or political subdivision to deny or abridge the right of any citizen of the United States to vote because he is a member of a language minority group.

(3) In addition to the meaning given the term under section 4(c) [subsec. (c) of this section], the term "test or device" shall also mean any practice or requirement by which any State or political subdivision provided any registration or voting notices, forms, instructions, assistance, or other materials or information relating to the electoral process, including ballots, only in the English language, where the Director of the Census determines that more than five per centum of the citizens of voting age residing in such State or political subdivision are members of a single language minority. With respect to section 4(b) [subsec. (b) of this section], the term "test or device", as defined in this subsection, shall be employed only in making the determinations under the third sentence of that subsection.

(4) Whenever any State or political subdivision subject to the prohibitions of the second sentence of section 4(a) [subsec. (a) of this section] provides any registration or voting notices, forms, instructions, assistance, or other materials or information relating to the electoral process, including ballots, it shall provide them in the language of the applicable language minority group as well as in the English language: Provided, That where the language of the applicable minority group is oral or unwritten or in the case of Alaskan Natives and American Indians, if the predominate language is historically unwritten, the State or political subdivision is only required to furnish oral instructions, assistance, or other information relating to registration and voting.

§ 5. Alteration of voting qualifications and procedures; action by State or political subdivision for declaratory judgment of no denial or abridgement of voting rights; three-judge district court; appeal to Supreme Court

Whenever a State or political subdivision with respect to which the prohibitions set forth in section 4(a) [*42 USCS § 1973b*(a)] based upon determinations made under the first sentence of section 4(b) [*42 USCS § 1973b*(b)] are in effect shall enact or seek to administer any voting qualification or prerequisite to voting, or standard, practice, or procedure with respect to voting different from that in force or effect on November 1, 1964, or whenever a State or political subdivision with respect to which the prohibitions set forth in section 4(a) [*42 USCS § 1973b*(a)] based upon determinations made under the second sentence of section 4(b) [*42 USCS § 1973b*(b)] are in effect shall enact or seek to administer any voting qualification or prerequisite to voting, or standard, practice, or procedure with respect to voting different from that in force or effect on November 1, 1968, or whenever a State or political subdivision with respect to which the prohibitions set forth in section 4(a) [*42 USCS § 1973b*(a)] based upon determinations made under the third sentence of section 4(b) [*42 USCS § 1973b*(b)] are in effect shall enact or seek to administer any voting qualification or prerequisite to voting, or standard, practice, or procedure with respect to voting different from that in force or effect on November 1, 1972, such State or subdivision may institute an action in the United States District Court for the District of Columbia for a declaratory judgment that such qualification prerequisite, standard, practice, or procedure does not have the purpose and will not have the effect of denying or abridging the right to vote on account of race or color, or in contravention of the guarantees set forth in section 4(f)(2) [*42 USCS § 1973b*(f)(2)], and unless and until the court enters such judgment no person shall be denied the right to vote for failure to comply with such qualification, prerequisite, standard, practice, or procedure: Provided, That such qualification, prerequisite, standard, practice, or procedure may be enforced without such proceeding if the qualification, prerequisite, standard, practice, or procedure has been submitted by the chief legal officer or other appropriate official of such State or subdivision to the Attorney General and the Attorney General has not interposed an objection within sixty days after such submission, or upon good cause shown, to facilitate an expedited approval within sixty days after such submission, the Attorney General has affirmatively indicated that such objection will not be made. Neither an affirmative indication by the Attorney General that no objection will be made, nor the Attorney General's failure to object, nor a declaratory judgment entered under this section shall bar a subsequent action to enjoin enforcement of such qualification, prerequisite, standard, practice, or procedure. In the event the Attorney General affirmatively indicates that no objection will be made within the sixty-day period following receipt of a submission, the Attorney General may reserve the right to reexamine the submission if additional information comes to his attention during the remainder of the sixty-day period which would otherwise require objection in accordance with this section. Any action under this section shall be heard and determined by a court of three judges in accordance with the provisions of section 2284 of title 28 of the United States Code and any appeal shall lie to the Supreme Court.

§ 14 (c) (3) Definitions.

(1)   The terms "vote" or "voting" shall include all action necessary to make a vote effective in any primary, special, or general election, including, but not limited to, registration, listing pursuant to this Act, or other action required by law prerequisite to voting, casting a ballot, and having such ballot counted properly and included in the appropriate totals of votes cast with respect to candidates for public or party office and propositions for which votes are received in an election.

(2) The term "political subdivision" shall mean any county or parish, except that where registration for voting is not conducted under the supervision of a county or parish, the term shall include any other subdivision of a State which conducts registration for voting.

(3) The term "language minorities" or "language minority group" means persons who are American Indian, Asian American, Alaskan Natives or of Spanish heritage.

PROCEDURES FOR THE ADMINISTRATION OF SECTION 5 OF THE VOTING RIGHTS ACT

28 C.F.R. PART 51 (2000) (selected sections)

Subpart A--General Provisions

Sec. 51.1 Purpose.

(a)   Section 5 of the Voting Rights Act of 1965, as amended, 42 U.S.C. 1973c, prohibits the enforcement in any jurisdiction covered by section 4(b) of the Act, 42 U.S.C. 1973b(b), of any voting qualification or prerequisite to voting, or standard, practice, or procedure with respect to voting different from that in force or effect on the date used to determine coverage, until either:

(1) A declaratory judgment is obtained from the U.S. District Court for the District of Columbia that such qualification, prerequisite, standard, practice, or procedure does not have the purpose and will not have the effect of denying or abridging the right to vote on account of race, color, or membership in a language minority group, or

(2) It has been submitted to the Attorney General and the Attorney General has interposed no objection within a 60-day period following submission.

(b)   In order to make clear the responsibilities of the Attorney General under section 5 and the interpretation of the Attorney General of the responsibility imposed on others under this section, the procedures in this part have been established to govern the administration of section 5.

Sec. 51.2 Definitions.

As used in this part--

Act means the Voting Rights Act of 1965, 79 Stat. 437, as amended by the Civil Rights Act of 1968, 82 Stat. 73, the Voting Rights Act Amendments of 1970, 84 Stat. 314, the District of Columbia Delegate Act, 84 Stat. 853, the Voting Rights Act Amendments of 1975, 89 Stat. 400, and the Voting Rights Act Amendments of 1982, 96 Stat. 131, 42 U.S.C. 1973 et seq. Section numbers, such as "section 14(c)(3)," refer to sections of the Act.

Attorney General means the Attorney General of the United States or the delegate of the Attorney General.

Change affecting voting means any voting qualification, prerequisite to voting, or standard, practice, or procedure with respect to voting different from that in force or effect on the date used to determine coverage under section 4(b) and includes, inter alia, the examples given in Sec. 51.13.

Covered jurisdiction is used to refer to a State, where the determination referred to in Sec. 51.4 has been made on a statewide basis, and to a political subdivision, where the determination has not been made on a statewide basis.

Language minorities or language minority group is used, as defined in the Act, to refer to persons who are American Indian, Asian American, Alaskan Natives, or of Spanish heritage. (Sections 14(c)(3) and 203(e)). See 28 CFR part 55, Interpretative Guidelines: Implementation of the Provisions of the Voting Rights Act Regarding Language Minority Groups.

Political subdivision is used, as defined in the Act, to refer to "any county or parish, except that where registration for voting is not conducted under the supervision of a county or parish, the term shall include any other subdivision of a State which conducts registration for voting." (Section 14(c)(2)).

Preclearance is used to refer to the obtaining of the declaratory judgment described in section 5, to the failure of the Attorney General to interpose an objection pursuant to section 5, or to the withdrawal of an objection by the Attorney General pursuant to Sec. 51.48(b).

Submission is used to refer to the written presentation to the Attorney General by an appropriate official of any change affecting voting.

Submitting authority means the jurisdiction on whose behalf a submission is made.

Vote and voting are used, as defined in the Act, to include "all action necessary to make a vote effective in any primary, special, or general election, including, but not limited to, registration, listing pursuant to this Act, or other action required by law prerequisite to voting, casting a ballot, and having such ballot counted properly and included in the appropriate totals of votes cast with respect to candidates for public or party office and propositions for which votes are received in an election." (Section 14(c)(1)).

Sec. 51.3 Delegation of authority.

The responsibility and authority for determinations under section 5 have been delegated by the Attorney General to the Assistant

Attorney General, Civil Rights Division. With the exception of objections and decisions following the reconsideration of objections, the Chief of the Voting Section is authorized to act on behalf of the Assistant Attorney General.

***

Sec. 51.6 Political subunits.

All political subunits within a covered jurisdiction (e.g., counties, cities, school districts) are subject to the requirement of section 5.

Sec. 51.7 Political parties.

Certain activities of political parties are subject to the preclearance requirement of section 5. A change affecting voting effected by a political party is subject to the preclearance requirement:

(a) If the change relates to a public electoral function of the party and

(b) If the party is acting under authority explicitly or implicitly granted by a covered jurisdiction or political subunit subject to the preclearance requirement of section 5.

For example, changes with respect to the recruitment of party members, the conduct of political campaigns, and the drafting of party platforms are not subject to the preclearance requirement. Changes with respect to the conduct of primary elections at which party nominees, delegates to party conventions, or party officials are chosen are subject to the preclearance requirement of section 5. Where appropriate the term "jurisdiction" (but not "covered jurisdiction") includes political parties.

***

Sec. 51.11 Right to bring suit.

Submission to the Attorney General does not affect the right of the submitting authority to bring an action in the U.S. District Court for the District of Columbia for a declaratory judgment that the change affecting voting does not have the prohibited discriminatory purpose or effect.

Sec. 51.12 Scope of requirement.

Any change affecting voting, even though it appears to be minor or indirect, returns to a prior practice or procedure, ostensibly expands voting rights, or is designed to remove the elements that caused objection by the Attorney General to a prior submitted change, must meet the section 5 preclearance requirement.

Sec. 51.13 Examples of changes.

Changes affecting voting include, but are not limited to, the following examples:

(a)   Any change in qualifications or eligibility for voting.

(b)   Any change concerning registration, balloting, and the counting of votes and any change concerning publicity for or assistance in registration or voting.

(c)   Any change with respect to the use of a language other than English in any aspect of the electoral process.

(d)   Any change in the boundaries of voting precincts or in the location of polling places.

(e)   Any change in the constituency of an official or the boundaries of a voting unit (e.g., through redistricting, annexation, deannexation, incorporation, reapportionment, changing to at-large elections from district elections, or changing to district elections from at-large elections).

(f)   Any change in the method of determining the outcome of an election (e.g., by requiring a majority vote for election or the use of a designated post or place system).

(g)   Any change affecting the eligibility of persons to become or remain candidates, to obtain a position on the ballot in primary or general elections, or to become or remain holders of elective offices.

(h)   Any change in the eligibility and qualification procedures for independent candidates.

(i)   Any change in the term of an elective office or an elected official or in the offices that are elective (e.g., by shortening the term of an office, changing from election to appointment or staggering the terms of offices).

(j)   Any change affecting the necessity of or methods for offering issues and propositions for approval by referendum.

(k)   Any change affecting the right or ability of persons to participate in political campaigns which is effected by a jurisdiction subject to the requirement of section 5.

***

Sec. 51.15 Enabling legislation and contingent or nonuniform requirements.

(a)   With respect to legislation (1) that enables or permits the State or its political subunits to institute a voting change or (2) that requires or enables the State or its political sub-units to institute a voting change upon some future event or if they satisfy certain criteria, the failure of the Attorney General to interpose an objection does not exempt from the preclearance requirement the implementation of the particular voting change that is enabled, permitted, or required, unless that implementation is explicitly included and described in the submission of such parent legislation.

(b)   For example, such legislation includes--

(1)   Legislation authorizing counties, cities, school districts, or agencies or officials of the State to institute any of the changes described in Sec. 51.13,

(2)   Legislation requiring a political subunit that chooses a certain form of government to follow specified election procedures,

(3)   Legislation requiring or authorizing political subunits of a certain size or a certain location to institute specified changes,

(4)   Legislation requiring a political subunit to follow certain practices or procedures unless the subunit's charter or ordinances specify to the contrary.

Sec. 51.16 Distinction between changes in procedure and changes in substance.

The failure of the Attorney General to interpose an objection to a procedure for instituting a change affecting voting does not exempt the substantive change from the preclearance requirement. For example, if the procedure for the approval of an annexation is changed from city council approval to approval in a referendum, the preclearance of the new procedure does not exempt an annexation accomplished under the new procedure from the preclearance requirement.

***

Sec. 51.18 Court-ordered changes.

(a)   In general. Changes affecting voting that are ordered by a Federal court are subject to the preclearance requirement of section 5 to the extent that they reflect the policy choices of the submitting authority.

(b)   Subsequent changes. Where a court-ordered change is not itself subject to the preclearance requirement, subsequent changes necessitated by the court order but decided upon by the jurisdiction remain subject to preclearance. For example, voting precinct and polling place changes made necessary by a court-ordered redistricting plan are subject to section 5 review.

(c)   In emergencies. A Federal court's authorization of the emergency interim use without preclearance of a voting change does not exempt from section 5 review any use of the practice not explicitly authorized by the court.

***

Subpart B–Procedures for Submission to the Attorney General

Sec. 51.20 Form of submissions.

(a) Submissions may be made in letter or any other written form.

(b) The Attorney General will accept certain machine readable data ....

***

Sec. 51.21 Time of submissions.

Changes affecting voting should be submitted as soon as possible after they become final.

Sec. 51.22 Premature submissions.

The Attorney General will not consider on the merits:

(a)   Any proposal for a change affecting voting submitted prior to final enactment or administrative decision or

(b)   Any proposed change which has a direct bearing on another change affecting voting which has not received section 5 preclearance.

However, with respect to a change for which approval by referendum, a State or Federal court or a Federal agency is required, the Attorney General may make a determination concerning the change prior to such approval if the change is not subject to alteration in the final approving action and if all other action necessary for approval has been taken.

Sec. 51.23   Party and jurisdiction responsible for making submissions.

(a)   Changes affecting voting shall be submitted by the chief legal officer or other appropriate official of the submitting authority or by any other authorized person on behalf of the submitting authority. When one or more counties or other political subunits within a State will be affected, the State may make a submission on their behalf. Where a State is covered as a whole, State legislation (except legislation of local applicability) or other changes undertaken or required by the State shall be submitted by the State.

(b)   A change effected by a political party (see Sec. 51.7) may be submitted by an appropriate official of the political party.

***

Sec. 51.25 Withdrawal of submissions.

(a) A jurisdiction may withdraw a submission at any time prior to a final decision by the Attorney General. Notice of the withdrawal of a submission must be made in writing, addressed to the Chief, Voting Section, as specified in Sec. 51.24 of this part. The submission shall be deemed withdrawn upon receipt of the notice.

***

Subpart C–Contents of Submissions

Sec. 51.26 General.

(a)   The source of any information contained in a submission should be identified.

(b)   Where an estimate is provided in lieu of more reliable statistics, the submission should identify the name, position, and qualifications of the person responsible for the estimate and should briefly describe the basis for the estimate.

(c)   Submissions should be no longer than is necessary for the presentation of the appropriate information and materials.

(d)   The Attorney General will not accept for review any submission that fails to describe the subject change in sufficient particularity to satisfy the minimum requirements of Sec. 51.27(c).

***

Sec. 51.27 Required contents.

Each submission should contain the following information or documents to enable the Attorney General to make the required determination pursuant to section 5 with respect to the submitted change affecting voting:

(a)   A copy of any ordinance, enactment, order, or regulation embodying a change affecting voting.

(b)   A copy of any ordinance, enactment, order, or regulation embodying the voting practice that is proposed to be repealed, amended, or otherwise changed.

(c)   If the change affecting voting either is not readily apparent on the face of the documents provided under paragraphs (a) and (b) of this section or is not embodied in a document, a clear statement of the change explaining the difference between the submitted change and the prior law or practice, or explanatory materials adequate to disclose to the Attorney General the difference between the prior and proposed situation with respect to voting.

(d)   The name, title, address, and telephone number of the person making the submission.

(e)   The name of the submitting authority and the name of the jurisdiction responsible for the change, if different.

(f)   If the submission is not from a State or county, the name of the county and State in which the submitting authority is located.

(g)   Identification of the person or body responsible for making the change and the mode of decision (e.g., act of State legislature, ordinance of city council, administrative decision by registrar).

(h)   A statement identifying the statutory or other authority under which the jurisdiction undertakes the change and a description of the procedures the jurisdiction was required to follow in deciding to undertake the change.

(i)   The date of adoption of the change affecting voting.

(j)   The date on which the change is to take effect.

(k)   A statement that the change has not yet been enforced or administered, or an explanation of why such a statement cannot be made.

(l)   Where the change will affect less than the entire jurisdiction, an explanation of the scope of the change.

(m)   A statement of the reasons for the change.

(n)   A statement of the anticipated effect of the change on members of racial or language minority groups.

(o)   A statement identifying any past or pending litigation concerning the change or related voting practices.

(p)   A statement that the prior practice has been precleared (with the date) or is not subject to the preclearance requirement and a statement that the procedure for the adoption of the change has been precleared (with the date) or is not subject to the preclearance requirement, or an explanation of why such statements cannot be made.

(q)   For redistrictings and annexations: the items listed under Sec. 51.28 (a)(1) and (b)(1); for annexations only: the items listed under Sec. 51.28(c)(3).

(r)   Other information that the Attorney General determines is required for an evaluation of the purpose or effect of the change. Such information may include items listed in Sec. 51.28 and is most likely to be needed with respect to redistrictings, annexations, and other complex changes. In the interest of time such information should be furnished with the initial submission relating to voting changes of this type When such information is required, but not provided, the Attorney General shall notify the submitting authority in the manner provided in Sec. 51.37.

Sec. 51.28 Supplemental contents.

Review by the Attorney General will be facilitated if the following information, where pertinent, is provided in addition to that required by Sec. 51.27.

(a)   Demographic information

(1)   Total and voting age population of the affected area before and after the change, by race and language group. If such information is contained in publications of the U.S. Bureau of the Census, reference to the appropriate volume and table is sufficient.

(2)   The number of registered voters for the affected area by voting precinct before and after the change, by race and language group.

(3)   Any estimates of population, by race and language group, made in connection with the adoption of the change.

***

(b)   Maps. Where any change is made that revises the constituency that elects any office or affects the boundaries of any geographic unit or units defined or employed for voting purposes (e.g., redistricting, annexation, change from district to at-large elections) or that changes voting precinct boundaries, polling place locations, or voter registration sites, maps in duplicate of the area to be affected, containing the following information:

(1)   The prior and new boundaries of the voting unit or units.

(2)   The prior and new boundaries of voting precincts.

(3)   The location of racial and language minority groups.

(4)   Any natural boundaries or geographical features that influenced the selection of boundaries of the prior or new units.

(5)   The location of prior and new polling places.

(6)   The location of prior and new voter registration sites.

(c)   Annexations. For annexations, in addition to that information specified elsewhere, the following information:

(1)   The present and expected future use of the annexed land (e.g., garden apartments, industrial park).

(2)   An estimate of the expected population, by race and language group, when anticipated development, if any, is completed.

(3)   A statement that all prior annexations subject to the preclearance requirement have been submitted for review, or a statement that identifies all annexations subject to the preclearance requirement that have not been submitted for review. See Sec. 51.61(b).

(d)   Election returns. Where a change may affect the electoral influence of a racial or language minority group, returns of primary and general elections conducted by or in the jurisdiction, containing the following information:

(1)   The name of each candidate.

(2)   The race or language group of each candidate, if known.

(3)   The position sought by each candidate.

(4)   The number of votes received by each candidate, by voting precinct.

(5)   The outcome of each contest.

(6)   The number of registered voters, by race and language group, for each voting precinct for which election returns are furnished. Information with respect to elections held during the last ten years will normally be sufficient.

(7)   Election related data containing any of the information described above that are provided on magnetic media shall conform to the requirements of Sec. 51.20 (b) through (e). Election related data that cannot be accurately presented in terms of census blocks may be identified by county and by precinct.

(e)   Language usage. Where a change is made affecting the use of the language of a language minority group in the electoral process, information that will enable the Attorney General to determine whether the change is consistent with the minority language requirements of the Act. The Attorney General's interpretation of the minority language requirements of the Act is contained in Interpretative Guidelines: Implementation of the Provisions of the

Voting Rights Act Regarding Language Minority Groups, 28 CFR part 55.

(f)   Publicity and participation. For submissions involving controversial or potentially controversial changes, evidence of public notice, of the opportunity for the public to be heard, and of the opportunity for interested parties to participate in the decision to adopt the proposed change and an account of the extent to which such participation, especially by minority group members, in fact took place. Examples of materials demonstrating public notice or participation include:

(1)   Copies of newspaper articles discussing the proposed change.

(2)   Copies of public notices that describe the proposed change and invite public comment or participation in hearings and statements regarding where such public notices appeared (e.g., newspaper, radio, or television, posted in public buildings, sent to identified individuals or groups).

(3)   Minutes or accounts of public hearings concerning the proposed change.

(4)   Statements, speeches, and other public communications concerning the proposed change.

(5) Copies of comments from the general public.

(6)   Excerpts from legislative journals containing discussion of a submitted enactment, or other materials revealing its legislative purpose.

(g)   Availability of the submission.

(1)   Copies of public notices that announce the submission to the Attorney General, inform the public that a complete duplicate copy of the submission is available for public inspection (e.g., at the county courthouse) and invite comments for the consideration of the Attorney General and statements regarding where such public notices appeared.

(2)   Information demonstrating that the submitting authority, where a submission contains magnetic media, made the magnetic media available to be copied or, if so requested, made a hard copy of the data contained on the magnetic media available to be copied.

(h)   Minority group contacts. For submissions from jurisdictions having a significant minority population, the names, addresses, telephone numbers, and organizational affiliation (if any) of racial or language minority group members residing in the jurisdiction who can be expected to be familiar with the proposed change or who have been active in the political process.

Subpart D—Communications From Individuals and Groups

Sec. 51.29 Communications concerning voting changes.

Any individual or group may send to the Attorney General information concerning a change affecting voting in a jurisdiction to which section 5 applies.

(a) Communications may be in the form of a letter stating the name, address, and telephone number of the individual or group, describing the alleged change affecting voting and setting forth evidence regarding whether the change has or does not have a discriminatory purpose or effect, or simply bringing to the attention of the Attorney General the fact that a voting change has occurred.

***

(d) Department of Justice officials and employees shall comply with the request of any individual that his or her identity not be disclosed to any person outside the Department, to the extent permitted by the Freedom of Information Act, 5 U.S.C. 552. In addition, whenever it appears to the Attorney General that disclosure of the identity of an individual who provided information regarding a change affecting voting "would constitute a clearly unwarranted invasion of personal privacy" under 5 U.S.C. 552(b)(6), the identity of the individual shall not be disclosed to any person outside the Department.
***

Subpart E—Processing of Submissions

***

Sec. 51.34 Expedited consideration.

(a) When a submitting authority is required under State law or local ordinance or otherwise finds it necessary to implement a change within the 60-day period following submission, it may request that the submission be given expedited consideration. The submission should explain why such consideration is needed and provide the date by which a determination is required.

(b) Jurisdictions should endeavor to plan for changes in advance so that expedited consideration will not be required and should not routinely request such consideration. When a submitting authority demonstrates good cause for expedited consideration the Attorney General will attempt to make a decision by the date requested. However, the Attorney General cannot guarantee that such consideration can be given.

(c)   Notice of the request for expedited consideration will be given to interested parties registered under Sec. 51.32.

Sec. 51.35 Disposition of inappropriate submissions.

The Attorney General will make no response on the merits with respect to an inappropriate submission but will notify the submitting authority of the inappropriateness of the submission. Such notification will be made as promptly as possible and no later than the 60th day following receipt and will include an explanation of the inappropriateness of the submission. Inappropriate submissions include the submission of changes that do not affect voting (see, e.g., Sec. 51.13), the submission of standards, practices, or procedures that have not been changed (see, e.g., Secs. 51.4, 51.14), the submission of changes that affect voting but are not subject to the requirement of section 5 (see, e.g., Sec. 51.18), premature submissions (see Secs. 51.22, 51.61(b)), submissions by jurisdictions not subject to the preclearance requirement (see Secs. 51.4, 51.5), and deficient submissions (see Sec. 51.26(d)).

***

Sec. 51.37 Obtaining information from the submitting authority.

(a)   If a submission does not satisfy the requirements of Sec. 51.27, the Attorney General may request from the submitting authority any omitted information considered necessary for the evaluation of the submission. The request shall be made by letter and shall be made within the 60-day period and as promptly as possible after receipt of the original submission. See also Sec. 51.26(d).

(b)   A copy of the request shall be sent to any party who has commented on the submission or has requested notice of the Attorney General's action thereon.

(c)   The Attorney General shall notify the submitting authority that a new 60-day period in which the Attorney General may interpose an objection shall commence upon the receipt of a response from the submitting authority that provides the information requested or states that the information is unavailable. The Attorney General can request further information within the new 60-day period, but such a further request shall not suspend the running of the 60-day period, nor shall the receipt of a response to such a request operate to begin a new 60-day period.

***

Sec. 51.39 Supplementary submissions.

(a)   When a submitting authority provides documents and written information materially supplementing a submission (or a request for reconsideration of an objection) for evaluation as if part of its original submission, or, before the expiration of the 60-day period, makes a second submission such that the two submissions cannot be independently considered, the 60-day period for the original submission will be calculated from the receipt of the supplementary information or from the second submission.

(b)   The Attorney General will notify the submitting authority when the 60-day period for a submission is recalculated from the receipt of supplementary information or from the receipt of a second related submission.

(c)   Notice of the receipt of supplementary information will be given to interested parties registered under Sec. 51.32.

Sec. 51.40 Failure to complete submissions.

If after 60 days the submitting authority has not provided further information in response to a request made pursuant to Sec. 51.37(a), the Attorney General, absent extenuating circumstances and consistent with the burden of proof under section 5 described in Sec. 51.52 (a) and (c), may object to the change, giving notice as specified in Sec. 51.44.

Sec. 51.41 Notification of decision not to object.

(a)   The Attorney General shall within the 60-day period allowed notify the submitting authority of a decision to interpose no objection to a submitted change affecting voting.

(b)   The notification shall state that the failure of the Attorney General to object does not bar subsequent litigation to enjoin the enforcement of the change.

(c)   A copy of the notification shall be sent to any party who has commented on the submission or has requested notice of the Attorney General's action thereon.

Sec. 51.42 Failure of the Attorney General to respond.

It is the practice and intention of the Attorney General to respond to each submission within the 60-day period. However, the failure of the Attorney General to make a written response within the 60-day period constitutes preclearance of the submitted change, provided the submission is addressed as specified in Sec. 51.24 and is appropriate for a response on the merits as described in Sec. 51.35.

Sec. 51.43 Reexamination of decision not to object.

After notification to the submitting authority of a decision to interpose no objection to a submitted change affecting voting has been given, the Attorney General may reexamine the submission if, prior to the expiration of the 60-day period, information indicating the possibility of the prohibited discriminatory purpose or effect is received. In this event, the Attorney General may interpose an objection provisionally and advise the submitting authority that examination of the change in light of the newly raised issues will continue and that a final decision will be rendered as soon as possible.

Sec. 51.44 Notification of decision to object.

(a)   The Attorney General shall within the 60-day period allowed notify the submitting authority of a decision to interpose an objection. The reasons for the decision shall be stated.

(b)   The submitting authority shall be advised that the Attorney General will reconsider an objection upon a request by the submitting authority.

(c)   The submitting authority shall be advised further that notwithstanding the objecton it may institute an action in the U.S. District Court for the District of Columbia for a declaratory judgment that the change objected to by the Attorney General does not have the prohibited discriminatory purpose or effect.

(d)   A copy of the notification shall be sent to any party who has commented on the submission or has requested notice of the Attorney General's action thereon.

(e)   Notice of the decision to interpose an objection will be given to interested parties registered under Sec. 51.32.

Sec. 51.45 Request for reconsideration.

(a)   The submitting authority may at any time request the Attorney General to reconsider an objection.

(b)   Requests may be in letter or any other written form and should contain relevant information or legal argument.

(c)   Notice of the request will be given to any party who commented on the submission or requested notice of the Attorney General's action thereon and to interested parties registered under Sec. 51.32. In appropriate cases the Attorney General may request the submitting authority to give local public notice of the request.

***

Sec. 51.48 Decision after reconsideration.

     (a)   The Attorney General shall within the 60-day period following the receipt of a reconsideration request or following notice given under Sec. 51.46(b) notify the submitting authority of the decision to continue or withdraw the objection, provided that the Attorney General shall have at least 15 days following any conference that is held in which to decide. (See also Sec. 51.39(a).) The reasons for the decision shall be stated.

     (b)   The objection shall be withdrawn if the Attorney General is satisfied that the change does not have the purpose and will not have the effect of discriminating on account of race, color, or membership in a language minority group.

     (c)   If the objection is not withdrawn, the submitting authority shall be advised that notwithstanding the objection it may institute an action in the U.S. District Court for the District of Columbia for a declaratory judgment that the change objected to by the Attorney General does not have the prohibited purpose or effect.

     (d)   An objection remains in effect until either it is withdrawn by the Attorney General or a declaratory judgment with respect to the change in question is entered by the U.S. District Court for the District of Columbia.

     (e)   A copy of the notification shall be sent to any party who has commented on the submission or reconsideration or has requested notice of the Attorney General's action thereon.

     (f)   Notice of the decision after reconsideration will be given to interested parties registered under Sec. 51.32.

Sec. 51.49 Absence of judicial review.

     The decision of the Attorney General not to object to a submitted change or to withdraw an objection is not reviewable. The preclearance by the Attorney General of a voting change does not constitute the certification that the voting change satisfies any other requirement of the law beyond that of section 5, and, as stated in section 5, "(n)either an affirmative indication by the Attorney General that no objection will be made, nor the Attorney General's failure to object, nor a declaratory judgment entered under this section shall bar a subsequent action to enjoin enforcement of such qualification, prerequisite, standard, practice, or procedure."

Subpart F—Determinations by the Attorney General

Sec. 51.51 Purpose of the subpart.

The purpose of this subpart is to inform submitting authorities and other interested parties of the factors that the Attorney General considers relevant and of the standards by which the Attorney General will be guided in making substantive determinations under section 5 and in defending section 5 declaratory judgment actions.

Sec. 51.52 Basic standard.

(a)   Surrogate for the court. Section 5 provides for submission of a voting change to the Attorney General as an alternative to the seeking of a declaratory judgment from the U.S. District Court for the District of Columbia. Therefore, the Attorney General shall make the same determination that would be made by the court in an action for a declaratory judgment under section 5: Whether the submitted change has the purpose or will have the effect of denying or abridging the right to vote on account of race, color, or membership in a language minority group. The burden of proof is on a submitting authority when it submits a change to the Attorney General for preclearance, as it would be if the proposed change were the subject of a declaratory judgment action in the U.S. District Court for the District of Columbia. See South Carolina v. Katzenbach, 383 U.S. 301, 328, 335 (1966).

(b)   No objection. If the Attorney General determines that the submitted change does not have the prohibited purpose or effect, no objection shall be interposed to the change.

(c)   Objection. An objection shall be interposed to a submitted change if the Attorney General is unable to determine that the change is free of discriminatory purpose and effect. This includes those situations where the evidence as to the purpose or effect of the change is conflicting and the Attorney General is unable to determine that the change is free of discriminatory purpose and effect.

Sec. 51.53 Information considered.

The Attorney General shall base a determination on a review of material presented by the submitting authority, relevant information provided by individuals or groups, and the results of any investigation conducted by the Department of Justice.

Sec. 51.54 Discriminatory effect.

(a)   Retrogression. A change affecting voting is considered to have a discriminatory effect under section 5 if it will lead to a retrogression in the position of members of a racial or language minority group (i.e., will make members of such a group worse off than they had been before the change) with respect to their opportunity to exercise the electoral franchise effectively. See Beer v. United States, 425 U.S. 130, 140-42 (1976).

      (b)   Benchmark.

      (1)   In determining whether a submitted change is retrogressive the Attorney General will normally compare the submitted change to the voting practice or procedure in effect at the time of the submission. If the existing practice or procedure upon submission was not in effect on the jurisdiction's applicable date for coverage (specified in the appendix) and is not otherwise legally enforceable under section 5, it cannot serve as a benchmark, and, except as provided in paragraph (b)(4) of this section, the comparison shall be with the last legally enforceable practice or procedure used by the jurisdiction.

      (2)   The Attorney General will make the comparison based on the conditions existing at the time of the submission.

      (3)   The implementation and use of an unprecleared voting change subject to section 5 review under Sec. 51.18(a) does not operate to make that unprecleared change a benchmark for any subsequent change submitted by the jurisdiction. See Sec. 51.18(c).

      (4)   Where at the time of submission of a change for section 5 review there exists no other lawful practice or procedure for use as a benchmark (e.g., where a newly incorporated college district selects a method of election) the Attorney General's preclearance determination will necessarily center on whether the submitted change was designed or adopted for the purpose of discriminating against members of racial or language minority groups.

Sec. 51.55 Consistency with constitutional and statutory requirements.

      (a)   Consideration in general. In making a determination the Attorney General will consider whether the change is free of discriminatory purpose and retrogressive effect in light of, and with particular attention being given to, the requirements of the 14th, 15th, and 24th amendments to the Constitution, 42 U.S.C. 1971(a) and (b), sections 2, 4(a), 4(f)(2), 4(f)(4), 201, 203(c), and 208 of the Act, and other constitutional and statutory provisions designed to safeguard the right to vote from denial or abridgment on account of race, color, or membership in a language minority group.

      (b)   Section 2. Preclearance under section 5 of a voting change will not preclude any legal action under section 2 by the Attorney General if implementation of the change demonstrates that such action is appropriate.

Sec. 51.56 Guidance from the courts.

In making determinations the Attorney General will be guided by the relevant decisions of the Supreme Court of the United States and of other Federal courts.

Sec. 51.57 Relevant factors.

Among the factors the Attorney General will consider in making determinations with respect to the submitted changes affecting voting are the following:

(a)   The extent to which a reasonable and legitimate justification for the change exists.

(b)   The extent to which the jurisdiction followed objective guidelines and fair and conventional procedures in adopting the change.

(c)   The extent to which the jurisdiction afforded members of racial and language minority groups an opportunity to participate in the decision to make the change.

(d)   The extent to which the jurisdiction took the concerns of members of racial and language minority groups into account in making the change.

Sec. 51.58 Representation.

(a)   Introduction. This section and the sections that follow set forth factors--in addition to those set forth above--that the Attorney General considers in reviewing redistrictings (see Sec. 51.59), changes in electoral systems (see Sec. 51.60), and annexations (see Sec. 51.61).

(b)   Background factors. In making determinations with respect to these changes involving voting practices and procedures, the Attorney General will consider as important background information the following factors:

(1)   The extent to which minorities have been denied an equal opportunity to participate meaningfully in the political process in the jurisdiction.

(2)   The extent to which minorities have been denied an equal opportunity to influence elections and the decisionmaking of elected officials in the jurisdiction.

(3)   The extent to which voting in the jurisdiction is racially polarized and political activities are racially segregated.

(4)   The extent to which the voter registration and election participation of minority voters have been adversely affected by present or past discrimination.

Sec. 51.59 Redistrictings.

In determining whether a submitted redistricting plan has the prohibited purpose or effect the Attorney General, in addition to the factors described above, will consider the following factors (among others):

(a)   The extent to which malapportioned districts deny or abridge the right to vote of minority citizens.

(b)   The extent to which minority voting strength is reduced by the proposed redistricting.

(c)   The extent to which minority concentrations are fragmented among different districts.

(d)   The extent to which minorities are overconcentrated in one or more districts.

(e)   The extent to which available alternative plans satisfying the jurisdiction's legitimate governmental interests were considered.

(f)   The extent to which the plan departs from objective redistricting criteria set by the submitting jurisdiction, ignores other relevant factors such as compactness and contiguity, or displays a configuration that inexplicably disregards available natural or artificial boundaries.

(g)   The extent to which the plan is inconsistent with the jurisdiction's stated redistricting standards.

Sec. 51.60 Changes in electoral systems.

In making determinations with respect to changes in electoral systems (e.g., changes to or from the use of at-large elections, changes in the size of elected bodies) the Attorney General, in addition to the factors described above, will consider the following factors (among others):

(a)   The extent to which minority voting strength is reduced by the proposed change.

(b)   The extent to which minority concentrations are submerged into larger electoral units.

(c)   The extent to which available alternative systems satisfying the jurisdiction's legitimate governmental interests were considered.

Sec. 51.61 Annexations.

(a)   Coverage. Annexations, even of uninhabited land, are subject to section 5 preclearance to the extent that they alter or are calculated to alter the composition of a jurisdiction's electorate. In analyzing annexations under section 5, the Attorney General only considers the purpose and effect of the annexation as it pertains to voting.

(b)   Section 5 review. It is the practice of the Attorney General to review all of a jurisdiction's unprecleared annexations together. See City of Pleasant Grove v. United States, C.A. No. 80-2589 (D.D.C. Oct. 7, 1981).

(c)   Relevant factors. In making determinations with respect to annexations, the Attorney General, in addition to the factors described above, will consider the following factors (among others):

(1)   The extent to which a jurisdiction's annexations reflect the purpose or have the effect of excluding minorities while including other similarly situated persons.

(2)   The extent to which the annexations reduce a jurisdiction's minority population percentage, either at the time of the submission or, in view of the intended use, for the reasonably foreseeable future.

(3)   Whether the electoral system to be used in the jurisdiction fails fairly to reflect minority voting strength as it exists in the post-annexation jurisdiction. See City of Richmond v. United States, 422 U.S. 358, 367- 72 (1975).

Subpart G—Sanctions

Sec. 51.62 Enforcement by the Attorney General.

(a)   The Attorney General is authorized to bring civil actions for appropriate relief against violations of the Act's provisions, including section 5. See section 12(d).

(b)   Certain violations of section 5 may be subject to criminal sanctions. See section 12(a) and (c).

Sec. 51.63 Enforcement by private parties.

Private parties have standing to enforce section 5.

***

Appendix to Part 51—Jurisdictions Covered Under Section 4(b) of the Voting Rights Act, as Amended

The preclearance requirement of section 5 of the Voting Rights Act, as amended, applies in the following jurisdictions. The applicable date is the date that was used to determine coverage and the date after which changes affecting voting are subject to the preclearance requirement.   Some jurisdictions, for example, Yuba County,

California, are included more than once because they have been determined on more than one occasion to be covered under section 4(b).